THE BUTTERFLIES OF COSTA RICA
AND THEIR NATURAL HISTORY

Philip J. DeVries

The Butterflies of Costa Rica

AND THEIR NATURAL HISTORY

VOLUME II

RIODINIDAE

Illustrated by Philip J. DeVries and Jennifer Clark

PRINCETON UNIVERSITY PRESS

Library of Congress Cataloging-in-Publication Data

DeVries, Philip J., 1952–
The butterflies of Costa Rica and their natural history.

Bibliography: p.
Includes index.
1. Butterflies—Costa Rica.   2. Insects—Costa Rica.   I. Title.
QL553.C67D48 1986   595.78′9′097286   85-28340
ISBN 0-691-02890-7
ISBN 0-691-02889-3 (pbk.)

This book has been composed in Baskerville

Princeton University Press books are printed on
acid-free paper and meet the guidelines for permanence
and durability of the Committee on Production
Guidelines for Book Longevity of the
Council on Library Resources

Printed in the United States of America
by Princeton Academic Press

2 4 6 8 10 9 7 5 3 1
2 4 6 8 10 9 7 5 3 1
(Pbk.)

CONTENTS

LIST OF FIGURES

LIST OF COLOR PLATES

(BY GENERA)

(following page 162)

LIST OF TABLES

PREFACE AND ACKNOWLEDGMENTS

Those members of society who revel in claims that stalking big game is a difficult endeavor have never attempted to make a study of the riodinid butterflies. This extraordinary group of butterflies melds all of the characteristics of a high tropical diversity with extreme rarity—something that, in my view, is distinctly and tragically the essence of Neotropical organisms.

This book was undertaken as an extension of my previous work on Costa Rican butterflies (*Butterflies of Costa Rica and their Natural History*, Princeton University Press, 1987), and I set out to write the present book for many of the same reasons as the previous one. First, despite their great diversity, comparatively little remains known about the riodinid butterflies. Through the years, a wide range of people have asked me what it is that I do in tropical forests. My response has been and continues to be that "I write epitaphs for a living." The complacent disregard shown by all human societies to the loss of tropical habitats and organisms has increased beyond rational bounds. So my second reason for writing this book is that perhaps it might be useful in the battle to understand and preserve tropical diversity before its complete extirpation. Third, if I am to be honest, the overwhelming reason for writing this book is that very few things in life give me as much pleasure as being immersed in a tropical forest and making discoveries about butterflies. Finally, I was blessed by a MacArthur Foundation Fellowship that allowed me to work unencumbered in tropical forests and make many of the observations on riodinid butterflies reported here—observations that I acknowledge may become elegies for many of the species.

The vital spark for the present volume began on the same rainy night and in the same field-worn jeep in San Jose, Costa Rica, as did my previous book. However, the seed of the present volume took a much longer time to germinate and come to term. Work on this book has left me with a series of experiences and memories that have become important parts of my life, and it is with the greatest pleasure that I recall making the acquaintance of the many riodinid butterflies in their own unique habitats and worlds. These recollections have made it all worthwhile, and my immersion into the realm of the riodinids has made me grow as a biologist and as a person.

Although no one is fond of reading the excuses authors feel compelled to write, completing this book has been difficult for a number of reasons. The great lepidopterist S. H. Scudder in 1887 encapsulated one reason why the present volume required a lot of time to complete.

Nestled in a short invited essay on riodinids that Scudder wrote for Godman and Salvin's *Biologia Centrali Americana* (pp. 110–112) we find this passage: "Our knowledge of the Lemoniinae (Riodinidae) is exceedingly meagre, that we can here draw no decided conclusions. There is, indeed, no greater desideratum in the study of butterflies than a knowledge of the transformation of the principal genera of this subfamily." These words, written a century ago, hold a special meaning for me because, after I have devoted a substantial portion of my time over the last ten years looking for them, the early stages for most of the butterflies treated in this book remain unknown. The fact is that less is known about most aspects of the riodinids than any other group of butterflies. A glance at the species accounts will show that much of our fauna is known, very imprecisely, from but a few specimens. Thus, my errors of fact and judgment concerning the taxonomic status and other details found here will, without doubt, provide a rich deposit of material for future workers to contend with, and hopefully correct.

Other delays in completing this book stemmed from the territorial jihads of some organizations involved in biodiversity, and from the cross fire between competitors in the conservation business. Apparently if they are not strongly and officially affiliated with one political side or another, independent researchers may find themselves on a Procrustean bed anesthetized by the bureaucratic processes that be. But everything else aside, this book was completed because I strongly believe that field guides are a documentation of the past, form a general basis upon which to start thinking about the future, and stimulate a broader interest in their subject matter. Should more future research and appreciation for the riodinid butterflies result from this book, then a major portion of my mission will have been accomplished.

ACKNOWLEDGMENTS

Books of this nature always have enormous help from institutions devoted to natural history, and from the people who staff them. The American Museum of Natural History has consistently encouraged and facilitated much of my work, and I wish to extend my thanks, especially to D. Grimaldi, J. Miller, F. Rindge, E. Quinter, C. Meyers, C. Snyder, J. ("PD") Carpenter, R. DeSalle, T. Schuh, the late G. E. Martinez, D. Yeates, and N. Platnick, for their support. A special thanks to S. Granato-Yeates who helped obtain many important references, and whose ability to find obscure literature is astounding. Much of the material illustrated in the identification plates is part of the G. B. Small, Jr., collection housed in the National Museum of Natural History, the Smithsonian Institution, and I extend thanks to R. Robbins, D. Furth, and D. Harvey for facilitating loans. For access to study material and lively discussions, I thank P. R. Ackery, I. J. Kitching, and R. I. Vane-Wright (Natural History Museum, London); L. Miller and J. Miller (Allyn Museum of Entomology, Florida); D. Spencer-Smith (Hope Entomological Collections, Oxford); B. Brown (Los Angeles County Museum); T. Emmel (University of Florida); G. Austin (Nevada State Museum), A. Young and S. Borkin (Milwaukee Public Museum); and J. Rawlins (Carnegie Museum, Pittsburgh). For assistance in getting through some of the taxonomic snarls and often intractable maze of nomenclature, the expertise of P. Ackery, C. Callaghan, D. Harvey, and especially that of G. Lamas and J. Hall is gratefully acknowledged.

This work could never have been completed without the help of many gracious and genuinely interested people. For collecting specimens, sharing natural history observations, and field assistance I thank A. Aiello, R. Aguilar, B. Bock, G. Broom, B. Brown, C. Callaghan, R. Canet, D. Campbell, I. Chacon, P. Chai, C. Covell, J. Clark, M. Cummings, M. deGoulain, O. Diorio, R. Dudley, E. Ericks, K. Fiedler, B. Finegan, the late E. Foster, Y. Gamara, N. Garwood, L. Gilbert, H. Greeney, N. Grieg, R. Hanner, B. Harris, R. Hesterberg, H. Hespenheide, R. Holzenthal, L. Jost, P. Knudsen, J. Longino, M. Lysinger, the late G. E. Martinez, Man Wah Tan, D. Murray, P. Opler, O. Pagels, J. Paul, C. Penz, E. Quinter, G. Ross, R. Rozyki, the late G. B. Small, N. G. Smith, A. Suarez, J. Thomas, C. D. Thomas, T. Walla, D. Windsor, K. Wolfe, D. Yeates, and M. Zumbado.

A number of people gave generously of their time and talents in helping me identify a variety of organisms that are important to this work on riodinid butterflies. For plant determinations I wish to acknowledge T. M. Aide, I. A. Chacon, R. Dressler, R. Foster, N. Garwood, the late A. Gentry, J. Gomez-Laurito, L. D. Gomez, M. Grayum, N. Greig, W. Haber, B. Hammel, D. Neil, L. Poveda, P. Sanchez, and N. Zamora. My thanks to B. Bolton, S. Cover, D. Feener, J. Longino, and R. Snelling for identifying ant specimens; D. Grimaldi and M. Wood for identifying Diptera; S. Shaw and D. Winsor for identifying Hymenoptera; and C. Covell, J. Miller, J. Rawlins, and C. Snyder for identifying moths that are involved in mimetic complexes with riodinids.

A special thanks goes to George Austin for performing the daunting task of sorting out and writing the entire section on *Calephelis*—a fine job on very short notice, and all while dealing with his many responsibilities and projects. Also I offer my thanks for allowing me access to his unpublished observations on Brazilian riodinids.

The illustrations in this book benefited from the assistance of a number of people. For generous help, encouragement, and for originally teaching me the photographic techniques for setting up the color plates, I thank the inimitable B. D'Abrera. I thank L. Jost and K. Winemiller for the use of their photos. Many thanks to S. Mustoe of the

University of Oregon's optics lab for patience and darkroom expertise. For help locating images and notes on important entomologists, I extend my thanks to M. Zíkan Cardoso, G. Lamas, N. Greig, J. Rawlins, and the Berlin Museum (H. Gaedicke), British Natural History Museum (J. Harvey and P. Ackery), and M. Epstein for ferreting around the U.S. National Archives. Again, my gratitude for helping me flesh out the "rogues' gallery" of entomologists and naturalists that contributed to our understanding of riodinid butterflies. A special thanks to B. Degner for providing the fine drawings in figures 15 and 18 on such short notice.

Amidst a torrent of her own responsibilities, Jennifer Clark has, in her usual unusual style, cheerfully created beautiful illustrations from my photographs. Her drawings clearly represent an imposing benchmark in caterpillar portraits. Thanks, Jennifer.

For various kinds of help and encouragement in my seemingly endless task of finishing this book I thank L. P. Brower, J. E. Cadle, T. Eisner, P. Ehrlich, D. Feener, M. Franklin, L. Friedlander, L. Gilbert, L. D. Gomez, N. Greig, D. Grimaldi, B. Hölldobler, K. Hope, P. Knudsen, G. Lamas, R. Lande, R. Mattoni, L. Mattoni, R. M. May, J. May, J. Miller, N. Pierce, G. Schaller, E. "Ike" Schwartz, M. Singer, C. Snyder, E. O. Wilson, and my parents, Helen and Hendrick DeVries. The following institutions helped facilitate my field and museum work: Smithsonian Tropical Research Institute, Organization for Tropical Studies, Museo Nacional de Costa Rica, Servicios Parques Nacionales de Costa Rica, Center for Conservation Biology, American Museum of Natural History, Museum of Comparative Zoology (Harvard University), University of Texas, and the University of Oregon.

I am indebted to several institutions and the many people who work in them for financial support toward completing this work. My thanks to the Smithsonian Tropical Research Institute and its entire staff for fellowships and support that was fundamental to many aspects of this book and my other research. My thanks to G. Tabor and S. McVey of the Geraldine R. Dodge Foundation for a fellowship that made significant contributions toward this work. My thanks to N. Pierce for facilitating my stay at Harvard in many ways, and to Ernst Mayr for a collections study grant. My profound gratitude for the receipt of fellowship support from an organization that is beyond category—the J. D. and C. T. MacArthur Foundation. Without the support of the MacArthur Fellowship and their complete understanding of my peripatetic methods, this book would never have been possible.

The manuscript was improved from comments provided by G. Austin, J. Cadle, J. Hall, H. Horn, P. Z. Goldstein, D. Grimaldi, N. Greig, R. Hanner, C. Penz, R. Raguso, and K. Willmott. I would like to thank E. Wilkinson at Princeton University Press for her patience, trust, and wickedly good cheer during the long gestation period of this book. Finally, I thank A. Calaprice for a terrific job of ferreting out the inconsistencies in the manuscript, and making the entire book a much more unified entity.

This book is dedicated to all tropical habitats that have been used so shabbily by humanity, and to the artists who were and remain sources of inspiration in the face of it all: Henry W. Bates, Miles Davis, Bill Evans, Lee Friedlander, J.B.S. Haldane, Joe Henderson, Ken Hope, Al Gentry, Dexter Gordon, Antonio Carlos Jobim, Steve Lacy, Cormac McCarthy, Thelonius Sphere Monk, George Russell, Gordon B. Small, Jr., Cecil Taylor, and Alfred Russel Wallace.

THE CONTENTS AND USE
OF THIS BOOK

This book treats over 250 species of Costa Rican butterflies in the family Riodinidae, with particular emphasis on their identification and natural history. The present work is meant to be a companion volume to my previous book that treated the Costa Rican Papilionidae, Pieridae, and Nymphalidae (DeVries 1987). In comparison to those families, however, the riodinids are much less well known in virtually all respects. Consequently, the present volume must be viewed as a first attempt to bring together a diffuse body of observations (published and unpublished) in the hope of stimulating future research on these distinctly Neotropical butterflies. Being confronted with the problem of treating a group of butterflies that is so poorly known motivated me to include topics, information, and illustrations that are typically not found in the field guide format. I took these liberties with format and information content in the hope of persuading others to examine butterflies, especially riodinids, in a different light. Because of the very real and widespread devastation of biodiversity, all biologists are engaged in writing epitaphs for the natural world. Therefore it is also my hope that the information in this book will stimulate others to produce field guides on many subjects that range beyond the boundaries of tradition, and perhaps help preserve tropical forests.

Area of Coverage

Although Costa Rica is geographically a small country (embracing an area of approximately 19,600 square miles) it contains tropical habitats that range from sea level to over 3,800 m that encompass more than fifteen distinct life zones. This geographical diversity is reflected in its rich flora and fauna. Costa Rica contains a large percentage of all the butterfly species known from Central America, and a substantial representation of the fauna of the Amazon Basin (see section on diversity). For example, I estimate that over 85 percent of the Central American species belonging to the family Riodinidae and about 70 percent of all Neotropical riodinid genera occur in Costa Rica. Hence, although this book is about Costa Rican riodinid butterflies, it covers a much larger portion of the Neotropical fauna than national boundaries might suggest.

Information Content and Sources

Although it is primarily a field guide to the identification of Costa Rican riodinid butterflies, this book includes information on their life cycles, morphology, systematics, natural history, ecology, evolution, and, as is my style, many anecdotes. In the opening chapters the reader will find introductions to these subjects, along with sections on habitats, climates, and how to collect and study riodinid butterflies. These sections contain an overview of references that will lead to a more detailed literature that should aid the field biologist and others in their research. Also included in this section is an overview of the family Riodinidae as it occurs throughout the world.

The generic accounts concentrate on the Neotropics and provide overviews that attempt to summarize what is known about systematics, geographical distribution, hostplants, early stages, natural history, and questions that require further study—a section that is lamentably thin. Although the literature cited under the generic accounts is not exhaustive, I have attempted to provide the researcher with references that will lead to a substantial portion of what has been published on the riodinids. The species accounts emphasize identification, distribution, and summaries of observations on both early stages and adults. Interspersed within the generic and species accounts are illustrations of early stages that will help in the identification and appreciation of caterpillars and pupae.

The information in this book derives from a diffuse literature and contains many field observations made by myself and others. For the geographical distribution of each species I have relied on the collections of the American Museum of Natural History, British Museum (Natural History) (BMNH), Museo Nacional de Costa Rica, Allyn Museum of Entomology, U.S. National Museum (USNM), Carnegie, Milwaukee Public Museum, and the private collections of R. Canet, B. Finegan, L. E. Gilbert, W. Haber, J. Hall, R. Hesterberg, T. Emmel, P. Knudsen, P. Opler, J. Paul, K. Willmott, K. Wolfe, and my own fieldwork. Observations on natural history and ecology are primarily from my own field experience, but have been, in some instances, generously supplemented by observations by A. Aiello, R. Aguilar, I. A. Chacon, P. Chai, L. D. Gomez, L. Gilbert, H. Greeney, N. Greig, R. Hesterberg, D. Janzen, J. Longino, the late G. B. Small, T. Walla, and M. Zumbado.

As in my previous field guide, the emphasis in this book is on species that inhabit forests at the expense of species that are most common in open second growth and pastures. I continue to believe that pastures have not played a significant role in the evolution of most Costa Rican butterflies, especially the riodinids. It is likely, however, that the only species left in the not too distant future will be those that inhabit open areas, but most if not all of the butterflies typical to pastures may be found at much lower densities along rivers and in forest light gaps. I find it difficult to contemplate a world where *Calephelis* and its allies will comprise the majority of the riodinid fauna, but then I recognize that many epitaphs are probably written in these pages. I hope that we have the sense to mourn.

The Color Plates

Each butterfly specimen illustrated in the color plates has a number that corresponds to a line of information on the facing page. Each line of information gives the name of the butterfly, its sex, orientation of the specimen, where the specimen originated, and where in the text that species is discussed.

The following abbreviations are used: ♂ = male; ♀ = female; D = dorsal: this means the *upperside* is illustrated; V = ventral: this means the *underside* is illustrated; CR = Costa Rica; [HT] = the *holotype* is illustrated; [PT] = a *paratype* is illustrated.

Wherever possible I have tried to illustrate specimens of Costa Rican origin. In many cases, however, this was not possible, and I used specimens from another Central American country, mainly Panama. Due to constraints imposed by the collections I was working with, it became necessary in some cases to illustrate specimens from South America.

Basic Nomenclature Used in This Book

Entire books are devoted to the subject of classification, taxonomy, and nomenclature, and the interested reader may turn to them (Mayr and Ashlock 1991; Simpson 1945, 1961; Wiley 1981). In discussing the riodinid butterflies of Costa Rica, we shall use the basic binominal or trinominal system of nomenclature.

Each species in this book has at least a two-part, and in many cases a three-part, Latin name. Following the last Latin name is the name of the author, or describer of the species, and a date. Each component part of a butterfly's scientific name is a shorthand method of access to systematic and natural history literature. For example, the butterfly name *Sarota gyas* (Cramer, 1775) indicates that this butterfly is currently placed in the genus *Sarota* and its species name is *gyas*, and it was first described by Cramer in 1775. The parentheses around the author's name indicate that *gyas* was originally placed in a different genus (in this case, *Papilio*) and was later transferred to the genus *Sarota*. A person searching the literature can look for *gyas* and be forewarned that information may be found under more than one genus. If there are no parentheses around the author's name, the investigator knows that the species was described in the genus appearing with the species name. In instances where there are three Latin names, the last Latin name refers to a subspecies or a geographically distinct form. For example, in breaking down the names *Setabis lagus jansoni* (Butler, 1870) we know the genus is *Setabis*, the species is *lagus*, and the subspecies is *jansoni*, which was described by Butler in 1870 under a different generic name.

The use of subspecies names is a mixed blessing. On one hand, a cursory examination of some taxonomic literature along with a collection of specimens shows that there appear to be many subspecies names that have little biological significance. In certain instances, subspecies names suggest the marking of territories by the taxonomists themselves (e.g., H. Stichel's later monographs, and the work of some present-day entomologists). On the other hand, after study, the subspecies may in fact be valid, and some subspecies will even, without doubt, turn out to be valid species, and thus their names will be available to taxonomists doing revisionary work. Hence, retaining subspecies names can be of assistance to future researchers.

How to Use the Species Accounts

As is typical of all illustrated field guides, the user matches the specimen in question with the illustration provided, then turns to the appropriate text pages that discuss that species. The diagnostic characters provided in each species account separate it from all others. However, because of the extensive mimicry in Costa Rican riodinid butterflies, the user should pay particular attention to the notes on similar species, and to the wing-length measurements, to make certain the identification is correct. For example, a specimen may look just like the illustration of female *Setabis cleomedes*, but upon closer examination it may actually turn out to be *Mesene silaris*, and it may bear a strong resemblance to several other species, including members of some families of moths. Be certain to compare your specimen to the similar species listed, and double-check your determinations. Never forget that mimicry really works!

The identification plates in this book differ from my previous field guide on Costa Rican butterflies in one significant manner: in order to make the patterns on the wings readily visible, some of the smaller species are magnified. In other words, the photographs in the color plates are not all to the same scale. Several hints will facilitate identification:

1. Remember to use the FW (forewing) length measurement to get an idea of size.
2. Read the species description to eliminate similar species.
3. Do not assume that this book represents a complete riodinid fauna of Costa Rica. You may have found species unreported

from the area. Consult an expert. I would be happy to help with any identifications.

The information provided for each species has five sections. The first includes the various names of the butterfly, its wing length in millimeters (measured from the base of the forewing to the apex), the plate on which the butterfly is illustrated, and the geographical distribution of the species and subspecies. The second section describes the host-plants and early stages, with a brief synoptic description of eggs, caterpillars, pupae, plus additional notes of potential interest. The next section provides diagnostic characters of the adult butterfly, including the similar species that the butterfly should be compared to, and at times there will be notes on the taxonomic nomenclature of that species. The fourth section on habits provides information on where the species occurs by elevation and associated habitat type, summarizes observations on behavior and seasonality, and, whenever possible, provides other biological commentary. Where available, a reference is provided to a paper on each species, but so little has been published on riodinids that most observations are distilled mainly from my own field experience. The final section comprises a list of localities and dates indicating where and in what month(s) the species has been collected in Costa Rica; if no dates are available, no month is given. The abbreviation [TL] in this section indicates the type locality. For example, in the account of *Euselasia matuta*, [TL] indicates that this species was described from specimens that originated from Juan Viñas. The locality abbreviations are as follows: [A] Alajuela, [C] Cartago, [G] Guanacaste, [H] Heredia, [L] Limon, [P] Puntarenas, [SJ] San Jose.

One further note on the species accounts. In this book I have included a number of species that have not been confirmed to occur in Costa Rica. I resolved to include these taxa for two reasons. First, a considerable number of species previously thought to be restricted only to South America (e.g., *Euselasia onorata*, *Euselasia subargentea*, *Chalodeta chaonitis*) are now known to have a much greater range, sometimes extending the full length of Central America and Mexico. Second, discussions with the late G. B. Small, the use of his collections, and my own experience in Panama influenced my decision to include certain taxa. Although these inclusions may evoke clamor from some quarters, due to the richness of the Costa Rican riodinid fauna and the paucity of information on most Central American species I suspect many of them are justified. However, as in all things, time will tell.

Classification of Costa Rican Riodinidae

In arranging the taxa covered in this book, I have followed, whenever possible, existing formal classifications and arrangements (see the section on Butterfly Systematics, pp. 64–73). Although unresolved questions remain with it, the higher-level classification followed throughout this book is that of Harvey (1987a). The sequential arrangement of taxa within these groups has tended to follow a combination of Stichel (1930–31) and the modifications made by Harvey's classification. As to the arrangements of certain groups, I have in some (but not all) instances followed the suggestions of C. Callaghan and G. Lamas, who are compiling a catalog of the Riodinidae. However, even the most cursory investigations on the riodinids will demonstrate that our understanding of their taxonomy and relationships is rudimentary at best, and in many instances dead wrong. It should be obvious that as our understanding of these butterflies increases, there will be many changes in how the group is presented in a systematic fashion; the flux of names should demonstrate that the group has attracted the attention of taxonomists. Diagnoses for the higher-level classification of Harvey (1987a) and a Costa Rican species list of our riodinid fauna are provided in Appendix III and IV, respectively.

Riodinid Butterflies and Habitat Associations

Butterfly biologists, botanists, herpetologists, mammologists, and naturalists tend to associate a particular species with a habitat within its geographical range. The delineation of a habitat typically reflects the experience of the field biologist, the labels on museum specimens, or both. In this sense, a species-habitat association is the sum of locality data and a bit of extrapolation on the part of the biologist who is familiar with the organism. Due to the fundamental nature of species habitat as a basic unit of communication among biologists, and because these units are often transmogrified by some into some sort of immutable law, I will briefly expand on the methods I used in associating a species with a habitat and a particular elevation.

Throughout its geographical range, the spectacular nymphalid *Morpho cypris* is restricted to areas of lowland rain forests (DeVries and Martinez 1993). However, on occasion individuals of this butterfly may be found in open areas, provided there is abundant forest nearby. When they are provided with corridors of an appropriate environment, butterfly species generally move across and between habitats. In this respect, riodinids are not exceptional, but there is a clear dearth of observations on these insects, making definitive statements impossible about what delimits their distributions, as in the case of *Morpho cypris*. Thus, while the habitat associations for the species in this book may represent general estimates of riodinid species distributions, they are most emphatically not hard-and-fast rules.

Although the riodinids are poorly understood, we can make some generalizations of their habitat associations. In this book I have associated a riodinid species with a habitat type and elevation by amassing all of the locality data I could find, and by making repeated observations at the same localities (in Costa Rica and Panama) over a number of years. I then calculated a mental average of elevations, localities, and associated life zones. Again, these habitat associations are in no way definitive, but they may serve as general guidelines and may be expected to change in response to habitat change (e.g., deforestation, succession) and as more people become interested in riodinid butterflies.

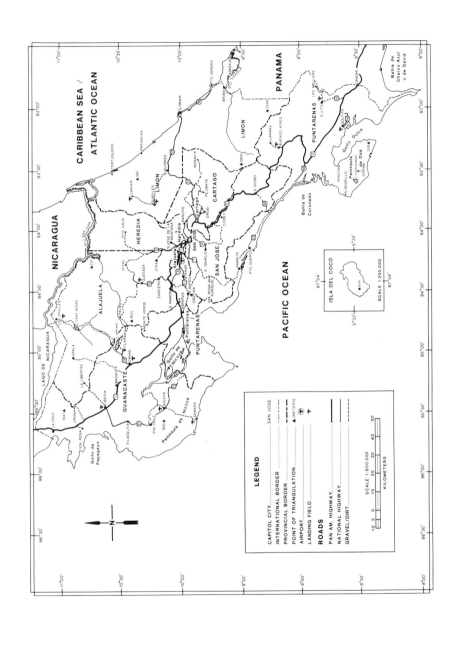

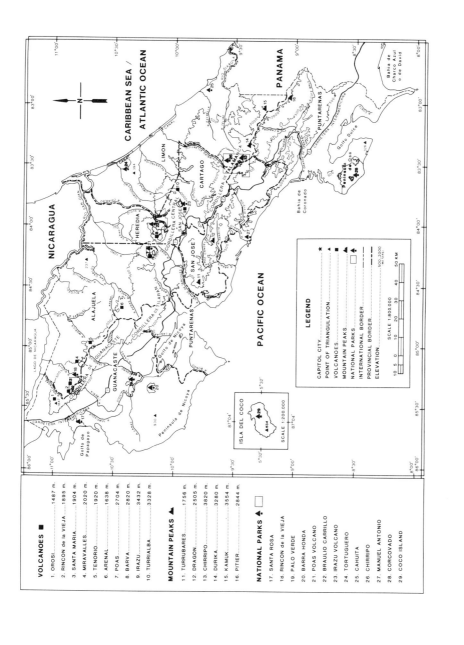

VOLCANOES ■

1. OROSI .... 1487 m.
2. RINCON de la VIEJA .... 1895 m.
3. SANTA MARIA .... 1904 m.
4. MIRAVALLES .... 2020 m.
5. TENORIO .... 1920 m.
6. ARENAL .... 1638 m.
7. POAS .... 2704 m.
8. BARVA .... 2820 m.
9. IRAZU .... 3432 m.
10. TURRIALBA .... 3328 m.

MOUNTAIN PEAKS ▲

11. TURRUBARES .... 1756 m.
12. DRAGON .... 2505 m.
13. CHIRRIPO .... 3820 m.
14. DURIKA .... 3280 m.
15. KAMUK .... 3554 m.
16. PITIER .... 2844 m.

NATIONAL PARKS ▲ □

17. SANTA ROSA
18. RINCON de la VIEJA
19. PALO VERDE
20. BARRA HONDA
21. POAS VOLCANO
22. BRAULIO CARRILLO
23. IRAZU VOLCANO
24. TORTUGUERO
25. CAHUITA
26. CHIRRIPO
27. MANUEL ANTONIO
28. CORCOVADO
29. COCO ISLAND

LEGEND

CAPITOL CITY .... ★
POINT OF TRIANGULATION .... ▲
VOLCANOES .... ■
MOUNTAIN PEAKS .... ▲
NATIONAL PARKS .... □
INTERNATIONAL BORDER .... — ·· —
PROVINCIAL BORDER .... – – –
ELEVATION .... 500 , 2000
                                   METERS

SCALE 1:800,000

10 5 0   10   20   30   40   50 KM

ISLA DEL COCO

SCALE 1:200,000

NICARAGUA

CARIBBEAN SEA /
ATLANTIC OCEAN

PANAMA

PACIFIC OCEAN

GUANACASTE

ALAJUELA

HEREDIA

SAN JOSE

CARTAGO

LIMON

PUNTARENAS

Bahía de
Coronado

Golfo Dulce

Península de Osa

Bahía de
Charco Azul
o de David

THE BUTTERFLIES OF COSTA RICA
AND THEIR NATURAL HISTORY

ONE. THE BIOLOGY AND SYSTEMATICS OF BUTTERFLIES

Across human history, people from many cultures have engaged in the study of butterflies. Although the curiosity about butterflies often begins early in childhood, as a person matures the interest generally wanes, to be replaced with an interest in more practical or weighty subjects. Nevertheless, the study of butterflies has contributed to a great many scientific disciplines and has maintained the interest of many persons who have made a mark on human history. I suggest that the readers who want a broad overview of butterfly biology and systematics consult the works of Vane-Wright and Ackery (1984) and Ackery and Vane-Wright (1984), both excellent primary sources. Their work encompasses some of the most thorough scholarship ever compiled on butterflies and will remain the standard for many years to come (see also Lamas et al. 1995).

Though this book concentrates on information relevant to an understanding of butterflies in the family Riodinidae as they occur in Costa Rica, it also includes more general topics that are applicable to riodinids elsewhere in the world, as well as to other butterfly groups. The first chapter of this book is divided into eleven subsections that will treat the butterfly's life cycle, morphology, symbioses with ants, enemies and defenses against them, and systematics, as well as suggestions on how to study butterflies.

BUTTERFLY LIFE CYCLE AND MORPHOLOGY

The development from egg to adult butterfly is called the "life cycle," which has four distinct stages:

1. *Egg*: the embryonic stage.
2. *Caterpillar* or *larva*: the feeding and growing stage.
3. *Pupa* or *chrysalis*: the stage in which larval tissues are broken down and redifferentiated to produce an adult.
4. *Adult butterfly*: the sexually mature stage in which the butterfly is capable of flight.

The morphology and behavior of butterflies in these four stages differ among species, and the study of their responses at each stage of the life cycle to environmental influences is the subject of natural history and ecology. Study of the comparative morphology or DNA sequences of the various life cycles as they respond to evolutionary change falls into the field encompassing systematics. Both ecology and systematics are disciplines with a firm basis in evolutionary theory, and they are not mutually exclusive. It is important to our understanding of butterflies to see these two disciplines as complementary, and to take into account all stages of the life cycle and the factors affecting them.

This section provides a brief overview of the morphology and biology of each stage in the life cycle of riodinid butterflies. The diagrams and figures depicting various morphological features or behaviors will aid in the identification and study of the riodinid butterflies. Finally, here I also cover various aspects of the little-understood ability of some riodinid butterflies to form symbiotic associations with ants.

The Egg

In much of the literature devoted to butterflies, the egg stage is considered to be little more than an unassuming but necessary part of the life cycle. The life of a butterfly, however, begins quite literally when the egg is laid, or *oviposited*, by the female on the host of the soon-to-be-born caterpillar. And while it is true that we know relatively little about them, butterfly eggs are surprisingly complex structures that nurture and protect the developing caterpillar enclosed within. I will provide a brief overview of riodinid eggs in the hope of stimulating further work on them. The reader interested in detailed study of eggs of the Lycaenidae and Riodinidae should consult Downey and Allyn (1980, 1981, 1984). These well-illustrated articles present the often complex terminology of egg morphology in a manner that is easy to assimilate, and they provide important insights into the structure and function of eggs. Those interested in comparative studies of insect eggs should consult the opus of Hinton (1981), the most comprehensive treatment ever compiled on the subject even though it is written in a turgid and somewhat user-hostile manner.

Butterfly eggs are typically laid either singly or in clusters that range from a few to many eggs; depending on the species, they may be laid on or off plant or arthropod hosts (Chew and Robbins 1984; Cottrell 1984; DeVries 1987). We know almost nothing about oviposition patterns and clutch sizes for most species of riodinids, but their egg-laying habits are similar to those of other butterflies. Rearing records suggest that the majority of riodinid caterpillars feed as solitary individuals, and that the females of these species lay single eggs. Observations also indicate that the females of some species of *Euselasia*, *Melanis*, and *Emesis* lay clusters of eggs, and females of *Eurybia*, *Ancyluris*, *Emesis*, *Thisbe*, *Theope*, and *Nymphidium* may, depending on the circumstance, lay either single eggs or small clusters (DeVries et al. 1994).

To the naked eye, a butterfly egg appears to be a tiny particle of white, yellow, orange, green, or blue matter. The outer shell, or *chorion*,

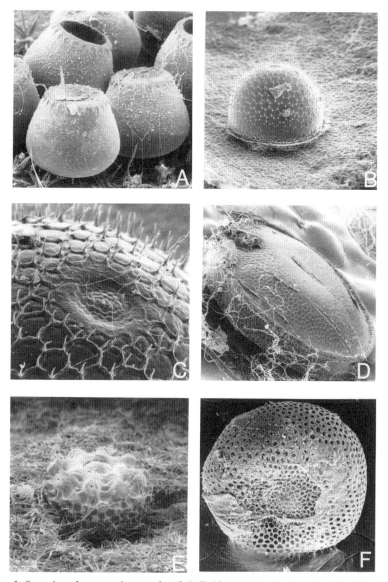

FIGURE 1. Scanning electron micrographs of riodinid eggs. (A) *Euselasia chrysippe*. This is but a portion of a cluster. Noteworthy is the fustrum shape (unusual in butterflies), and the distinct lack of sculpturing on most of the egg. The first instars have hatched in the eggs with missing tops. (B) *Leucochimona vestalis*. An example of an echinoid-shaped egg. Note the stalks protruding from the sculpturing. (C) *Leucochimona vestalis*. Detail of the micropylar region and sculpturing. (D) *Eurybia lycisca*. Note the pie shape that is typical of the genus and bears a striking resemblance to diatoms in the genus *Stephanodiscus*. (E) *Symmachia tricolor*. An example of the crown or tiarate shape. The egg has been deposited in the damage made by a first instar larva in the dense mat of trichomes on the leaf surface. Note the aeropyles (black spots) located in the center of the large tubercles. (F) *Sarota gyas*. A basic echinoid shape. Note the dense covering of residue that may be important in gluing the egg to the substrate. (Photos by P. J. DeVries)

FIGURE 2. Scanning electron micrographs of riodinid eggs. (A) *Helicopis cupido*. Although this butterfly is a strictly South American species, its egg shows yet another aspect of riodinid egg shapes. Note the intricate network of sculpturing that extends along the perimeter of the cakelike egg. This egg is typically laid on hostplants that grow in oxbow lakes, suggesting that the sculpturing may aid egg respiration in extremely wet habitats. (B) *Emesis tenedia*. This echinoid-shaped egg with long, stalked aeropyles looks very much like a cactus. Note the long threadlike scales deposited there during oviposition by the female. (C) *Thisbe irenea*. Note the meshlike chains of sculpturing that bear stalked aeropyles at their interstices and the distinctive micropylar area. (D) *Juditha dorilas*. Of special note here is the presence of *plastrons* between the links of the meshlike chains of sculpturing. Plastrons are rarely found in riodinid eggs. (E) *Synargis phylleus*. An echinoid shape with distinctly stalked aeropyles. Note the nipplelike micropylar area. (F) *Synargis phylleus*. Detail of the micropylar area. The four micropyles are distinctly visible on the inside perimeter of the "nipple," whereas various aeropyles are visible outside the perimeter. (Photos by P. J. DeVries)

FIGURE 3. Scanning electron micrographs of riodinid eggs. (A) *Synargis mycone*. The beautiful form of this egg is perhaps best described as a "soccer ball in a mesh bag." (B) *Synargis orestes*. Although strictly a South American species, note the heavy crust of sculpturing that shows the variation within *Synargis*. (C) *Menander menander*. Note the large hole where the first instar has emerged from the egg. (D) *Nymphidium ascolia*. Note the heavy covering of residue on the top of the eggs that give them the appearance of a frosted pastry. (E) *Theope virgilius*. Note the lateral compression and extensive micropylar area that imparts an appearance not unlike a car tire encased in mesh. (F) *Theope matuta*. The obvious lateral compression, flat micropylar area, and netlike sculpturing of these eggs bear a similarity to those of *Nymphidium*. Note that these eggs have hatched and have a covering of mold on them. (Photos by P. J. DeVries)

is composed of complex proteins and is frequently covered with an elaborate sculpturing that is especially prominent in eggs of the Nymphalidae, Lycaenidae, and Riodinidae. Viewing an egg under high magnification (especially the scanning electron microscope) reveals the intricate chorionic sculpturing that is often astonishing to behold (Figs. 1–3). Amid the ridges and waves of chorionic sculpturing are two types of minuscule pores of fundamental importance to the egg and the developing caterpillar. The first type consists of one to four tiny pores, each of which is termed a *micropyle* and located invariably on top of the egg (Figs. 1–3). By way of the micropyles, the sperm pass through the chorion into the egg during fertilization, and the *micropylar* region is typically surrounded by delicate sculptured rosettes. The form and sculpturing of the micropylar region may be flat, raised on a slight dome, raised into an ornate nipple-like projection, or recessed into several types of depressions (Figs. 1–3). The second type of pores, termed *aeropyles*, are generally scattered over the surface of the egg and frequently have openings to the atmosphere located on stalks or columns (Figs. 1–3). These tiny *aeropyles* are part of the "air-conditioning" system of the egg and play an integral role in respiration.

High magnification may also reveal a residue that covers all or portions of the chorion (particularly at the base) which, in some cases, may look like the moist frosting on an elaborate pastry (Figs. 2a, 3e). This residue is deposited on the egg upon being laid, and it is thought to function in gluing the egg to the substrate and aid in hardening the chorion. In cases where the egg is covered in a frothy mass, the hardened residue may act as physical protection against egg parasitoids and help protect the egg from desiccation (Downey and Allyn 1981).

Riodinid eggs are remarkably varied. Even though some of them may resemble those of the Lycaenidae, a significant number are utterly distinct from the eggs of all other groups of butterflies. In addition to taking some artistic license, the basic terminology developed for lycaenid eggs by Downey and Allyn (1981) is useful for describing riodinid eggs. Seven general forms of eggs are covered here: (1) the "echinoid shape," that is, those resembling the test of a sea urchin (as in *Emesis tenedia, Synargis phylleus*; Fig. 2b,e,f); (2) a "fustrum shape," resembling a cone with the top sliced off (as in *Euselasia*; Fig. 1a), which is highly unusual among butterflies; (3) "tiarate," or crown shaped (as in *Symmachia tricolor*; Fig. 1e); (4) a single flattened pie that resembles diatoms in the genus *Stephanodiscus* (*Eurybia*; Fig. 1d); (5) appearing as two stacked pies (as in *Lasaia*; see Downey and Allyn 1981); (6) a form that resembles an ornate pastry (as in *Helicopis* and *Nymphidium*; Figs. 2, 3); and (7) a form that resembles a soccer ball or automobile tire enclosed in a net bag (as in *Thisbe irenea, Juditha dorilas, Synargis mycone*; Figs. 2, 3).

A perennial parallel has been drawn between riodinids and ly-caenids, including the form of their eggs. The difference between riodinid and lycaenid eggs was first pointed out by Downey and Allyn (1980), who noted, among other things, that one major difference is that *plastrons*—the highly porous areas of the chorion (abundant on lycaenid eggs) that may act like a gill for taking oxygen from rain-water—are typically absent on riodinid eggs (but see *Juditha dorilas*, Fig. 2d). Moreover, their study of merely thirteen riodinid species (within six genera) revealed a greater diversity of form than surveys of many more species, genera, and tribes of lycaenid eggs (Clark and Dickson 1971; Downey and Allyn 1980, 1981, 1982). Our understanding of riodinid eggs is very much in its infancy; but as more material becomes available, an even greater diversity of egg forms is certain to be found. It should be evident that a brief consideration of only a few riodinid eggs shows a truly remarkable diversity of form, and that a detailed comparative survey of riodinid eggs could add much to our under-standing of butterfly eggs in general and the relationships between the riodinids and lycaenids in particular.

The eggs of all butterflies are prone to be eaten by parasitoids and predators, and a number of defenses appear to have evolved that aid in keeping eggs out of harm's way. Many riodinids conceal their eggs by laying them in fissures and cracks in bark, in damaged portions of leaves, or off the hostplant (e.g., *Ancyluris, Symmachia, Mesenopsis, Synargis, Thisbe*). Another means of protection involves the instance when a female butterfly (e.g., *Euselasia chrysippe*) spends considerable time investigating an oviposition site rather than hastily laying an egg on the first appropriate plant, perhaps inspecting a plant for predators. One might make a case for parental care in instances when an egg is laid only in the presence of particular species of guardian ants (*Juditha, Lemonias*). Here the female must locate particular ant species, lay her eggs, and then leave the "babysitters" to protect the eggs (and the re-sulting caterpillars) from enemies. Although our understanding of riodinid eggs is rudimentary compared to other butterfly groups (e.g., Chew and Robbins 1984; Hinton 1981), as studies on riodinids increase a greater number of potential defenses used by adults to protect their eggs will certainly come to light.

The Caterpillar

As a beginning university student, I once overheard a botany professor proclaim that "zoology is the study of plants and their parasites." Al-though this is a distinctly botanicocentric viewpoint, it is nonetheless a concept whose simplicity rings true. Butterflies do not exist outside of the context of caterpillars—one cannot have one without the other, and one cannot have either without plants. The study of caterpillars is one of the most fascinating aspects about working with butterflies. How satisfying to observe a butterfly and be able to associate it with a host-plant and a series of interactions within a habitat; how indolent to simply swing the net and collect a specimen. Focusing on caterpillars permits an understanding of the interactions between butterflies, cater-pillars, and the plants they depend on for survival.

The study of caterpillars has greatly enriched our understanding of insect-plant interactions, symbiotic associations, defenses against para-sitoids and predators, behavior, evolution, systematics, and ecology. The number of ecological and evolutionary interactions that take place during the caterpillar stage strongly suggests that a rudimentary knowl-edge of caterpillars is fundamental to understanding butterflies. Those interested in an overview of ecological and evolutionary topics should see Stamp and Casey (1993) for a truly enjoyable and stimulating col-lection of articles on caterpillars. Those with an interest in caterpillar morphology should consult Peterson (1962), Stehr (1987), and Scoble (1992) for general treatments, while the papers of Miller (1991, 1996) are models for using comparative caterpillar morphology in system-atics. This section will focus briefly on caterpillar biology with special emphasis on the riodinids.

The Caterpillar or Larval Stage. The larval stage of all members of the order Lepidoptera is commonly known as a caterpillar. In functional terms the caterpillar is a chitonized head with mandibles for biting food into manageable fragments, and a soft, ambulatory body that houses a long gut for processing food.

Caterpillars show a remarkable diversity of form that reflects how they go about making a living. The outward appearance of caterpillars may range from extremely cryptic to brightly aposematic, they may bristle with spines and/or hairs, appear to be naked, or, as is clearly marked within the riodinids, some may parody caterpillars from other groups—a mimicry among caterpillars of distantly related groups (e.g., *Ancyluris, Necyria, Napaea, Chalodeta*). Caterpillars of papilionids or pierids exhibit the traditional, cylindrical shape and spend their lives crawling about on plants feeding on leaves in exposed positions. Others, such as the riodinid genera *Symmachia* and *Mesenopsis*, have slightly flattened bodies and spend much of their lives within the curled edge of a leaf, reflecting habits of certain moth families like Pyralidae and Tortricidae, while *Menander* appears much like a syrphid fly maggot, a trilobite, or a marine chiton (Figs. 4a,b, 53). The diet of butterfly caterpillars may range from the traditional fare of vegetable matter, to the flesh of other insects, to feeding entirely on secretions

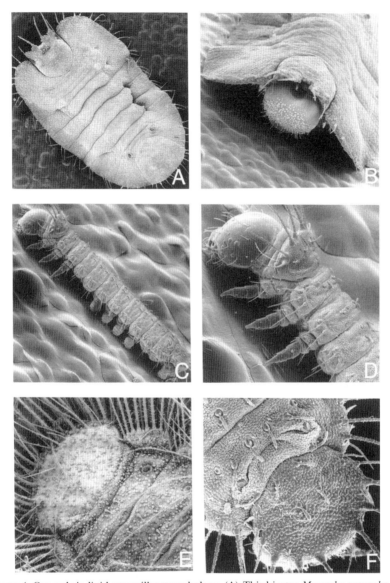

FIGURE 4. General riodinid caterpillar morphology. (A) Third instar *Menander menander* (dorsal view) showing a highly modified carapace. Note the locations of the anterior tentacle organs, tentacle nectary organs, and the anal plate. Also note that the right side of the carapace has been damaged in this specimen. (B) Frontal view of third instar *Menander menander* showing the head and how the carapace wraps around the body. (C) First instar *Synargis mycone* showing the three body regions: head, thorax, and abdomen. Note the position of the true legs on the thoracic segments, and the prolegs on the abdominal segments. (D) Detail of first instar *Synargis mycone* showing position of the stemmata, thoracic shield, true legs, and primary and secondary setae. (E) Detail of the anal plate of third instar *Mesenopsis melanochlora*, a non-myrmecophilous species. Note the position of the spiracles on abdominal segment 8, and the well-developed setae. (F) Detail of the anal plate on first instar *Synargis mycone*, a myrmecophilous species. Note position of spiracles on segment 8, and the areas where the tentacle nectary organs will become functional at the third instar. (Photos by P. J. DeVries)

produced by other insects (Cottrell 1984; Ackery 1988, 1990, 1991; Thomas et al. 1989; Fiedler 1991; DeVries et. al 1994).

Depending on the species, butterfly caterpillars feed either as solitary individuals or in gregarious groups. Typically those caterpillars that feed as solitary individuals are cryptic (e.g., *Leucochimona*) and those that feed as social groups are more obvious, or even aposematically colored, as in the lycaenid genus *Eumaeus* (DeVries 1977). Recent reviews suggest that the reasons for gregarious feeding or social assemblages include benefits that enhance their survivorship and aid in resource utilization (Fitzgerald 1993; Costa and Pierce 1996). For example, young caterpillars may be unable to attack a tough leaf surface alone; or, in the face of predation, there may be a better chance of some individuals attaining maturity in a gregarious group than if they were alone. Typically, a social group of caterpillars results from a single mass of eggs, but in some species a group may result from the eggs laid by several females (Chew and Robbins 1984). Caterpillars that live in social groups are frequently synchronous in their molting cycles, and often for good reason. If an individual caterpillar delays molting a day or two after the group, that individual is at risk of being eaten when it is immobile during the molting process. In the riodinids, gregarious caterpillars are known in the subfamily Euselasiinae, and semi-gregarious caterpillars are in the subfamily Riodininae from the tribes Eurybiini, Riodinini, Emesini, Lemoniini, and Nymphidiini (DeVries et al. 1994).

Caterpillar Morphology. Despite their diversity of form, color, and behavior, all caterpillars have the same basic body plan. A knowledge of a few morphological landmarks common to all caterpillars is useful in communicating effectively with biologists. A butterfly caterpillar is composed of three main divisions: a head, three thoracic segments (T1–3), and ten abdominal segments (A1–10); riodinid caterpillars have important features found on these three divisions (see Figs. 4 and 5).

Head (Figs. 4d, 7e, 8a). As the only extensively hardened or sclerotized portion of the caterpillar, the head provides attachment points for muscles and contains the stoutly armored mandibles that possess molars and incisor areas. The mandibles articulate laterally to function as shears where the cutting edge of one mandible plays against the edge of the other mandible, resulting in a "bite" of food being snipped off. In herbivorous caterpillars, these symmetrical bites of leaf can be discerned later in the compacted frass pellets. The cutting surfaces become worn down as the caterpillar matures, but these are replaced at each molt so each instar begins life with sharp new mandibles. An apparently unique character of riodinid mandibles is the presence of more than two mandibular setae (Harvey 1987b).

Along the side of the head, behind and above the antennae, are the group of simple eyes termed the *stemmata* (often incorrectly called ocelli). The stemmata typically consist of six tiny hemispherical warts, where five are arranged in a curve that opens to the posterior and the sixth is located posterior to the rest (Fig. 4d). The stemmata contain light-sensitive pigments that allow the caterpillar to distinguish light and dark as well as discriminate between the horizontal and vertical, and they probably produce a well-focused image as well (Dethier 1963). Among Lepidoptera, the arrangement of the stemmata can be an important taxonomic character.

Between the maxillary and labial palpi is located a slender horny tube called the spinneret, which serves a number of important functions. When the caterpillar walks, it sways its head from side to side, laying down a zigzag of silk that is subsequently grasped by the legs as the caterpillar moves forward. This silk acts as a "safety line" that guards against being knocked off a hostplant leaf or other substrate— an important tool for early instars that could starve to death if knocked off their plant. In *Anteros, Symmachia, Thisbe,* or *Theope,* caterpillar's silk may be used for securing rolled leaves or attaching leaf shelters to the hostplant where the caterpillars hide when not feeding. Prior to pupation, the silk gland provides the "button of silk" to attach the pupa to the substrate, the silk girdle to bind the pupa to the substrate, or, as in the case of *Sarota* and *Anteros,* to spin a cocoon.

Sutures. There are two obvious suture lines on the head. One is the *ecdysial line* and forms an inverted V-shape circumscribing the triangular frons (the face); the other is the *epicranial suture* and runs from the apex of the triangular frons to the top of the head or *epicranium* (Figs. 7e, 8a). Both of these sutures split apart during molting (or *ecdysis*) to allow the head of the next instar to be withdrawn. After molting, the cast head capsule consists of two halves of the head (split along the epicranial suture) and a triangular plate (split along the ecdysial suture), all loosely held together by threads of connective tissue. The sutures and the areas around them are often useful for describing caterpillars, or for comparing the differences between instars in a particular life cycle.

Thorax. The first three segments (T1–3), located immediately behind the head, comprise the thorax. Each of the thoracic segments bears a pair of *true legs* that terminate in a hard tarsal claw. The first thoracic segment (T1), termed the *prothorax*, is frequently the smallest

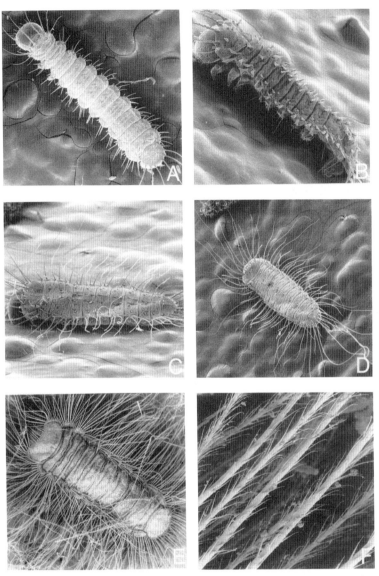

FIGURE 5. General riodinid caterpillar morphology and setae. (A) First instar *Synargis mycone* (dorsal view) showing the segmentation of head, thorax, and abdomen. Note also the primary and secondary setae. (B) First instar *Synargis phylleus* showing the head and how the carapace wraps around the body. (C) Lateral view of first instar *Symmachia tricolor* showing body segmentation and the long secondary setae. (D) Dorsal view of first instar *Symmachia tricolor* detailing the exaggeration of the secondary setae typical of nonmyrmecophilous species. (E) Dorsal view of third instar *Mesenopsis melanochlora* showing the dense and exaggerated profusion of secondary setae; these setae almost certainly function to keep potential predators away from the body. (F) Detail of secondary setae of *Mesenopsis melanochlora*. Note the accessory barbs on the shaft of the setae that are likely to impede arthropod predators like ants. (Photos by P. J. DeVries)

segment that may have unusual features of particular interest in the riodinids: functional spiracles, tufts of setae, the vibratory papillae, bladder setae; or it may bear the exaggerated prothoracic shield (Figs. 4d, 5b). The second thoracic segment (T2), or *mesothorax*, although distinct, is not particularly specialized. The third thoracic segment (T3), or *metathorax*, is where the extrusible anterior tentacle organs arise on some myrmecophilous species (see section on ant organs). Another feature of T3 is that it shares a spiracle with the boundary of T2 that is located under the cuticle.

Abdomen. Immediately posterior to T3 are the ten abdominal segments (designated A1 through A10) that form the bulk of the body (Fig. 4c), and these segments bear a number of important features. The primary means of caterpillar locomotion is through use of the *prolegs* located on segments A3 through A6 and then on A10. The prolegs function by hydraulic pressure and by means of some muscles that move them in and out, and they grip the substrate by means of a terminal rosette of microscopic hooks called *crochets*. The form and arrangement of the crochets separates the riodinids from other groups of butterflies (Harvey 1987b).

Abdominal segments 1 through 8 bear the external orifices of the respiratory system called *spiracles*. The spiracles open and close to allow gas exchange with the atmosphere, and each spiracle may act independently of the others. The position of the spiracles in riodinid caterpillars differs from that of all other butterflies by having the spiracle on T1 distinctly lower than the rest; caterpillars in other groups have all the spiracles essentially arranged in line. Segment A8 is important in myrmecophilous species as it bears the pair of extrusible tentacle nectary organs (see the section on ant-organs). Segments 9 and 10 are fused together and form the *anal plate*, a structure that may be conspicuous in the myrmecophilous species (Figs. 4f, 7a,b).

Setae. All caterpillars have bristlelike hairs, or *setae*, located on all of their segments. Depending on the species, the density, length, and type of setae may vary dramatically (Figs. 4–6). For example, caterpillars may range from those that appear almost naked (e.g., *Thisbe, Calospila, Menander, Eurybia*) to those that have so many setae that they resemble ambulatory powder puffs (e.g., *Anteros, Symmachia, Apodemia*). Nevertheless, it is typical for the first instar caterpillar of any species to have a reduced number of setae, even those that may be extremely hirsute in later instars.

Quite a few types of setae have been described in Lepidoptera caterpillars (Stehr 1987); two are important for our purposes: the primary and secondary setae. The *primary setae* are relatively few in number, and

FIGURE 6. Adding insult to herbivory. This mature *Juditha molpe* caterpillar is seen here drinking at an extrafloral nectary of its hostplant while being tended by *Dolicho-derus bispinosus* ants. Note that the caterpillar has almost completely eaten away the young leaf that is attached near the base of the nectary. (Photo by P. J. DeVries)

their position remains constant as a caterpillar undergoes its molting sequence from first to final instar. As a general rule, first instar caterpillars have the primary thoracic setae curving forward and the primary abdominal setae directed to the rear (see Figs. 4–5). The *secondary setae* generally develop in second and subsequent instars, and their number may increase dramatically with successive molts. The form of both primary and secondary setae may change during the molt sequence.

The study of caterpillar setae, especially the position and form of the primary setae (called *chaetotaxy*) has been important in systematic studies of butterflies and moths (Scudder 1889; Kitching 1984, 1985; Stehr 1987; Miller 1991). Although primary setae are valuable in systematic work, relatively few specimens of first instar caterpillars are available for most butterfly and moth species, and systematists typically have to rely upon secondary setae in their studies.

A few examples of primary setae from our riodinid fauna show how different they can be even among congeners. For example, consider the primary setae in first instar *Synargis mycone* and those in *Synargis phylleus* (Figs. 5a,b). Here the flattened primary setae of *S. phylleus* are in strong contrast to the typical bristle-like setae found on *S. mycone* and elsewhere among the Lemoniini and Nymphidiini. Observing the length and density of setae is often a convenient way of telling whether a riodinid caterpillar is myrmecophilous or not. Typically, caterpillars with obvious setae do not have associations with ants, and of course they do not have secretory organs or produce calls, as do the myrmecophiles. The long setae may serve a defensive function by keeping ants and other potentially dangerous arthropod predators at bay. For example, the long setae of *Sarota gyas* can be directed toward any area of the body that is stimulated. When ants come in contact with the caterpillar, they withdraw almost immediately, spend time cleaning their antennae, and then avoid the caterpillar (DeVries 1988a), and I have made similar observations on caterpillars of *Mesenopsis melanochlora*, *Anteros formosus*, and *A. acheus*. When the ants groom themselves after contacting a caterpillar, it is likely that they are trying to remove the minute auxiliary barbs that occur on the long setae (Figs. 5e,f), which may break off and adhere to the head of the ant. Thus, such setae are likely to be a defense against small arthropod predators. Finally, long setae may also serve as a barrier to potential predators in the pupal stage when they are used to form a cocoon that entirely envelops the pupae (e.g., *Anteros, Sarota, Mesenopsis*).

Caterpillar Growth. After a caterpillar reaches a certain size, it stops eating and undergoes a molting process during which the skin and head split and are sloughed off to permit the emergence of the next instar. The duration of the caterpillar's life prior to each molt is called a *larval instar*, and it is worthy of note that the onset of each larval molt is signaled by the production of wet frass instead of the typical dry pellets produced between molts. As is typical for most groups of butterflies, the larval stage of riodinids is punctuated by five molts; the caterpillar emerging from the egg is the first instar, which grows until it molts into a second instar, and so on until the fifth instar, which, upon molting, produces the pupa, or *chrysalis*. Furthermore, each instar may have a distinctive appearance, a trait seen best in some groups of papilionids and nymphalids (DeVries 1987; DeVries and Martinez 1993), but also occurs within some riodinids (e.g., *Ancyluris, Emesis*).

The caterpillar is effectively an eating machine characterized by a voracious appetite and rapid growth. Consider that during their itinerary from egg to mature fifth instar caterpillars, some moth species may increase their weight 200-fold or more (Reavey 1993). A more modest example from our riodinid fauna is *Thisbe irenea*, whose caterpillars may increase their weight 60-fold during the growth phase from first to fifth instar—all in less than two weeks.

Growth is not simply a steady increase in weight from first to fifth instar but a dramatic fluctuation of weight that is forecast by the onset of each molt. As a particular instar grows, it steadily increases in weight and size until physiological conditions signal the onset of the molt to the next instar. At this point, the gut is voided of its contents (heralded by the presence of wet frass), and the weight of the caterpillar drops below the maximum attained by that particular instar. After emergence from the cast skin, the newly molted caterpillar weighs less than the maximum weight of the previous instar. However, once this instar begins eating, its weight will quickly increase and soon exceed the maximum weight of the previous instar. A dieter's nightmare no doubt, but a remarkably efficient way for a caterpillar to attain maximum size and proceed to the pupal instar.

Caterpillar Behavior and Feeding. After molting, caterpillar behavior may also change in several important ways. For example, one subtle behavioral change after molting that is common among most species is when they feed. Caterpillars are often thought to feed almost constantly throughout life, and those with experience rearing them will agree that this is a reasonable assumption. However, under field conditions, diurnal feeding typically diminishes drastically or stops entirely in the mid to late fourth instar, and subsequent feeding activity takes place entirely during the night. This is probably the result of pressure by visually hunting predators. Larger caterpillars are more obvious than small ones, and so they hide during the day. Indeed, my own observations suggest that diurnal vespid wasps have keen eyesight, and can easily detect a fifth instar *Thisbe irenea* or similar-sized caterpillar from over 15 cm away. Of interest is to note that only the few species in the wasp genus *Apoica* are active nocturnally, whereas the other hundreds of species in the family Vespidae hunt caterpillars during the day.

A more dramatic example of behavioral change is the molt to third instar in myrmecophilous species, a time when the ant-organs become functional. The third and subsequent instars are persistently tended by ants and show all of the behaviors necessary to maintain their association with ants (see the section on myrmecophily). Even though these caterpillars are typically surrounded by a guard of ants, there is also a switch in feeding times as the caterpillars mature. The timing of when caterpillars drink extrafloral nectar goes hand in hand with when they feed on leaves (Figs. 6, 59); early instars are found at the nectaries constantly, whereas later they are generally found at the nectaries only during the night (DeVries and Baker 1989).

Except for some peculiar species in the Riodinidae and Lycaenidae (see Cottrell 1984; DeVries et al. 1994), butterfly caterpillars feed typically on plant material. The fact that butterfly caterpillars may, overall, feed on a great many plant families with tissues containing toxic secondary compounds has proven fertile ground for understanding how insects detoxify poisons in their food. Of interest is that riodinids and lycaenids have the greatest host breadth among all groups of butterflies (Pierce 1987; DeVries et al. 1994), even though the life histories of most of the species remain unknown. It is clear that butterflies will remain important in the development of research into the evolution of insect-plant interactions (Futuyma and Slatkin 1983; Stamp and Casey 1993).

It has long been known that there are patterns of host use among butterflies, patterns that gave rise to the term coevolution (Brues 1924; Ehrlich and Raven 1965). Butterfly caterpillars that feed on a restricted set of plant species are termed *monophagous*, or specialist feeders. An example of a monophagous species would be *Thisbe irenea*, a riodinid that feeds only on a few species of the genus *Croton* (Euphorbiaceae) throughout its geographical range. Species that feed on a wide range of unrelated plant families are termed *polyphagous* or generalist feeders, and good examples of this type would be the riodinids *Juditha molpe* and *Synargis mycone*. Within a small area of their geographical distribution (even a single hectare at some sites) the caterpillars of these butterflies may feed on plants embraced by over a dozen families. Although in widespread use in the ecological literature, these terms may not always paint an accurate picture of the diet breadth of all butterflies. Some butterfly species may change their diets depending on their geographical locality and be monophagous at one locality and polyphagous at another. For thoughtful analyses of this phenomenon, see Singer (1983, 1984), Singer and Parmesan (1993), and Singer et al. (1994).

Ant-Organs and Myrmecophily

Like most other organisms, butterfly caterpillars are intolerant of the presence of other species. In some cases, however, butterfly caterpillars form intimate symbiotic relationships with ants, wherein the ants protect them from enemies while they are feeding, molting, or moving about in a caterpillarly fashion. Although it has been known for over one-hundred years that butterfly caterpillars form associations with ants (Edwards 1878; Lamborn 1915; Farquharson 1921; Jackson 1937; Eliot 1973; Cottrell 1984), and modern studies have provided both theoretical and empirical insights into these complex associations, our understanding of these types of symbioses remains rudimentary. The fact is that out of potentially 6,000 riodinid and lycaenid species, the natural history of only a tiny fraction of them has been examined in any detail (summarized in Cottrell 1984; DeVries 1991a; DeVries et al. 1994; Fiedler 1991). Given the nature and complexity of caterpillar-ant symbioses, there is clearly much to be learned from their study that will be relevant to all branches of biology, and I genuinely hope that more research is directed toward this area of biology.

In butterflies the ability to form symbioses with ants (termed *myrmecophily*, meaning ant loving) is found only among members of the Riodinidae and Lycaenidae. The basis of these symbioses is that caterpillars provide food secretions to ants in exchange for protection against arthropod predators (Pierce et al. 1987; DeVries 1991b; Wagner 1993). In addition to protection, the association with ants may provide caterpillars with other benefits that include faster development times, shelter, overwintering sites, and food (Ross 1966; DeVries and Baker 1989; Thomas et al. 1989; Baylis and Pierce 1991; Elmes et al. 1991a,b; Wagner 1993; Cushman et al. 1994).

As one might guess from the unusual nature of this symbiosis, these caterpillars have evolved a number of specialized adaptations that enhance this intimate association. Working with European lycaenids, Malicky (1969, 1970) made important contributions to the topic by pointing out that caterpillars of myrmecophilous species tend to (1) lack a thrashing or beat reflex when the caterpillar is molested; (2) have a thick cuticle (a tough hide) compared to other Lepidoptera, which probably helps withstand the bites of ant mandibles; and (3) possess tiny secretory pits scattered on the epidermis that appear to emit substances important for mediating ant association, the *perforated cupola organs* (abbreviated PCOs). While myrmecophilous riodinids do not have the thrashing reflex, no study has examined the thickness of their cuticles relative to other Lepidoptera, and the function of the PCOs is not understood in any lycaenid or riodinid.

Other more conspicuous specializations that become functional upon molting to the third instar consist of organs peculiar to myrmecophilous caterpillars (collectively termed "ant-organs"; Figs. 7, 8). These include organs for producing sound, food secretions, and semiochemicals, all of which work in concert to modify ant behavior and enhance the protective attitude of ants toward caterpillars. Several types of adaptations to myrmecophily in butterflies have been reviewed and described by Cottrell (1984) and DeVries (1988b, 1991a,b,c), while still others are treated in this book.

Much of our perception of riodinid myrmecophily and evolution has typically been inferred from what we know of the lycaenids. For example, because the riodinids were lumped within the lycaenids, myrmecophily in butterflies was long considered to have evolved only a single time (e.g., Hinton 1951; Vane-Wright 1978; Pierce 1987), mainly because although the caterpillars of both groups were known to produce secretions for ants, few riodinid caterpillars had been examined critically. However, a simple comparison between riodinid and lycaenid caterpillars (Fig. 9) shows that the ant organs of lycaenids and riodinids are analogous (that is, they have similar functions), but they are not homologous (they arise from different areas on the body). Elsewhere (DeVries 1988b, 1991c) I have used caterpillar ant-organs to argue that it is most probable that myrmecophily evolved at least twice in butterflies, i.e., once in the lycaenids and independently in the riodinids (Fig. 10).

Regardless of their phylogenetic relationships, myrmecophilous riodinid and lycaenid caterpillars form symbioses with similar ants,

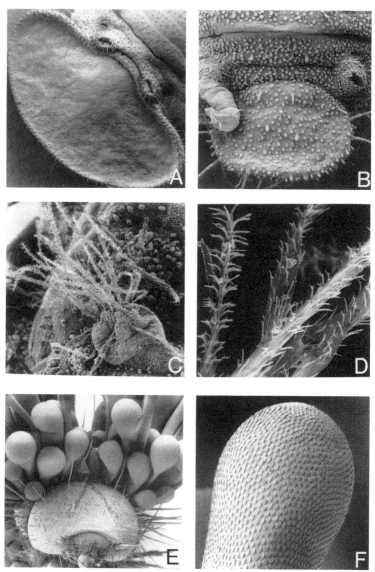

FIGURE 7. Caterpillar ant-organs of the Riodinidae. (A) Fifth instar *Theope eleutho* showing extremely well-developed anal plate. Note position of the orifices where the tentacle nectary organs arise, and the position of the abdominal spiracle. (B) Fifth instar *Lemonias caliginea* showing the anal plate. Note position of the tentacle nectary organs, and that the one on the left is extruded. (C) Detail of an extruded anterior tentacle organ of *Lemonias caliginea* showing the brushlike setae. (D) Detail of the brushlike setae of *Lemonias caliginea* showing the surface structure. Note that it is likely that this surface structure aids in dissemination of volatile chemicals. (E) Frontal view of the head of *Theope eleutho* showing the exaggerated corona of balloon setae. (F) Detail of the surface of a balloon seta of *Theope eleutho* showing the covering of scale-like structures. Although it remains to be demonstrated, it is likely that the balloon setae disseminate volatile chemicals that mediate associations with ants. (Photos by P. J. DeVries)

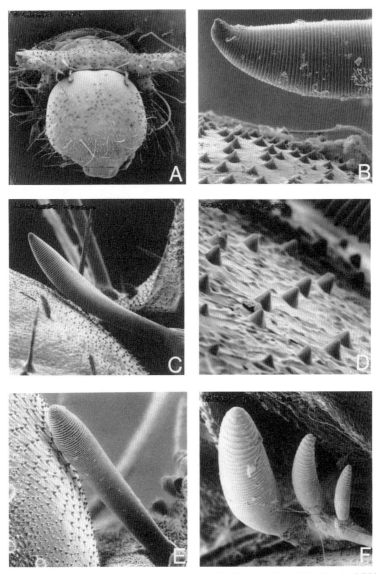

FIGURE 8. Caterpillar ant-organs of the Riodinidae. (A) Frontal view of the head of fifth instar *Synargis gela* showing position of the vibratory papillae against the epicranium. (B) Detailed lateral view of a vibratory papilla of *Lemonias caliginea* and the thornlike ridges on the epicranium. It is easy to imagine how these structures function to produce stridulations. (C) Detailed lateral view of a vibratory papilla of *Synargis mycone* and the epicranial granulations. (D) Detailed view of the epicranial granulations in *Synargis mycone*. Note the grooved surface of the vibratory papilla in upper right of the photograph. (E) Detailed lateral view of the vibratory papilla of *Audre* nr *aurina* and the well-developed epicranial granulations. (F) Detailed lateral view of one set of vibratory papillae on *Theope matuta*. Note that this is the only riodinid species known that consistently bears six vibratory papillae—three per set. (Photos by P. J. DeVries)

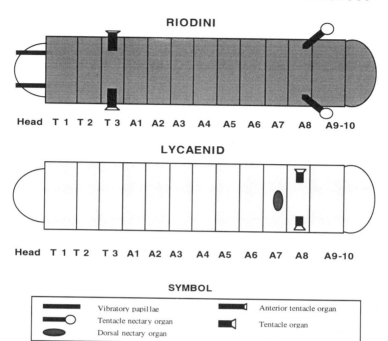

FIGURE 9. Schematic diagram comparing the ant-organs on riodinid and lycaenid caterpillars. Note that the positions on the body of the caterpillars indicate that riodinid and lycaenid ant-organs are analogous but not homologous. (After DeVries 1991a)

namely those ant species whose foraging ecology indicates that they forage on secretions (DeVries 1991b). Furthermore, the same ant species that tend butterfly caterpillars also tend Homoptera and plants with extrafloral nectaries. Hence, in any habitat where they occur, multiple species of butterfly caterpillars, Homoptera, and plants all share the same ant symbionts. Naturally, a broad understanding of myrmecophily in butterflies demands an understanding of their ant symbionts, something that is well beyond the scope of this book. The interested reader is strongly encouraged to consult Hölldobler and Wilson (1990) and Bolton (1994) for excellent means of becoming familiar with the systematics and biology of ants. The following section focuses on the specialized features found exclusively on members of the Riodinidae and provides notes on their form and function within the context of myrmecophily.

Tentacle Nectary Organs: Paying for Protection. When observing a riodinid caterpillar that is being tended by ants, one will notice that

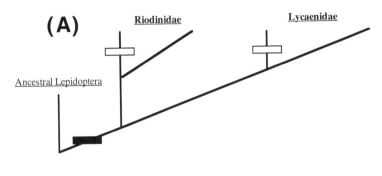

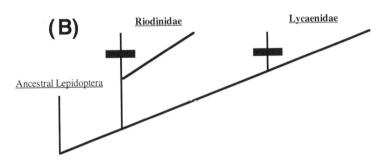

FIGURE 10. Evolution of butterfly myrmecophily. Solid bars indicate myrmecophily, open bars indicate the loss of myrmecophily. (A) A long-standing hypothesis of ancestral myrmecophily in butterflies where the trait was lost at least twice. This is inconsistent with homologies of ant-organs. (B) The simplest hypothesis that is consistent with ant-organ homologies indicating that butterfly myrmecophily arose at least twice. (After DeVries 1991a)

the ants pay close attention to a pair of ant-organs on the abdominal segment 8. These are termed the *tentacle nectary organs* (commonly abbreviated TNOs), and can be extruded individually or simultaneously. The position of the TNOs is marked by two orifices, and, depending on the group, the orifices may be almost indistinguishable from the surrounding tissue (*Eurybia* and *Nymphidium*), marked by a slight indentation (*Synargis* and *Thisbe*); or, in genera like *Theope* and *Audre*, the orifices may be on stalks and form part of an exaggerated and flattened anal plate (Fig. 7a,b).

Typically, when ants antennate (tap with their antennae) the anal plate or around the orifices, the translucent TNOs extrude from the body and yield a drop of clear secretion at the tip of what looks like the finger of a miniature surgical glove (Figs. 7b, 11). As soon as the drop of secretion appears, it is enthusiastically imbibed by the ant, and then

FIGURE 11. *Ectatomma ruidum* ants drinking secretion from the everted tentacle nectary organs of a mature *Thisbe irenea* caterpillar. Note that this photo was taken moments before a tachinid fly maggot emerged from the body of the caterpillar (see Fig. 14). (Photo by P. J. DeVries)

the organ is withdrawn back into the body. The ants, however, are so enthralled by the secretion that they constantly antennate the caterpillar to solicit more. For example, I estimate that a tending *Ectatomma* ant will solicit secretions from a fourth or fifth instar *Thisbe irenea* caterpillar at least once every minute. When a caterpillar has had enough of these unrelenting solicitations, the caterpillar will tap the posterior segments on the substrate several times, a signal that is sometimes audible. Afterward the ants may cease their attentions for a time, but they generally resume solicitations for the secretion within a few moments.

The ants' stubborn persistence in collecting tentacle nectary organ secretions can be remarkable, and it is common to observe ants avidly tending a caterpillar while ignoring the extrafloral nectaries of the caterpillar's hostplant. Part of the reason for this behavior seems to lie in the chemical content of the caterpillar secretion, which may be very different from that of the extrafloral nectar offered by the caterpillar's hostplants. For example, the caterpillar secretions of *Thisbe irenea* contain much higher concentrations of amino acids than those found in *Croton* extrafloral nectar. While the extrafloral nectar may contain a sugar concentration of approximately 33 percent, there are almost no detectable sugars in the caterpillar secretion (DeVries 1988b; DeVries and Baker 1989). In this case it appears that ants obtain a more nutritious secretion from caterpillars than that provided by plant extrafloral nectaries, even if it is not as sweet. Caterpillar-ant interactions provide a good example of a common rule in the evolution of symbiotic associations—"you scratch my back and I'll scratch yours." In other words, the caterpillar secretion produced by the TNOs may be viewed in an evolutionary context as a payment to ants for protection against predators (Pierce 1987; DeVries 1991b).

The secretions produced by some lycaenid caterpillars appear to differ substantially from those of *Thisbe*. However, because the secretions of so very few riodinid or lycaenid caterpillar species have ever been analyzed, it is hardly surprising that different species have different secretions. Lycaenid secretions apparently contain low concentrations of amino acids, but have sugar concentrations similar to plant extrafloral nectar (Baker and Baker 1975, 1976; Maschwitz et al. 1975; Pierce 1983; Fiedler 1991).

The attractiveness of caterpillar secretions to ants is influenced by the individual plant that a caterpillar feeds upon. For example, Baylis and Pierce (1991) demonstrated that caterpillars of *Jalmenus evagoras* (Lycaenidae) which fed on fertilized hostplants were tended by more ants than those which fed on nonfertilized plants. This implies that the attractiveness of secretions produced by a caterpillar depends on the quality of its diet, and this in turn may translate directly into protection against predators (see also Peterson 1995). Using the old economic adage "you get what you pay for," it seems that the degree of tending by ants may be related to the rate of pay. In other words, if given a choice, why should an ant tend a caterpillar that pays less than the one next to it?

There are likely to be other factors in the variations of caterpillar secretions. It is quite possible that the chemistry of secretions varies depending on what type of ant symbionts typically tend a caterpillar (DeVries and Baker 1989). For example, the high amino acid concentration (with no sugars) found in *Thisbe* secretions may be the result of generally forming symbiotic associations with ants that are, effectively, once-removed carnivores; *Ectatomma* is unusual among ponerine ants in that it feeds in large part on secretions, whereas close relatives are typically carnivores. On the other hand, caterpillars of *Theope* that typically associate only with secretion-foraging ants like *Azteca* may have secretions that are lower in amino acids but higher in sugar concentrations than *Thisbe* (DeVries and Baker 1989).

Variation in the chemical composition has been documented for secretions produced by plants (Baker et al. 1978), Homoptera (Auclair 1963), and caterpillars (Maschwitz et al. 1975; DeVries and Baker 1989), and ants have been shown to be able to discriminate among sugars and amino acids in liquids (Lanza 1988). Given that the vast majority of caterpillar-ant symbioses have never been studied, we may expect that overall caterpillar secretions will be shown to have a greater chemical variety than is currently documented. An interesting study would be to explore for a correlation between the chemistry of caterpillar secretions and the types of ants that tend them. Such a study may help explain in part why some caterpillars appear to associate only with particular ants (e.g., *Theope* and *Azteca*)—similar to the correlation between flower nectar and type of pollinator (Baker and Baker 1976). Although this topic has never been explored, it is probable that, in addition to sugars and amino acids, caterpillar secretions also contain compounds like phenols and/or lipids that are important in mediating interactions with ants.

Anterior Tentacle Organs. Many myrmecophilous riodinid caterpillars have, in addition to the tentacle nectary organs, a pair of extrusible subdorsal glands on the third thoracic segment called *anterior tentacle organs.* In some cases (*Menander*), the location of the anterior tentacle organ orifices is well marked, while in others (*Thisbe, Synargis*) the location is difficult to discern. With a little patient observation in the field, however, one can see the anterior tentacle organs being momentarily extruded and quickly withdrawn back into the body. As far as I can determine, ants seldom antennate the orifices of the anterior tentacle organs, and the timing of when these organs are extruded appears to be entirely under the control of the caterpillar (DeVries 1988b).

When the anterior tentacle organs are extruded out of the body, they too resemble the finger of a surgical glove. However, instead of yielding a drop of secretion like the tentacle nectary organs, the tip bears a set of distinct setae that overall looks like a tiny feather duster (Fig. 7c,d). When these organs extrude from the body they cause a dramatic change in the behavior of attending ants (Fig. 12). For example, in

FIGURE 12. A *Camponotus sericieventris* ant reacting to the eversion of the anterior tentacle organs from a mature *Synargis mycone* caterpillar. Note the defensive posture of the ant. The anterior tentacle organs can be seen protruding from thoracic segment 3, just in front of the ant's head. (Photo by P. J. DeVries)

Thisbe irenea and *Ectatomma*, the ants near the caterpillar will snap to attention with their mandibles agape, and curl the abdomen under their body in what is clearly a defensive posture. While in this posture, moving a small piece of wood or thread near the caterpillar typically releases an aggressive attack by the ants—they rush at the object, bite it, and attempt to sting it (DeVries 1988b).

The reaction of ants suggests that the anterior tentacle organs emit a volatile chemical similar to ant alarm pheromone—something that was postulated for lycaenid caterpillars some time ago (Clark and Dickson 1956; Malicky 1970; Claassens and Dickson 1977; Cottrell 1984; DeVries 1984a). Under high magnification, each of the setae on the anterior tentacle organs is covered with numerous branches and flaps (Fig. 7d). One might expect such structural arrangement from an insect organ that disseminates a volatile chemical (see Boppré 1984; Vane-Wright and Boppré 1993), and these setae also bear a strong resemblance to osmophores—glands on plants that disseminate volatile scents to attract pollinators (see Stern et al. 1987; Fahn 1988; Curry et al. 1991). In a behavioral sense, it appears that the anterior tentacle organs function by seizing the attention of ants through chemical means and helping to keep it focused on the caterpillars. Although a number of workers provide observations on these types of organs in both riodinids and lycaenids (Cripps and Jackson 1940; Henning 1983; Cottrell 1984; DeVries 1988b), the chemical composition of caterpillar emissions and how they compare to ant alarm pheromones remains unknown.

The Balloon Setae of Theope *and* Nymphidium. In an important early paper on butterflies of Trinidad, Guppy (1904) noted that the caterpillars of two *Theope* species possessed a corona of inflated setae around the head. Subsequent investigations have shown that among riodinids this trait is typically found only on caterpillars of the genera *Theope* and *Nymphidium*. These *balloon* setae (or bladder setae of Harvey 1987a) are typically found in two or more sizes, and depending on the species may be composed of several different colors (see species accounts of *N. mantus, T. eleutho, T. virgilius*). The setae taper dramatically from their bulbous tips down to their attachment points, and when examined at high magnification they resemble an elongate balloon whose surface appears to be covered in flat, overlapping scales (Fig. 7e,f).

With one exception (i.e., *mantus*) the balloon setae on *Nymphidium* caterpillars are generally reduced in number and size (Figs. 58, 59), while they may be very conspicuous on *Theope* caterpillars. In fact, some species of *Theope* (e.g., *eleutho, virgilius*) have such exaggerated setae that they impart a comical "balloon-headed" appearance to the caterpillar (Fig. 7e).

Although the existence of balloon setae on *Theope* caterpillars has been known for nearly a century, their function has not been investigated. As so little is known about balloon setae, I here provide a few observations that may intrigue future investigators. My observations on various species of *Theope* suggest that the balloon setae play a role in mediating symbioses with ants. For example, *Azteca* ants will frequently antennate the balloon setae of *Theope* and then briefly seize one of the setae with their mandibles. After biting a seta the ant will run about for a few moments in an agitated manner and cause a markedly increased activity in nearby ants—an analogous behavior can be simulated by crushing an individual ant near its nestmates. This suggests that the balloon setae secrete some chemical substance that causes a brief alarm response in the attending ants and thus function in a manner similar to the anterior tentacle organs.

Much like a tautly inflated balloon that has been squeezed between two fingers and then released abruptly, the body of a balloon seta bends inward when seized in an ant's mandibles and springs outward upon release, returning to its original shape. This seems to indicate that balloon setae are not solid structures but composed of some resilient material that retains its turgidity after being compressed. Further attesting to their resiliency, the balloon setae retain their structural integrity in caterpillars preserved in alcohol and in the dried cast skins. However, when squeezed too hard with forceps, the setae lose some of their integrity and take on a permanent, semideflated appearance. The morphology of balloon setae, the contents of the setae, and their function in caterpillar-ant symbioses remain to be explored.

Vibratory Papillae: Sound Production Organs. The vibratory papillae are a pair of mobile, rodlike appendages arising from the distal edge of segment T1 of caterpillars in the tribes Lemoniini and Nymphidiini (Callaghan 1977, 1982a, 1986a; Schremmer 1978; Harvey 1987a; DeVries 1991c). These organs were first noted on Argentinean caterpillars of the genus *Audre* by Bruch (1926) and Borquin (1953), and were subsequently described in greater detail for a species of *Lemonias* by Ross (1964), who termed them *vibratory papillae* (Fig. 8).

Ross (1966) showed that the vibratory papillae are ringed with annulations along their shafts, and that they have well-developed abductor and adductor muscles that move them rapidly up and down. He suggested that the beating motion of *Lemonias* vibratory papillae might convey vibrations to ants. A later study (DeVries 1988b) used the morphology of the vibratory papillae, head movement, and specialized epicranial granulations of *Thisbe irenea* caterpillars to develop a model of how all of these components function in concert to produce an acoustical call. The model proposed that sound is produced when the head is moved in and out, and the ringed shaft of each vibratory papilla

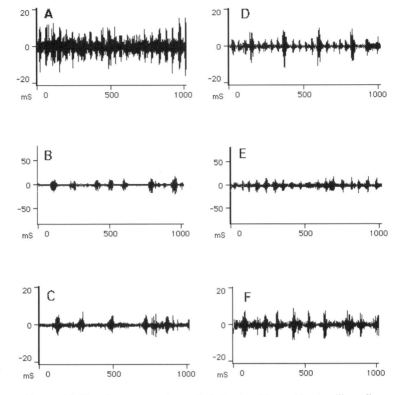

FIGURE 13. Wave-form comparisons of riodinid and lycaenid caterpillar calls.
(A) *Lemonias zygia* (Riodinidae). (B) *Synargis mycone* (Riodinidae). (C) *Theope lycaenina*
(Riodinidae). (D) *Thereus pedusa* (Lycaenidae). (E) *Arawacus lincoides* (Lycaenidae).
(F) *Panthiades bitias* (Lycaenidae). Note the general similarity of the calls among all of
these species.

grates on the specialized epicranial granulations, effectively akin to
how the Latin American percussion instrument, the *güiro*, is played in
accompaniment to salsa, merengue, or bossa nova music.

Several lines of evidence established that this model was correct.
First, caterpillars with vibratory papillae produce calls that can be detected and recorded with a sensitive microphone (see Fig. 13). Second,
the call is diminished when one vibratory papilla is removed, elimi-
nated when both are removed, but returns when the vibratory papillae
are replaced at the next molt (DeVries 1990, 1991c). Third, caterpillars
found in nature without the vibratory papillae developed are mute,
even though they have epicranial granulations and move their heads
normally. Finally, experimental evidence indicates that caterpillar calls
function to attract and maintain ant symbionts (DeVries 1990).

The number of vibratory papillae may vary with respect to individuals and species. Typically, caterpillars have two (e.g., *Thisbe irenea, Synargis mycone*), but some species may have two pairs (one large and one very small) (Fig. 8). Some may have three or none at all, and at least one species, *Theope matuta,* has six vibratory papillae—a pair with three shafts per attachment point. Vibratory papillae appear to divide roughly into two morphological types: (1) those with annulations distributed evenly along the distal two-thirds of the shaft and with the cusp surfaces radiating out from the central axis, as in *Thisbe, Juditha, Synargis, Calospila,* and *Menander*; and (2) those with annulations of varying widths at the distal one-third, with the cusps directed in either an anterior or a posterior direction, as in some species of *Theope* and *Nymphidium.*

Members of the tribes Lemoniini and Nymphidiini have rows of specialized granulations on the epicranium, and it is on this surface, covered in plectralike teeth, where the vibratory papillae strike (Fig. 8). Available evidence (DeVries 1991c) suggests there are at least five general types of specialized epicranial granulations. The granulations may consist of (1) irregular rows of sharp, roughly conical granulations that project forward (*Thisbe, Synargis*); (2) longitudinally flattened disks that are directed slightly forward (*Calospila*); (3) sharp, erect wedges with the bases buttressed on two sides (*Menander*); (4) a raised, pointed edge with heavy buttressing at the posterior edge of the base (*Nymphidium mantus, Theope*); or (5) blunt hemispheres (*Nymphidium*).

Call Production and Vibratory Papillae. As outlined above, the possession of vibratory papillae in riodinid caterpillars is strongly correlated with the ability to produce a call. There are, however, two exceptions for call production with vibratory papillae among the riodinids. First, *Eurybia* caterpillars produce distinct calls yet do not possess vibratory papillae or granulations on the epicranium. The ability to produce calls in *Eurybia* caterpillars has evolved differently, and thus independently, from members of the Lemoniini and Nymphidiini, perhaps through shivering as in the lycaenids (DeVries 1991c). Second, some caterpillars in the genus *Nymphidium* that possess vibratory papillae and epicranial granulations, and exhibit head oscillation behavior, do not produce calls. Here it appears that vibratory papillae are prevented from contacting the epicranial granulations due to a dense covering of mushroom-like setae on the epicranium. Consequently, *Nymphidium* is the only riodinid genus known thus far in which the possession of vibratory papillae is not correlated with the ability to produce calls (see DeVries 1991c).

Caterpillar and Ant Calls. Until recently the notion that caterpillars could produce acoustic calls was an idea that seemed preposterous. It is now known that many butterfly caterpillars in the Riodinidae and Lycaenidae typically produce acoustic signals that function in the formation of symbioses with ants. A survey of many caterpillar species showed that only riodinid and lycaenids have the ability to produce calls (Fig. 13), and that this trait is strongly correlated with those species that form symbioses with ants (DeVries 1990, 1991c, and unpublished). Are caterpillar calls unique to myrmecophilous caterpillars, or do they occur elsewhere in nature? Various lines of evidence suggest that such calls occur elsewhere. Several studies have shown that ants produce acoustic signals that function to attract nestmates to resources (see Baroni-Urbani et al. 1988; Hölldobler and Wilson 1991). Another study compared the calls produced by lycaenid caterpillars to those of their obligate host ant species (DeVries et al. 1993) and found that although caterpillar calls were not identical to those of ants, their calls were similar to those produced by ants—no mean feat for a caterpillar! The calls of both caterpillars and ants are low amplitude and substrate borne. This means that the energy and characteristics of the calls (Fig. 13) travel in substrate like wood, leaves, or bark, and that a sensitive microphone and amplifier are required for humans to hear or record them (DeVries 1991d). That the calls are substrate borne is not so odd if we consider that ants do not hear per se but are extremely good at detecting vibrations in the substrates they walk on. What is exciting about riodinid and lycaenid caterpillar calls is that it serves as an example of how the call of one species evolved to attract another, unrelated species only in the context of forming symbiotic associations. Although there is a great deal more work to be done, it is likely that caterpillar calls evolved to enhance the symbioses between themselves and ants.

Protection by Ants. Experimental studies have shown that forming symbiotic associations with ants provides caterpillars with protection against arthropod predators, and that the most important predators include social wasps, spiders, Hemiptera, and parasitoids in the wasp families Braconidae and Ichneumonidae (Pierce 1987; Pierce et al. 1987; DeVries 1988b, 1991b; Thomas et al. 1989; Wagner 1993). In the case of myrmecophilous riodinids, parasitoid flies in the family Tachinidae are seldom deterred by the presence of ants. The tachinid flies circumvent ant guards by either ovipositing on the caterpillar too quickly for the ants to notice, or they lay microtype eggs on the leaves which are ingested by the caterpillar. However, there appears to be a price for this circumvention. Typically the full complement of caterpillar ant-organs remains functional right up to the time when the tachinid maggot emerges from the body of the host (Figs. 11, 14), thus assuring a constant attendance of ants (DeVries 1988b). My observations from Panama and Ecuador strongly suggest that few tachinid flies

FIGURE 14. An *Ectatomma ruidum* ant with a tachinid fly maggot seized in its mandibles. This photograph was taken moments after the tachinid fly maggot emerged from the body of the *Thisbe irenea* caterpillar on the left, and these are the same caterpillars and ants as in Figure 11. (Photo by P. J. DeVries)

reach adulthood after attacking a myrmecophilous riodinid caterpillar. While the tachinid maggot is squirming its way out of its host's body, what invariably happens is that the ants seize the maggot, kill it, and carry the carcass back to their nest (Fig. 14)—an unforeseen and lethal consequence of attacking a myrmecophile.

The Pupa

After a final instar caterpillar has grown to its maximum size, it stops eating and begins voiding the gut of all food (as wet frass) in preparation for its final molt. This phase is called a *prepupa*. Because its physiological machinery is very active, the prepupa stage is generally attended by a noticeable change in coloration, and a wandering phase where the caterpillar will crawl ceaselessly for a time before finding a place to settle down to its final molt. This wandering phase serves to disperse the caterpillar away from its hostplant and from potential parasitoids and predators that may cue in on damaged leaf tissue and kill the prepupa. Incidentally, it is during the noticeable wandering phase that many casual entomologists take note of caterpillars and subsequently confine them in containers. Often such caterpillars will pupate, but instead of a butterfly, a parasitoid emerges from the pupa. It may be that such caterpillars are more obvious to the observer because of a behavioral change induced by the interaction of their defenses and that of the parasitoid within to prolong the wandering phase (see Shapiro 1976; Smith-Trail 1980; Stamp 1981). The reasoning is simple: if the casual entomologist can frequently find such caterpillars, it is also likely that they are readily found by predators that eat the caterpillar (which is effectively dead anyway), but in the process will also kill the parasitoid within—an evolutionary last laugh on the part of the caterpillar.

When a prepupal caterpillar molts, the result is an almost sessile stage called the *pupa*, or, as it is commonly known in butterflies, the *chrysalis*. Often described as the resting stage, the pupa is decidedly anything but resting. Within the pupal shell the tissues of the caterpillar are being broken down by biochemical means and reconstructed through the process known as *metamorphosis* into an organism that bears little resemblance to either caterpillar or pupa—the adult butterfly. The chrysalis is divided into three well-marked areas—the head, thorax, and abdomen—each bearing the outline of the appendages that will become important in the adult stage (Fig. 15). Close examination of the ventral area of the thorax will reveal the legs and wingpads, plus the location of the proboscis and antennae. The general morphology of butterfly and moth pupae has been treated in detail by Moschler (1916) and Hinton (1946).

The pupa is attached to the substrate by a series of hooks located on

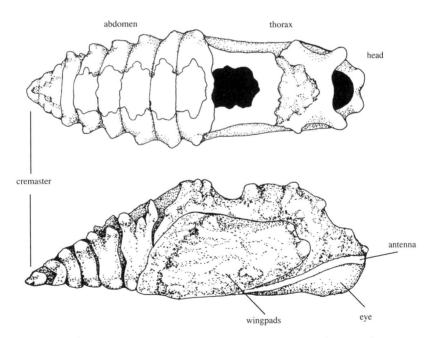

FIGURE 15. Schematic diagram of the pupa of *Thisbe irenea* indicating some important morphological landmarks. *Top*: Dorsal view. Note that the black areas on the head and thorax are heavily pigmented spots. *Bottom*: Lateral view.
(Drawing by B. Degner)

segment A10, the *cremaster* (Fig. 15), that embed into the button of silk that was spun by the prepupal caterpillar. Each major group of butterflies typically has a characteristic pupal shape and manner of pupation. For example, the habit of pupating with the head suspended downward and attached only by the cremaster is typical of members of the family Nymphalidae, whereas pupae of the Papilionidae are typically attached by the cremaster with head upward, but held in place by a girdle of silk over the third thoracic segment, a character unique to the Papilionidae. As in their other characteristics, the riodinid pupae's overall shape and their manner of pupation are variable. Riodinid pupae may be roundly squat (*Euselasia*), blocky and angular (*Leucochimona, Mesosemia*), bear lateral spines (*Ancyluris, Necyria*), smoothly elongate (*Theope*), strikingly similar to lycaenid pupae (*Chalodeta*), have extremities to enclose the greatly exaggerated proboscis (*Eurybia*), or be enclosed within a cocoon composed of the long setae from the caterpillar (*Anteros, Sarota*). Some may even have suspended pupae recalling the Nymphalidae (*Emesis, Lepricornis*), a trait that led Bates (1868) to reject his original systematic divisions within the riodinids

As diverse as they may be, riodinid pupae have characteristics that are unique unto themselves. The study of Harvey (1987a) suggested four characters to separate riodinid pupae from those of other groups. These characters are summarized as follows:

1. Spiracle on A3 is concealed in all Riodininae, except some *Emesis*.
2. Silk girdle passes across A1 in most Riodinidae and all Pieridae.
3. Silk girdle passes across A2 only in members of the Mesosemiini.
4. Silk girdle passes across the interface of T3 and A1 in *Apodemia*, and some *Emesis*.

In the field, confusion may arise when trying to discriminate between a riodinid pupa and that of a lycaenid or nymphalid. Generally, I find that a quick way to distinguish riodinid pupae from other groups is to note that the cremaster of riodinids is often broader than that of other butterflies. For example, the pupa of *Chalodeta lypera* is similar to the pupae of many Lycaenidae, but its broadly flattened cremaster immediately indicates that it is a riodinid. The suspended pupa of *Lepricornis strigosa* is similar to some members of the Melitaeinae (Nymphalidae), but again the nymphalid pupae tend to have a cremaster that is much more slender than those of the riodinids.

As one might imagine, the relatively immobile pupa is susceptible to predation and mechanical injury. Since most injuries to the pupa are seriously debilitating or fatal, butterfly pupae are almost invariably cryptic. As far as I am aware, this is always the case in the riodinids. The site where riodinid butterflies pupate may include leaf litter, nooks and crannies in tree bark, rolled leaves, and even ant nests—all sites that enhance their crypticity. Although most riodinids appear to pupate as solitary individuals, some may form small groups (if the density of caterpillars is sufficiently high on a given plant), and a few are decidedly gregarious (e.g., some species of *Hades, Euselasia, Emesis*).

It has long been known that the pupae of the Lycaenidae are capable of sound production by possession of a rasp and file system located on some of the abdominal segments (see Downey and Allyn 1973, 1978; Elfferich 1988a,b). The production of sound in pupae is considered to be a defense against predators who might be frightened away by a whirring, clicking, or buzzing noise (Downey 1966). Some riodinid pupae appear to have abdominal stridulatory organs (Downey and Allyn 1973), but their ability to produce sound remains to be demonstrated (DeVries 1991c).

When the adult inside the pupa is fully formed, its color changes, and within a day or two the pupa splits along its ventral surface and the adult butterfly emerges, or more properly, *ecloses*. It has been my experience that most butterflies tend to emerge early in the morning. Upon eclosion the wings are merely soft buds and the butterfly requires the help of gravity to pump fluids into the wing veins. After emerging from the pupa, the butterfly must hang from the pupal shell or an area nearby and expand its wings, and allow them to dry into their final, hardened form. If a butterfly cannot hang up almost immediately after emerging from the pupa, the wings will dry in a crumpled state and be useless for flying. Since a butterfly that cannot fly is effectively dead, the period immediately after emergence from the pupa marks it as one of extreme vulnerability.

After the wings have fully expanded, the butterfly expels a red, cream, or brown fluid (termed *meconium*) that constitutes the metabolic waste products of the pupal stage. There is ample evidence from the Papilionidae and Nymphalidae that female butterflies are mated soon after *eclosion* from the pupa (Platt et al. 1984), or in some cases even before they emerge from the pupa (Gilbert 1976). This phenomenon has never been investigated in riodinid butterflies. However, the general trend among insects is for females to be mated soon after emergence, suggesting one of the most potent laws of evolution—nature abhors a virgin.

The Adult

The adult stage of the butterfly's life cycle is the fully mature insect that is incapable of further growth but is capable of flight, mating, and reproduction. As in all insects, the butterfly is composed of the head,

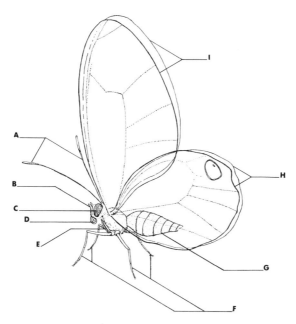

FIGURE 16. Major morphological areas of the adult butterfly (*Cithaerias menander*: Nymphalidae). (A) Antennae. (B) Labial palpi. (C) Compound eye. (D) Proboscis. (E) Forelegs (reduced in all nymphalids and in male riodinids). (F) Walking legs. (G) Abdomen. (H) Hindwings. (I) Forewings. (Drawing by N. Greig)

thorax, and abdomen (Fig. 16), all of which are largely covered with scales of various types. As the most obvious stage in the life cycle, the adult butterfly has received by far the most attention. Here I describe general aspects of butterfly morphology, go over the terminology used in this book, provide diagrams that are intended to help in using this book as an identification guide, and discuss hostplant relationships. Those concerned with detailed morphological studies may wish to consult Ehrlich (1958 a,b) as an excellent starting point.

Head. The most obvious features of the butterfly head are the large compound eyes. The eyes are composed of numerous facets (*ommatidia*) that are incapable of focusing but may be extremely sensitive to movement, light, and certain colors. A dorsal pair of *antennae*, each of which terminate in a thickened *club*, arise from between the eyes. The antennal club varies in thickness and shape according to the species or group. The antennae function as sensory organs for finding food, for mating, and for balance during flight, and they are sensitive to volatile chemicals. The chemical receptors are located in pits that are concentrated primarily on the antennal club. Ventrally and between the eyes there is a pair of heavily scaled *palpi*, which may show considerable variation in form (and thus are important in classification; e.g., Reuter 1896), and can be articulated laterally across the eyes. Even though every butterfly has them, the function of palpi in butterflies is unknown. Elsewhere (DeVries 1987) I have suggested that the palpi are used as cleaning organs in those nymphalid butterfly groups that feed on rotting fruits (e.g., the Charaxinae). Perhaps worth mentioning here is that long palpi in the riodinid butterflies appear to be characteristic of those species that form symbiotic associations with ants.

Between the palpi lies the *proboscis*, a hollow tube composed of two interlocking halves. This feeding organ, which is coiled like a watch spring when not in use, can be extended and inserted into flowers and may be sufficiently stout to penetrate soft fruit tissues. By virtue of having only "soda straw" mouthparts, all butterflies are restricted to a diet of liquids that may include flower nectar, extrafloral nectar, rotting fruit juices, carrion, dung, water, or digested pollen (Norris 1936). The length of a butterfly's proboscis may vary according to the species or group. It is within the riodinid genus *Eurybia* that we find perhaps the most exaggerated proboscis length of any butterfly: it may be over one and a half times the length of the butterfly's body. With such a long proboscis, these butterflies can take nectar from a wide range of flowers, including those of their main hostplant genus, *Calathea*.

Thorax. Behind the head is a region composed of three fused segments that bear the wings and legs and contain the locomotory muscles and various other internal organs. This region is the *thorax*—the toughest part of the butterfly. As in all insects, the adult butterfly has six legs, one pair per segment. The families Papilionidae, Pieridae, and Lycaenidae have six walking legs, and in the Nymphalidae the *forelegs* are reduced. The Riodinidae are unique, however: depending on the sex of the butterfly, the forelegs are of different sizes—the female bears six *walking legs*, whereas the males have reduced forelegs that are modified into brushlike organs that probably function in mating.

Attached to the thorax are the all-important wings. A butterfly has four—a pair of *forewings* and a pair of *hindwings*—all of which are typically covered in scales. These scales give butterflies their characteristic colors and patterns. Beneath the scales, the wings are membranous and supported by a system of *veins* that run from the *wing base* out to the *distal margins* (see Fig. 17). The forewing *costa*, or leading edge, is heavily reinforced by the confluence of many *veins*. The arrangement of the *venation* has been used extensively in classification (see Miller 1970), especially the radial venation associated with the forewing and hindwing *cells*.

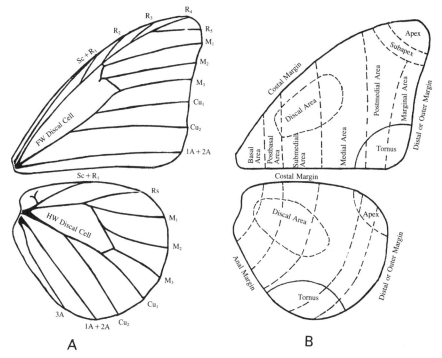

FIGURE 17. (A) Wing venation of the butterfly following the modified Comstock system of numbering. (B) Names of the major wing areas referred to in this book. (Drawing by P. J. DeVries)

The patterns and the colors on the wings of butterflies are mainly the result of a dense covering of scales that are arranged like overlapping roof tiles; in a few species, wing membrane colors are also important. Each scale is attached to a thin shaft that is inserted into a socket in the wing membrane in a fashion analogous to the feathers of birds. The surface of each scale has fine longitudinal ridges cross-linked with finer ridges, giving the appearance of a honeycomb or certain breakfast cereals. There are three main types of scales: pigmentary scales, structural scales, and the scent scales used by males to disseminate odors, termed *androconia*. The pigmentary scales are rather flat and are colored mainly by the deposition of melanin pigments, but they may also be colored by the presence of pterins (especially in the Pieridae) or other chemicals. The various color patterns of butterflies (especially the Nymphalidae) that often appear radically different have been demonstrated to follow a developmental ground plan, or homology system (see Nijhout 1991), and recent molecular studies have demonstrated that the developmental systems for color patterns are similar in both butterflies and fruit flies (Carroll et al. 1994). The structural scales are found mainly on male butterflies and typically generate colors like blue, violet, copper, or green by reflecting particular wavelengths of incident light. For a detailed account of colors and the structural morphology of butterfly scales, see Downey and Allyn (1975). The androconial scales may be connected to secretory cells and generally store chemical compounds (termed *pheromones*) that are used in mating. Certain androconial scales appear to be nonsecretory and are physically transferred to the female during mating (Vane-Wright 1972). Structurally the androconial scales can be very elaborate; their biochemistry and function has been investigated in some of the danaine and ithomiine nymphalids (see Ackery and Vane-Wright 1984; Boppré 1984).

Abdomen. The abdomen contains the digestive and reproductive tracts and terminates with the reproductive organs termed the *genitalia.* The abdomen is composed of ten segments: seven or eight form the longest portion, and two or three form the genitalia. Except for the segments pertaining to the genitalia, the abdomen is capable of stretching when the gut becomes filled with liquid food, and the distension of the abdomen can become considerable in nymphalids like the Charaxinae that feed on rotting fruits.

The genitalia of butterflies are used extensively in systematics and identification, and much has been written on their configuration, treatment for study, and homologies (Klots 1931; Callahan and Chapin 1960; Tuxen 1970; Clench and Miller 1976; Mitter 1988). Here I mention only the most rudimentary of the genitalic structures to assist the reader in distinguishing the sexes. The penultimate segment of the abdomen in the male bears two ventral *valvae,* or, as they are commonly called, the *claspers.* The claspers open to expose the *aedeagus* (penis) and other organs (see below) and literally clasp the end of the female's abdomen during mating. The morphology of the male genitalia has been used extensively in taxonomic studies, and dissection of genitalia for comparative study is relatively easy (see Clench and Miller 1976). The interested reader will find some of the more important landmarks detailed in Figure 18. The female abdomen terminates in three openings: the anus, the egg pore, and the copulatory pore. Those wishing more detail on the morphology of female genitalia should consult Callahan and Chapin (1960) and Miller (1987).

Secondary Sexual Characters. The differences between male and female butterflies can often be discerned easily without examination of the genitalic openings. In most species in which the sexes are similar, the female has a more robust abdomen that terminates bluntly, her forewing apex is more rounded, and her coloration is typically more som-

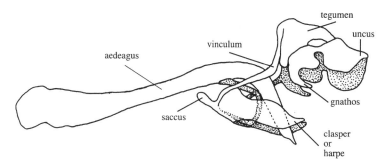

FIGURE 18. The configuration of the male genitalia in riodinids (*Thisbe irenea*). Note that only some of the important parts used in taxonomic work are indicated. Note also that the stippled areas indicate the far side of the three-dimensional genitalic capsule. (Drawing by B. Degner)

ber. However, in many species of butterflies, the males and to a limited extent, females bear *secondary sexual characters*. Such characters can include the configuration of the forelegs, but they are commonly found to be specialized androconial scales or scent organs. These scales and organs are widespread among butterflies (see Longstaff 1912 for illustrations), and may be located on the wings, the forelegs, and on or within the abdomen (Boppré 1984). Elsewhere I have provided examples of these characters in the papilionids, pierids, and nymphalids of Costa Rica (DeVries 1987). However, with the exception of the universally modified male forelegs, I am aware of only two secondary sexual characters found on riodinids.

1. *Androconial patches*, or *alar patches*, are usually located on the forewing near the cell and stand out from the surrounding scales by being darker or having a mealy appearance. As far as I am aware, such scales are found in some but not in all, of the species of the Mesosemiini, the genus *Eurybia*, and the genera *Setabis*, *Pandemos*, *Adelotypa*, and *Theope* in the Nymphidiini.
2. *Androconial tufts*, which are tufts of scales, are found occasionally on the hindwings and always on the abdominal segments in members of the tribe Symmachiini. These tufts are thought to be erected during courtship.

Hostplant Relationships. Plants are of paramount importance to the existence of butterflies, and a great many butterfly species feed only on a few closely related plant species. Hence an extremely critical aspect in the life cycle of the butterfly is the ability of the ovipositing female to find, and the caterpillars to feed on, particular hostplants. Indeed this *hostplant relationship* is so strong that on an evolutionary scale we find that a particular lineage of butterflies is typically associated with particular plants or plant compounds, but other plants are unacceptable to caterpillars or ovipositing females. The broad patterns of host-plant relationships among insects in general and butterflies specifically gave rise to the idea of coevolution between insect and plant lineages (Brues 1924; Ehrlich and Raven 1965), a major concept of evolutionary biology (Futuyma and Slatkin 1983).

The term "coevolution" has come to have various meanings (Futuyma and Slatkin 1983), but with respect to butterflies we mean that there are predictable patterns of hostplant relationships that may be used to generate hypotheses about the systematics and ecology of butterflies. For example, within the papilionid tribe Troidini there is a strict hostplant relationship with the Aristolochiaceae. This pattern is so well established everywhere in the world that *any* record of a troidine caterpillar feeding on any other plant family is immediately suspect, and demands proof. This relationship extends to our concepts of mimicry and insect defenses—all troidines are considered to be unpalatable to vertebrate predators due to the poisons they accrue from their Aristolochiaceae hostplants. Many times when a butterfly is shown to have a hostplant relationship outside of its "normal" plant family, analysis has shown that the different plant family may contain certain chemicals in common with the usual hostplant. An example of this would be butterflies in the family Pieridae feeding on Brassicaceae as a normal host and the distantly related Tropaeolaceae; both contain mustard oils. Remember that "herbivorous insects do not feed on Latin binominals, they feed on plants or plant parts" (Janzen 1973a), and since butterflies make their living at it, they are extraordinarily good chemists, and even better botanists.

Although broad hostplant relationships are well known for the Papilionidae, Pieridae, and Nymphalidae, those for the Lycaenidae and Riodinidae are not. Pierce (1985) and more recently Fiedler (1991) brought together a large and diffuse literature that provides the best available synthesis of host use patterns for the Lycaenidae, showing that broad patterns are emerging for the family. However, a recent summary of riodinid host records (DeVries et al. 1994) indicated that (1) riodinid host records include monophagy and polyphagy, caterpillar benefits accrued from drinking extrafloral nectar (see the *Thisbe irenea* account), and a modicum of aphytophagy; (2) only members of the tribes Eurybiini and Incertae Sedis show what may be considered circumscribed host use patterns; and (3) the overall host use patterns for the Riodinidae remain elusive mainly due to the fact that host records for three quarters of the species are unknown. Another consideration is that most of the riodinid host records originate from a single geographic locality, and/or consist of single rearing records. In sum, our eventual understanding of host use patterns in the riodinid butterflies will depend on many more observations than are currently available. (See Appendix 2 for a summary of riodinid hostplants.)

There is, however, one unusual hostplant pattern found within the riodinid butterflies that appears to be robust. Available evidence suggests that, depending on the species, myrmecophilous riodinid caterpillars may be monophagous or feed on a variety of plant families, but almost invariably their hostplants possess extrafloral nectaries (DeVries 1991a; DeVries et al. 1994). These caterpillars not only devour new leaf tissue and use the ants for their own protection, but it has been demonstrated that they gain growth benefits by drinking extrafloral nectar (Fig. 6). In this situation, the riodinid caterpillars appear to be invading and exploiting a two-species mutualism because the extrafloral nectaries are the basis of the symbiosis between the plants and ants. Thus, the caterpillars have the ability to drink extrafloral nectar, and this benefit allows myrmecophilous riodinid caterpillars to add insult to herbivory (DeVries and Baker 1989).

Enemies and Butterfly Defenses against Them

As with all insects, a newly laid butterfly egg's chance for survival into adulthood in nature is slim, very slim. During all stages of their life cycle, butterflies are at risk from many factors that influence their chances for survival. Little is known for most aspects of the ecology of Neotropical butterflies, especially the riodinids, including the mortality factors that affect them. Much of our understanding of the subject has been extrapolated from studies conducted in the temperate zones. Here I outline briefly the effects that parasites, parasitoids, and predators may have on the lives of butterflies, and I place them in the context of defenses that butterflies have evolved against them. The material supplements the information covered in the sections on the butterfly life cycle and myrmecophily.

For our purposes here, the reader should bear the following definitions in mind: *Pathogens* cause diseases that eventually may kill the butterfly host. A *parasite* is an organism that feeds on portions of the host but does not directly cause its death. A *parasitoid* (usually wasp or fly larvae) devours the butterfly host slowly, from the inside, eventually killing it. Depending on the species of parasitoid, one or more adult individuals may emerge from a single butterfly host. A *predator* kills its prey by devouring it, and a predator kills many individual prey during its lifetime.

Pathogens

Anyone who has reared butterfly caterpillars knows that unless the rearing containers are cleaned regularly, the caterpillars are prone to become moribund, die, and quickly putrefy. This is typically the effect of contagious viral pathogens that may rapidly kill all caterpillars in a particular culture. The best-known viral pathogens of butterfly caterpillars are polyhedrosis viruses that have received laboratory study (Smith 1967), but little is known about their effects on caterpillars in the field. Neogregarine protozoans are reported to infect caterpillars and adults of two species of *Danaus* butterflies (Nymphalidae) and a tortricid moth (see McLaughlin and Myers 1970; Munster-Swendson 1991; Leong et al. 1992). However, the effects of these pathogens, their mode of transmission, and how widespread they may be among butterflies in a natural setting has not been explored.

Fungal pathogens also effect butterflies, especially entomophagous fungi in the genus *Cordyceps*. As reviewed by Evans (1982), it has been established that *Cordyceps* may attack and kill eggs, caterpillars, pupae, or adult insects, and different species of *Cordyceps* may show some host specificity. Although demonstrated to be important mortality factors in some insect groups, its importance to butterflies is effectively unexplored. Over the years in Costa Rica, Panama, and Ecuador, I have occasionally observed live adult papilionids, satyrine nymphalids, and hesperiids with fungal infections on the tips of their antennae. I happened to notice that these insects flew in an odd manner for the individual species (altered behavior is a characteristic of hosts infected with *Cordyceps*). I have reared *Leucochimona, Emesis, Thisbe, Synargis,* and *Theope* caterpillars that have turned into rubbery white mummies of mold just prior to pupation, but whether riodinids contract fungal infections as adults is apparently unknown.

Another type of fungal infection appears to be restricted to riodinid and lycaenid caterpillars. Species of these caterpillars that form symbioses with ants may contract a lethal fungal infection associated with the glands that produce food secretions for the ants (Farquharson 1921; Jackson 1937; Clark and Dickson 1971). Under laboratory conditions, whether or not a caterpillar is tended by ants and persistently "groomed" does not seem to affect the chances of contracting an infection, but such infections may be lethal to both caterpillars and pupae (Fiedler and Saam 1995).

Parasites

A parasite weakens but does not kill its host because its own fate is tied to the survival of the host. True parasites have rarely been reported in butterflies. In Costa Rica perhaps the most common ones are flies in the family Ceratopogonidae, or, as they are commonly known, the biting midges. These midges feed on the hemolymph of caterpillars and on the wing veins of the adults (Lane 1984). In Costa Rica they are most frequently observed on Nymphalidae, especially *Caligo* caterpillars, or on the wing veins of various Ithomiinae. In Brazil, Lane (1984) reports these midges from the riodinid genera *Helicopis*, *Leucochimona*, and *Stalachtis*, but there are no reports for any Central American riodinids to date. The effects of these midges on their butterfly hosts is unknown, but it is conceivable that they transmit diseases.

Parasitoids

The term "parasitoid" typically refers to certain families of wasps and flies that lay their eggs on or in an early stage of the butterfly life cycle, and whose larvae devour internal tissues of the host, eventually killing it. Parasitoids have been shown to be important in regulating the population of many insects, including butterflies (Dempster 1984; Godfray 1994; Hawkins and Sheehan 1994), and although we know very little about the effects of parasitoids on populations of tropical butterflies, they are almost certainly a force to reckon with. The various parasitoids and predators that are known to attack riodinid butterflies in Costa Rica are presented in Table 1.

Butterfly egg parasitoids typically belong to the wasp families Trichogrammatidae, Scelionidae, Eupelmidae, and Encyrtidae, and as many as sixty individual adult wasps may emerge from a single butterfly egg. The potential of these parasitoids for regulating butterfly populations, along with aspects of their biology are discussed in Salt (1937), Malo (1961), Godfray (1994), and Hawkins and Sheehan (1994).

Parasitoids that attack the caterpillars or pupae of butterflies include wasps in the family Braconidae, Chalcidae, and Ichneumonidae, and flies in the families Tachinidae and Sarcophagidae. Braconid wasps lay eggs in the body of the caterpillar (in which the parasitoid larvae develop). At maturity, the wasp larvae emerge from the butterfly host to pupate, frequently leaving a distinctive cottony mass of cocoons on the outside of the immobilized and dying host. This is especially true of the important parasitoids in the genus *Apanteles*. Important braconid parasitoids of certain myrmecophilous riodinid caterpillars are members of the genus *Rogas* (Rogadiinae), which leave the caterpillar host in a mummified state (see species account of *Thisbe irenea*). Chalcid wasps lay eggs inside the body of the caterpillar or pupa while the host cuticle is still soft immediately following a molt. Chalcids develop inside the host and, when mature, they chew holes through the side of the host pupa to escape. In contrast to the Ichneumonidae, where typically only one wasp develops per host, in both braconids and chalcids many individuals may emerge from the same host.

Flies in the family Tachinidae attack butterfly caterpillars either by depositing eggs directly on caterpillars, or by scattering minute "micro-

TABLE 1
Some Important Parasitoids and Predators of Costa Rican Butterflies

INSECTA (insects)		REPTILIA (reptiles)	
Order	Hymenoptera (ants and wasps)	Family	Teiidae
Family	Formicidae (E, L, P)	Genus	Ameiva (L, P, A)
	Vespidae (L, P)	Family	Iguanidae
	Sphecidae (L, A)	Genus	Anolis (L, A)
	Braconidae (L)		
	Chalcidae (L, P)	MAMMALIA (mammals)	
	Ichneumonidae (L)	Family	Cebidae
	Trichogrammatidae (E)	Genus	Saimiri (L, P, A)
	Scelionidae (E)		Cebus (L, P, A)
	Encyrtidae (E)	Family	Muridae
	Eupelmidae (E)	Genus	Oryzomys (L, P)
Order	Diptera (flies)		Nyctomys (L, P)
Family	Tachinidae (L, P)	Family	Didelphidae
	Sarcophagidae (L, P)	Genus	Philander (L, P)
	Asilidae (A)		Marmosa (L, P)
Order	Orthoptera (mantids, katydids)		
Family	Mantidae (A)	AVIFORMES	
	Tettigoniidae (E, L, P)	Family	Momotidae (A)
			Galbulidae (A)
ARACHNIDA (spiders, scorpions)			Bucconidae (A)
Family	Araneidae (A)		Capitonidae (A)
	Uloboridae (A)		Cotingidae (A)
	Ctenidae (L, A)		Tyramidae (A)
	Thomisidae (A)		Vireonidae (A)
	Salticidae (A)		Parulidae (A)
	Lycosidae (L, A)		Furnariidae (L, A)
Order	Scorpiones (L)		Formicaridae (A)
			Troglodytidae (L, P, A)

NOTE: Abbreviations: E = egg, C = caterpillar, P = pupa, A = adult. These correspond to the stage of the butterfly life cycle most frequently attacked by the parasitoid or predator.

type" eggs on the hostplant leaves. In the latter case, the caterpillars ingest the eggs when they feed, and the eggs hatch within the body. In all tachinid flies the maggots feed on internal tissues of the host until they are ready to pupate. At this time the maggot bores though the body of the host, falls to the ground, and pupates (or more correctly, pupariates) in the soil. In most cases a caterpillar with a tachinid maggot inside will be killed; however, records of nonlethal tachinids do exist (DeVries 1984b). Since we know so little about the life histories of tropical Tachinidae, care should be taken when rearing caterpillars in case this phenomenon is more common than assumed (see also pp. 32–33).

Butterfly caterpillars that harbor parasitoids are frequently found by casual observation. This is witnessed by the number of parasitized caterpillars that are found in field collections. Again, finding parasitized caterpillars may be the result of behavioral changes invoked by the internal parasitoids that make the caterpillar more obvious to a human observer. Shortly before the parasitoids emerge from the host, parasitized caterpillars typically go through a short wandering phase that recalls the wandering phase prior to pupation. It has been speculated that the caterpillar makes itself more conspicuous to predators in a last attempt to rid itself of the parasitoid (see section on pupae).

Predators

A predator is defined here as any organism that kills any life stage of a butterfly and depends on killing more than a single individual to stay alive and reproduce. This definition allows us to discriminate them from parasitoids, which rely upon only a single host to complete their life cycle. Predators of butterflies include both vertebrates and invertebrates (Table 1), and in terms of overall effect, the latter are probably vastly more important (Pierce et al. 1987; DeVries 1991b). Vertebrate predators include birds, lizards, amphibians, and mammals that consume all of their prey, or, in the case of adult butterflies, may eat the body and discard the wings, or eat the gut contents and discard the rest of the body. Arthropod predators include spiders, mantids, wasps, ants, flies, beetles, and Heteroptera, and, depending on the arthropod, these predators may consume all or a portion of their prey (as in mantids, wasps, and beetles) or suck its juices and discard the carcass (as in spiders, flies, and Heteroptera). Although predators are extremely important forces in butterfly ecology, when one considers the species richness in the tropics there are surprisingly few published observations of predation events on most Neotropical butterflies by specific predators (see Calvert et al. 1979; Chai 1986, 1990; Ehrlich and Ehrlich 1982; Sherry 1983; Alonso-Mejia and Marquez 1994).

Butterfly Defenses against Parasitoids and Predators

The defenses of butterflies may result from natural selection brought about by a specific or generalized suite of predators. There are many generalized defenses in butterflies (myrmecophily, spines, crypsis, noxious chemicals), but it is only from field observations that we can infer which defenses are possibly directed at specific predators. For example, spiny nymphalid or fuzzy riodinid caterpillars may be equipped to avoid being eaten or killed by predaceous ants, but the same caterpillars are unlikely to be touched or eaten by white-faced monkeys, even though they may be palatable. However, the same caterpillars may be tasty morsels to some birds, or to squirrel monkeys, after their spines or hairs have been removed. In this example we cannot be certain what specifically promoted the evolution of caterpillar spines or long setae, only that it helps in some instances but not in others to have such defenses. Too few observations have been made on butterfly defenses in the context of their natural habitats and natural enemies to know with certainty (if anything ever is certain) whether such defenses are directed at subsets of predators, specific predators, or predators in general. The evolution of defense by butterflies is undoubtedly complex and involves appearance, physical armaments, behavioral and chemical weapons, and symbioses with ants, and many probably work in concert. This section focuses on some important defenses of butterflies, while myrmecophily is treated in a separate section (pp. 19–33).

Appearance. There are two major ways in which all stages of butterflies utilize appearance to avoid being eaten: *protective resemblance* (or *crypsis*) and *mimicry*. Of the two, mimicry is, in concept and evolution, more complex and is dealt with in a separate section. Protective resemblance may be defined as a camouflage that allows an organism to blend into its background and make its presence difficult to detect; it is cryptic.

The eggs of butterflies are often laid in inconspicuous places on or off the hostplant, making them difficult to find. Eggs may be laid, for example, at the junction of leaf veins (*Caria*), in fissures on the stem of the host (*Euselasia*, *Eurybia*, and *Ancyluris*), on epiphyls growing on other plants (*Sarota*), on detritus associated with the hostplant (*Thisbe*), in damaged portions of host leaves (*Symmachia*), or in the leaf litter (*Charis*).

Generally, butterfly caterpillars show a protective resemblance to their environment and have behaviors that enhance their camouflage (see DeVries 1987). The distinctive coloration of *Ancyluris inca* caterpillars in tandem with their habit of resting on the underside of damaged *Miconia* leaves makes them look as if they are part of the vegetation, even when many caterpillars are on the same leaf. Even large, gregarious groups of *Euselasia* caterpillars may be difficult to find because of their cryptic coloration, and because they rest at the base of a tree during the day. Countershading can play an important part in the crypsis of *Leucochimona*, *Juditha*, and *Nymphidium* caterpillars. In a countershaded caterpillar, one side is paler than the other, and under natural illumination these caterpillars are extremely cryptic because they blend in with their background. However, when the caterpillar is turned over from its natural resting position, the lighting makes it stand out against its background. For a discussion of countershading, see Wickler (1968) and Owen (1980).

A related form of defense is when caterpillars build shelters or structures that further reduce their chances of being detected by visually oriented predators. Several excellent examples of this are found within the Costa Rican fauna. The inordinately fuzzy caterpillars of *Anteros* roll the edge of their leaves and hide within these shelters, making them very difficult to see. The caterpillars of *Mesenopsis melanochlora* tightly roll the edge of their host leaves and live inside them; these tubes are often filled with frass that further enhances the appearance that nothing is there. Even so, I have observed vespid wasps investigating rolled leaves and chewing through the tubes to eventually kill and carry away the caterpillar from its snug hiding place.

As in other butterfly groups, protective resemblance plays an important part in the defenses of adult riodinids. In fact, most riodinid species appear cryptic on their undersides whether they are aposematically colored or not. For example, many species of *Euselasia, Mesosemia*, and *Theope* have colors and patterns on the underside of the wings that blend incredibly well into the vegetation they rest upon, yet even on brightly colored species (e.g., *Lyropteryx, Melanis*) the scales on the underside of the wings lack the sheen of the upperside and thus reflect less light. To this widespread crypsis add the outstanding behavioral characteristic of resting on the underside of leaves and playing "hide and seek" to further enhance crypsis, and the distinct suggestion of strong selective pressure by visually oriented predators.

When a predator does locate a butterfly and attack it, certain types of patterns on the underside of the wings may act as target areas to deflect attacks away from vital parts of the body. An attack by a bird or lizard may focus on an eyespot or other prominent wing marking and result in the predator getting a mouthful of wing while the butterfly escapes. For example, in members of *Euselasia* it is not uncommon to find lizard bites or bird beak marks over the prominent spots at the hindwing tornus indicating that these markings function to deflect predator attacks. This type of defense falls under what has been termed the "false head" hypothesis for the Lycaenidae (Robbins 1981).

Physical Armaments. Physical means of protection against enemies are widespread in many insects groups (e.g., stings and mandibles of wasps, ants, beetles), but are not generally well developed in butterflies. In the riodinids the most obvious physical armaments are the long, dense setae of members of *Sarota* and *Anteros* that are likely to serve as protection against certain arthropods. These long setae bear many little barbs on their shafts that may break off and adhere to the head and antennae of the attacking arthropod, thus deterring it (Fig. 5). The possession of long setae almost certainly deters some vertebrate predators as well. For example, captive capuchin monkeys (*Cebus capuchinus*) are quite willing to eat a large variety of insects in their diets. However, they will not even touch slightly hairy or spiny caterpillars even though the caterpillars may not urticate in the least. In such a situation, a fuzzy *Anteros* caterpillar is almost certainly gaining protection through its resemblance to urticating moth caterpillars in the family Megalopygidae.

Chemical Defenses. Perhaps the most commonly encountered defense in butterflies involves "chemical warfare," and noxious chemicals have been found in all stages of the butterfly life cycle. These defenses may take the form of toxins in or on eggs, caterpillar regurgitations or chemicals secreted from glands, and chemicals stored in the bodies of caterpillars or adults. Investigations into chemical defenses of butterflies has proved important to the development of both empirical and theoretical considerations in the evolution of insects, plants, and predators. The large literature on some aspects of this subject has been reviewed by Eisner (1970), Ackery and Vane-Wright (1984), Brower (1984), Ackery (1988, 1991), Price et al. (1991), and Stamp and Casey (1993).

Chemical defenses in butterflies may be considered to be the deployment, by any means imaginable, of noxious chemicals that help a butterfly, at any stage of its life, avoid being killed. Butterfly caterpillars known to have chemical defenses include members of the Papilionidae (Eisner and Meinwald 1965; Honda 1983), Danainae and Ithomiinae (Ackery and Vane-Wright 1984; Brower 1984), Heliconiinae and Acraeinae (Narstedt and Davis 1981, 1983), Brassolinae (DeVries 1987), and the Morphinae (DeVries and Martinez 1993). Nothing is known about possible chemical defenses in any species of riodinid.

In adult butterflies, chemical defenses are typically acquired in two ways: active storing of plant-derived compounds from the caterpillars, or de novo synthesis as adults. The classic work on the monarch butterfly (*Danaus plexippus*) by Jane Van Zandt Brower (1958a,b) and Lincoln Brower and Jane Van Zandt (1964) demonstrated that these butterflies may store nasty chemicals acquired from their hostplants through feeding as caterpillars. Other studies (e.g., Narstedt and Davis 1981, 1983; Boppré 1984; Brown 1984) have shown that some Heliconiinae, Danainae, and Ithomiinae butterflies acquire and/or enhance their chemical arsenals by feeding as adults on the nectar, pollen, or secretions of particular plants. In view of these studies there are potentially many more unpalatable species of butterflies than we currently recognize (see Brower 1984; Ritland and Brower 1991; DeVries 1994).

Judging by their color pattern and behavior, certain groups of

MIMICRY

FIGURES 19, 20, AND 21

FIGURE 19

Black and yellow mimicry complexes in Costa Rican riodinids, and in arctiid and dioptine moths. Abbreviations are: m = male, f = female.

1. *Pachythone gigas* f (Riodinidae)

2. *Micropus* nr. *ochra* (Geometridae: Sterrhinae)

3. *Setabis cleomedes* f (Riodinidae)

4. *Monethe rudolphus* f (Riodinidae)

5. *Xenorma grandimaeula* (Arctiidae)

6. *Chamaelimnas villagomes* m (Riodinidae)

7. *Mesenopsis bryaxis* m (Riodinidae)

8. *Josia ligata* (Notodontidae: Dioptinae)

9. *Josiomorpha triangulifera* (Arctiidae)

10. *Mesenopsis melanochlora* f (Riodinidae)

11. *Erbessa salvini* (Notodontidae: Dioptinae)

12. *Chamaelimnas villagomes* f (Riodinidae)

13. *Josides* nr. *celena* f (Arctiidae: Lithosiinae)

14. *Xenandra caeruleata* m (Riodinidae)

15. *Pterographium elegans* f (Riodinidae)

16. *Isapis agyrtus* m (Riodinidae)

17. *Josides* nr. *celena* m (Arctiidae: Lithosiinae)

18. *Mitradaemon pseudena* (Notodontidae: Dioptinae).

(Photo by P. J. DeVries)

FIGURE 19

FIGURE 20

Black mimicry complexes involving Costa Rican riodinids, acrtiid and dioptine moths, and nymphalid butterflies. Abbreviations are: m = male, f = female.

1. *Uraneis ucubis* f (Riodinidae)

2. *Pterographium elegans* m (Riodinidae)

3. *Esthemopsis colaxes* f (Riodinidae)

4. *Ithomeis eulema* m (Riodinidae)

5. *Stalachtis magdalaenae* m (Riodinidae) from Panama

6. *Hypocritta aletta* m (Arctiidae)

7. *Erbessa lindigii* (Notodontidae: Dioptinae)

8. *Isostola* nr. *nigrivenata* (Arctiidae: Lithosiinae)

9. *Lepricornis strigosa* m (Riodinidae)

10. *Phanoptis cyanomelas* (Notodontidae: Dioptinae)

11. *Calithomia hezia* f (Nymphalidae)

12. *Hypothyris euclea* m (Nymphalidae).

(Photo by P. J. DeVries)

FIGURE 20

FIGURE 21

Black, red, and orange mimicry complexes involving Costa Rican riodinids, geometrid and zygaenid moths, and nymphalid butterflies. Abbreviations are: m = male, f = female.

1. *Mesene margaretta* f (Riodinidae)

2. *Eudule* sp. (Geometridae: Laurentiinae)

3. *Symmachia rubina* f (Riodinidae)

4. *Lyropteryx cleadas* f (Riodinidae)

5. *Cariomothis poeciloptera* m (Riodinidae)

6. *Calospila asteria* m (Riodinidae)

7. *Euclimacia* nr *tortricalis* (Zygaenidae)

8. *Mesene croceella* m (Riodinidae)

9. *Calospila zeurippa* f (Riodinidae)

10. *Ansorgia ephestris* (Geometridae: Laurentiinae)

11. *Eudulophasia invaria* (Geometridae: Laurentiinae)

12. *Biblis hyperia* m (Nymphalidae).

(Photo by P. J. DeVries)

riodinids will almost certainly be found to be chemically defended. For example, based on characteristics of other groups of Lepidoptera, it is difficult to imagine any member of the Costa Rican fauna in the genus *Melanis* to be anything other than unpalatable. Another example is the widespread *Hades noctula* (p. 114) whose adults I have noticed reflexively bleed hemolymph from the thorax upon being handled—a characteristic of some distinctly unpalatable insects. The only direct tests of riodinid palatability (Chai 1990) showed that caged rufous-tailed jacamars rejected *Hades noctula*, *Ancyluris inca*, and *Esthemopsis clonia*, but *Eurybia patrona* and *Juditha molpe* were eaten readily. Unfortunately, even as diverse as the riodinids are, very little work directed at their possession of chemical defenses has been done. Clearly, this is an area in which an enormous amount of work is to be done.

MIMICRY: MIMICS DON'T HIDE, THEY ADVERTISE

Consider a butterfly in the fruit-feeding nymphalid genus *Zaretis* (Charaxinae). When one of these butterflies lands on the forest floor to feed on the juices of a rotting fruit, it looks extremely similar to a dead leaf—herbivore damage included. When this insect is feeding it appears to melt into the background. This is an excellent example of protective resemblance. Now, if a bird happens to notice, attack, and subsequently eat our *Zaretis* butterfly, the bird might appear complacent for a few moments, and in the interests of another meal, it would probably then give dead leaves more careful scrutiny—at least for a while. If, however, the same bird happens to attack and eat a *Tithorea tarricina* (Ithomiinae) that is lazily flying by, its reaction will be different. If it swallows the butterfly, the bird may regurgitate the contents of its crop, fluff its feathers, wipe its bill on its perch, and give the appearance of having ingested something disagreeable. Should another *Tithorea tarricina* fly past, the bird would probably ignore it. Likewise, the bird would ignore *Heliconius hecale* and any other butterfly that looked like *Tithorea tarricina*. The bird has learned to associate a color pattern and behavior with a nasty experience. Those butterflies that resemble *Tithorea tarricina* gain some immunity from attack by this bird through their mimicry.

Both protective resemblance and mimicry are the result of natural selection, but they are not the same thing, and it is important to bear the distinction in mind. Protective resemblance occurs when an organism resembles its environmental surroundings and gains protection from predators through crypsis—by being overlooked. Protective resemblance can be thought of as a passive defense. Protective mimicry, on the other hand, implies that one species of organism closely resembles another species that is avoided by predators. Mimics gain protection from predators by appearing to be unpalatable. In other words, mimics do not hide, they advertise.

A great deal has been written on mimicry, and it is a subject that has acquired a diversity of meanings and nuances. In this book I define mimicry in a narrow sense, and the interested reader is encouraged to sample from the development of mimicry theory and the variety of views as expressed by Poulton (1908, 1924); Punnett (1915); Swynnerton (1915); A. H. Turner (1924); Vane-Wright (1976, 1980); Pasteur (1982); Gilbert (1983); J.R.G. Turner (1984); Guilford (1986); Mallet and Singer (1987); L. P. Brower (1988); A.V.Z. Brower (1995); Mallet and Gilbert (1995); Chai (1996). This section presents a brief introduction to mimicry in Neotropical butterflies, discusses the role of mimicry in riodinids, and provides examples from the Costa Rican riodinid fauna.

Protective mimicry in butterflies may be divided into two general classes: *Batesian mimicry*, where there is an unpalatable model species and a palatable species that mimics it; and *Müllerian mimicry*, where several unpalatable model species share the same color pattern. Despite the differences in the types of mimicry, both rely on advertising a conspicuous color pattern to predators. Of the two types, Müllerian mimicry is most common among Neotropical butterflies in the families Papilionidae, Pieridae, Nymphalidae, and Lycaenidae, and it is likely (although not tested) to occur in the Riodinidae. Batesian mimics occur unambiguously in the nymphalid subfamily Charaxinae, Lycaenidae, and the Riodinidae.

Batesian Mimicry

The first theory of mimicry was presented by H. W. Bates (1862) in an attempt to explain why members of the pierid genus *Dismorphia* look and behave like ithomiine and *Heliconius* butterflies. After more than a decade of field observations in the Amazon basin, Bates concluded that the *Dismorphia* butterflies mimic the warningly colored and unpalatable ithomiine and *Heliconius* butterflies to gain protection from predators. Batesian mimicry, then, involves a palatable species (the mimic) that closely resembles an unpalatable species (the model). Often, but not always, the model species is more common in a particular habitat than the mimetic species, thus serving to educate predators repeatedly of the nasty taste associated with the warning color pattern. One line of reasoning is that if the mimics are too common, predators would not associate the color pattern with a nasty experience, and they would begin selecting against butterflies of that color pattern until a time when the models became more abundant. However, if the model is sufficiently nasty and brightly colored, the mimics may be more abundant than the model. Under these conditions, the model's color and nasty taste work in concert to strengthen the learned aversion reaction of predators, and the mimics still gain a strong benefit (e.g., Guilford 1986).

As the mimetic species confers no advantage to the model species (actually a disadvantage), a Batesian mimic may be thought of as a parasite of the model's color, or signaling pattern—a sheep in wolf's clothing. Considered as such, model species should evolve defenses to rid themselves of their Batesian parasites. The interested reader should see Fisher (1930) and Gilbert (1983) for reviews along this line of thought, and also Turner (1984) and L. P. Brower (1984) for reasons why this may not be possible.

Müllerian Mimicry

In 1879, F. Müller presented a paper on mimicry to explain why so many unpalatable butterfly species look alike. He reasoned that convergence of color patterns in distasteful species more effectively serves to educate birds and other vertebrate predators of the nasty taste associated with that color pattern. Müllerian mimicry does not require one species to be more abundant than another, and more importantly, protection of one mimetic species does not imply that another species will be put at a disadvantage. Even though there is a palatability spectrum among Müllerian mimics, natural selection will favor this association (Poulton 1908; Fisher 1930; Turner 1984). In the Neotropics the most common Müllerian color patterns among ithomiines, danaines. and heliconiine butterflies are black-and-orange tiger stripes, transparent, or blue and white. Among the Neotropical Papilionidae the Müllerian patterns are black, white, and red.

Studie Mimicry in Butterflies

One of the foremost pr ents for the study of mimicry as a means of understanding evolut as E. B. Poulton. Almost consumed with the idea of showing th erflies were eaten by predators, Poulton encouraged many r s to publish their findings, and he frequently wrote review p rshaling evidence for the power of mimicry in the wild. Po responsible in large part for showing that birds attack butt d established them as important selective agents (see Pou ; Eltringham 1910; Carpenter 1942). The later experimenta of Lincoln and Jane Van Zandt-Brower demonstrated that earn to recognize and avoid color patterns that are associate a bad taste or nasty experience, and that palatable, Batesian benefit from resembling bad-tasting models (see references in

J.V.Z. Brower 1958a,b; L. P. Brower et al. 1967, 1984; Walbauer and Sternberg 1975).

One of the first field studies showing that natural selection acts on Müllerian mimics was done by Benson (1971, 1972), who worked with *Heliconius* butterflies in Costa Rica. This study took advantage of *Heliconius* roosting behavior to show that individuals with Müllerian color patterns receive a reduced number of attacks by birds, and that Müllerian mimics live longer. In Panama, Boyden (1976) was able to show experimentally that under field conditions *Ameiva* lizards can learn to avoid eating butterflies with an aposematic pattern. Subsequent studies by Chai (1986, 1990, 1996) examined the visual and gustatory responses of a specialist predator bird, the rufous-tailed jacamar (Galbulidae), to a community of Costa Rican butterflies found in Parque Corcovado—perhaps the largest and most complex experimental study of its type ever done. Chai's elegant field study tested the ideas of Bates (1862), Müller (1879), Poulton (1908), and Turner (1984), and it points to further avenues in mimicry and bad taste.

Riodinid Butterflies and Mimicry

The papilionids, pierids, and nymphalids hav⌐   ⸜vided fertile ground for experimental and theoretica¹   ⸜nimicry in butterflies. Although their existence was rec⸜   ⸜any years ago (Bates 1859; Seitz 1916–20), we know almost   ⸜ about obvious mimicry complexes involving the riodinids—⸜⸍   certainly due to their small size, general scarcity in the field, ⸜   ⸜he historical precedent set by the butterfly subjects of early w   ⸜ on mimicry. Nevertheless, unexplored mimetic complexes frc⸜.⸜ the Costa Rican fauna (see Figs. 19, 20, 21) involve the riodinid genera *Esthemopsis, Brachyglenis, Mesene, Symmachia, Pterographium,* and the day-flying moth genera *Erbessa, Phanoptis, Phaenochlaena, Josia* (Notodontidae: Dioptinae), *Sagaropsis, Mitradaemon, Hypocritta, Josiodes* (Arctiidae), *Eudulophasia,* and *Calippia* (Geometridae). Many of the species involved in these complexes show an uncanny similarity, have overlapping geographical distributions, and fly at the same time of day—classic earmarks for tightly evolved mimicry pairs. Given that arctiid moths are well known to be unpalatable, and there is evidence that *Eudulophasia* (Geometridae) may be unpalatable to arthropods (L. Gilbert, unpublished), these riodinid-moth complexes are likely to involve both Müllerian and Batesian mimicry. Of interest is to note that like other families of Costa Rican butterflies, mimicry in riodinids is mainly found in lowland and mid-elevation rain forest habitats, and negligible or absent in the Guanacaste lowlands and the high-elevation forests (DeVries 1987, 1994).

Our understanding of riodinid mimicry systems is very limited (Miller 1996). There is a real need for studies to examine the responses of both vertebrate and invertebrate predators to members of the Riodinidae and the moths they mimic. In fact, simply accruing observations on the natural history of these species would add new dimensions to both theoretical and empirical considerations of mimicry in butterflies.

BUTTERFLY BIOLOGISTS IN THE NEW WORLD

As coined by Alfred Russel Wallace in his work on biogeographic regions, the word "Neotropics" signifies the New World tropics. It derives from "the new world," or the Americas as "discovered" by Cristobal Colon in 1492. Soon after Colon brought back news of his discovery to Spain, the "new world" became renown, especially its tropical portions, for its unexplored regions teeming with an interesting and uncanny flora, fauna, and human culture. It was indeed very much a new world that had little in common with previously explored realms.

Over five hundred years have passed since Colon's discovery, yet in terms of biodiversity the Neotropics remain the largest bastion of the terrestrial unknown. For a few more years, one might still, with a certain amount of determination, find expanses of tropical nature that are relatively unscathed by the ravages of human activities. In short, the Neotropics remain the last large biogeographic region where animals and plants new to science can consistently and abundantly be found. As was the case over five centuries ago, making discoveries about the natural world and bringing them to the attention of the world at large remain the realm of pioneers—individuals who go forth with sufficient curiosity, interest, and inclination to make discoveries relevant to humanity. Such discoveries have been and will be mulled over by future generations as part of the process called learning; in the larger picture, these discoveries will provide us with images of what the natural world once was, and how much is left to learn.

Clearly, the foundation of our knowledge of Neotropical butterflies in general, and the riodinids in particular, rests on the labors of naturalists and entomologists who continue to provide the world with collections and observations. Anyone who has used a museum collection or sought knowledge about Neotropical butterflies from a book or technical paper owes a special debt of gratitude to these naturalists. Consider what it must have been like to work in an area where almost everything was new to science, and where almost no end was in sight to the variety of animals and plants. Furthermore, consider an era when, unlike today, exploratory natural history was considered important enough to be reported in the everyday mass media, and when the layman was conversant in at least a few of the discoveries of the day.

Early Workers in the Neotropics

The early workers in the Neotropics have had a tremendous influence on the developmental history of entomology as a field of study, and on our current view of Neotropical butterflies. It was the willing task of the pioneers to observe, collect, describe, and catalog the fauna of the New World. As an acknowledgment, I mention here a number of these pioneers by name, along with a few words about their contributions. For some of them, I am including a photographic portrait to round out the "species account" (Figs. 22, 23). Although this list is incomplete, the reader should recognize that the work of the people mentioned here, both living and dead, bears directly upon the Costa Rican fauna.

Henry W. Bates (b. 8 February 1825, d. 16 February 1892). Batesian mimicry was named for this preeminent Neotropical explorer and naturalist. Bates was the first person to work on higher riodinid systematics, and his writings about working in the Amazon Basin added much to our understanding of Neotropical natural history (see O'Hara 1995). His extremely important collections are housed in the British Museum of Natural History, London.

Fritz J.F.T. Müller (b. March 1822, d. May 1897). This neotropical explorer and distinguished naturalist had a wide-ranging interest in organisms, but is perhaps best known as the originator of the theory of Müllerian mimicry. His ideas and contributions to a wide variety of biological subjects besides Lepidoptera remain fresh today.

Otto Staudinger (b. 2 May 1830, d. 13 October 1900). Staudinger was an eminent European entomologist and butterfly taxonomist whose material is found in many museums, but especially in the Berlin Museum, where the majority of his riodinid types are housed.

Thomas Belt (b. 27 November 1832, d. 21 September 1878). Belt's skill as a naturalist and observer of nature is perhaps best summed up by Charles Darwin, who praised his book, *A Naturalist in Nicaragua*, as the best natural history journal ever published up to that time. Belt's Central American butterflies are found in the British Museum of Natural History and form the basis for many of the riodinid observations made by Godman and Salvin.

Frederick D. Godman (b. 15 January 1834, d. 19 February 1919) and Osbert Salvin (b. ?, 1835, d. 1 June 1898). These are the celebrated naturalists and taxonomists who not only edited and produced the thirty-nine volumes of *Biologia Centrali Americana* concerned with insects, but together

FIGURE 22. (A) H. W. Bates. (B) F. Müller in Brazil circa 1890. (C) O. Staudinger. (D) T. Belt. (E) F. D. Godman. (F) O. Salvin. (G) H. Fruhstorfer. (H) A. Seitz. (I) H. Fassl (left) and G. Garlepp (right) in a photographic studio setting circa 1915; exact whereabouts unknown.

FIGURE 23. (A) H. Stichel. (B) C. H. Lankester in Cartago circa 1968. (C) W. Schaus near Turrialba circa 1908 or 1909. (D) W. Schaus. (E) J. Barnes. (F) G. B. Small, Jr., near San Vito de Java, Costa Rica, circa 1978. (G) B. D'Abrera at the Museo Nacional, San Jose, Costa Rica in 1979. (H) G. Lamas at the Museo Nacional de Historia Natural, Lima, Peru, circa 1993. (I) I. A. Chacon (*right*) and P. J. DeVries (*left*) at La Montura, Parque Nacional Braulio Carrillo, Costa Rica, circa 1980.

also treated the butterfly fauna of this region. Their contributions to Central American butterflies is enormous, and their collections form an important part of the holdings in the British Natural History Museum (BNHM), London.

Hans Fruhstorfer (b. 7 March 1866, d. 9 April 1922). This prodigious collector, taxonomist, and natural historian of butterflies wrote extensively on the Nymphalidae the world over (especially in Ceylon and Java), and also collected riodinids in the Neotropics. Much of his writing is found in the species and generic accounts found in the Seitz catalogs. His material is found in virtually all of the world's major museums, and he was one of the first taxonomists to utilize morphology of genitalia in discerning taxonomic relationships and diagnosing species from one another.

Adalbert Seitz (b. 24 February 1860, d. 5 March 1938). The great lepidopterist is best known for editing his celebrated series, *The Macrolepidoptera of the World*, a work consisting of sixteen large and lavishly illustrated volumes covering all of the then known butterflies and moths. This work remains as the principal reference work for the Lepidoptera for most regions of the world and has influenced every lepidopterist since its publication. Of particular interest here is that in volume 5 Seitz contributed the treatment for what was then the entire Neotropical riodinid fauna.

Anton H. Fassl (b. 1876, d. 4 October 1944). Fassl provided an exceptional amount of important material to museums throughout the world. His collecting sites ranged throughout the Amazon Basin, and he provided museum specimens with labels from Costa Rica and Panama as well. In addition to adult butterflies, Fassl also sent specimens of caterpillars and published field observations on their natural history. For some butterfly species, his observations of long ago are the only recorded natural history accounts in existence.

Hans F.E.J. Stichel (b. 16 February 1862, d. 2 October 1936). Although employed by the State Railroads in Germany, Stichel's real vocation was the production of the largest extant body of work on systematics of the riodinids. Hence, he may be considered the "father" of riodinid taxonomy. His collection is now housed in the Museum für Naturkunde, Berlin.

William Schaus (b. 11 January 1858, d. 20 June 1942) and Jack Barnes (no information available). These important figures in Neotropical Lepidoptera were constant companions throughout most of their adult lives.

Their close collaboration resulted in the large and important Schaus collection that forms the basis of the U.S. National Museum's (USNM) Neotropical Lepidoptera collections. Both of them collected extensively in Costa Rica (and elsewhere) at the turn of the century, and today Schaus and Barnes material is found in museums throughout the world.

Jose F. Zikán (b. 19 March 1881, d. 23 May 1949). Born in Bohemia (now the Czech Republic), Zikán worked in Brazil (mainly around Itatiaia), and published on the natural history, taxonomy, and ecology of beetles, wasps, ants, flies, butterflies, and moths of this area, including the riodinids. He played an important role in developing Brazil's first national park (Itatiaia), and his collections are housed at the Instituto Oswaldo Cruz in Rio de Janeiro.

Charles H. Lankester (b. 14 June 1879, d. 10 July 1969). An important naturalist who lived in Costa Rica early in this century, Lankester often hosted biologists visiting Costa Rica, who stayed with him at Cachi or traveled into the field with him. He maintained an active correspondence with biologists interested in birds, Lepidoptera, and plants (e.g., O. Ames, M. A. Carriker, H. Pittier, N. D. Riley, W. Schaus). His collections of Costa Rican plants, animals, and insects are found in many major museums. The Lankester Botanical Garden in Cartago testifies to his skills as a botanist and naturalist.

Other entomological pioneers whose discoveries were pertinent to our understanding of Neotropical butterflies include A. Alfaro, E. Arcé, P. Biolley, P. Calvert, G. C. Champion, P. and A. Calvert, A.G.M. Gillott, W. B. Richardson, H. Rogers, E. Trötsch, H. Ribbe, and C. F. Underwood.

Modern-Day Workers in the Neotropics

The early pioneers had an important effect on the field of natural history through the publication of treatments on tropical butterfly faunas that were readily available to subsequent generations of entomologists. Two publications with arguably the largest impact on Neotropical butterfly natural history were the Godman and Salvin volumes in the *Biologia Centrali Americana* series, and A. Seitz's volume 5 in the *Macrolepidoptera of the World* series. After the interruptions imposed by the great world wars, our understanding of Neotropical butterflies in general, and the Costa Rican fauna in particular, has advanced considerably. During this time, a great many people made contributions in a variety of areas, and many of them continue their work today. The following provides brief biographical sketches of some but not all the workers of this century who have advanced our understanding of Neotropical butterflies, particularly the Costa Rican butterfly fauna.

Gordon B. Small Jr. (b. 1934, d. 22 January 1989). This peerless modern collector made unparalleled collections and observations on Panamanian and Costa Rican butterflies. Although he seldom published, Small's letters, personal encouragement, observations, and collections have influenced most Neotropical butterfly biologists and taxonomists living today. A truly exceptional individual whose efforts have just begun to be appreciated. His collections are housed in the USNM and at the Universidad de Panama.

Paul R. Ehrlich (b. 29 May 1932). Ehrlich is a biologist of prodigious breadth and output, and his work has had an effect on butterfly ecology, conservation biology, and systematics at many levels.

Keith S. Brown, Jr. (b. 1 October 1938). This energetic field and laboratory biologist has contributed widely to our understanding of South American butterflies and has been an important force in the field of biogeography and conservation biology.

Daniel H. Janzen (b. 18 January 1939). During the last twenty years, Janzen's work as an ecologist and organizer of insect collectors and collections has had a truly large impact on the Costa Rican biological scene at many levels. His work has also influenced much of tropical biology, entomological and otherwise.

Bernard D'Abrera (b. 28 August 1940). Based on British Museum of Natural History material, D'Abrera's regional biogeographic catalogs are famous for their lavish illustrations. Although idiosyncratic in places, his books provide the only readily accessible references to global butterfly biodiversity.

Annette Aiello (b. 1 May 1941). A biologist known for her meticulous life history work on Lepidoptera, Aiello has long been a resident naturalist at the Smithsonian Tropical Research Institute in Panama. Her work serves as a model to those interested in caterpillar and hostplant biology.

Allen M. Young (b. 23 February 1942). In addition to his studies on general insect ecology, during the last twenty years Young has produced many papers on the natural history and hostplant associations of Costa Rican butterflies. His collections are housed at the Milwaukee Public Museum.

Richard I. Vane-Wright (b. 26 July 1942). Vane-Wright, an unusual and ebullient systematist at the BNHM, has a great breadth of interests and insights that have ranged across a great diversity of topics concerned with butterfly biology and systematics.

Lawrence E. Gilbert (b. 22 November, 1942). Primarily known for his contributions to the ecology of *Heliconius* butterflies and their hostplants, Gilbert has been a strong source of encouragement to many students of Neotropical butterfly ecology.

George Austin (b. 10 July 1943). Through his energetic inventory work and his taxonomic studies on the skippers (Hesperiidae), Austin has made important contributions toward understanding Neotropical butterflies.

Luis D. Gomez (18 July 1944). This Costa Rican botanist's role in the development of the Museo Nacional and the blossoming of the "age of naturalists" in Costa Rica cannot be overstated. Gomez has helped many biologists (the present author included) develop a lasting interest in all branches of Costa Rican biology. His collections are housed mainly in the Museo Nacional, but are found in many other major museums as well.

Phillip R. Ackery (b. 22 October 1946). No one who has had contact with the BNHM can fail to have noticed the enormous assistance provided by Ackery. Much of his careful and often voluminous work serves as a model for systematic and bionomic studies on butterflies.

Gerardo Lamas (b. 29 May 1948). Lamas, whose taxonomic work and labors in cataloging Neotropical butterfly biodiversity are certain to be of great importance to all branches of entomology, is considered by the cognoscenti as the foremost living scholar of Neotropical butterfly nomenclature and the history of Neotropical lepidopterology. He has made large and important collections of butterflies that reside in the Museo de Historia Natural in Lima.

Curtis J. Callaghan (b. 1943). Callaghan has consistently published papers on the natural history and taxonomy of South American riodinids, and has for some years been engaged in formally cataloging all of the species in the family.

Isidro A. Chacon (b. 31 January 1956). An energetic and gifted field naturalist, Chacon has made profound contributions to our understanding of Costa Rican butterflies, plants, and birds. His collections are housed in the Museo Nacional de Costa Rica.

Other recent biologists who have made significant contributions to our understanding of Neotropical butterflies, especially the Costa Rican riodinid fauna, include R. Aguilar, W. W. Benson, F. M. Brown (deceased), A.V.Z. Brower, L. P. Brower, J. Llorente-Bousquetes, R. Canet, P. Chai, H. K. Clench (deceased), R. Cubero, R. F. D'Almeida (deceased), R. del la Maza, J. de la Maza, T. C. Emmel, R. M. Fox (deceased), N. Greig, W. Haber, J. Hall, D. J. Harvey, R. Hesterberg, V. King (deceased), P. Knudsen, J. Longino, J. B. Mallet, D. Murray, A. Muyshondt, J. Miller, L. D. Miller, P. Opler, C. Penz, R. Raguso, R. K. Robbins, G. N. Ross, M. C. Singer, D. Spencer-Smith, F. G. Stiles, K. Willmott, K. Wolfe, and M. Zumbado.

A brief and excellent history of Costa Rican natural history may be found in Gomez and Savage (1983), which describes the social climate that fostered the development of biological science within the country. In the meantime, let us hope that the Neotropics, and Costa Rica in particular, continues to produce enthusiastic naturalists.

BUTTERFLY SYSTEMATICS

Systematics is a scientific discipline concerned with recognizing and describing organisms, placing them into groups, and understanding their relationships by ordering them in a hierarchical fashion. The ability to discern and recognize differences and similarities includes most aspects of human life: virtually everyone recognizes that, although they are different, tigers and house cats, wolves and dogs, hummingbirds and ostriches, and butterflies and moths are related. I believe that cognizance of systematics, including taxonomy, is an integral part of being aware of one's surroundings. The interested reader who wishes to pursue the historical development of systematics may wish to consult Huxley (1940); Simpson (1945, 1961); Hennig (1966); Wiley (1981); Mayr and Ashlock (1991); and Forey et al. (1992). This section highlights certain aspects of systematics that have a an influence on our understanding of butterflies, with special reference to the riodinids.

Early Butterfly Systematics

The first classification of butterflies appeared with the publication of the tenth edition of *Systema Naturae* in 1758 by Carolus Linnaeus, the creator of the binominal nomenclature system. At the inception of Linnaeus's classification system, all butterflies (as well as some members of the family Ascalaphidae in the order Neuroptera) were placed under the generic name *Papilio*. Roughly fifty years after the first use of the binominal system, generic names other than *Papilio* began to be employed for butterflies. At this point in history, although it was not explicitly part of the then current philosophy to catalog nature *ad ma-*

jorem Dei gloriam, an innate recognition of relatedness became important simply by recognizing that papilionids were in one group, nymphalids in another, and so forth. That is to say, that recognition of "birds of a feather" set the tone for all subsequent systematic work.

As is the case for most groups of Neotropical organisms, our current understanding of riodinid butterflies rests in large part on the efforts of the Victorian British and German naturalists who explored the Neotropics. The discoveries of these naturalists were eagerly described, published, and read by scientists at European museums and academic societies. During this period, museum systematists, academic scholars, and field naturalists (in some sense, workers needed to be all three) began to influence one another in profound ways, particularly in the context of development of a field of organismal biology. Some of the most important Neotropical naturalists to influence our understanding of tropical biodiversity in general, and the riodinid butterflies in particular, include H. W. Bates, T. Belt, C. R. Darwin, W. Müller, F. Müller, and E. Möschler.

Perhaps the most important landmark in the study of the Central American butterfly fauna was the publication of the *Biologia Centrali Americana*, volumes 1 and 2, by F. D. Godman and O. Salvin. This work drew upon the studies of H. W. Bates, A. G. Butler, H. Doubleday, H. Druce, J. O. Westwood, W. C. Hewitson, C. and R. Felder, O. Staudinger, and J. A. Boisduval, all of whom were important pioneers of butterfly systematics. Furthermore, Godman and Salvin's use of the morphology of genitalia to separate species, delimit genera, and indicate systematic problems (especially in the riodinids) foreshadowed the importance of these characters in modern works: the morphology of the genitalia remains an extremely important part of virtually all current systematic revisions of Lepidoptera (e.g., Klots 1956; Miller 1991, 1996; Miller and Otero 1994).

The early part of the twentieth century marks a time influenced by German workers who assembled prodigious entomological catalogs. Volume 5 of *The Macrolepidoptera of the World,* edited by A. Seitz, remains the most important single encyclopedic treatment of Neotropical butterflies. Although the section on riodinid butterflies (authored by Seitz) has serious taxonomic and nomenclatural problems, it nevertheless remains an important starting point for any work on the riodinids. Close on the heels of Seitz's work came the work of H. Stichel, who published more on the riodinid butterflies than any other person before or since. It is upon the work of Stichel that all modern systematic and taxonomic knowledge of riodinids is based.

Early systematists did not employ an exacting methodology to construct hypotheses of relationships, or *phylogeny,* that were reflected in their classifications. Rather, they were more concerned with enumeration and description of species, called *alpha taxonomy*, and a personal interpretation to put together a classification. The past four decades has seen a rebirth of systematic thought, and a great interest in the methodology to construct hypotheses that reflect the evolutionary history. Thus, there was a shift away from enumeration to a more formal and rigorous application of evolutionary theory. The major schools of systematics during the last forty years include *evolutionary systematics* (Huxley 1940; Simpson 1945, 1961; Mayr and Ashlock 1991), *numerical taxonomy* or *phenetic systematics* (Sokal and Sneath 1963), and *phylogenetic* or *cladistic systematics* (Hennig 1966).

Modern Butterfly Systematics

As mentioned above, systematics is a formal scientific discipline that is concerned with ordering the natural world into groups or categories, usually in a manner reflecting phylogenetic relationships. The importance of systematics (including taxonomy) is simply that intelligent comparisons of organisms cannot be conducted in a scientific manner unless their taxonomy has been established (Simpson 1945). In essence, when a biologist wishes to understand something about a particular organism, often the most readily available information will be found in a systematic treatment of the group to which the study species belongs. For example, if, for a comparative study, one wished to find the caterpillars of a rare species of *Eurybia*, the systematic hostplant patterns summarized in this book strongly suggest searching flowers of Marantaceae or Zingiberaceae in the area where the butterfly has been reported. Thus, by using systematics we may make predictive guesses about this hypothetical *Eurybia*, even though nothing may be known of its early stages.

When the systematic relationships between organisms have been established by any modern method, their hypothetical phylogeny may be expressed as a classification system in which the categories are ordered hierarchically (i.e., family, subfamily, tribe, genus, species). These evolutionary relationships can also be presented schematically as a branching diagram called a *dendrogram* or, as it is called in modern systematics, a *cladogram*. As systematics and taxonomy have matured as a discipline, dendrograms have evolved in the form, use, and meaning to reflect changes in other areas of biological science. For example, the spidery branches showing butterfly relationships in Reuter's (1896) classification contrast sharply with the angular lines of Ehrlich's (1958a) classification, and both differ from that of Kristensen (1976). As one might guess, there are considerable differences in the shape of the diagrams and how the evolutionary history of the butterflies is depicted. Reuter's hypothesis of relatedness was done through the study of a single structure (the palpi) and by his individual interpretation of the observed patterns. Ehrlich's hypothesis was done using a large number of character sets, based on an overall statistical similarity (phenetics). Finally, Kristensen's hypothesis employed cladistic analyses of shared-derived characters (*synapomorphies*) alone. Though different, all three hypotheses share similarities, especially at the higher levels, suggesting that higher-level classification in butterflies is to some extent stable.

The appeal of phylogenetic or cladistic systematics as a logical method of reconstructing phylogeny (see Hennig 1966; Wiley 1981; Forey et al. 1992) is that it uses homologous, shared-derived characters to establish relationships across taxa to develop evolutionary hypotheses. Furthermore, cladistics requires that all aspects of systematic work be defined in a manner explicit enough to allow other workers to reproduce the analysis, and to add more characters of their own. Effectively, this means that any systematic work based upon gestalt or "trust me, I know" methods without defining precisely why two or more organisms are placed together in some manner of relationship is suspect, because the method is based on subjective overall similarity, not homologous, shared-derived characters. Inasmuch as all other schools of systematics do not require such methods, a portion of the work in phylogenetic systematics research may involve reevaluating previous systematic ideas and classifications. The search for shared-derived characters is on, and we are presently in a healthy time, when all classifications and systematic treatments of the butterflies are under question. A critical feature of cladistics is that shared-derived character states must be identified, and these characters alone form the basis of a phylogenetic hypothesis. The differences among the results of using different systematic analyses may easily be seen by comparing Ehrlich (1958a) and Kristensen (1976), Munroe (1953) and Miller (1987), and Brown (1981) and Brower (1994a). The future will no doubt produce exciting work that will challenge some of our currently held ideas about the tree of life in general, and the evolution of butterflies in particular.

Each of the two common types of diagrams found in modern systematic works, the unresolved and the resolved dendrogram, expresses different types of systematic information. In the hypothetical examples here (Fig. 24), the unresolved dendrogram has four separate branches indicating four taxa (a, b, c, d) that might, for example, represent genera or subfamilies of riodinid butterflies. Note, however, that the relationships of the branches to one another are not shown explicitly, or resolved. In other words, the unresolved dendrogram shows that the four branches represent apparent monophyletic taxa, but do not illustrate the hierarchical relationship of one to another. In the resolved dendrogram, however, the four branches are ordered so that the rela-

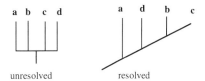

FIGURE 24. Two common styles of dendrograms used for depicting systematic relationships. Note that the resolved dendrogram shows an explicit order of relationships. (Drawing by P. J. DeVries)

tionships among the taxa are explicit: they provide an explicit hypothesis of relatedness. In other words, closely related taxa share a more recent common ancestor than distantly related ones. Here we can easily see that taxon (b) is more closely related to taxon (c) than to taxa (d) and (a), and the hypothesis of the relationship is that taxon (a) is basal (or most primitive) to taxon (d), that the taxa (b) and (c) form a sister group, and that relative to the other taxa, this sister group (b and c) is most derived.

Overall interest, number of workers, and human history are, of course, important to the development of systematic ideas, and typically the current schools of systematic thought have the benefit of learning from the strengths and weaknesses of earlier ones. For historical notes on the systematics of butterflies, especially tropical ones, see Ackery (1984, 1988), DeVries (1987), and Miller (1987); Tyler et al. (1994) provide interesting and amusing contrasts of the various systematic schools and their various quirks. Here I give an overview of systematics and classification that bears on our understanding of the riodinid butterflies.

Higher Systematics of the Riodinidae

Historically, there has never been disagreement that the group of butterflies treated in this book form a natural, or monophyletic, group, even though they have been known under the family names Lemoniidae, Erycinidae, Nemobiidae, and finally the Riodinidae. The first major systematic treatment of the riodinids was done by H. W. Bates (1868), who not only produced the first classification of the riodinids but suggested they form a natural group. Corroboration of many of Bates's ideas came from Reuter's (1896) classification of all butterflies based on a detailed examination of only the labial palpi—a work of over five hundred pages! Then came the most ambitious riodinid worker, H. Stichel, who, between 1910 and 1930, cataloged all of the known species, divided the group into subfamilies, tribes, and sections, and described many taxa. Taken as a whole, Stichel's work provided a framework for building all subsequent classifications, and many of the ideas within it will no doubt continue to be important.

The first modern classification embracing all groups of butterflies is that of Ehrlich (1958a), which is a far more critical and thorough analysis of butterfly systematics than had occurred previously. On the basis of statistical similarity, the riodinids were treated by Ehrlich as a subfamily of the Lycaenidae, and the view that the riodinids form a sister-group relationship with the lycaenids remains the most conventional yet uncorroborated systematic hypothesis (see Ackery 1984). However, there are several outstanding questions concerning the riodinids that stem directly from Ehrlich's work and from Kristensen's (1976) reanalysis of it: (1) Do the riodinids form a sister-group relationship to the Lycaenidae? (2) If a sister-group relationship exists, what is the relationship of the riodinids with respect to the overall phylogeny of the Lycaenidae? and (3) If there is no sister-group relationship between the riodinids and lycaenids, what is the sister-group of the riodinids?

At the time of this writing, we still have no phylogeny of the butterflies as a whole, but a number of studies bear upon our systematic concept with respect to the position of the riodinid butterflies within the context of the lycaenids. Actually, a number of studies on various characters suggest that the riodinids and the lycaenids may not be closely related (Table 2). Some recent examples are worth relating. Although he does not address riodinid-lycaenid relationships explicitly

TABLE 2

Some Comparative Differences between Riodinid and Lycaenid Butterflies

1. Lycaenids with six walking legs, all riodinid males with modified forelegs (Bates 1859)
2. Differences in the morphology of palpi (Reuter 1896)
3. Androconia rare in the riodinids, widespread in lycaenids (Müller in Longstaff 1912)
4. Position of spiracles and silk girdle on riodinid pupae (Harvey 1987a)
5. Riodinid female trichoid sensilla on foretarsi, genitalia without posterior apophyses (Harvey 1987a)
6. Differences in the morphology of foreleg coxae and trochanter (Robbins 1988)
7. More than two mandibular setae, arrangement of crochets, and position of spiracles unique in riodinid caterpillars (Harvey 1987b)
8. Differences in the homologies of caterpillar ant-organs (DeVries 1991a)
9. Differences in acoustic frequencies of caterpillar calls (DeVries 1991c)
10. Differences in chromosome compliments (Lorkovic 1990)
11. Eye pigment chemistry (Bernard 1979)
12. Several molecular data sets (Martin and Pashley 1992; Campbell and Pierce, pers. comm.)

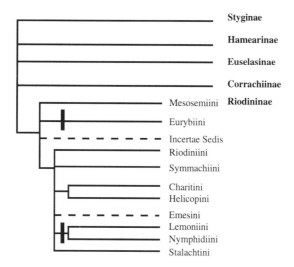

Styginae

Hamearinae

Euselasinae

Corrachiinae

Mesosemiini   Riodininae

Eurybiini

Incertae Sedis

Riodiniini

Symmachiini

Charitini

Helicopini

Emesini

Lemoniini

Nymphidiini

Stalachtini

FIGURE 25 The phylogeny of the subfamilies and tribes within the Riodinidae (after Harvey 1987a). Dotted lines represent groups thought not to be monophyletic; black vertical bars indicate myrmecophilous lineages. The substructure of the entire Old World Hamearinae has been collapsed from the original in this diagram.

(Fig. 25), Harvey (1987a) maintained the riodinids as a family separate from the Lycaenidae on the basis of early-stage and adult characters. The study of foreleg characters from all butterfly families by Robbins (1988) implied that the riodinids are most closely related to the Nymphalidae, not the Lycaenidae. A comparative study of caterpillar ant organs (DeVries 1991a) showed that riodinid and lycaenid ant organs are not homologous, thus suggesting that myrmecophily evolved independently in the two groups. Martin and Pashley's (1992) work using molecular markers found no evidence for a sister-group relationship between riodinids and lycaenids, but they found that the riodinids cluster with the Pieridae or Nymphalidae. Most recently, a continuing study using mitochondrial DNA analysis by N. Pierce and her coworkers suggests that the riodinids and lycaenids may, or may not be closely related (D. Campbell and N. Pierce, pers. comms.). Clearly, such questioning of previous systematic work should be taken as a strong indication of a healthy interest in resolving the phylogeny of the riodinids and lycaenids.

There is little doubt that future understanding of riodinid phylogeny and classification will come from the use of modern molecular techniques, expanded sets of morphological characters, and the repeated testing and refinement of our concepts of particular groups. We are now in an age when many research efforts in systematics concentrate on the use of molecular data for reconstruction of phylogeny. Although they are powerful tools for adding an important independent source of phylogenetic information, molecular techniques cannot provide much-needed information on the behavior, habitats, symbiotic interactions, and conservation ecology of living riodinids. Such fundamental information must come from fieldwork, collecting, experiments, and observations.

The Phylogeny of the Riodinidae

One of the most useful paradigms of cladistic systematic methods is that, provided with a character matrix, one can evaluate explicitly any phylogenetic hypothesis, meaning that systematic work can be constantly reevaluated in much the same way as findings in experimental science have been modified through time. In light of modern systematic methods, how confident are we that the subfamily and tribal classification followed in this book reflect the evolutionary relationships of the riodinids?

Unfortunately, assessing the higher-level classification of the riodinids becomes problematical because no explicit methods were provided in Harvey (1987a) stating how the classification was derived. Although we cannot reproduce that work precisely, we can extract characters from it, test some of the hypotheses using cladistic methods, and get an approximation of how confident we should be in the overall phylogeny. To do this we can ask which of the characters found in Harvey (1987a) are informative about the relationships among higher taxa (tribes or subfamilies) of riodinids. For example, characters found only within one higher taxon, or those shared by all higher taxa, would not help us understand relationships among the higher taxa. We need characters that vary among the tribes so that the potential for discovering shared-derived characters linking two or more groups is possible. Of course, a character that is uninformative at this higher level may well be phylogenetically informative at a lower level. In other words, some characters can provide information within groups (e.g., the genera within a tribe), but they cannot be used to address our question because they are not shared among groupings at the higher level.

Upon inspection it was found that twenty-three of the sixty-four total characters used by Harvey (1987a) were informative for phylogenetic analysis at the higher level. These characters (eleven early-stage characters and twelve adult characters) were placed in a data matrix (Table 3) and analyzed cladistically with the computer program PAUP, version 3.1.1 (Swofford 1993) using a heuristic search. To explore both adult and early-stage characters independently for building a phylogeny, three separate analyses were performed on the data in Table 3: one

TABLE 3

Characters Used for a Cladistic Assessment of the Higher Classification of the Riodinidae

Taxon	3	4	9	11	12	13	14	15	19	21	26	36	37	38	39	41	45	47	48	49	50	52	53
Styginae	?	?	?	?	?	?	?	?	?	?	?			0	0	0	1	0	0	0	0	1	0	0	0
Hamaeris	?	0	0	0	0	0	0	0	3	0	0		1	1	1	1	0	0	0	0	1	0	0	0
Zemeros	?	0	0	0	0	0	0							1	2	0	0	0	0	1	0	0	0
Abisara	?	0	0	0	0									1	1	0	0	0	1	0	0	0
Euselasiinae	1	1	0	0										1	1	0	0	1	0	0	0
Corrachiinae	?	?	?	?										0	0	0	0	1	0	0	0
Mesosemiini	0	?	?												0	1	1	0	1	0	0
Eurybiini	1	1	1												0	1	1	0	0	0	0
Incertae sedis	1	1	1												0	1	1	0	0	0	0
Riodina sec	1	1	1												0	1	1	0	0	1	1
Ancyluris sec	0	?	?												?	?	?	0	1	1
Symmachiini	?	?	?												0	1	1	0	0	0	0
Charitini	1	1	1												0	1	1	0	0	0	0
Helicopini	1	1	1												1	1	0	0	0	0	0
Emesini	?	?	1												0	1	1	0	0	0	0
Lemoniini	1	1	2	1										1	0	1	1	0	1	0	0
Nymphidiini	1	1	2	1	1									1	0	1	1	0	0	0	0
Stalachtini	?	?	?	?	?	?								1	1	0	1	1	0	0	0	0

NOTES: The top row of numbers refers to the characters as listed in Harvey (1987a). The first eleven characters (beginning 3 and ending 26) are derived from the early stages, while the remaining characters (beginning 36 and ending 53) are derived from the adults. A question mark indicates no information was available for that character.

using adult characters only, one using early stage characters only, and one using a combination of both character sets. Due to the large number of equally parsimonious trees generated from the data (over 3,000 for the total data set), a strict consensus option was employed to derive the three unrooted dendrograms (Fig. 26).

Although the dendrogram published in Harvey (1987a) cannot be reconstructed without his exact methods, the cladistic analysis resulting from his data does provide some insights into the classification of the Riodinidae. The highest-order groupings (subfamilies) remain stable no matter which of the character sets are used to derive the dendrograms and suggest the five subfamilies represent stable monophyletic groups. Note that the dendrogram for only early-stage characters (Fig. 26c) does not include the Styginae or Corrachiinae because there is no information available on them. The groupings (or tree topology) of some tribes within the Riodininae do, however, vary from Harvey (1987a) and among themselves (Figs. 25, 26). This variation includes the complete separation of the Charitini and Helicopini branch, and

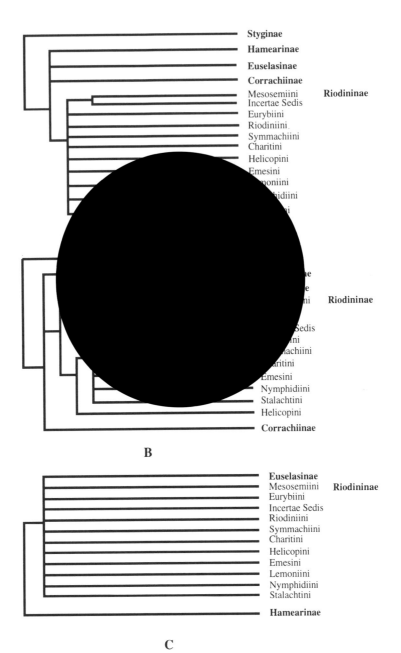

Styginae

Hamearinae

Euselasinae

Corrachiinae

Mesosemiini   **Riodininae**
Incertae Sedis

Eurybiini

Riodiniini

Symmachiini

Charitini

Helicopini

Emesini

...oniini

...idiini

...i

...e

...e

...ni   **Riodininae**

...edis

...ni

...achiini

...ritini

Emesini

Nymphidiini

Stalachtini

Helicopini

Corrachiinae

B

Euselasinae
Mesosemiini   **Riodininae**
Eurybiini

Incertae Sedis

Riodiniini

Symmachiini

Charitini

Helicopini

Emesini

Lemoniini

Nymphidiini

Stalachtini

Hamearinae

C

FIGURE 26. Hypotheses of relatedness among riodinid subfamilies and tribes resulting from a cladistic reanalysis of the characters in Harvey (1987a). These are unrooted, strict consensus trees. The substructure of the Hamearinae has been collapsed into a single branch, as have the two sections of the Riodinini. (A) Dendrogram based on twenty-three total characters (twelve from the adults and eleven from the early stages). (B) Dendrogram based on twelve characters of the adults only. (C) Dendrogram based on eleven early-stage characters only, where the Styginae and Corrachiinae were omitted because the early stages are unknown. Note the differences in the hypotheses of relatedness between the dendrograms here and the one in Figure 24.

the complete separation of the Lemoniini-Nymphidiini branch; the Mesosemiini are most closely related to Incertae Sedis on the one hand, and to the Lemoniini on the other. Without involving the technical details of cladistic analyses and interpretation (see Forey et al. 1992), we can say that when taken together these simple analyses (figs. 25 and 26) do suggest two things: there are too few informative characters to resolve branching patterns, and much more systematic work is needed before we can be confident of understanding riodinid phylogeny.

Like Stichel's work before him, Harvey's work on the higher classification of the riodinids provides a framework upon which to build more refined systematic hypotheses—a sign of progress in riodinid systematics. I believe that a more profound understanding of the riodinids will come from a synthetic grasp of their morphology, early stages, ecological relationships, behavior, and molecular biology (e.g., see A.V.Z. Brower 1994a,b). As we face the very real threat of almost complete devastation of intact tropical and temperate biodiversity— which will probably happen before this book is out of print (e.g., Myers 1986; World Wildlife Conservation Monitoring Center 1992; Lande et al. 1994; Lawton and May 1995)—we owe it to future generations to gain a better understanding of the biology of the living organisms that currently inhabit our planet. Since we still do not have a resolved phylogeny of the butterflies, one important means of providing for future generations is by actively practicing systematics now.

COLLECTING AND STUDYING BUTTERFLIES

A major part of our understanding of butterflies comes from collections. Although I am not considered very good as insect collectors go (I spend too much time chasing caterpillars), I nevertheless recognize the great importance of making and studying collections. This field guide owes a large part of its existence to the Costa Rican riodinid butterflies that are in museum and personal collections. Without access to these collections I could never have derived a species list of Costa Rican riodinids, assessed the rarity of certain species, learned their geographical distributions, found their distinguishing characters, or provided many of the questions and comments that are strewn throughout this book. In fact, the scope and utility of all future field guides on tropical butterflies will depend on the extent and quality of the collections that have been consulted.

It is my hope that this guide will encourage people to collect and study riodinid butterflies. Even though my views on collecting may not be shared, I remain firm in my belief that studying collections, collecting, and observing butterflies in their natural habitats provide the main sources of understanding these organisms. By collecting I mean earnest field and museum work to advance our interest, concept, and understanding of biodiversity—not casual social activities or endless bouts of networking around a conference table. After all, one can, in the name of "development projects," completely eradicate all traces of organisms on large tracts of land, and even be encouraged to do so in the name of creating short-term gains and jobs. In the face of the increasing number of development projects that unalterably destroy nature, why is a serious effort to collect and study organisms so vigorously penalized?

For the serious student of butterflies, making a collection entails a great deal of hard work, patience, personal expense, learning, open-mindedness, and dedication. A well-made collection of butterflies will eventually be passed on to museums, where it will be part of a larger collection and of use to future generations for centuries. Although they typically receive less funding, staff, and resources than other institutions of higher learning, natural history museums are wonderful libraries where serious students of nature can go in search of knowledge. This knowledge is the product of the past generations who created the collections, and thus it is a natural and logical fact that those who use natural history museums eventually add to the knowledge housed there by donating collections, equipment, time, and support.

We now live in an age where the twilight of wild nature can easily be seen, and where saving tiny remnant fragments of nature from the planned destruction of tropical forests is already a matter of course. The tropics of the New World that H. Bates, W. Schaus, and A. R. Wallace reveled in has gone forever, most of it without a trace. In the end, natural history museums and their collections will be one of the few places in the world where students of nature can learn, even if only through dead material and the written word. Had I begun the work for this book one hundred years later, I am convinced that my only resources for understanding the diversity of riodinids in Costa Rica would be the mute testimonies left in museums. This hypothesis can and should be tested. Although I certainly will not be alive to see it, I believe that the museum diversity of Costa Rican riodinids will be much higher than the living diversity a century from now, and I further predict that there will be someone interested enough in nature to test this notion.

Consider what a facile understanding of the natural world will result if future generations do not possess enough curiosity to grapple with organisms. Understanding and appreciating nature doesn't emerge from a passive walk in the woods, giving donations to a nature tour agency, or reading a book. Such an understanding takes curiosity, time, and a lot of effort. A deeper understanding of biodiversity demands hard work and personal experience from the real natural world. If we

are to pass a small understanding of biodiversity to the next genera-
tion, now is the time for deeds, not words.

Collecting and Preserving

Part of making a collection of butterflies for documentation and study
entails learning how to properly collect, kill, and preserve the insects.
There is a variety of methods commonly used by different entomologists to collect butterflies, and due to considerations of size, toughness,
and activity, the various families of butterflies are treated differently.
Provided in this section are a few methods that I have found to be
useful for my work specifically with the riodinids. The reader may wish
to consult other treatments on collecting and studying insects (e.g.,
Oldroyd 1958; Common and Waterhouse 1972; Scott 1986; Stehr 1987;
Borror et al. 1989; Woodhall 1992).

Nets. When collecting riodinids, use only very fine, limp netting for
the net bag. Using a net bag that may work well for other groups of
butterflies will typically scuff or damage delicate riodinids. Experience
and practice is the best teacher. Serviceable nets can be purchased
from entomological supply houses in both the United States and in the
United Kingdom. Depending on the supplier, nets are available in
white, green, or black material and may be fitted to either circular or
triangular (kite-style) frames. For standard work, I use circular, custom-
made, white silk bags, 60 cm in diameter by 90 cm deep, set on at least
a 2-meter pole. For specialized work that entails the use of extensions
over 4 meters, I have both small- and larger-diameter net bags, and I
generally include a small folding net without a handle in my gear for
emergencies. Again, regardless of what type of net is employed, it is
important always to use the softest and most limp material for the net
bags when collecting riodinids.

Notebooks. One of the most important pieces of equipment the student of butterflies owns is a notebook. Notes on butterflies should include the date, the place where observations are made, the subject of
the notes, and any observations, however trivial, on behavior, hostplants, predators, or thoughts that may be useful in the future. Remember that you may be writing observations that represent the sum
total of our knowledge about a particular butterfly. A notebook should
be on hand at all times, and the notes should always be written in
indelible ink.

Plastic Bags and Containers. To collect caterpillars in the field, plastic
bags are essential to carry on your person at all times. Plastic bags can

be suspended along a clothesline inside a building or tent back at camp to rear caterpillars conveniently. The line will keep the specimens out from under foot, and also out of the way of animals that may devour them. Plastic containers with tight-fitting lids are useful for transporting live material between field sites. A label placed into the plastic bag or container can be referred to when taking notes on caterpillar development or behavior.

Incidental Equipment. Several other items are useful both in the field and in the field laboratory. Blunt forceps for handling delicate specimens without damaging them and a pair of needle-nosed watchmaker's forceps are useful for picking up ants or taking tissue samples (see below). A ten-power hand lens will come in handy for examining tiny structures, and a pair of good binoculars is extremely useful for observing butterflies at a distance, such as those that are visiting flowers or ovipositing in the canopy. Reversing the binoculars and using them like a hand lens works extremely well for close work.

Killing Jars. Typically, lepidopterists use killing jars for most if not all specimens. Generally one of two chemicals is used as a killing agent: ethyl acetate or cyanide. Some prefer to use a jar containing a small piece of absorbent card or plaster of Paris dotted with a few drops of ethyl acetate. Presumably ethyl acetate is chosen because it may be easier to obtain than other poisons. However, because ethyl acetate evaporates very quickly, it is necessary to carry a small bottle of it at all times to be able to recharge the killing jar frequently. Many entomologists, however, prefer to charge their killing jars with sodium or potassium cyanide. When used properly, cyanide is effective and safe to use. While in the field, I generally carry two cyanide jars with me at all times. Carrying two jars minimizes the chance of having to put two insects in the same jar simultaneously—a practice that typically results in damage to both specimens.

Making a Cyanide Jar. For riodinids or other small butterflies, I prefer killing jars made with the 4 to 6 ounce straight-sided, wide-mouth glass containers such as those that originally contained herbs and spices (Fig. 27). Similar size, heavy polypropylene tubes also work well. Jars of this size are easily carried in the pockets, field vest, or apron; they have reasonably well made screw cap lids and are readily available in most supermarkets. However, when choice is not an option, virtually any jar will do. To make a killing jar, place about half an inch of potassium cyanide crystals on the bottom of a jar that is thoroughly dry. Cut a circle of paper that will fit inside the jar and more or less cover the cyanide. Pour about one inch of vermiculite or fine, very dry sawdust

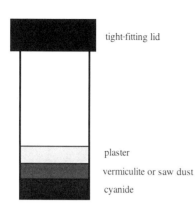

tight-fitting lid

plaster

vermiculite or saw dust

cyanide

FIGURE 27. Schematic diagram of how to make a cyanide bottle for killing insects. As a safety measure, always cover the bottom of the bottle with strong tape before use, and treat the bottle with the respect due to all poisons. (Drawing by P. J. DeVries)

on top of the paper, and tamp the vermiculite to compress it slightly. Pour about one inch of freshly made plaster of Paris that has a smooth and not too runny consistency over the vermiculite. As the plaster begins to harden gently, tap the bottom of the jar on the floor or table to allow air bubbles to escape. Tapping the bottom will yield a smooth, white plaster surface that is free of lumps or craters. Set the topless jar outdoors in a dry place to allow the plaster to set rigidly. The setting time will vary depending on the ambient humidity, the amount of water in the plaster, and the quality of the plaster itself, but generally 24 hours is more than enough. After the plaster has set, screw the top on to contain the cyanide gas vapors that are slowly being released; recall that potassium cyanide reacts with water to produce cyanide gas. (In rare instances, the process will need to be started by adding a few drops of water to the plaster.) The bottom of the jar should be securely taped with masking or fiber tape before use. Should the jar be accidentally broken, taping the bottom will make disposal easier and safer by containing the cyanide crystals and glass shards. Periodically, the inside of the jar should be wiped with tissue paper to remove moisture and detritus. It is a good idea to make five to ten jars at a time. That way one always has spares in storage that can be called into use should the need arise. (*Note*: *Cyanide is a deadly poison.* When working with cyanide crystals, do so outdoors or in a well-ventilated area, and make absolutely certain that all jars, spoons, and materials are dry.)

Depending on the ambient humidity and degree of use, a well-made cyanide jar will function for a year or more. When the jar no longer produces cyanide gas in sufficient quantity to effectively kill specimens, the jar can no longer be used. Some entomologists dispose of old killing jars by leaving them outdoors with the tops off, or burying them long enough to allow all of the cyanide to dissipate, then disposing of them. However, when all cyanide has dissipated, old jars may be reused after chipping out the plaster of Paris, cleaning them, and starting from scratch. *Always* treat the killing jar with care, and mark it as a poison; a caricature of the death's head will do nicely.

Pinching. Many butterflies and moths can be killed by a concise and sharp pinch to the thorax while the insect is still in the net. Although it can be effective for other groups of butterflies (e.g., Papilionidae, Nymphalidae), the pinching method seldom yields riodinid specimens of high quality: often, legs come off in the process or the thorax becomes severely deformed, and later it is difficult to set them properly. However, with practice and a "feel" for the procedure, the proper amount of pressure can be applied without damaging the specimen. In a situation where it is absolutely necessary to kill riodinids by pinching, remember to do so very carefully. If possible, however, use a killing jar whenever collecting riodinids.

Temporary Storage. Immediately after a specimen has been killed, it should be removed from the killing jar and protected against damage that can occur during subsequent transport and storage. This must be done carefully, always bearing in mind how fragile the wings are. Remember that a considerable time may pass between the time a specimen is collected and when it is set and then finally entered into a collection. Two highly satisfactory methods for storing or papering specimens are possible. One method involves placing the butterflies in glassine envelopes that are available commercially from stamp-collecting stores. Glassine envelopes are resistant to damage, their flaps will generally keep the specimen from slipping out, and they can be neatly stacked in large numbers in airtight boxes for transport. The envelopes come in a variety of sizes, but often the smallest size is the most useful.

The second way to store butterflies is to use paper triangles that were either constructued beforehand, or are made up as the need arises. Any paper is suitable for making triangles except for heavy card or waxed paper, but perhaps the best paper is glassine. Glassine paper can be purchased from most stores that sell technical-drawing materials. A simple diagram of how to fold paper triangles is shown in Figure 28.

As soon as possible after the butterfly has been placed in the envelope or triangle, all information relevant to that specimen should be written directly on the storage paper. For example, as soon as a specimen is placed in an envelope, I write the time of capture and a few abbreviated notes on the butterfly's behavior. Because the activity time of many riodinid species may be extremely short, you can write this useful information directly on the permanent label later. Often it is not convenient to keep the freshly killed specimens in the field, so all of the material needs to be processed for storage and transport. At the end of a working day, then, place all specimens in individual envelopes or papers and, at minimum, label them with the locality, date, and year.

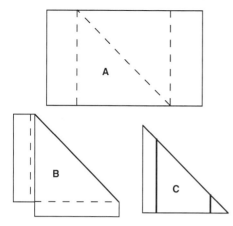

Figure 28. Making paper triangles for temporary storage of butterflies. (A) A rectangle of paper to be folded along the dotted lines. (B) A semifolded paper triangle. At this stage the specimen can be carefully placed inside with the wings folded over its back and the antennae positioned properly. (C) A completely folded paper triangle with the corners folded over to contain the specimen. Specimens can be stored indefinitely in this manner.

At this point, critical notes concerning a particular specimen can be added. The information that accompanies each specimen is of fundamental importance, especially so when treating voucher specimens. Never trust your memory for the details about a specimen. Make a habit of writing information on the papers at least at the end of every day, if not immediately upon collecting the specimen. Remember that a specimen is a time capsule of future material importance.

Pinning and Setting. All riodinid specimens should be pinned using the highest quality number 2 pins: smaller pins bend, and larger pins tend to distort the thorax. There are various methods for setting Lepidoptera (Oldroyd 1958; Borror et al. 1989), and perhaps the most widespread one entails the use of a setting board and strips of paper. However, although this method is fine for large butterflies, the delicate riodinids are often damaged unless the utmost care is taken while setting them, especially specimens that have been relaxed.

The method that I find easy to use, and which produces excellent results, entails the use of pinning blocks. A pinning block can be constructed and used with great ease and convenience. In its simplest form, it is a small wooden block with a groove cut into the top; a small hole in the middle of the groove allows the pin to pass through, and a pinning substance underneath helps keep the pin upright. Instead of paper strips, use a length of thread to open the wings and hold them in the proper position against the top of the pinning block (see below). A design that I find gives excellent results is depicted in Figure 29.

Making and Using the Pinning Block. As riodinid butterflies have different wing shapes, wing lengths, and body widths, it is a good idea to

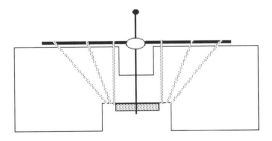

Cross Section

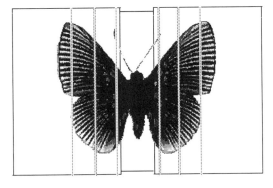

Dorsal View

FIGURE 29. A schematic diagram of a specimen properly set on a pinning block. *Top*: cross section. *Bottom*: dorsal view. (Drawing by P. J. DeVries)

make several sizes of blocks with grooves of several widths cut into them. Drill a small hole into the center of the groove to accommodate the pin and thus center the specimen on the block. If you vary the overall size of the blocks from one to four square inches, with body grooves ranging from three to ten millimeters, you will be able to accommodate most species of riodinids and lycaenids. Make certain that the top surface of the block (the surface on which the wings will be laid) is smooth and without any trace of burrs or splinters. I use a cotton thread (mercerized) to bind the wings because in my hands synthetic thread seems to chafe specimens. Nicking the top and bottom edges of the block in several places with a razor blade, and then running the thread into these nicks as the wings are bound, helps to keep the thread in place. The following step-by-step instructions may be useful to the beginner.

1. With a specimen in hand, choose a block that is wide enough for the spread wings (and long enough for tails) and has a groove wide enough to accommodate the body (not too narrow,

not too wide). Place the pin into the butterfly and adjust for proper height, set the pin into the hole in the center of the groove, and make certain that the articulation point of the wing is at the horizontal surface of the block, not below it (Fig. 29).

2. Bring the string between the wings and the pin (close to the body) and pull gently downward so that the wing on one side meets the block surface. While maintaining a slight tension on the string to restrain the wings against the block, adjust the wings into desired position with a fine needle.

3. Bind the wings into position with two to three wraps of string, being careful not to bind too tightly and mark the wings. At this point, be sure to place the wing angles in the desired position and the body parallel in the groove. Adjust and brace the body with pins if necessary.

4. Repeat the procedure on other pair of wings.

5. Support the abdomen and adjust the antennae into proper position if necessary. To the block, attach the data that will be on the final label, so that it does not get separated from the specimen.

6. Allow the specimen to dry for 48 hours in an air-conditioned place, 24 hours in a laboratory drying oven set on low, or for several hours in a household oven at 150 degrees. It can be air dried for a week or more depending on ambient conditions. Do not use too much heat when drying specimens. Again, experience is the best teacher.

7. Gently unbind the specimen by unwinding the thread, taking care not to damage the antennae or wings. Slowly remove the pinned specimen by grasping the head of the pin in one hand and restraining the block with the other. Once the specimen has been removed from the block, label it at once.

Relaxing Specimens. Setting butterflies before they have had time to dry out and become rigid produces, without question, the finest specimens. However, when staying for extended periods in the field this is not practical simply because transporting pinned, dried specimens under such conditions greatly increases the chance of damaging them. Most people will be confronted with dried specimens in papers that need to be relaxed or rehumidified prior to setting the specimen. Relaxing dried specimens requires only a container with a flat bottom and a tight-fitting lid. Flexible containers designed for food storage that come in a variety of sizes are excellent for this purpose.

After you have selected the specimens to be relaxed, place a damp paper towel on the bottom of the container, place the specimens in their papers flat on the bottom towel, cover them with another damp paper towel, and seal the lid. If many specimens are to be relaxed, use a large container and make several layers of damp towels and butterflies. Do not pack too tightly. It is advisable to put Chloral-creosote, paradichlorobenzene, or other chemicals in the container to prevent mold. Leave the specimens in the relaxing container for 24 hours, and then check them to see if they are sufficiently relaxed to set. Anything left after 24 hours should be checked every five hours or so. Typically, riodinids can be set after 24 hours, but the amount of time depends on the size of the specimen and the dampness of the towels. Again, experience is the best teacher. Note that you *must not* leave specimens in the relaxing container for extended periods of time because they will mold and/or rot.

Shipping Specimens. In some instances, it may be necessary or desirable to ship specimens to experts for identification, as loan material to a taxonomist doing revisionary work, or to return material that you have borrowed. Although dried insects, especially butterflies, are extremely fragile, set specimens can be shipped without sustaining damage if they are packaged properly. Packing and shipping pinned butterflies can be accomplished with a minimal amount of effort and a few double-checks (see Borror et al. 1989).

Basically, the specimens need to be shipped in two boxes: one small pinning box fitted with a proper foam or carton pinning bottom and a top that encloses the sides, and another larger packing box that will act as a buffer against the hazards of shipping through the postal service. The pinning box can be a special carton box made for shipping museum specimens (called Mailmasters) or a wooden insect box. Or you can make your own carton out of stiff cardboard and pinning foam.

Into the small box, carefully and firmly pin each specimen into the bottom. Push the pin all the way into the pinning surface, using pinning forceps if necessary. Though specimens can be layered, it takes extra care to extract them later. Double-check to make certain that the specimens do not touch each other. Once all the specimens have been pinned into the box, check for "spinners" by gently touching the forewing costa with a pin. A spinner is a specimen that will rotate around the axis of the pin, invariably come to pieces while in transit, and of course cause damage to other specimens. Spinners need to be braced with two pins to maintain them in place: one at FW costa, and the other either at the distal margin or at the posterior edge of the tornus. Imagine that a loose specimen or abdomen acts like a wrecking ball turned loose on your box of other prized specimens, and you will get the picture: it can destroy the lot, or as is common, at least the most valuable ones. Remember to check all specimens before shipping. The safest method is to brace all of the specimens and place additional pins in spaces between specimens.

Once you have pinned the specimens into the small box and double-checked them, place a heavy card, or better, a foam insert so it rests on the heads of the pins, and place the cover on the box. The insert will take up the space between the heads of the pins and the top of the box. The box of specimens is now placed into the center of the larger box in such a manner that it is completely surrounded with packing material (plastic bubbles, Styrofoam peanuts, excelsior). Seal the large box well. In bold words indicate that the contents are fragile and contain scientific material that is of no commercial value. Packaged in such a manner, specimens can be sent short distances or around the world to arrive in pristine condition.

Eggs. Collecting and preserving eggs is simple. Small vials filled with alcohol that have tight-fitting tops are all that is required. I find that 2-ml screw-cap polypropylene vials manufactured for the medical industry are excellent for this purpose. The egg is simply dropped into the alcohol, along with a data label, and the egg will be preserved for future study. Although virtually any type of alcohol will do (including cheap rum), 70% ethanol seems to be the preferred elixir; 100% should be avoided because it may cause deformation of the specimen. If an egg is collected immediately after oviposition, Downey and Allyn (1980) recommend allowing it to air dry for about 24 hours before placing it into alcohol. This will prevent the chorion from collapsing. However, I have frequently deposited eggs in alcohol within minutes of oviposition without any damage to them. When collecting tiny riodinid eggs, I generally slice off a small fraction of the plant material upon which they were deposited and drop the entire assemblage into the alcohol. This will avoid damaging the eggs and preserves the matrix of glue that holds the eggs to their substrate.

Caterpillars. Collecting and preserving properly identified caterpillars is an extremely important aspect of butterfly biology, and one that should be vigorously encouraged. It is a pleasure to rear caterpillars and discover life histories. I always carry a supply of plastic bags with me in the field to collect and transport both the caterpillars and pieces of the host plant. Later the same bags may be suspended on a line at base camp (out of the sun), and observations on life history changes can be noted and photographed.

Very few riodinid species in collections have associated preserved caterpillars. By getting into the habit of rearing them, one can make large contributions to our understanding of a riodinid's early stages. From the numerous methods of preserving caterpillars (see Stehr 1987), I suggest three that are useful to the field worker.

The simplest but least desirable method is to drop the living caterpillar into a vial with 70–80% alcohol (again, cheap rum will do in a pinch). Although it is quick and easy, this method generally yields poor specimens because they curl tightly and may turn black because the alcohol doesn't permeate them quickly. However, there will be times when this method is the only recourse.

If conditions permit, use a second method, as follows. First, drop the live caterpillar into a pan of water that has just come off the boil, and leave it until the body sinks to the bottom. Generally a minute or two is sufficient. Then remove the caterpillar from the water, drop it into alcohol, and after a few days transfer it to the final vial of alcohol. Dropping the caterpillar into hot water kills the enzymes and micro-organisms in its gut, and the transfer to the second vial will ensure that most of the water in the specimen has been replaced with alcohol. This method will produce satisfactory specimens.

A third method, which is more involved but yields beautifully pre-served material, derives from Peterson (1962) and was modified by E. Quinter at the American Museum of Natural History in New York. Many of the cognoscenti, including myself, refer to it as "Quinter's solution." Make a basic solution of equal parts xylene and 95% ethanol and add a dash of glacial acetic acid (no more than 5% by volume). Make up a quantity of this stock solution for the lab, and carry a smaller container of it into the field. Quinter notes that this mixture works fine if the caterpillar is somewhere in the middle or toward the end of its stadium, but if the specimen has recently molted the solution needs to be modified. Quinter suggests adding drops of water (one at a time) until the solution starts to turn milky but does not separate (xy-lene is not miscible in water). If the solution does separate, add more of the basic solution. Once the solution is made, simply drop the cater-pillar into it and watch carefully as the solution permeates the speci-men (this will be obvious as the water streams out of the body) until such a time as the caterpillar inflates and straightens out. (Note that small caterpillars such as riodinids that are left in the solution too long will burst. Be careful.) When the caterpillar has inflated with the pro-legs directed outward and the body is straight, remove it from the solu-tion and drop it into 70% alcohol. After about a week, transfer the caterpillar to another vial of 70% alcohol to remove all the xylene. This method is far superior to the other two, and should be used whenever possible.

Collecting Tissue for Molecular Techniques. Recent trends in systematics may employ techniques developed for the field of molecular biology. Even though DNA can be extracted from long-dead museum material, including fossils many millions of years old (DeSalle et al. 1992; Gri-maldi 1993, 1995, 1996), current wisdom indicates that fresh tissue is the best because it yields the best sequences. Luckily, field collecting specimens for later molecular analysis is simple. All that is required are some small polypropylene vials with screw tops that have a gasket seal and are filled with absolute alcohol (100% ethanol), a permanent marking pen to mark the vials, a pair of fine watchmaker's forceps, and perhaps a razor blade. Select a freshly killed specimen, carefully remove pieces of tissue from the abdomen, thorax, or head with the forceps, drop all immediately into the absolute alcohol, and seal the vial. Tearing the specimen into pieces allows the alcohol to permeate all of the tissue and stop decomposition. However, I have found that simply tearing the abdomen from fresh material and dropping it into the alcohol works well, and this method has the added benefit that the voucher specimen will be intact for pinning. Store the wings as vouchers in an envelope that has been marked with the same code as the vial containing the tissue (numbers work well) so that the samples can always be cross-referenced. Material preserved in this manner can be maintained at ambient temperatures in the tropics for several months, and in the laboratory they can be stored in the freezer.

TWO. FAUNAL REGIONS, HABITATS, AND RIODINID DIVERSITY

Because of its equatorial position (between 8° and 11°9″ north latitude), interactions between surface wind patterns, a backbone of rugged mountains, and oceans on two sides, Costa Rica has an enormous diversity of terrestrial habitats for the relatively small area it occupies on the planet. Furthermore, the country forms a biological and geological bridge between Central and South America by connecting with Nicaragua on the north and Panama on the south. Consequently, the patchwork of weather patterns, topography, microhabitats, and biogeographical position interact to produce an area that supports a high biotic diversity. The climate of Costa Rica is discussed in some detail by Coen (1983), but a few examples from that work will serve to illustrate how diverse the climate of Costa Rica can be. The mean annual rainfall ranges from 1.5 meters along the northwest coast of Guanacaste to over 6 meters in the central portion of the Cordillera de Talamanca. Depending on the locality and the month, the number of hours of sunshine may range from 2.0 to 9.7 per day. Likewise, depending on the elevation and the month, temperatures may range from over 30 degrees centigrade during the day in the northwest at Guanacaste to zero degrees or less on the high peaks of the Talamancas.

The biotic diversity of Costa Rica has been explored by many field biologists over the last century. Even though biological studies are currently a cottage industry, a staggering amount of exploration remains to be done. The efforts of the Museo Nacional, the Instituto Nacional de Biodiversidad, and the various staff and associates of those institutions have been significant in making major advances in our understanding of Costa Rica's habitats and organisms. Very good general overviews of Costa Rica's climate, flora, and fauna include Janzen (1967, 1983) and McDade et al. (1994).

For the purpose of describing Costa Rican fauna, we can divide the country into the Pacific and Atlantic slopes, the various elevations along these slopes, and their associated life zones as defined by Holdridge (1967). Although there are no data to completely correlate Holdridge life zones and butterfly species (butterflies move and go extinct, and no complete inventories for any site exist), the life zone system is useful in making generalizations about the likely occurrence of butterfly species within Costa Rica. In my previous work on butterflies (DeVries 1987), I divided Costa Rica into six large units, termed *faunal regions*, that were distinguished by characteristic species and species assemblages. These faunal regions are retained in this book as well, but I have added to them examples of particular interest relating to the riodinid butterflies (see Figs. 30–36). These faunal regions are described in terms of elevation, life zones, butterfly species that are both typical of and peculiar to them, and certain aspects of the overall biology of the butterflies for each region are highlighted. From my own experience, and through the experience of other biologists, I further subdivided these regions into what I term *zones of endemism, boundary zones,* and *species pockets.* I conclude this section by comparing riodinid species richness and diversity in the six faunal regions of Costa Rica, and then compare the Costa Rican fauna to other Neotropical sites.

FIGURE 30. Pacific lowland deciduous forest. (A) Early rains of the season sweeping the lowlands. Photo taken on road ascending to Monte Verde. (B) Ridge forest in the dry season, Parque Santa Rosa. (Photos by P. J. DeVries)

Pacific Slope

The major characteristic of the Pacific slope is its well-defined seasonality. The first rains of the wet season fall in May, and there is almost daily rainfall until October. By November the dry season has begun in earnest, and little or no rain falls until the following May. The changes of season are strong environmental cues for flowering, fruiting, and growth of vegetation (Opler et al. 1976), and strongly influence population fluctuations of insects (Janzen 1973b). The severity of the dry season varies along the Pacific slope, being most strongly pronounced in the lowland deciduous forests of Guanacaste. This region fluctuates between a lush green environment with a high abundance of insects during the wet season, to an almost desert brown with reduced insect abundance in the dry season. The southern lowlands and midelevations of this region also exhibit seasonality, but as these areas are typically wetter, the seasonal effects on vegetation and insect abundance seem more moderate and less pronounced to the casual observer. Butterfly species richness and overall abundance are strongly tied to the annual precipitation on the Pacific slope, and there is a general trend for all areas in the north (e.g., Parque Santa Rosa) to have fewer species than those in the south (e.g., Parque Corcovado).

Pacific Lowland Deciduous Forest (sea level–600 m). This area extends from Nicaragua south to just southeast of the city of Puntarenas, and it is composed of tropical dry, tropical dry transition, and some tropical moist forest life zones. In this book I frequently refer to this area as the "lowland Guanacaste" forest. The prominent characteristic of this entire area is its strong seasonality. The dry season is a time when most of the vegetation is leafless, and this is followed by the rainy season with its lush vegetative growth. During the dry season, butterfly abundance and species richness are reduced, with some resident butterflies passing this environmentally harsh period in riparian forest. About four weeks after the first rains have fallen, the entire area erupts with butterfly species (Fig. 30). As the rainy season progresses there is a noticeable procession in the appearance of butterfly species (although mostly undocumented for riodinids). Some butterflies, such as the genus *Eurytides* (Papilionidae), are most abundant for the first two weeks of the rainy season, whereas others, such as the genera *Archaeoprepona*, *Zaretis*, and *Memphis* (Nymphalidae), are most abundant much later. Some of the resident butterflies in this area—e.g., *Eurytides* (Papilionidae), *Eurema* (Pieridae), *Marpesia* (Nymphalidae), *Celaenorrhinus* (Hesperiidae)—may show a reproductive diapause during the dry season (DeVries et al. 1987; Odendaal 1990), and some exhibit regular patterns of seasonal migration (see DeVries 1987). Although we lack direct observations, the riodinids will likely show marked seasonal patterns with respect to various aspects of their biology.

On the whole, the lowland deciduous forest has fewer butterfly species than other Costa Rican habitats below 1600 m (DeVries 1987, 1994), including the riodinids. Conspicuously low in richness are the nymphalids in the subfamilies Ithomiinae, Brassolinae, and Satyrinae, and the riodinids. Perhaps because this area has extensive expanses of agricultural lands, an abundance of wide-ranging species is able to thrive in these open areas (DeVries 1994). Another notable feature of the deciduous forest is that there are relatively few mimetic butterfly species compared to other lowland areas—almost certainly due to the lack of ithomiines (DeVries 1987), and, in the case of the riodinids, perhaps due to a lack of appropriate moth species as models.

Compared to other lowland sites, the Pacific deciduous forest has relatively few or no riodinid species from the Euselasiinae, Mesosemiini, Incertae Sedis, Charitini, and Nymphidiini. This paucity of species and the proportions of the species and tribes that are represented (or absent) are similar to particular sites in Mexico. The riodinids that are typical to this area, or appear to reach their southern geographical ranges, include *Pandemos godmanii* and the species in *Apodemia, Lasaia, Calydna,* and *Pachythone*—strengthening the idea that the lowland deciduous forest shares biological affinities with certain types of Mexican forest. However, the reader should bear in mind that we know very little of the riodinid fauna from this area except that comparatively few species occur there (see also pp. 102–110). See DeVries (1987) for other butterfly species typical of the lowland deciduous forest, including those that reach their southern range in this area.

Pacific Lowland Evergreen Forest (sea level–800 m). This area extends roughly from the Rio Grande de Tarcoles near San Mateo southward to Panama and embraces the following life zones: tropical moist, moist transition, premontane wet transition, and tropical wet forest. Although this entire area experiences a dry season (especially the northern portion), it never dries out to the extent of the Guanacaste lowland forest, and is most clearly observed in the forests on the Osa Peninsula (Fig. 31). Because of the more moderate climate, the seasonality of the butterflies is not as marked as in the deciduous forest areas to the north.

This area appears to have two distinct divisions for butterflies: the drier area north of Punta Quepos, and the more diverse, wetter area to the south. Although much overlap of species occurs, each area contains a distinct fauna. The butterflies that occur in the evergreen forest

FIGURE 31. Pacific lowland evergreen forest. (A) Interior of floodplain forest, Parque Corcovado. (B) Trail through the interior of the Corcovado basin, Parque Corcovado. (C) Mangrove-estuary forest, Sirena, Parque Corcovado. (Photos by P. J. DeVries)

exhibit extensive mimicry and some endemism, and overall the area contains a moderate species richness (DeVries 1987), including the riodinid fauna.

Taken as a whole, this region represents a transition zone in which a number of subspecies more typical of the Panamanian fauna occur, and it contains faunal elements representative of South America. Some unusual riodinid species that are found here or are apparently endemic to the area include *Euselasia leucophryna, Euselasia euoras, Euselasia eucrates, Mesenopsis melanochlora, Phaenochitonia ignicauda,* and *Synargis palaeste.* Of special interest is the boundary effect between those areas north and south of San Mateo. The change in the butterfly fauna is perhaps most dramatically illustrated by the brown and blue forms of the showy nymphalid *Morpho peleides,* which change abruptly on either side of this boundary (see DeVries 1987).

Pacific Mid-Elevation (700–1600 m). This region is very complex with respect to habitats and microhabitats and embraces the following life zones: tropical moist, premontane belt transition, lower montane moist, lower montane wet, premontane wet, premontane wet-rain transition, and premontane rain forest (Fig. 32). The region may be divided into two parts: the drier areas of the Cordillera de Guanacaste and the Meseta Central (with fewer species), and the species rich, wetter areas south along the Cordillera Central and Talamanca. These areas also differ with respect to the composition of butterfly species. For example, we find populations of *Papilio torquatus* and *Morpho polyphemus* in the Cordillera de Guanacaste (DeVries 1987), but few if any of the riodinid species are peculiar to this area except perhaps *Euselasia inconspicua.* In the Cordillera de Talamanca we ▓▓▓▓▓▓*le grandis, Memphis lankesteri, Memphis elara,* very differe▓▓▓▓▓▓*o peleides* and *Morpho theseus* (DeVries 1987), and ▓▓▓▓▓▓*sia gyda, Sarota acantus, Calephelis sodalis,* and *Adelo*▓▓▓▓▓

The Meseta Central appears to act as an eco▓▓▓▓▓a-nacaste forest and the wetter mid-elevation for▓▓▓▓▓a migrational corridor between the Atlantic and Pa▓▓▓▓▓ere that we find mix zones where species typical of one ▓▓▓▓▓c other fly together (e.g., *Heliconius pachinus, Heliconius cydno, Melinaea lilis, Melinaea scylax*). Also notable in this respect are the areas around Villa Colon, Santa Maria de Puriscal, and the Dota Valley (DeVries 1987). However, I am unaware of examples of our riodinid fauna that are peculiar to these areas.

High-Elevation Pacific and Atlantic (1800 to above 3000 m). There is a great similarity between the high-elevation faunas and floras on the Atlantic and Pacific slopes, especially above 2000 m. With few excep-

FIGURE 32. Pacific mid-elevation. (A) Wind savanna at Ujaraz de Buenos Aires in El Valle General. (B) Forest interior along the Rio Coton, Las Alturas. (C) Forest interior in Valle de Copey. (Photos by P. J. DeVries)

tions, all habitats within this region receive daily precipitation and markedly reduced solar radiation compared to other areas in Costa Rica (sometimes weeks may pass without sunshine), and a few areas are subject to freezing temperatures at night. The life zone forest types in this region include premontane wet transition, premontane rain, montane wet, montane rain, and subalpine rain paramo (Fig. 33). The butterfly fauna found here includes species that are endemic to the Talamancas, a high proportion of genera that reach their highest diversity in the South American Andes, and some species that are typical of the North American temperate zone. The habitats above 2000 m have the lowest butterfly species richness in all of Costa Rica.

A characteristic of the high-elevation fauna is that there is a pronounced reduction in the number of nymphalids that feed on rotting fruits as adults. At these elevations, there is a shift from exclusive fruit feeders to those that feed on dung, or, as in the pronophiline satyrines, feed on fruits when they can but typically supplement their diets with flower nectar. The assortment of conspicuous butterflies in our high-elevation habitats include *Papilio abderus* (listed as *garamas*), *Catasticta cerberus, Lymanopoda euopis,* and *Catargynnis dryadina* (DeVries 1987).

Very few riodinids occur at elevations above 1800 m (Table 6). The total of six species occurring at high elevations are drab little butterflies with ranges that include most of the Central American cordilleras. Although high elevations may seem to have a rather boring riodinid fauna, to the cognoscenti high-elevation habitats conjure up one of the most enticing of all Central American species, *Corrachia leucoplaga*, a singular butterfly that is endemic to a small area of the Talamancas, and whose natural history is cloaked in mystery (p. 113). It is interesting to note that of the meager numbers of riodinid species at high elevations, none associate with ants. This, of course, in part reflects the fact that ants, especially secretion-foraging species, are typically rare or absent above 1800 m (W. L. Brown 1973; Olson 1994), and points to the importance of myrmecophily in the evolution and ecology of certain riodinids (see section on Diversity).

Atlantic Slope

The major characteristic of the Atlantic slope is that it is always wet. This is due to the westerly air masses that move off the Caribbean Sea and come up against the backbone of high mountains. The condensation that results from this interaction produces constant humidity and precipitation. Although the weather patterns are not as predictable or as pronounced as those on the Pacific slope, a general seasonal weather sequence for the Atlantic slope might be described as follows. The driest months (those with the most sunshine) are February and

FIGURE 33. High-elevation habitats. (A) Rain paramo near Cerro Chirripo. (B) Chusquea thickets on Cerro de la Muerte. (C) Elfin forest below Cerro de la Muerte. (D) Talamancan forest near Madre Selva. (Photos by P. J. DeVries)

March, and occasionally a few weeks into April. The rains begin sometime in April (or at the latest in May), and this is followed by a brief dry period in September and/or October. This dry spell (the inveranillo de San Juan) is then followed by the heaviest rains in November and December. In my experience, both butterfly abundance and species richness are highest during the dry periods of the year and lowest during the periods of heaviest rains.

Atlantic Lowland (sea level–700 m). This region extends from Nicaragua south across the Panamanian border, and perhaps has the greatest range of all the Central American habitat types between South America and Mexico. In Costa Rica this region contains the following life zones: tropical wet, tropical moist, and premontane wet forest transition, all of which are habitats that never dry out during the year and include areas like Tortuguerro that are large tracts of swamp forest (Fig. 34). The butterflies in this region are, for the most part, wide-ranging species that occur throughout Central and South America (see DeVries 1987). Components of the riodinid fauna found here include: *Cremna thasus, Cyrenia martia, Stichelia sagaris tyriotes, Mesenopsis bryaxis,* and *Lepricornis strigosa.* Overall, the Atlantic lowland region is species rich and has many well-developed examples of mimicry, including complexes involving the riodinids (see pp. 51–55; Figs. 19–21).

Atlantic Mid-Elevation (800–1500 m). This region is very species rich, embraces a great diversity of microhabitats, is very wet throughout the year, and contains the following life zones: tropical wet, premontane transition, premontane wet, and premontane rain forest (Fig. 35). This region exhibits endemism and range disjunctions, and is perhaps the most diverse region in all of Costa Rica. Due to the presence of a number of unusual and endemic species, I have applied the term "Carrillo Belt" to the portion of this region that extends from the Reventazon Valley along the Cordillera Central and Tilaran.

Members of the butterfly fauna that are characteristic of this area include *Battus laodamas, Eurytides pausanias* (Papilionidae), *Agrias aedon, Memphis aureola, Eunica norica, Epiphile eriopis, Dynamine hoppi, Antirrhea pterocopha,* and *Cissia drymo* (DeVries 1987). Some of the riodinids that are peculiar to this area may include *Euselasia matuta, Euselasia chrysippe, Euselasia subargentea, Mesosemia esperanza, Eurybia cyclops, Monethe rudolphus, Metacharis umbrata,* and *Nymphidium lenocinium.*

Faunal Subzones

The six major regions of Costa Rica also contain subzones of interest to understanding biodiversity. These subzones distinguish themselves from the whole by having elements of endemism or rarity, or they appear to be boundary zones where butterflies show a mixture of color patterns that may be distinct from those in other areas. Our understanding of butterfly distribution and ecology of Costa Rican butterflies is too meager, especially with respect to the riodinids, to say with certainty where all of these subzones occur. However, such areas do exist, and in many cases their peculiarities with respect to butterflies is reflected by peculiarities of the flora, other insect groups, birds, reptiles, and amphibians. The reasons why such areas are biologically unusual

FIGURE 34. Atlantic lowland forest.
(A) A logging boat on the Rio
Tortuguero. (Photo by P. J. DeVries)
(B) Aerial view of the Tortuguero
lowland forests. (Photo by K.
Winemiller) (C) The Rio Sucio in
Parque Braulio Carrillo near where
the old train station in Carrillo used
to stand. (Photo by P. J. DeVries)

FIGURE 35. Atlantic mid-elevation. (A) La Montura, Parque Braulio Carrillo. (Photo by P. J. DeVries) (B) Once an extremely important site for riodinid butterflies along Rio Angel near Colonia del Socorro, now destroyed. (Photo by P. J. DeVries) (C) Forest interior at Parque Braulio Carrillo. (Photo by L. Jost)

are unknown, although they should be of great interest to population geneticists. Certain areas appear to be mediated by local climates, as is the case for rain shadow valleys. Other areas, such as the Corcovado Basin, may be the result of geological factors such as soils that may influence the forest community. No matter how these subzones, came to be, they deserve particular study. Based on my field experience with butterflies and other organisms and from my interactions with other biologists, I recognize three types of subzones in Costa Rica.

Zones of Endemism. These areas can be fairly sizable in Costa Rica. They contain butterfly faunas that are unique to Costa Rica and western Panama, and are distinguished by having a high percentage of endemics. There are at least three zones of endemism in Costa Rica: the high montane Talamanca zone, the Carrillo Belt, and the Chiriqui-Talamancan zone, which has two subdivisions. The high Talamancan zone runs from the Cordillera Central south through the Cordillera de Talamanca into Panama, and includes habitats above 2400 m. The butterfly fauna of this zone is apparently derived from the South American Andean fauna; the genus *Catasticta* (Pieridae) and most of the satyrine tribe Pronophilini have a high percentage of species that are endemic to these mountains. The riodinid *Corrachia leucoplaga* is of course also endemic here. The Carrillo Belt is effectively the Atlantic slope midelevation habitat that follows the Talamancan zone, but at a lower elevation (500–1700 m). Butterflies characteristic of this area include *Eurytides pausanias prasinus* (Papilionidae), *Dismorphia zaela oreas* (Pieridae), *Doxocopa excelsa, Ithomia bolivari, Perisama barnesi, Adelpha stilesiana, Antirrhea pterocopha* (Nymphalidae), and the riodinids *Mesosemia albipuncta, Sarota turrialbensis,* and *Nymphidium lenocinium.* The Chiriqui-Talamancan zone is centered around Volcan Chiriqui in Panama. The higher elevation portion of this zone corresponds well with the premontane wet forest and the rain forest transition life zone, and ranges from about 1000 to 2000 m elevation. Notable species from this area include *Prepona lygia, Memphis elara, Epiphile grandis* (Nymphalidae), and the riodinids *Euselasia gyda, Euselasia inconspicua, Euselasia portentosa, Calephelis sodalis,* some populations of *Sarota acantus,* and *Mesene croceella.* The lower portion of this zone encompasses the Osa Peninsula and surrounding areas (including Panama) and was at one time known as the legendary forests of Bugaba, which have been effectively extirpated within the last two decades. Butterflies characteristic of this area include *Heliconius hewitsoni, Callithomia hydra, Antirrhea tomasia* (Nymphalidae), and the riodinids *Phaenochitonia ignicauda, Calospila zeurippa,* and *Theope eleutho.*

Boundary Zones. Observations of non-riodinids (DeVries 1987) reveal at least five boundary zones in Costa Rica. All have the property of

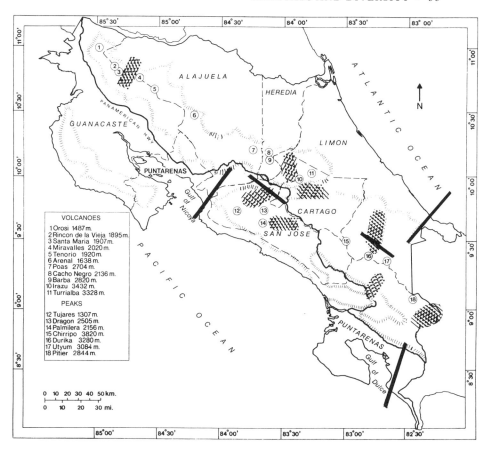

FIGURE 36. Approximate locations of boundary zones (solid black lines) and species
pockets (hatched areas) in Costa Rica.

being areas in which species show a mixture of phenotypes, or where
species composition abruptly changes (Fig. 36). There is a very noticeable boundary effect on the Pacific slope between the areas north and
south of the Rio Tarcoles that is best exemplified by the color changes
in *Morpho peleides*. The area to the northwest and southwest of the
Golfo Dulce exhibits a change in the phenotypes of several subspecies
of Ithomiinae (among other nymphalids) from Costa Rican to the Panamanian forms. The area in the Atlantic lowlands around Bribri also
shows a change from phenotypes characteristic of Costa Rica to those
characteristic of Panama, perhaps best illustrated by *Heliconius cydno*
(Nymphalidae). There is an area on the Atlantic slope between 2000
and 1000 m (corresponding to the Fila Bugu) where species from the
highlands and the lowlands mix. Finally, there is a mix-zone located
along the western slope of the Meseta Central, and although it is al-

most devoid of mature vegetation, here the butterfly fauna may show a mixture of Atlantic and Pacific slope species, and many of the species show a noticeable phenotypic plasticity. It is not known whether these areas exhibit peculiar trends for the riodinid butterflies.

Species Pockets. Based on my observations of mainly nymphalids (DeVries 1987), I found particular habitats in Costa Rica that contain rare or unusual species and thus can be distinguished from the surrounding areas. These species pockets are usually small and have certain climatic characteristics: they fall in rain shadows, sun shadows, particular valleys, rivers, and mountain tops. It is unknown how many such areas exist in Costa Rica, but these types of areas are the stuff of organismal and conservation biology. They include the following: all habitats classified as subalpine rain paramo; the rain shadows of Valle de Copey; Las Alturas; Las Mellizas; Ujarras de Buenos Aires; the extremely wet areas around Tapanti and the Rio Grande de Orosi; the area around Villa Colon; the mountain passes between Volcan Santa Maria and Volcan Mirravalles; and the passes between Volcan Irazu and Volcan Barba (see Fig. 36). Again, it is not known whether riodinid butterflies exhibit peculiar trends in these areas.

Diversity of the Riodinidae

Species diversity is a measure of the number of species within a community, where communities may range in size from a tiny square of habitat to large biogeographic regions encompassing thousands of kilometers. Even a cursory glance at the natural world reveals that the simplest habitats contain many species, and some of the earliest written documents recognize and enumerate species of both animals and plants. However, during the last fifty years, efforts have been devoted to developing methods of measuring, modeling, and comparing species diversity in different habitats and communities. The measurement and description of diversity is now a wide-ranging part of the ecological and evolutionary literature (e.g., Huston 1979; Rhode 1992; Ricklefs and Schluter 1993), and Lande (1996) has recently reviewed much of the pertinent literature on the methods of measuring diversity, and their properties and applications.

There are two common measurements of species diversity. The first measurement attempts to estimate the number of species in a community along with an assessment of the abundance of each species. The second measurement considers only the species richness or the number of the species reported from a particular community, but does not consider commonness or rarity of the species comprising that community. It is easy to imagine why obtaining the former measurement is more difficult than the latter. Furthermore, most available estimates of species diversity are based on species counts, including the patterns of riodinid butterfly diversity mentioned here.

Butterfly Diversity within the Forest. Within any forest habitat there are two major layers of vegetation, the forest canopy and the forest understory, and one can imagine that they represent differing biological communities. One study of fruit-feeding nymphalid butterflies from the Atlantic lowlands in Costa Rica suggested that stratification by species of forest butterflies breaks down in forests that have been disturbed (i.e., forests with a high percentage of light gaps or second growth), and there is a strong edge effect at the interface of forest and pastures (DeVries 1988c). Recent studies from several Ecuadorian rain forest sites show these and other effects on butterfly stratification. Furthermore, these studies suggest that our understanding of even the basic biology of the most conspicuous tropical butterflies is very poor (DeVries, Murray, and Lande, unpub.; DeVries et al., unpub.). Although they are not well understood, light environments clearly play an important role in determining the distributions of forest butterflies. A thoughtful analysis of light environments and their effects on diversity is provided by Endler (1993).

Getting a handle on the vertical stratification of riodinids in forest communities is more difficult than conspicuous nymphalids because they cannot be trapped. However, it is evident that one reason some riodinid species are typically rare is that they spend a great deal of their adult lives in the canopy. My observations indicate that some species (e.g., *Euselasia gyda, Hermathena candidata, Ancyluris jurgensenii, Sarota gamelia, Synargis palaeste, Calospila* spp) are not infrequently observed visiting flowers or perching in the canopy, and furthermore, T. Erwin (pers. comm.) indicates that riodinids are important fractions of the butterfly fauna in canopy fogging samples. However, direct observations on stratification are unavailable for the bulk of the riodinid species. The recent surge of interest in the forest canopy (e.g., Erwin 1982; Farrell and Erwin 1988; Longino and Nadkarni 1990) may eventually provide answers, especially studies designed to examine the effects of deforestation on the dynamics of insect stratification.

Regardless of how little is known about riodinids and their natural history, one thing is clear—riodinids are *the* Neotropical group of butterflies. The world fauna of butterflies is comprised of the families Papilionidae, Pieridae, Nymphalidae, Lycaenidae, and Riodinidae (and some also include skippers, Hesperiidae), and it is well known that these groups show tropical distributions—the diversity of each group increases toward the equator. Leaving the other groups aside, consider what happens to the diversity of riodinids and lycaenids within major

TABLE 4

Distribution of Species Numbers for the Lycaenidae and Riodinidae by
Major Biogeographic Regions (after DeVries, 1991a)

Family	Australian	Asian	Palearctic	African	North American	Neotropical
Lycaenidae	420	1200	>95	1300	>100	1100
Riodinidae	21	32	10	14	20	1200

biogeographic regions (Table 4). This simple estimate makes it obvious
that the lycaenid butterflies have a relatively even diversity among the
tropic regions, whereas the diversity of riodinids outside the context of
the Neotropics is trivial.

Riodinid Diversity within Costa Rica. The riodinids are difficult subjects
by which to pinpoint patterns of local faunal region diversity for two
reasons: no site inventory of the riodinids approaches the complete-
ness of other butterfly groups, and riodinid faunas may differ between
two similar or even adjacent sites. Bearing these caveats in mind we
can, however, make a first attempt at describing the diversity of the
riodinid fauna within the context of the faunal regions described for
other butterfly groups (DeVries 1987). To compare riodinid diversity
within Costa Rica, two sites that are moderately well known were
pooled to represent each of five faunal regions, and the sixth region
(high elevation) was arrived at by pooling four, less well known sites.
The sites representing the six faunal regions include (1) Chilamate
and Finca La Selva (Atlantic lowland); (2) Turrialba and Virgen del
Socorro (Atlantic mid-elevation); (3) Volcan Irazu, Volcan Poas, Volcan
Turrialba, and Cerro de la Muerte (high elevation); (4) San Vito de
Java and Las Alturas (Pacific mid-elevation); (5) San Mateo and Parque
Corcovado (Pacific evergreen); and (6) Parque Santa Rosa and Cañas
(Pacific deciduous). Several patterns of diversity emerge when the re-
gions are compared (Table 5).

In addition to being the quintessential group of Neotropical butterflies (Table 4), the riodinids may also contribute significantly to the
butterfly diversity of a particular faunal region. Consider the contribution to species diversity by members of the Papilionidae, Pieridae, Nymphalidae, and Riodinidae among the six faunal regions (Pacific
deciduous, Pacific evergreen, Pacific mid-elevation, high elevation, Atlantic mid-elevation, and Atlantic lowland). Among the groups used in
the comparison, the riodinids account for between 18 to 31 percent of
the species diversity in the mid-elevation and lowland regions (Table
5), indicating they are an important component of Neotropical butterfly diversity.

TABLE 5
Faunal Regions of Costa Rica

Family	PD	PE	PM	HE	AM	AL
Papilionidae	14	17	17	3	21	16
	(7.8)	(5.7)	(5.0)	(3.7)	(5.6)	(4.5)
Pieridae	31	26	45	18	30	26
	(17.4)	(8.8)	(13.3)	(22.2)	(8.0)	(7.3)
Nymphalidae	101	174	205	54	205	219
	(56.7)	(58.8)	(60.8)	(66.6)	(54.8)	(61.2)
Riodinidae	32	79	67	6	117	97
	(18.0)	(26.7)	(20.7)	(7.4)	(31.4)	(27.1)
Total species	178	296	334	81	373	358

NOTES: Note the contribution of riodinids to species diversity within the six faunal regions. The numbers in parentheses represent the percentage of the total species within a region. Data for non-riodinid families from DeVries (1987). Abbreviations: PD = Pacific deciduous; PE = Pacific evergreen; PM = Pacific mid-elevation; HE = high elevation; AM = Atlantic mid-elevation; AL = Atlantic lowland.

It is evident from the comparison in Table 5 that riodinid diversity changes with respect to faunal region. Ranked from the highest to the lowest numbers of species they contain, the faunal regions are Atlantic mid-elevations, Atlantic lowlands, Pacific evergreen, Pacific mid-elevations, Pacific deciduous, and, finally, high elevations. Note, however, that this rank does not follow those for the families Pieridae and Nymphalidae, and that the riodinids have a decidedly higher diversity on the Atlantic slope.

Considering the identity of the taxa within the faunal regions (Table 6) and extrapolating their geographical distributions suggest several apparent faunistic patterns. Many of the species found in the Atlantic low- and mid-elevation regions are the same (see species accounts) or have close relatives that are typical components of Amazonian forests (e.g., *Chalodeta, Exoplisia, Synargis, Menander*). The Pacific deciduous region has only a few more species than what is characteristic of northern Mexico or the southern USA, and some of the species are shared among these areas (e.g., *Apodemia, Calydna*). The high-elevation fauna has a low diversity that is composed primarily of wide-ranging species (e.g., *Emesis tenedia, E. cypria, E. mandana*) and one endemic (*Corrachia leucoplaga*). Finally, there is variation with respect to the proportion that each higher-level taxon contributes to the total riodinid diversity among each region. For example, depending on the region, the Euselasiinae may contribute from 0 to nearly 15 percent of the diversity, and the Mesosemiini may contribute between 0 and nearly 12 percent

TABLE 6

Comparison of Riodinid Diversity among the Six Faunal Regions

Taxon	CR	PD	PE	PM	HE	AM	AL
Corrachiinae	1	0	0	0	1	0	0
	(0.3)				(16.6)		
Euselasiinae	29	2	10	10	0	15	4
	(11.5)	(6.2)	(12.6)	(14.9)		(12.8)	(4.1)
Mesosemiini	19	1	6	8	0	13	11
	(7.5)	(3.1)	(7.6)	(11.9)		(11.1)	(11.3)
Eurybiini	6	1	3	1	0	5	6
	(2.4)	(3.1)	(3.8)	(1.4)		(4.3)	(6.2)
Incertae sedis	8	1	2	4	0	6	4
	(3.2)	(3.1)	(2.5)	(5.9)		(5.1)	(4.1)
Riodinini	61	9	16	21	3	29	22
	(24.2)	(28.1)	(20.2)	(31.3)	(50.0)	(24.8)	(22.7)
Symmachiini	27	0	8	4	0	8	13
	(9.5)		(10.1)	(5.9)		(6.8)	(13.4)
Charitini	18	2	6	4	1	10	10
	(6.7)	(6.2)	(7.6)	(5.9)	(16.6)	(8.5)	(10.3)
Emesini	22	7	5	8	1	7	4
	(8.7)	(21.8)	(6.3)	(11.9)	(16.6)	(5.9)	(4.1)
Lemoniini	15	4	6	2	0	9	7
	(5.9)	(12.5)	(7.6)	(2.9)		(7.7)	(7.2)
Nymphidiini	50	5	17	5	0	15	16
	(19.8)	(15.6)	(21.5)	(7.4)		(12.8)	(16.5)
Total species	252	32	79	67	6	117	97

NOTES: The numbers within parentheses represent the percentage of the total number of species in a region. In the CR column, the number in parentheses represents the percentage of the total Costa Rican fauna. See Table 5 for abbreviations.

of the diversity. However, the only strong ecological trend suggested by these comparisons is that few riodinids occur at high elevations.

Myrmecophily and Diversity

Together the riodinids and lycaenids account for a major fraction of total butterfly diversity (Vane-Wright 1978; Robbins 1982), and without doubt these groups embrace the greatest diversity of life histories among all butterflies (Cottrell 1984; Pierce 1987; Thomas et al. 1989; DeVries et al. 1994). One life history facet that has shaped our thinking about the diversity of these butterflies is their ability to form symbioses with ants (see Pierce 1984; Pierce and Elgar 1985). Although myrmecophily has probably evolved separately in the Riodinidae and Lycaenidae (e.g., DeVries 1991a,c), both families may be divided conveniently into two ecological groups: the myrmecophilous species, and the amyrmecophilous species. Dividing them in this manner has provided a basis for comparisons central to exploring the hypothesis of Pierce (1984) that the evolution of myrmecophily has fostered a higher species diversity in the lycaenoid (Riodinidae + Lycaenidae) butterflies (Pierce 1985, 1987; Harvey 1987a; DeVries 1991a; Fiedler 1991).

Myrmecophilous Riodinids. Adapting the comparison of Downey (1961) for the lycaenid butterflies, Harvey (1987a) divided the Neotropical riodinids into myrmecophilous species (Eurybiini + Lemoniini + Nymphidiini) and amyrmecophilous species (all other riodinid groups) to estimate that 24 percent of the total Riodinidae were expected to be myrmecophilous, and that at four separate Neotropical sites, 21 to 42 percent of the riodinids were estimated to be myrmecophiles. Partitioning the Costa Rican riodinids in this manner, and asking what overall contributions myrmecophilous species make to the diversity of faunal regions and the individual sites within these regions, allows a different view of riodinid diversity.

Once again, elevation has a significant influence on the contribution of myrmecophilous species to faunal region diversity (Table 7). Here the diversity of myrmecophilous species declines dramatically with increasing elevation such that there are simply none that occur at high elevations. Incidentally, this phenomenon reflects the well-documented decline in ant species diversity with elevation (e.g., Olson 1994). The Atlantic lowland and mid-elevation regions tie for the most myrmecophilous species, then the ranks decline from the Pacific evergreen, the Pacific deciduous, the Pacific mid-elevation, and lastly the high elevations with zero myrmecophilous species. This comparison suggests that overall the myrmecophilous species are marginally more diverse on the Atlantic slope.

This comparison can also be used to ask what proportion of the total fauna in each region is myrmecophilous (Table 7). Ordering the re-

TABLE 7
The Proportion of Myrmecophilous Riodinids in Faunal Regions

Faunal Region	Total Species	Myrmecophilous	Proportion of Fauna (%)
AL	97	29	29.9
AM	117	29	24.8
HE	6	0	0
PM	67	8	11.9
PE	79	26	32.9
PD	32	10	31.2

NOTE: See Table 5 for abbreviations.

gions by proportion of myrmecophiles from highest to lowest yields the following: (1) Pacific evergreen (33%); (2) Pacific deciduous (31%); (3) Atlantic lowland (30%); (4) Atlantic mid-elevation (25%); (5) Pacific mid-elevation (12%); and (6) high elevation (0%). Note that here the proportion of myrmecophily remains relatively even for the low- and mid-elevation sites—between 25 and 33 percent. Note also that the least diverse lowland habitat (Pacific deciduous) has a high proportion of myrmecophilous species, showing that the contribution of myrmecophily may remain high in the face of low overall diversity.

At this point the following question arises: What contributions do the myrmecophilous species make to the overall diversity of the twelve sites comprising the faunal regions? Here we must include caveats that are common to virtually all species lists that are currently available, namely that the inventories for each site are incomplete, and sampling effort is not equal among sites.

The patterns for site diversity are similar to those found for the faunal regions (Table 8). The low-elevation sites (both Atlantic and Pacific) have a higher proportion of myrmecophilous species than do other sites, ranging from 25 to 40 percent myrmecophily in the lowland sites to nearly 12 to 26 percent at mid-elevations. Again, this points out that myrmecophily falls off with an increase in elevation. The exceptional site is Monte Verde. Here I suspect the estimate of twenty species is low (due to insufficient data at the time of this writing), and that the actual number of nonmyrmecophilous species (especially Euselasiinae, Riodinini and Charitini) will be found to be much higher. As observed for faunal regions, those sites with the highest diversity do not necessarily contain the highest proportion of myrmecophilous species (e.g., compare Las Selva and Turrialba with Sirena and Cañas).

Depending on geographical proximity and habitat, I suspect that taxonomic proportions could be informative for developing local site lists, especially in adjacent areas where one suspects an overlap of faunas. For example, Cañas and Santa Rosa have similar numbers of species (22 and 26, respectively) and nearly equal proportions of myrmecophilous species (27%); but the Lemoniini and Nymphidiini contribute different proportions to this total. Due to similarity in habitat and elevation, the proportion of myrmecophiles in Santa Rosa accounted for by the Lemoniini (Table 8) suggests that this group has been underestimated for Cañas. Likewise comparing La Selva and Chilamate (Table 8), based on the La Selva fauna we might suspect (and almost certainly correctly) that the Charitini is underestimated at the Chilamate site.

Other considerations aside, the comparison in Table 8 suggests that in Costa Rica myrmecophilous species contribute from 25 to 40 per-

TABLE 8

Species Numbers Reported at Twelve Costa Rican Sites

Taxon	LS	CH	TU	PL	CB	MV	LA	SV	SM	SIR	CA	SR
Euselasiinae	3 (3.7)	2 (3.4)	13 (12.4)	1 (2.7)	6 (11.8)	3 (15.0)	9 (17.6)	5 (11.6)	6 (17.1)	4 (7.3)	1 (4.5)	2 (7.8)
Mesosemiini	11 (13.6)	7 (11.9)	11 (10.5)	5 (13.8)	8 (15.7)	2 (10.0)	5 (9.8)	6 (13.9)	1 (2.8)	6 (10.9)	1 (4.5)	1 (3.8)
Eurybiini	6 (7.4)	3 (5.1)	5 (4.8)	4 (11.1)	4 (7.8)	1 (5.0)	1 (1.9)	1 (2.3)	1 (2.8)	3 (5.4)	1 (4.5)	1 (3.8)
Incertae sedis	4 (4.9)	3 (5.1)	5 (4.8)	0	3 (5.8)	2 (10.0)	3 (5.8)	3 (7.0)	0	2 (3.6)	1 (4.5)	0
Riodinini	17 (21.0)	16 (27.1)	25 (23.8)	8 (22.2)	12 (23.5)	5 (25.0)	15 (29.4)	17 (39.5)	9 (25.7)	10 (18.2)	8 (36.4)	8 (30.8)
Symmachiini	10 (12.3)	4 (6.8)	8 (7.6)	6 (16.6)	4 (7.8)	0	2 (3.9)	2 (4.6)	2 (5.7)	7 (12.7)	0	0
Charitini	9 (11.1)	4 (6.8)	10 (9.5)	6 (16.6)	5 (9.8)		4 (7.8)	2 (4.6)	5 (14.3)	2 (3.6)	0	2 (7.8)
Emesini	3 (3.7)	3 (5.1)	6 (5.7)	3 (8.3)	5 (9.8)	4 (20.0)	7 (13.7)	4 (9.3)	3 (8.6)	2 (3.6)	5 (22.7)	6 (23.1)
Lemoniini	5 (6.2)	6 (10.2)	8 (7.6)	1 (2.7)	2 (3.9)	2 (10.0)	1 (1.9)	1 (2.3)	2 (5.7)	6 (10.9)	3 (13.6)	4 (15.4)
Nymphidiini	13 (16.0)	11 (18.6)	14 (13.3)	2 (5.5)	2 (3.9)	1 (5.0)	4 (7.8)	2 (4.6)	6 (17.1)	13 (23.6)	2 (9.1)	2 (7.8)
Total species	81	59	105	36	51	20	51	43	35	55	22	26
% myrmecophily	29.6	33.9	25.2	19.4	15.7	20.0	11.7	9.3	25.7	40.0	27.3	26.9

Note that sampling intensity among these sites is not equal, and that these counts are certainly underestimates. Abbreviations: LS = La Selva (50–100 m); CH = Chilamate (100 m); TU = Turrialba (600 m); PL = Plastico (600 m); CB = Cariblanco (850 m); MV = Monte Verde (1300–1600 m); LA = Las Alturas (1400–1700 m); SV = San Vito (1000–1300 m); SM = San Mateo (500 m); SIR = Sirena (0–100 m); CA = Cañas (100 m); SR = Parque Santa Rosa (0–100 m). The numbers in parentheses refer to the elevation of the site, in meters.

TABLE 9

Successive Years of Collecting in Cacaulandia, Rondonia, Brazil

Taxon	1989	1991	1992	1993
Euselasiinae	21	29	48	54
Mesosemiini	23	30	37	41
Eurybiini	8	8	8	8
Incertae sedis	8	8	8	8
Riodinini	34	40	54	60
Symmachiini	10	13	21	22
Charitini	5	6	8	10
Emesini	11	14	23	29
Lemoniini	11	13	18	20
Nymphidiini	41	58	65	68
Stalachtini	2	2	2	2
Total species	174	221	292	322
% myrmecophily	34.5	35.7	31.2	29.8

NOTES: Data from Emmel and Austin (1990), and G. Austin (unpublished). Note that the proportion of myrmecophiles gets close to 30% as the site becomes better known.

cent of the riodinid diversity in lowland habitats, and less than 25 percent in mid-elevation habitats and above. At this point, two questions arise: If this pattern holds in Costa Rica, how general is it with respect to other Neotropical sites? How do these proportions change as a particular fauna becomes increasingly better known? A tabulation of the species lists developed across four sampling periods from Cacaulandia, Rondonia, Brazil, perhaps the most diverse site in the Neotropics, sheds some light on these questions (Table 9). The observations indicate that even though more species were recorded at each successive period, the proportion of myrmecophiles ranged between 30 and 36 percent regardless of sampling intensity. As the site became better known, the proportion of myrmecophilous species fell to a midpoint between the ranges found in Costa Rican lowland sites.

Given the proportional similarity of myrmecophilous species in Costa Rica and Cacaulandia (Tables 8 and 9), we can ask: How do these proportions compare to other sites across the Neotropics? In other words, should we expect riodinid faunas from any lowland Neotropical sites to be composed of between 25 and 35 percent myrmecophilous species regardless of latitude? A tabulation of species lists from eleven lowland sites ranging from Mexico to Brazil (Table 10) provides some intriguing observations.

The myrmecophilous species tabulated from eleven distinct comparisons (Table 10) account for between 16 and 44 percent of the riodinid

TABLE 10

Comparative Neotropical Riodinid Diversity by Site

Taxon	ET	TIK	LS	BCI	TRIN	JS	GC	PAK	TAM	SJ	CL	Neotropics
Euselasiinae	0	3 (5.9)	3 (3.7)	3 (5.1)	4 (3.4)	29 (17.4)	15 (10.3)	34 (13.7)	49 (20.7)	2 (4)	54 (16.8)	136 (11.8)
Mesosemiini	4 (25.0)	3 (5.9)	11 (13.6)	4 (6.9)	4 (3.4)	28 (16.8)	20 (13.7)	33 (13.3)	35 (14.8)	6 (12)	41 (12.8)	136 (11.8)
Eurybiini	1 (6.2)	0	6 (7.4)	3 (5.1)	5 (4.2)	9 (5.4)	10 (6.8)	10 (4.0)	7 (2.9)	1 (2)	8 (2.5)	23 (2.0)
Incertae sedis	2 (12.5)	2 (3.9)	4 (4.9)	2 (3.4)	4 (3.4)	5 (3.0)	5 (3.4)	4 (1.6)	8 (3.3)	3 (6)	8 (2.5)	37 (3.2)
Riodinini	1 (6.2)	17 (33.3)	17 (21.0)	14 (24.1)	21 (18.0)	30 (17.9)	28 (19.2)	46 (18.5)	38 (16.0)	15 (31)	60 (18.7)	297 (25.8)
Symmachiini	1 (6.2)	1 (2.0)	10 (12.3)	8 (13.8)	11 (9.3)	6 (3.6)	7 (4.8)	13 (5.2)	13 (5.5)	4 (8)	22 (6.9)	129 (11.1)
Charitini	2 (12.5)	2 (3.9)	9 (11.1)	3 (5.1)	7 (5.9)	6 (3.6)	5 (3.4)	13 (5.2)	9 (3.8)	1 (2)	10 (3.1)	27 (2.3)
Emesini	1 (6.2)	9 (17.6)	3 (3.7)	3 (5.1)	15 (12.7)	12 (7.2)	9 (6.2)	23 (9.3)	16 (6.7)	10 (20)	29 (9.0)	107 (9.2)
Lemoniini	3 (18.7)	5 (9.8)	5 (6.2)	7 (12.1)	10 (8.5)	8 (4.8)	11 (7.5)	10 (4.0)	11 (4.6)	4 (8)	20 (6.2)	70 (6.0)
Nymphidiini	1 (6.2)	6 (11.8)	13 (16.0)	11 (19.0)	37 (31.4)	34 (20.3)	34 (23.3)	62 (25.0)	51 (21.5)	3 (6)	68 (21.2)	190 (16.5)
Total species	16	48	81	58	118	167	144	248	237	49	320	1152
% myrmecophily	31.2	22.9	29.6	36.2	44.1	30.5	38.2	33.1	29.1	16.3	30.0	24.5

Notes: The Styginae, Corrachiinae, and Stalachtini were omitted from this comparison, and the Helicopini has been collapsed into the Charitini. The numbers in parentheses refer to the percentage of the total group in question. Site abbreviations are in square brackets, and sources of the data are as follows: [ET] Estacion Los Tuxlas, Mexico (Raguso and Llorentes 1991); [TIK] Tikal, Guatemala (G. Austin, unpubl.); [LS] La Selva, Costa (present volume); [BCI] Barro Colorado Island, Panama (DeVries, unpubl.); [TRIN] Trinidad (Barcant 1970; M. Cock, unpubl.); [JS] Jatun Sacha, Ecuador (D. Murray, unpubl.); [GC] Garza Cocha, Ecuador (DeVries, unpubl.); [PAK] Pakitza and [TAM] Tambopata, Peru (Lamas 1981,1985; Lamas and Robbins, unpubl.); [SJ] Serra do Japi, Brazil (Brown 1992); [CL] Cacaulandia, Rondonia, Brazil (G. Austin, unpubl.); entire Neotropics (Harvey 1987a).

diversity at these sites. Although these estimates reflect those derived from the lowland Costa Rican sites (Table 8) and fall within the range of myrmecophilous species reported by Harvey (1987a) in his comparison of four Neotropical areas, the low proportion of myrmecophiles for Serra do Japi, Brazil, is peculiar. On one hand, this might suggest that Serra do Japi is unusually depauperate in myrmecophiles due to ecological reasons having to do with the composite of cloud forests, scrub forest, and savanna habitats found there. Although unlikely (K. Brown, pers. comm.), the low proportion of myrmecophilous species might be due to insuficient sampling of the Serra do Japi fauna. The suggestion of Harvey (1987a) that Trinidad contains an unusually high proportion of myrmecophilous species is completely corroborated here. However, Trinidad shows proportions similar to some observed at other sites (Tables 8 and 9). The proportion of myrmecophilous species at each site may reflect the overall proportion in the family (24% in Harvey 1987a), a phylogenetic effect (see Harvey and Pagel 1991) and/or underlying ecological and phylogenetic effects. Unfortunately, these ideas need to be tested with data sets that include much greater detail than only species counts. Nevertheless, based on the site-dependent variation observed in this comparison (Tables 8, 9, and 10), it would appear that myrmecophiles may be expected to account for about 30 percent of the riodinid diversity in many lowland communities.

The simple comparisons provided here show unequivocally that myrmecophilous species comprise an extremely important portion of the total riodinid butterfly fauna in lowland habitats. Whether one cares to argue from a phylogenetic or ecological standpoint, why the proportion of myrmecophilous species at these sites seems to converge on 30 percent of the total is unknown. Many more comparative sites must be investigated. However, consideration of myrmecophilous species does highlight a fundamental component of lowland tropical forest diversity: diversity, as well as our understanding of it, rests upon multispecies symbiotic associations. This of course points to the need for comparative data on host use and ant symbionts from a variety of sites—about which we know virtually nothing.

A GUIDE TO THE RIODINIDAE OF COSTA RICA

Subfamily CORRACHIINAE Stichel, 1928

This monobasic subfamily is characterized on the basis of a unique fusion between veins Sc and R1 that extends to the edge of the wing, and dissection of museum specimens which shows that they have a fustrum-shaped egg (Harvey 1987a). The configuration of the male genitalia in *Corrachia* is similar to another monobasic subfamily, the Styginae, containing the peculiar butterfly *Styx infernalis* that occurs only in a small area of the Peruvian high Andes. As smooth fustrum-shaped eggs are unusual among Lepidoptera, finding them in *Corrachia*, *Euselasia*, and *Styx* suggests a potentially close relationship. Virtually nothing is known of the Costa Rican endemic *Corrachia*.

Corrachia leucoplaga
(Schaus, 1913)
FW length: 15.5–16.0 mm   **Plate 1**
Range: Costa Rican endemic
Hostplant: Unknown
Early stages: Unknown
• **Adult:** Sexes similar. Upperside dark gray-brown with a conspicuous white medial area on FW that intrudes in the cell and broadly ends at the inner margin. Underside mottled drab gray with whitish areas in the FW, and an indistinct row of postmedial white spots. The tips of the antennae are somewhat flattened like members of the family Nymphalidae. In overall appearance this butterfly recalls a drab moth in the families Noctuidae, Geometridae, or Pyralidae.
Habits: This butterfly is known only from a handful of localities, all of which are above 1600 m in the Sierra de Talamanca south of Cartago and north of San Isidro General. The butterfly tends to fly throughout the day dur-

ing the driest part of the year at the canopy level, has a weak, fluttery flight, and resembles a nondescript moth while on the wing (I. Chacon, pers. comm.). The only flower record I am aware of comes from B. Harris, who collected a male feeding at the white flowers of a shrub which also attracted various arctiid moths and lycaenids (Asteraceae?). The scarcity of this butterfly is quite likely due to the typically cloudy weather at high elevations, an undetermined seasonality, and its unassuming, or rather eminently dull, appearance. Given the peculiar systematic position of this butterfly and its restricted range, any information regarding its early stages or general ecology should be published. Rare in collections.
Localities: [C]: Palmital de Guarco [TL]. [SJ]: Tablazo (March), Cerro de la Muerte (April), Valle de Copey (April), Madre Selva (May). [P]: North of Buenos Aires de San Isidro (June, July).

Subfamily EUSELASIINAE Kirby, 1871

The members embraced by this subfamily are united on the basis of having a smooth juncture where vein M2 joins m1, m2 at the forewing cell, giving the appearance of a single vein. Only members of the Euselasiinae have such a distinct junction of these veins. Furthermore, depending on the species, all of the genera may show a sexual dimorphism with respect to the number of radial veins in the forewing (in such cases the males may have five radial veins, whereas the females have only four; Stichel 1928). Finally, the male genitalia bear scales on the lateral surface of the valvae, and lateral projections on the tegumen (Harvey 1987a).

Three genera are currently placed in the Euselasiinae (*Euselasia*, *Hades*, and *Methone*), and the group contains more than 140 species, some of which are extremely rare. Many of the Euselasiinae are difficult to identify (especially in *Euselasia*), and judging from material in museums and field collections, there are without doubt numerous species yet to be described. The pertinent taxonomic literature for this cohesive but complicated group includes Godman and Salvin (1879–1901), Stichel (1910–11, 1928, 1930–31), Bridges (1988), plus many isolated articles scattered throughout the English, Spanish, French, and German literature. Hostplant families reported for the Euselasiinae include Melastomataceae, Anacardiaceae, Myrtaceae, Clusiaceae, and Sapotaceae. The caterpillars are covered in a dense pile of setae, and some of the gregarious species show an extraordinary synchronous processional behavior.

Genus **HADES** Westwood, 1851

The butterflies in this genus are immediately recognized by the extensive black ground color bearing patches of red at the base of the wings and a striated ray pattern that is prominent on the underside of the hindwings. Members of *Hades* are found from Mexico throughout Central and South America. There are two species in the genus, one that occurs in Costa Rica, and another that is entirely South American.

The coloration, behavior, and even the name *Hades* suggest that these butterflies are aposematic. Furthermore, when fresh individuals of *H. noctula* are handled, they bleed drops of brown fluid from the thorax like the reflexive bleeding exhibited by some arctiid moths and blister beetles in the family Meloidae. These observations strongly suggest that *Hades* butterflies defend chemically against predators. As originally noted by Godman and Salvin (1885), *Hades noctula* strongly resembles members of the unpalatable lycaenid genus *Eumaeus* throughout Central and NW South America, and the curious nymphalid butterfly *Anemeca ehrenbergi* (Geyer, 1833), which is confined entirely to southern Mexico. For modern biologists it is a matter of course to think about the evolution and consequences of mimicry in terms of biogeography, population dynamics, predation, and habitat destruction (e.g., Gilbert 1983; Turner 1984; Endler 1993). However, similar ideas were expressed over a century ago by Godman and Salvin (1885) who, when discussing the resemblance between *Hades* and *Anemeca*, suggested: "If these two forms assumed similar coloring of the wings by mimicry, they must have for a long time coexisted in the same area. Their distribution now would show either that the *Morpheis* [= *Anemeca*] has been largely exterminated, or that the *Hades* has vastly extended its range." A century later, Godman and Salvin's questions concerning these butterflies and their evolutionary history remain fresh and intriguing. Before habitat destruction makes it impossible, a study of the *Hades* and *Anemeca* system using modern ideas and techniques might provide major advances in our understanding of mimicry and molecular evolution.

The early stages of *Hades* are incompletely known, but judging from their gregarious caterpillars and pupae the females must lay clusters of eggs. The only available host record is from the family Anacardiaceae (D. H. Janzen, pers. comm.). In Costa Rica, and elsewhere, the butterflies occur in a wide range of habitats, but typically they are found to be abundant locally.

Hades noctula
Westwood, 1851
FW length: 22.0–23.5 mm **Plate 1**
Range: Mexico to Colombia and Venezuela
Hostplant: *Spondias mombin* (Anacardiaceae)
Early stages: *Mature caterpillar*—head capsule dull orange without ornamentation; body densely covered in short black setae interspersed with longer whitish setae. The caterpillars are gregarious throughout their life and pupate in groups. *Pupa* (Fig. 37a)—brown with broken black bands on all segments, eyes black, anterior edge of thorax with a conspicuous black crescent, and wing veins and distal margins of wings trimmed in black. Overall not unlike the pupa of *Lepricornis*. Pupation takes place in gregarious masses numbering from ten to eighty pupae, generally on the underside of a large leaf.
• **Adult:** Sexes similar. Upperside of both wings black with thin white distal margins. Underside black with a white ray pattern. Conspicuous red area at base of wings.
Habits: This common, wide-ranging species occurs from sea level to 1800 m on both slopes in habitats ranging from second-growth to primary forest. The butterfly is one of the most commonly collected of our riodinid species, and it is decidedly most abundant at middle elevations. The adults may be found throughout the year, except in the Pacific dry forest, where they appear to fly during the wetter periods. The conspicuous fluttery flight of these butterflies strongly resembles that of the unpalatable lycaenid *Eumaeus godartii* that usually flies in the same habitats. If handled or squeezed gently, fresh individuals produce a drop of brownish liquid from the thorax near the base of the wings which has a faintly oily texture and taste—at least to my tongue. Depending on the site, the males are encountered perching along forest edges and rivers between 08:00 and 10:00 hrs on vegetation about 3 to 5 m above the ground, not infrequently in small colonies. The solitary females are found typically from midday to early afternoon in shaded forest or along forest edges. Both sexes visit flowers of herbs, shrubs, and trees that bear small white flowers.
Localities: [A]: Cariblanco (September), Atenas (December). [C]: Moravia de Chirripo (February, April), Turrialba (June–August). [SJ]: Carrillo. [P]: San Vito (April–June), Las Alturas (March–May, July, September, December), Sirena (April), Llorona (March, April, July), Rincon (February, March), Monte Verde (September). [L]: Hitoy Cerere (January). [G]: Santa Rosa (January, December), Upala nr Bijagua (September).

Genus **METHONE** Doubleday, 1851

These butterflies may be immediately recognized by their rich yellow and orange coloration and the toothlike lobes on the hindwing distal margin. The butterflies have been referred to under the name *Methonella* in much of the older literature. The butterflies in *Methone* range from Costa Rica south through Ecuador, and to the eastern slope of the Andes. There is a long-standing question as to whether the genus contains either a single, variable species, or two species (Godman and Salvin 1885; Seitz 1916). Although the problem remains unresolved, I treat it here as a single species.

During flight these butterflies are rather clumsy and may frequently be observed to settle on the underside of leaves where they may remain for prolonged periods, sometimes for over 12 hours. Their conspicuous black and orange coloration and clumsy flight behavior suggests that they may be aposematic. However, the butterflies are easily damaged by the slightest handling, and in some areas (Las Alturas, San Vito) I have frequently found beak-marked wing fragments on the forest floor, suggesting they are palatable to birds. Although in certain localities these butterflies are fairly common, nothing is known of their early stages or their hostplants.

Methone cecilia chrysomela
(Butler, 1872)
FW length: 20–25 mm   Plate 1
Range: Costa Rica to Amazon Basin
Subspecies: Costa Rica to Colombia
Hostplant: Unknown
Early stages: Unknown
• **Adult:** Sexes dimorphic. *Male*—upperside with a fiery orange medial area bordered broadly with jet black. *Female*—upperside medial area yellow-orange with broad, indistinct black margins, a conspicuous pale yellow crescent in FW submargin, and pale yellow submarginal band on distal portion of HW.
Habits: This striking butterfly occurs in mid-elevation forest areas on both slopes from 400 to 1600 m in association with moist and cloud forest habitats. On sunny days both sexes may be encountered as solitary individuals in shady forest understory, or along shaded streams and trails between 08:30 and 13:00 hrs. Occasionally found to be locally abundant for a few weeks at a time. I have never noted behavior suggesting that the males maintain perches or engage in energetic chases. Common.
Localities: [A]: Cariblanco (February–May, September), Peñas Blancas (January). [C]: Rio

Chitaria (March, October). [SJ]: Carrillo (July). [P]: San Vito (February–June, September, November), Brujo de Buenos Aires (September), north of San Isidro (July, August), Las Alturas (March, April, July–September). [G]: Volcan Santa Maria (April).

Genus **EUSELASIA** Hübner, 1819

The butterflies in this genus are united by characteristics of their wing venation and have been divided into sections according to the number of subcostal veins in the forewing (e.g., Godman and Salvin 1885). The butterflies in *Euselasia* may be readily recognized by their large eyes, small palpi, wing shape, and the generally somber but distinct underside patterns. The genus comprises a substantial fraction of Neotropical riodinid species, and with the many cryptic and undescribed species that are coming to light, *Euselasia* may eventually be found to contain more than 150 species. The fundamental taxonomic literature for *Euselasia* remains that of Stichel (1930–31), and his general arrangement is followed here. In some older literature these butterflies were placed under the name *Eurygona*. Members of the genus are found from the southwestern USA, throughout Central and South America, with by far the greatest number of species found in the Amazon Basin. There are at least twenty-eight species reported from our area, a substantial number of which are rare and little known.

When the geographic range of the genus is considered in its entirety, only a few species of *Euselasia* appear to be widespread and common, whereas the majority of the species may be considered to be rare and restricted to particular habitats. It is evident that in the Costa Rican fauna some species are extremely localized, some may be crepuscular, and a substantial fraction of the species are known from only a few museum specimens. The rarity and extreme localization of these butterflies is probably even more pronounced than we think, and I would not be surprised to find that eventually the total number of *Euselasia* species from Costa Rica will increase by 10 to 15 percent. The nature of these butterflies and our fragmentary knowledge of the Costa Rican fauna make it obvious that the treatment here is far from complete. The users of this book are in a position eventually to provide a better understanding of *Euselasia* in general and the Costa Rican fauna in particular.

For a group of this magnitude, there is re-

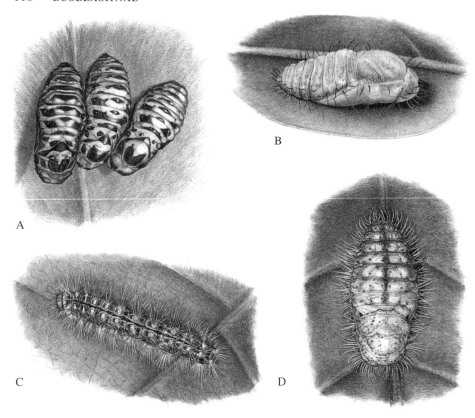

FIGURE 37. (A) *Hades noctula* pupa. (B) *Euselasia eubule* pupa. (C) *Euselasia procula* caterpillar. (D) *Euselasia procula* pupa. (Drawings by J. Clark)

markably little information on its early stages. Thus far the hostplant families reported for *Euselasia* include Myrtaceae, Clusiaceae, Sapotaceae, and Melastomataceae (DeVries et al. 1994), and it is likely that the list of hostplant families will increase as the group becomes better known. Available evidence suggests that the eggs are all of a fustrum shape (Fig. 1), the caterpillars are typically covered in downy setae, they may be solitary or gregarious, and no species of *Euselasia* forms associations with ants. The gregarious caterpillars of some species move about in synchronous head-to-tail processions, feed at night, and rest during the day on the base of tree trunks.

In the field, these butterflies rest with the wings folded over the back as in the Lycaenidae and Nymphalidae. Indeed, most casual entomologists frequently mistake these butterflies as lycaenids, both in the field and in museums. It has been suggested that some *Euselasia* species may rub their hindwings together like many species of Lycaenidae (e.g., Robbins 1981, 1985). However, I have never observed this behavior in any species from Central America, Ecuador, or Argentina. These butterflies visit a variety of small flowered plants and occasionally wet sand, and I have also seen them feed at extrafloral nectaries found on leaves and emerging buds.

Discrete activity times, frequently of short duration, are the rule for these butterflies. Many *Euselasia* species are active only in the early morning, others during midday, others in late afternoon, and regardless of when they fly, their activity is typically restricted to short windows of time during the day. In Costa Rica I found that males of several species may use the same tree to perch on, but that the species show a pronounced vertical stratification. For example, one species will perch only on the highest portions of a tree, other species lower, and others fairly close to the ground. Add to this the variable temporal component, and a single perching site may have ten or more species perching at it during the course of the morning. The activity times of males and females may be very different, so the sexes almost never fly together. For example, during the course of one year at Las Alturas, I observed at least five hundred individual males of *Euselasia argentea* at one particular tree along a roadcut, and a total of only three females. Despite searching for 500 m in either direction along the road (within virtually identical habitat), I found no other perching sites for these butterflies at this locality.

Euselasia bettina
(Hewitson, 1869)
FW length: 15–17 mm   Plate 1
Range: Nicaragua to Ecuador
Hostplant: Unknown
Early stages: Unknown
• **Adult:** Sexes dimorphic. *Male*—upperside velvet black, with the underside a uniform golden brown (often with a sheen), and marked only by a spot at the HW tornus. *Female*—upperside gray-brown with the underside as in the male.
Habits: This species occurs locally from 400 to 1200 m on both slopes in association with cloud forest habitats. The males are encountered from 07:00 hrs until about 09:00 hrs along forest edges and light gaps in small groups of five to ten individuals. A typical perching locality is typically confined to a single tree or small area of vegetation from 2 to 10 m above the ground. For example, for over ten years I found that the same 10 m of trail served as a traditional perching area for discrete populations at La Virgen del Soccoro de Cariblanco. In recent years this site has been severely deforested to make way for a hydroelectric project, almost certainly resulting in the elimination of an important historical courtship site that was used by this and other butterflies. While perching, the males engage in spectacular whirling aerial interactions that may last from 10 to 20 sec. After these rapid flights, each male will typically return to its own individual leaf.
Localities: [A]: Reserva San Ramon (April), Cariblanco (April, June, July, October). [C]: Orosi (December), Moravia de Chirripo (February, April), Tapanti (June), Juan Viñas, Cachi. [SJ]: Patarra (May), Carrillo. [H]: Plastico (March, October), La Cinchona (September).

Euselasia aurantia
(Butler and Druce, 1872)
FW length: 12–15 mm   Plate 1
Range: Costa Rica to Colombia
Hostplant: Unknown
Early stages: Unknown
• **Adult:** Sexes dimorphic. *Male*—upperside bright orange confined by broad, jet-black margins and costa; entire underside silvery white. *Female*—upperside dirty brown with a yellow patch in the FW medial area, and a faint yellow blush on the HW (occasionally the HW yellow forms an indistinct ray pattern); underside as in the male. Compare with *chrysippe*.
Habits: This butterfly occurs from sea level to 1600 m on both slopes, generally in association with wet forest habitats. The males are encountered in small assemblies of five to ten individuals perching from 4 to 10 m above the ground along forest edges from 08:00 to 08:45 hrs. At any given locality, the male assemblies are typically concentrated near one particular tree, and this site may be used consistently for several years. In my experience, females occasionally fly at the perching sites along with males.
Localities: [A]: San Mateo. [SJ]: Santa Rosa de Puriscal (January). [C]: Moravia de Chirripo (April, June, August). [P]: Monte Verde, Golfito (February), Rincon (February, August), Las Alturas (April, September, November), San Vito (September–November), Santa Maria de Pittier (September), Rio Chirripo de Pacifica, 5 km N. Rivas (September), Agua Buena.

Euselasia leucophryna
(Schaus, 1913)
FW length: 15.8–17.6 mm   Plate 1
Range: Costa Rican endemic
Hostplant: Unknown
Early stages: Unknown
• **Adult:** Sexes presumably dimorphic. *Male*—upperside warm, reddish brown that darkens at FW apex and along costa, and at the HW costa; underside entirely silvery white with a very thin, slightly curvy postmedial line running from FW costa to HW inner margin. The undersides of some specimens have a postmedial black dot in the FW tornus and some black marginal spots on the HW. *Female*—apparently unknown, and in need of description. Compare with *inconspicua, matuta, eucrates*.
Habits: This distinctive and rare butterfly is known only from a few specimens found within an elevational range of 500 to 1100 m

in rain forest habitats. The holotype in the U.S. National Museum was taken over eighty years ago by William Schaus on the Atlantic slope, remaining the only known specimen until a second specimen was taken in 1978 by K. Wolfe on the Pacific slope. More recently, several more males were taken by W. Haber on the Atlantic slope near Monte Verde. The former of these localities has been deforested in recent times, whereas the Peñas Blancas site has reasonable intact forest habitat. It would be of interest to know if this butterfly survives in present-day remnant patches of forest between these widely disparate localities. Given its apparent endemicity and rarity, observations on its natural history would be worth publishing.

Localities: [A]: Peñas Blancas (July). [C]: Cachi [TL] (October). [SJ]: Santa Rosa de Puriscal (February).

Euselasia chrysippe
(Bates, 1866)
FW length: 13–15 mm   Plate 1
Range: Guatemala to Colombia
Hostplant: *Miconia elata, M. calvescens* (Melastomataceae)
Early stages: *Egg* (Fig. 1)—pale green, entirely smooth with dark area surrounding the micropyle; frustum-shaped base broader than the flattened top, giving the overall appearance of a gumdrop; eggs are laid in tight crescent-shaped clusters on which the eggs may be one on top of another. *Mature caterpillar*—body pale yellow (almost transparent) with ten pairs of conspicuous black dorsal spots on the abdominal segments (and a pair on the third thoracic segment) that are divided by a dark midline; thoracic segments darker yellow than other body segments; all segments bear a sparse covering of long yellowish and black setae, with the black ones arising mainly from the dark dorsal spots and the yellowish setae arising laterally; head capsule shiny amber with a sparse covering of setae, and often bearing two dark spots on the epicranium. As in other congeners, the caterpillars of this butterfly are processionary and synchronous in their feeding, movements, resting, and molting.
• **Adult:** Sexes dimorphic. *Male*—FW upperside bright orange with broad black costa and margin, and a thin black inner margin; HW upperside bright orange with black costa and apex and a thin black margin; underside an almost uniform pale yellow with separated black spots along HW submargin. *Female*—similar to the male except the upperside is pale yellow instead of orange. Compare with *aurantia*.

Habits: Occurs commonly from sea level to 1500 m on both slopes in association with primary to second-growth rain forest habitats. The males are generally found as solitary individuals perching along forest edges from 08:30 to 09:30, and then again from 13:00 to 14:00 hrs. I found that the females fly along forest edges from 12:45 to 15:00 hrs, and on several occasions I watched females search for oviposition sites along a second growth edge between 13:00 and 15:00 hrs. The females tap the forelegs on the underside of leaves, then walk about while dragging the tip of the abdomen on the surface of the leaf. When a female begins laying eggs, she occasionally pulses the wings open and may lay twenty to thirty eggs during the course of 15 min. During oviposition the females are not skittish and may be approached very closely. Both sexes visit the sticky leaf buds of *Ficus* and the extrafloral nectaries of *Inga, Passiflora*, and other plant species.

Localities: [A]: Cariblanco (February, October). [C]: Juan Viñas (October), Turrialba (January, July), Tuis (September, October), Moravia de Chirripo (February). [SJ]: Carrillo, La Selva (July, September). [H]: Chilamate (March, August, September). [P]: Las Alturas (September). [L]: Guapiles.

Euselasia matuta
(Schaus, 1913)
FW length: 12–14 mm   Plate 1
Range: Costa Rican endemic(?)
Hostplant: Unknown
Early stages: Unknown
• **Adult:** Sexes dimorphic. *Male*—FW upperside reddish brown with broad dark brown costa and margin, and a bright orange triangular patch posterior to the cell; underside silvery white (the orange triangle on FW upperside shows through), with a faint, thin brown medial line. *Female*—upperside ground color paler brown with no trace of reddish, and the triangular patch more yellowish; underside as in the male. Compare with *aurantia, chrysippe*.
Habits: This butterfly has been reported in our area only from a few rain forest localities in the Turrialba Valley that range in elevation between 600 and 1200 m. Most of the specimens were collected over 50 years ago, before widespread deforestation, and thus it is possible that the habitat of this apparently endemic species may have been extirpated. I have never seen it alive. Rare.
Localities: [C]: Juan Viñas [TL] (October), Turrialba (January, May, June), Orosi (May).

Euselasia regipennis regipennis
(Butler and Druce, 1872)
FW length: 16–20 mm   **Plate 3**
Range: Mexico to Colombia. **Subspecies:** Costa Rica and Panama
Hostplant: Unknown
Early stages: Unknown
- **Adult:** Sexes dimorphic. *Male*—FW upperside black with deep, resplendent purple that is best seen when viewed obliquely; HW upperside black with purple along the distal margin; underside gray brown with a straight, red-brown medial line that may or may not be bordered distally by an ill-defined white band, and a prominent blue submarginal spot on HW. *Female*—two forms that fly together: (1) upperside light brown, generally with a prominent wide, white band across both wings that gives the insect the appearance of the satyrines *Cissia hesione* and *C. metaluca* (Nymphalidae); and (2) upperside almost entirely brown, and in appearance like other members of the genus *Cissia*. *Note.* Small specimens that bear a white medial band on the underside have been named *eupepla* Godman and Salvin, 1885. Compare with *euoras*, *arbas*.
Habits: Occurs locally from sea level to 800 m on both slopes in association with rain forest habitats, typically during sunny, dry periods. Typically encountered as solitary males perching in small light gaps or along shady forest edges from 09:00 to 12:00 hrs from 2 to 8 m above the ground, although they may perch lower at times. The flight is fast, erratic, and of short duration when an individual moves between perches.
Localities: [C]: Turrialba (June–August, October). [SJ]: Carrillo (June, September), Santa Rosa de Puriscal (May). [H]: La Selva (April–June). [P]: Llorona (March–May), Sirena (February). [L]: Hitoy Cerere (January), Siquirres, Madre de Dios (September), Germania (April), Tortuguerro.

Euselasia euoras
(Hewitson, 1855)
FW length: 17.5 mm   **Not illustrated**
Range: Costa Rica, Colombia, Ecuador, and Peru
Hostplant: Unknown
Early stages: Unknown
- **Adult:** Sexes presumed dimorphic. *Male*—upperside black with deep iridescent purple on FW distal area, costa, and distal margin; HW with purple along distal margin; underside washed with a bright, warm ochre, especially the medial line; HW distal submargin with distinct ochre rays; distal margin with a conspicuous, dark submarginal ocellus that bears a purple iridescence when viewed obliquely; dis-

tal margin of ocellus trimmed in white. *Female*—unknown from our area. *Note:* The unique specimen before me is very similar to the type specimen of *euoras*. However, given the apparent geographical range of *euoras* and the absence of more material from our area, I am uncertain as to the identity of this butterfly. It may be that the butterfly in question here is *eupepla* Godman and Salvin, 1892, and perhaps should be considered a full species. Compare with *regipennis*.
Habits: This butterfly is known in our area from a single specimen taken by K. Wolfe in Pacific lowland rain forest. Whether the butterfly referred to here is properly named, is an aberrant specimen of *regipennis*, or represents an undescribed taxon requires confirmation and more material.
Localities: [SJ]: Santa Rosa de Puriscal (February).

Euselasia corduena anadema
Stichel, 1927
FW length: 17–22 mm   **Plate 1**
Range: Costa Rica to Peru, Bolivia. **Subspecies:** Costa Rica to Colombia
Hostplant: Unknown
Early stages: Unknown
- **Adult:** Sexes dimorphic. *Male*—upperside velvety black with reflective blue patches on basal one-third of FW and at the HW tornus; underside white with distinct gray-brown medial and postmedial bands that traverse both wings, and a distinct yellow patch at the HW distal margin that bears a conspicuous black spot. *Female*—upperside dark brown with a broad white patch on FW that runs from costa almost to tornus; underside as in the male. Compare with *labdacus*.
Habits: This butterfly has been recorded in our area from 500 to 1600 m on both slopes in association with rain forest habitats. The solitary males perch on the upper or underside of leaves along forest edges and streams from 07:30 to 09:00 hrs when they may be observed making sorties about every 2 min from a low branch. The male typically uses the same perch for about 15 min before moving on and occupying another branch. This suggests that an individual may move continually through a habitat during its lifetime. The females fly from midday until early afternoon along forest edges and rivers. In Colombia the observations of Velez and Salazar (1991) suggest that this species generally flies at the subcanopy level. Uncommon in our area.
Localities: [A]: Reserve San Ramon (July), Cariblanco (June, August), Peñas Blancas (July). [C]: Navarro, Moravia de Chirripo (April),

Orosi (December). [P]: Las Alturas (August, September), San Vito (May, September, December).

Euselasia gyda gydina
Stichel, 1919
FW length: 116–19.5 mm   **Plate 2**
Range: Costa Rica to Colombia, Brazil. **Subspecies:** Costa Rica and Panama
Hostplant: Unknown
Early stages: Unknown
• **Adult:** Sexes dimorphic: *Male*—upperside a gorgeous golden yellow with broad black on FW costa, apex, and distal margins. Underside of both wings an almost immaculate luminous, pearly white with golden fringe. *Female*—upperside white with indistinct gray costa and distal FW margin, and some yellow near base of costa; underside as in male. This beautiful species cannot be confused with any other riodinid in our area.
Habits: In Costa Rica this butterfly is known from a single montane, rain shadow area on the Pacific slope at 1400 m. The males are encountered as solitary individuals, or in small groups of three to five along forest edges, light gaps, and streams from 08:30 to 09:30 hrs on bright, sunny days. There they perch between 5 and 15 m above the ground on the underside of leaves attached to overhanging branches that project outward from the forest along edges. I found that emergent *Cecropia* trees were a favorite perch, and that the underside of its leaves provide an extremely cryptic background for the butterfly to rest on. While perching, the males fly out and interact with males and females of the same species. However, the males also vigorously interact with passing individuals of *Morpho theseus* (Morphinae) that fly in their characteristic floating fashion. To observe the males tenaciously courting a butterfly that is at least fifteen times larger than itself is comical, but it does suggest that the whitish color of *M. theseus* probably serves as a superstimulus in *gyda* courtship. Although the flight is rapid and erratic, it is not as rapid as many other *Euselasia* with which I am familiar, and the wonderful alternating flicker of gold and pearly white flashing in the sunlight makes individual males easy to follow with the naked eye (or binoculars). The females fly from 2 to 5 m above the ground along forest edges and streams between 08:30 and 11:15 hrs, and their slow and steady flight is similar to white, day-flying moths *Cabera* (Geometridae) that are common in this habitat. These butterflies are quite rare in Costa Rican collections but

present almost throughout the year at Las Alturas.
Localities: [P]: Las Alturas (March–May, August–December).

Euselasia procula
(Godman and Salvin, 1885)
FW length: 12–13 mm   **Not illustrated**
Range: Mexico to Panama, and Colombia
Hostplant: *Eugenia* sp. (Myrtaceae)
Early stages: *Mature caterpillar* (Fig. 37c)—head capsule orange with a sparse covering of white and black setae; body overall color greenish brown; all abdominal segments with a pair of raised, orange dorsal lumps (one on either side of the midline) from which arise sparse tufts of whitish yellow setae; dorsal midline very dark, undulate, and bounded on either side by a thin white band at the interface of venter and lateral portion of each segment that is lobed outward slightly with a pale green skirt from which arise tufts of setae that are directed outward and down toward the substrate. The caterpillars are gregarious, rest on tree trunks during the day about 0.5 m above the ground, and in confinement they feed during the day. *Pupa* (Fig. 37d)—dorsolaterally compressed as in other *Euselasia*; golden yellow except for a black triangle at the interface of the thorax, abdomen, and wing pads; lateral areas sparsely covered with white setae that curve toward the substrate. Pupation takes place on the dorsal surface of leaves, typically near the leaf midvein.
• **Adult:** Sexes similar. Entire upperside dark gray-brown with no reddish anywhere; leading edge of FW costa yellow-orange at basal one-third. Underside ground color gray-brown with a distinct red-brown medial line running across both wings; postmedial line dark gray; FW distal margin dark gray; HW distal margin dark gray except for the tornal margin, which has a thin red-brown margin. Compare with *inconspicua*, *sergia*, *hieronymi*.
Habits: This butterfly is known in our area from sea level to about 1000 m on both slopes in association with wet and rain forest habitats. N. Greig reared this species from a group of caterpillars she found on a medium-sized *Eugenia* tree in primary rain forest on the Osa Peninsula. I have never seen it alive. Uncommon in Central American collections.
Localities: [C]: Cachi (October). [SJ]: Guatuso, San José, La Montura (April), Patarra (November). [P]: Corcovado (March).

Euselasia sergia sergia
(Godman and Salvin, 1885)
FW length: 13–16 mm   **Not illustrated**
Range: Mexico to Panama, Colombia. **Sub-species:** Mexico to Panama
Hostplant: Unknown
Early stages: Unknown
• **Adult:** Sexes dimorphic. This species is distinguished from similar ones by the distinct tornal pattern on the HW underside that is set toward the medial line instead of near margin of HW. *Male*—dorsal ground color black with orange intrusion into the FW and HW. *Female*—dorsal coloration appears washed out, almost brown. Compare with *mystica*.
Habits: This butterfly has been recorded in our area from sea level to 1200 m on both slopes in association with forest habitats. It apparently flies during the end of the rainy season.
Localities: [A]: San Mateo. [C]: Moravia de Chirripo (April), Tres Rios, Juan Viñas, Cachi, Turrialba (May, July–September). [SJ]: Santana (July), San Jose (March). [G]: Santa Rosa (October–December), Rincon de la Vieja (December), N of Santa Cruz.

Euselasia mystica
(Schaus, 1913)
FW length: 12.5–14.5 mm   **Plate 2**
Range: Costa Rican endemic(?)
Hostplant: *Psidium* spp. (Myrtaceae)
Early stages: *Egg*—deposited in clusters of 5 to 20 on underside of old leaves. *Mature caterpillars*—body greenish brown with two darker subdorsal lines, and densely covered with soft, medium-long white setae. The caterpillars remain in gregarious masses throughout their life, and they are synchronous in behaviors; they feed nocturnally, and rest at the base of the hostplant tree during the day. *Pupa*—overall brown with two dark spots on thorax, flattened ventrally, and squat in general shape.
• **Adult:** Sexes slightly dimorphic. *Male*—FW upperside reddish brown with broad black costa, apex, distal margin, and tornus; HW upperside reddish brown with broad black at costa, apex, and one-half of distal margin. Underside gray-white with a red-brown medial line that angles strongly to HW inner margin; patterns in HW tornus are smeary and pulled to margin, and black triangle at HW margin is bordered by pale yellow. *Female*—upperside dull orange-brown with indistinct black margins; underside as in the male. Compare with *sergia, inconspicua, hieronymi*.
Habits: Reported in our area from sea level to 1200 m on both slopes in association with a diversity of habitats that range from lowland

forest to cloud forest, and second-growth vegetation in rural areas. The butterflies are generally encountered as solitary individuals during the rainy season. In various parks within the city of San Jose I found the males active between 08:00 and 10:00 hrs on sunny days. Although I never found this species to be abundant, it is typically found in local populations in close proximity to the hostplant trees. Since the hostplant is cultivated widely throughout our area, this butterfly may, in some sense, be considered part of the domesticated insect fauna whose range and abundance are influenced by human activities.
Localities: [A]: San Mateo [TL] (June, February). [C]: Moravia de Chirripo (April), Rio Macho (March, April), Turrialba (July). [SJ]: Santana, San Jose (March, April, June–September, November). [P]: Monte Verde (December). [G]: Rincon de la Vieja.

Euselasia hieronymi
(Godman and Salvin, 1868)
FW length: 14–16 mm   **Plate 2**
Range: Mexico to Panama
Hostplant: *Eugenia capuli* (Myrtaceae)
Early stages: (Kendall 1976) *Egg*—laid in clusters. The caterpillars feed gregariously; early instars graze the epidermis away from the leaf, later instars feed on the entire leaf.
• **Adult:** Sexes dimorphic. *Male*—FW upperside black with red-orange that extends in an elongate triangle from base almost to tornus, and along the distal margin of cell, and some red-orange that extends into the cell; HW tornus is elongated; HW upperside black with red-orange beginning narrowly near base, and widening as it meets the tornus. Underside gray-brown with elongate, smeared ocelli in HW tornus, and a roundly triangular spot at distal margin that is bordered in yellow. *Female*—FW upperside dirty gray-brown, with indistinct black costa, apex, and distal margin; HW upperside entirely dirty gray-brown; underside pattern as in the male. Compare with *sergia, inconspicua, amphidecta, mystica*.
Habits: This butterfly has been recorded in our area from 500 to 1600 m on both slopes in association with montane forest habitats. The males are encountered typically in small groups from 07:15 to 08:00 hrs while perching between 2 and 5 m above the ground along forest edges and streams. The focal point of these semisocial groups is generally an isolated shrub or tree that is in direct sunlight. Individuals make sorties every few minutes, vigorously interact with other males (and species) on their rapid and erratic flights, and then return

to the perch. However, during these interactions these butterflies generally do not fly very high above the ground. Unlike similar Costa Rican species, the males of this butterfly perch *under* leaves. My observations at Las Alturas suggest that a perching spot (a tree or shrub) is not used traditionally for long periods as in other species (e.g., *chrysippe, bettina*), but rather these perching spots appear to change frequently. Also at Las Alturas I found individual females flying between 08:00 and 09:10 hrs along the interface of forest edge and pasture, almost a kilometer from where I had been observing the males perch.

Localities: [A]: Reserva San Ramon (March), Cariblanco. [C]: Moravia de Chirripo (April). [SJ]: Carrillo. [P]: San Vito (March, April, June), Las Alturas (July–September).

Euselasia inconspicua
(Godman and Salvin, 1878)
FW length: 13–14.5 mm   Plate 2
Range: Costa Rica to Panama
Hostplant: Unknown
Early stages: Unknown
• **Adult:** Sexes dimorphic. *Male*—FW upperside dull red-brown with broad, indistinct black on costa, apex, and distal margin; HW upperside dull red-brown with indistinct black radial veins; underside of both wings off-white with red-brown medial lines, and FW with red-brown postmedial line. *Female*—upperside light brown with an indistinct dark brown FW apex and distal margin; underside pattern as in the male. This species can generally be separated from similar ones by the small size, rounded overall wing shape, and the FW apex cut at a slight angle. Compare with *procula, hieronymi, mystica, sergia.*
Habits: This butterfly has been reported in our area from 500 to 1600 m on the Pacific slope in association with montane forest habitats. I have observed individual males twice in nature, and both times they were perching about 4 m above the ground along forest edges between 11:00 and 12:30 hrs. Uncommon in Costa Rican collections.
Localities: [SJ]: Puriscal Mountains (November). [P]: Las Cruces (April, September, December), Las Alturas (August, September).

Euselasia leucon
(Schaus, 1913)
FW length: 17–18 mm   Plate 2
Range: Costa Rica to Panama
Hostplant: Unknown
Early stages: Unknown
• **Adult:** Sexes dimorphic. *Male*—FW upperside black with red-brown from base along inner margin to areas posterior to cell; HW upperside bright red-brown with broad black costa and distal margins; underside pale orange-brown with a distinct red-brown medial line that begins at the FW costa, runs across HW, and curves basally just posterior to HW cell, loops toward HW tornus, and then terminates at HW inner margin. *Female*—FW upperside brown with a large golden yellow patch in the discal area, and HW tornal margin with a reddish blush; underside with a more yellow cast than the male. Compare with *amphidecta, eucrates, onorata, portentosa.*
Habits: This butterfly is known in Costa Rica from two montane localities: one on the Atlantic slope, and one on the Pacific slope. Judging by the original label ["Turrialba," 5800 ft] the butterfly was probably collected on the slopes of Volcan Turrialba, and recently W. Haber found this distinctive species in Monte Verde at 1300 m. In Panama, G. Small collected several individuals of this species at about the same elevation on Cerro Colorado (1450 m). On the strength of these records I assume that this rare butterfly occurs typically in a range of montane forest habitats.
Localities: [C]: Turrialba [TL] (October, September). [P]: Monte Verde (August).

Euselasia labdacus reducta
Lathy, 1926
FW length: 15–18 mm   Plate 2
Range: Costa Rica to Colombia, Bolivia. **Subspecies:** Costa Rica and Panama
Hostplant: *Mammea americana* (Clusiaceae)
Early stages: Seitz (1916), referring to the description in Sepp (1848–52), reports that the caterpillar is bright brick red with broad black-green subcostal [lateral?] stripes and white points behind the head. *Pupa*—green with brown markings.
• **Adult:** Sexes dimorphic. *Male*—upperside deep orange with all margins broadly black; underside white with reddish brown postbasal, medial, and postmedial lines, and a submarginal row of black spots that are especially evident on the FW. *Female*—upperside dirty brown with a greenish white sheen on the medial areas of both wings; underside as in male, but with the reddish brown markings less distinct. Compare with *corduena.*
Habits: In Costa Rica this butterfly is recorded from a single locality at 1200 m on the Atlantic slope in association with rain forest. From locality data it appears that this species may be active during the rainy season. In Panama, G. Small found the males perching at about

15:00 hrs in several localities that range from sea level to over 1000 m. Rare in Costa Rican collections.
Localities: [C]: Moravia de Chirripo (April, June, July).

Euselasia argentea argentea
(Hewitson, 1871)
FW length: 14–15.5 mm   **Plate 2**
Range: Mexico to Colombia, Bolivia. **Subspecies:** Nicaragua to Panama
Hostplant: Unknown
Early stages: Unknown
• **Adult:** Sexes dimorphic. *Male*—FW upperside black with a bright orange patch posterior to the cell that extends from the base to the distal end of cell; HW upperside black with an orange band that runs from base to distal margin of tornus, and costa with an ill-defined patch of white; underside typically glossy white with gray distal margins, two brown medial lines running from FW costa to HW tornus or inner margin, HW with two more brown lines that start at base of costa and run almost to the tornus, and a fused, double orange triangle in HW tornus. *Female*—upperside brown with a prominent round, yellow spot on FW discal area posterior to the cell; underside pattern as in the male. Compare with *leucon, corduena.*
Habits: This butterfly has been recorded in our area from 500 to 1600 m on both slopes in association with a variety of forest habitats. The males are frequently, but not always, found in gregarious assemblages perching from 3 to 10 m above the ground along forest edges and streams between 06:00 and 09:00 hrs (depending on weather conditions). My observations suggest that a single tree may be used as a perching spot for long periods of time. For example, during a period of one full year I noted that one particular tree at Las Alturas had been used every sunny morning as a focal point for male assemblies. However, although I observed literally hundreds of males at this site, I saw only three females during this time. Common.
Localities: [C]: Juan Viñas (June, September), Moravia de Chirripo (July, August). [P]: Las Alturas (March, April, May, July, August, September, October, November, December), San Vito (September).

Euselasia eucrates leucorrhoa
(Godman and Salvin, 1878)
FW length: 15.5–17 mm   **Plate 2**
Range: Costa Rica to Bolivia. **Subspecies:** Costa Rica to Venezuela
Hostplant: Unknown

Early stages: Unknown
• **Adult:** Sexes dimorphic. *Male*—FW upperside a rich, red-brown with distinct black costa, apex, and distal margin; HW upperside almost uniformly rich, red-brown except for thin black distal margin; HW tornus elongated with relatively smooth margins; underside pearly white with indistinct combinations of gray and white at distal margins; the FW is gray-brown distal to the medial line, the anterior half of HW is gray-brown, whereas the posterior half of HW is pearly white, and there is a distinct, thin orange margin along tornus. *Female*—FW upperside black with a yellow-orange medial patch that changes to golden brown near base and inner margin; HW upperside with a golden-brown cast, and costa and distal margins indistinctly black; underside pattern as in the male. Compare with *hieronymi, onorata, amphidecta, portentosa.*
Habits: This butterfly is known locally from sea level to 1200 m on both slopes in association with forest habitats. Judging by collections, and the one time I encountered it in the field, this butterfly may be locally abundant upon occasion.
Localities: [C]: Cachi (October), Moravia de Chirripo. [P]: Villa Neily (July), Rio Canasta de Coto Brus (September).

Euselasia portentosa
Stichel, 1927
FW length: 17.5 mm   **Not illustrated**
Range: Costa Rica and Panama(?)
Hostplant: Unknown
Early stages: unknown
• **Adult:** Sexes presumably dimorphic. *Male*—FW upperside entirely black; HW upperside black with a distinct and very broad red-brown costa that runs from base to subapex, and encompasses most of the cell and all of the apex; underside silvery white on basal half of wings, dull gray-brown on distal half of wings, both wings with a distinct brown, wavy medial line, and HW distal margin at tornus with a thin border of orange. *Female* —unknown, and in need of description. *Note.* Many thanks to C. Callaghan who provided a photo of the unique type specimen on which I based the above description. Compare with *eucrates, onorata.*
Habits: This distinctive butterfly is apparently known only from the type specimen deposited in the Berlin Museum among the Stichel material, and bears a label "Costa Rica" (C. Callaghan, pers. comm.). Obviously this butterfly is exceedingly rare and worthy of study when more material becomes available.

Euselasia amphidecta
(Godman and Salvin, 1878)
FW length: 14.5–16 mm   **Plate 2**
Range: Costa Rica to Panama
Hostplant: Unknown
Early stages: Unknown
• **Adult:** Sexes dimorphic. *Male*—FW upperside rich, red-brown confined to medial area nearly posterior to cell by broad black costa, apex, and margin; HW upperside with a long, rich red-brown patch that runs from inside cell near base to tornal margin, and is confined by a broad black costa, apex, and distal margin; the HW margin is distinctly undulate. Underside gray-brown and decidedly overshot with purple; HW tornus with distinct red-orange distal margin and a series of marginal white spots. *Female*—FW upperside light brown with broad, indistinct black costa, apex, and distal margin; HW distal margins white within the undulations; underside pattern as in the male. Compare with *eucrates, portentosa, onorata.*
Habits: This butterfly has been recorded in our area from sea level to 200 m on both slopes in association with rain forest habitats. The males are encountered as small, gregarious groups perching from 2 to 10 m above the ground, and they are rather noticeable in that they engage in long, high-speed erratic chases. When abundant, the frantic activity of the males almost resembles a small swarm of bees. This butterfly may be active during clear or overcast weather. Typically found in locally abundant populations during the dry season along forest edges and streams during the late afternoon between 16:00 and 17:30 hrs. Uncommon in Costa Rican collections.
Localities: [H]: La Selva (April), Magsaysay (August). [P]: Sirena (January–March), Llorona (May, June).

Euselasia eubule
(Felder, 1869)
FW length: 12–17 mm   **Plate 2**
Range: Mexico to Panama
Hostplant: Unknown
Early stages: *Pupa*—in overall shape as in *procula*, but uniformly pale green with dark, dorso-lateral bristle-like setae on head, wing-pads, and abdomen (Fig. 37b).
• **Adult:** Sexes dimorphic. *Male*—upperside orange-brown with black FW apex and margins; several indistinct yellowish spots in FW cell area; HW distinctly squared at tornal margin; underside almost appears to have no distinct markings, but the gray-brown ground color is paler distal to a thin, angular medial line traversing both wings. *Female*—upperside brown with black FW margins and apex, and 2–3 prominent white spots in distal area of FW cell that are distinctly obvious on the underside as well. *Note.* The taxon *hypophaea* (Godman and Salvin, 1878), which differs from *eubule* by having an upperside with slightly broader black margins and an underside with even fewer markings, is considered by some authors to be a separate species. Compare with *eucrates, amphidecta.*
Habits: This butterfly has been recorded in our area from 500 to 1600 m on both slopes in association with a variety of forest habitats. Although many museums have abundant material from areas north of Costa Rica, it is uncommon in Costa Rican collections. I have never seen it alive.
Localities: [A]: San Mateo (September, November, December). [SJ]: Carrillo (June). [H]: Magsaysay (August).

Euselasia onorata
(Hewitson, 1869)
FW length: 16–17 mm   **Plate 3**
Range: Costa Rica to Colombia and Ecuador
Hostplant: Unknown
Early stages: Unknown
• **Adult:** Sexes presumably dimorphic. *Male*—upperside a beautiful opalescent brown orange; FW costa, apex, and distal margin black; a distinctive square, black intrusion at the end of the cell which is separated from the black apex by a thin band of orange; underside with bright white on most of the HW discal area, extending to the inner margin and tornus; a distinct oblong ocellus near the end of the HW cell. *Female*—apparently unknown. Compare with *eucrates, aurantiaca, portentosa.*
Habits: This butterfly has been recorded in our area from a single specimen collected on the Atlantic slope at about 500 m in a rain forest habitat. Judging from museum collections and the literature, this species is apparently rare throughout its range.
Localities: [SJ]: Carrillo (June).

Euselasia midas crotopiades
Stichel, 1919
FW length: 16.5–20 mm   **Plate 3**
Range: Costa Rica to Peru, Brazil. **Subspecies:** Costa Rica and Panama
Hostplant: Unknown
Early stages: Unknown
• **Adult:** Sexes dimorphic. *Male*—upperside typically deep purple with indistinct black FW margin and apex. However, specimens from the Pacific slope may be entirely brown. Underside gray-brown with purple cast that is

seen at oblique angles, a distinct red-brown medial line, FW submargin with a series of brown triangles between veins, and a black medial spot at inner margin near tornus. *Female*—larger than male; upperside light brown with indistinct gray areas surrounding the cells of both wings, and darker patches in cells of both wings; underside pattern as in male. Compare with *rhodogyne, angulata, regipennis*.

Habits: This butterfly has been recorded in our area from sea level to 1400 m on both slopes in association with rain forest habitats. I found males perching from 3 to 10 m above the ground along forest edges between 09:00 to 10:30 hrs. Uncommon in Costa Rican collections.

Localities: [A]: San Mateo (July). [C]: Moravia de Chirripo (April, September). [P]: Golfito (August). [L]: Sixaola.

Euselasia rhodogyne patella
Stichel, 1927
FW length: 17–20 mm   **Plate 3**
Range: Costa Rica to Colombia. **Subspecies:** Costa Rica and Panama
Hostplant: *Clusia odorata* (Clusiaceae)
Early stages: *Caterpillars*—gregarious in groups of up to fifty individuals, all of the same instar. *Mature caterpillar*—head capsule black; body dull black (especially noticeable in lateral view) with conspicuous maroon dorsal squares on all segments except T1 and T2, which are yellowish; the interface between each segment is ringed with two silver-white lines; all abdominal segments with sparse tufts of white lateral and subdorsal setae; segment T1 bears two prominent tufts of white subdorsal setae that project well beyond the head and give the caterpillar the overall appearance of a moth caterpillar in the family Lymantriidae. The caterpillars are gregarious and processionary. *Pupa*—uniformly green with a scattering of short, stiff lateral setae, and a small black dot at the interface of the thorax and the wing-pads.
• **Adult:** Sexes dimorphic. *Male*—upperside dark brown with a prominent orange FW band running from costa almost to the tornus; underside warm brown with a distinct red-brown medial line; HW elongate and acuminate at tornus. *Female*—upperside and underside pattern similar to male but larger in overall size; HW especially large with an angular distal margin. *Note. Patella* was originally described as a full species. See *leucon, midas, Emesis cypria*.
Habits: This butterfly has been recorded in our area from various rain forest habitats on the Atlantic slope between 200 and 600 m. How-

ever, considering that it has been reared several times from Barro Colorado Island in Panama but never collected there as adults—despite butterfly collectors visiting the island for over seventy years—this butterfly is likely to have a larger distribution within Costa Rica, including habitats on the Pacific slope. It is probable that this butterfly is common in the forest canopy, but that it seldom descends to the ground. In my experience this butterfly is encountered as rare, solitary individuals perching along forest edges from 4 to 8 m above the ground both in bright sunlight and in shaded situations. While flying, this butterfly strongly resembles the common *Emesis cypria*. Uncommon in Costa Rican collections.

Localities: [C]: Turrialba (August, November, December). [H]: Chilamate (March, April, July, August). [L]: Rio Estrella, south of Limon (April).

Euselasia aurantiaca aurantiaca
(Salvin and Godman, 1868)
FW length: 16.5–23 mm   **Plate 3**
Range: Mexico to Venezuela. **Subspecies:** Nicaragua to Panama
Hostplant: Unknown
Early stages: *Mature caterpillar*—overall the body is cross-banded with yellow and black; head capsule shiny black; body covered densely with setae with lateral setae very long and covering the legs. *Pupa*—pale green, and squat in general shape as in other congeners, with two black spots on dorsum of first abdominal segment. The single individual I found of this species pupated on top of a leaf, a trait shared by other congeners.
• **Adult:** Sexes dimorphic. *Male*—FW upperside radiant to dull orange with broad black on apex and distal margins; the black in tornus intrudes into the orange to create a small lobe near inner margin; HW upperside orange with some black on apex and distal margin; underside off-white with a pearly sheen. *Female*—much larger than male; FW upperside orange-brown with black apex, and a pale yellow-orange band that runs from costa almost to tornus; HW upperside orange-brown with the apex indistinctly black; underside pale orange-brown with a distinct medial line. See *gyda, aurantiaca*.
Habits: This butterfly has been recorded in our area from a few males collected in montane forest on the Atlantic slope, and a single female from the Pacific lowlands on the Osa Peninsula. Judging from museum collections, this species may be abundant in areas north of Costa Rica, especially Mexico. Although it has

long been considered rare in our area (Seitz 1916), it may be that this butterfly typically inhabits the forest canopy and thus goes largely unobserved. *Note*—D. Harvey has pointed out that some of the males from our area differ from typical *aurantiaca* by having broad black borders, and red-orange medial areas on the upperside, and may represent an undescribed species.
Localities: [C]: Turrialba (June), Moravia de Chirripo (April, July, August). [P]: Llorona (August).

Euselasia angulata
Bates, 1868
FW length: 18.2 mm   **Plate 3**
Range: Mexico, Costa Rica, Colombia to Brazil
Hostplant: Unknown
Early stages: Unknown
• **Adult:** Sexes presumably dimorphic. *Male*— Upperside dark brown overshot with some dull purple, and a distinctive tooth on the distal margin of the HW; underside gray-brown with a somber purple cast, and a wide, distinctly darker purple medial band that begins broadly at the FW costa and tapers dramatically to the HW inner margin. *Female*—apparently unknown from Central America and in need of description. Compare with *midas*.
Habits: Reported in Costa Rica from a single specimen in the U.S. National Museum collected by W. Schaus in the Turrialba Valley. Seitz (1916) indicated that all the subspecies (all were considered under *angulata* Bates, 1868) were entirely South American, and all quite rare. Recently, de la Maza and de

la Maza (1980) reported this species from Mexico, thus extending its range considerably. K. Brown (in lit.) observes that in Brazil its relative (*angulata*) flies after dusk and before dawn. Considering the breadth of its apparent range, it is possible that the butterfly is more common in Central America than previously supposed, but that it has escaped detection due to its crepuscular habits. Alternatively, the Mexican and Central American butterflies may represent a different species altogether.
Localities: [C]: Tuis (June).

Euselasia subargentea
(Lathy, 1904)
FW length: 21.5–25 mm   **Plate 3**
Range: Costa Rica to Colombia
Hostplant: Unknown
Early stages: Unknown
• **Adult:** Sexes similar. Immediately distinguished from all other species in our area by its exaggerated size and the elongated HW tornus. *Male*—upperside uniformly dull black; underside pearly white with gray on the distal half of the FW. *Female*—based on Colombian material, it is similar to the male but duller brown on upperside.
Habits: This unusual species has been reported in Costa Rica from a single specimen taken by R. Hesterberg from a montane Atlantic habitat. He informs me that the butterfly was perched very high (over 10 m above the ground) in a light gap deep in the forest. Obviously rare in Central American collections.
Localities: [C]: Moravia de Chirripo (April).

Subfamily **RIODININAE** Grote, 1895

The characters defining this subfamily were summarized by Harvey (1987a) as follows: all taxa have a pedicel connecting the aedeagus to the base of the valve; the presence of a costal vein on HW basal margin; an antero-ventral placement of first abdominal spiracle on the caterpillar; and the contact of pupal segments M2 and A1. This is the largest and most diverse higher grouping of the Riodinidae.

Tribe **MESOSEMIINI** Bates, 1859

The butterflies embraced by this tribe are characterized by having a silk girdle on the pupa that crosses A2; male genitalia have a split base at the pedicel; eyes are consistently hairy; and tibial spurs are absent. As presently conceived, there are over 130 species placed within five genera: the wide-ranging *Perophthalma*, *Leucochimona*, and *Mesosemia*, plus *Mesophthalma* and *Semomesia*, which are South American. In the field, all of these butterflies may be easily recognized as members of this tribe on the basis of their flight and peculiar behavior upon alighting: they act like clockwork toys. In passing, it is worth noting that this behavior mirrors that of the Old World genera *Saribea*, *Abisara*, *Praetaxila*, and *Laxita*. All known hostplants for this tribe are from the Rubiaceae, and the caterpillars are nonmyrmecophilous, bearing a sparse covering of setae.

Genus PEROPHTHALMA
Westwood, 1851

The butterflies in this genus are easily recognized by their tiny size, a prominent eyespot in the forewing subapex, and the brown pattern on the discal area of the hindwing. Members of *Perophthalma* are found from Mexico throughout Central and South America, and the genus has been considered to contain but a single species (Seitz 1916; Stichel 1930–31), with five described subspecies (Bridges 1988). However, the genitalia of the two forms as found in Costa Rica show differences in the valvae and aedeagus, and are here treated as distinct species.

The only hostplant record for these butterflies is for members of the family Rubiaceae. The caterpillars have a sparse covering of setae and are similar to those of *Mesosemia*. In the field, these butterflies have the same "clockwork" movements as *Leucochimona* and *Mesosemia*.

Perophthalma tullius
(Fabricius, 1787)
FW length: 12–13 mm   **Plate 3**
Range: Mexico to Brazil
Hostplant: *Palicourea guianensis* (Rubiaceae)
Early stages: *Egg*—tiny, white, and deposited singly on underside of leaves or in leaf axils. *Mature caterpillar*—head capsule shiny green; body pale green, sparsely covered with short white setae. The caterpillar feeding damage creates windows in the leaf.
• **Adult:** Sexes similar. FW upperside dirty brown with an indistinct white medial band; HW upperside dirty brown with two orange-yellow bands on discal area. Compare with *lasus*.
Habits: In Costa Rica this butterfly is recorded on both slopes in association with lowland rain forest. I have observed this butterfly on three occasions at La Selva along a shaded forest trail between 12:30 to 13:30 hrs. Its habits are similar to those described for *lasus*.
Localities: [A]: Rio Macho (September), Rio Virilla (September), Atenas (March, October, December). [C]: Turrialba (July). [H]: La Selva (April, July), Chilamate (March), Santa Clara (September, October). [P]: Rio Cacao (September), Rio Coton (September), Brujo de Buenos Aires (September), Rio Catarata (September). [L]: Germania (April, September), Bannanito (September), Puerto Viejo (March, September), La Bomba (September).

Perophthalma lasus
(Westwood, 1851)
FW length: 12–13 mm   **Plate 3**
Range: Costa Rica to Panama
Hostplant: Unknown
Early stages: Unknown
• **Adult:** Sexes similar. FW upperside dirty brown with a distinct white medial band. HW upperside dirty brown with yellow-orange bands on discal area, and entire wing with a white cast. Compare with *tullius*.
Habits: In our area this butterfly occurs commonly from sea level to 1400 m on both slopes in association with rain forest or associated second-growth habitats. Typically encountered as solitary individuals between 08:00 and 15:00 hrs along trails, forest edges, and small forest streams. Both sexes fly low to the ground and perch on the upperside of leaves in the shaded forest understory. When two individuals interact, they perform slow spiraling flights that typically ascend from 2 to 5 m above the ground. I have never noticed that this butterfly maintains perching spots. Common.
Localities: [C]: Turrialba (June, July), Orosi. [SJ]: Santa Rosa de Puriscal (November), Carrillo. [H]: Plastico (March, August), Chilamate (September). [P]: Golfito (April), Rincon de Osa (March, August), Llorona (June, July), Sirena (February–April, July, December), Las Alturas (August), San Vito (July–October), Villa Neily (October), Carrara (May), Chacarita (September), Rio Catarata (September), Palmar Norte, [L]: Limon (September), Guapiles (March), Germania (April, October), Tortuguerro, Bribri, Sixaola.

Genus LEUCOCHIMONA
Stichel, 1909

The butterflies in this genus are small, delicately marked with gray and black spots or lines over a white ground color. In older literature these butterflies were referred to under *Mesosemia* and *Diophthalma*. Members of *Leucochimona* are found from Mexico throughout Central and South America, and the genus is thought to embrace nine species, and at least as many subspecies have been named. The similarity and apparent variation among the Central American species makes many of them difficult to identify, and the jumbled state of museum collections reflects this taxonomic un-

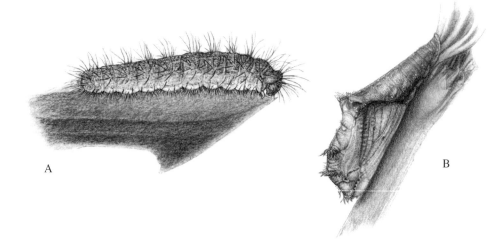

FIGURE 38. (A) *Leucochimona vestalis* caterpillar. (B) *Leucochimona vestalis* pupa. (Drawings by J. Clark)

certainty. It goes without saying that our understanding of *Leucochimona* would benefit from a revisionary study of this genus. Using the diagnoses of Godman and Salvin (1885) and taking into consideration the nomenclatural changes provided by Stichel (1930–31), I treat three species here.

All known hosts are small, sprawling plants in the family Rubiaceae (DeVries et al. 1994; see also summary in Harvey 1987a). The caterpillars are sparsely covered in stiff setae as in *Mesosemia*, and they strongly resemble those of the Old World genus *Abisara* (see illustration in Johnston and Johnston 1980). In overall form, the pupae are reminiscent of certain nymphalids in the genus *Euptychia* (Satyrinae), except they have a very broad cremaster.

In Costa Rica, members of the genus are found in all forest habitats from sea level to over 1200 m elevation, and are typically present throughout the year.

Leucochimona vestalis leucogaea
(Godman and Salvin, 1885)
FW length: 15–18 mm   **Plate 4**
Range: Guatemala to Ecuador. **Subspecies:** Guatemala to Panama
Hostplant: *Diodia* sp., *Borreria* sp., *Coccocypselum* (Rubiaceae)
Early stages (Fig. 1): *Egg*—tiny, white, deposited singly in leaf axils. Almost hemispherical in shape with a netlike sculpturing from which

spiny projections erupt. *Caterpillars* (Fig. 38a)—body and head of all instars pale green with a scattering of tiny white dots; body with a sparse covering of bristlelike setae with the most prominent ones arising laterally near the venter. All instars are wonderfully cryptic and difficult to detect on the plant. The caterpillars feed by removing leaf tissue from below, and leaving a "window" of the epidermis. *Pupa* (Fig. 38b)—overall shape resembles a pale green "monkey in a dunce cap" with tufts of hairs at the eyebrows, nose, mustache, and beard; base of cremaster pale with brown area on dorsum, very broad at attachment point; brown trim along wingpads, head, and edge of thorax and abdomen.

• **Adult:** Sexes similar. Upperside white with a distinct eyespot in the FW cell, thin brown margins on both wings set with a submarginal row of black spots, but no eyespot at the distal margin. *Note.* In the field this butterfly can be confused with the nymphalid genus *Euptychia*. Compare with *lagora, lepida.*

Habits: This butterfly occurs commonly in lowland forest areas from sea level to 800 m on both slopes, and it is typically present throughout the year. Encountered as solitary individuals or small populations along forest edges, light gaps, and small clearings, flying low to the ground and frequently alighting on vegetation. This butterfly often flies in the company of *Euptychia* species (Nymphalidae). Both sexes perform jerky, semicircular movements while walking on vegetation. Females oviposit during midday, often on plants that grow at the base of trees or along fallen tree trunks. **Localities:** [A]: Cariblanco. [C]: Turrialba (June). [SJ]: La Montura (June). [H]: La Selva (June). [P]: San Vito (February, April, May). [L]: Guapiles.

Leucochimona lepida
(Godman and Salvin, 1885)
FW length: 15–17 mm   Plate 4
Range: Nicaragua to Panama
Hostplant: *Diodia* spp, *Palicourea guianensis* (Rubiaceae)
Early stages: *Caterpillars*—pale green, including head capsule, with a sparse covering of bristlelike hairs. The caterpillars feed by removing leaf tissue from below, and leaving a "window" of the epidermis, and like its congeners, they are very difficult to find on the plant. *Pupa*—overall shape as described for *vestalis*.
• **Adult:** Sexes similar. Upperside white with the distal third of the FW brown set with an eyespot that does not have a pupil, and no eyespots in the FW cell. The brown on the FW is variable. Compare with *vestalis, lagora*.
Habits: This butterfly can be locally common in forest habitats from sea level to 1000 m on both slopes. Encountered along forest edges, light gaps, and small, sunny clearings, and, in my experience, found mainly during the wet seasons. As with its congeners, both sexes of this butterfly fly low to the ground and perform jerky, semicircular clockwise movements while walking on vegetation. Females oviposit during midday on plants growing in large light gaps and along forest edges.
Localities: [A]: Cariblanco (February, April, June, September, November), Chachagua de San Carlos (June). [C]: Turrialba, Juan Viñas. [SJ]: Zapote (January, March, November). [H]: Chilamate (July), La Selva (February, September). [P]: San Vito (March, July), Sirena (November). [L]: Siquirres, Zent.

Leucochimona lagora
(Herrich-Schäffer, 1853)
FW length: 16–17 mm   Plate 4
Range: Nicaragua to Ecuador and the Guianas
Hostplant: Unknown
Early stages: Unknown
• **Adult:** Sexes slightly dimorphic. Upperside white with thin brown FW margin set with a single black marginal spot, and the HW with a very small black submarginal spot. Underside of FW with a distinct black eyespot in cell that is ringed in yellow and bears a central pupil

(this eyespot may show through to the upperside in some specimens), and HW with a series of straight brown lines across the discal area. The male tends to have heavy dark markings on the underside, whereas the female has more white. This butterfly is variable with respect to the extent of the brown markings. Compare with *vestalis, lepida*.
Habits: This butterfly is common in lowland forest habitats from sea level to 800 m on both slopes during both rainy and dry seasons. Encountered as solitary individuals or in small groups along forest edges, and in light gaps. As other congeners, both sexes perform jerky, semicircular movements while walking on vegetation. In the field this species can easily be confused with the satyrines *Euptychia jesia* and *Euptychia westwoodi* (Nymphalidae).
Localities: [A]: La Libertad (February), Reserva San Ramon (June), Cariblanco (February, March, June, November). [C]: Rio Chitaria (March), Bajo Pacuare (October), Turrialba, Juan Viñas. [SJ]: Zapote (January–March, May, June, November), Carrillo (September, November). [H]: Plastico (April, May, August–October), Chilamate (March, April, July, September), Magsaysay (January, September), La Selva (February, May–July, September). [P]: San Vito (July), Sirena (November). [L]: Puerto Viejo (March, September), Bannanito (September), Guapiles (March), Germania (March, April, October), Siquirres, Zent.

Genus **MESOSEMIA** Hübner, 1819

The butterflies in this genus are recognized by their rather square wing shape, the presence of an eyespot in the forewing cell that generally contains one to three pupils (in some cases the ocellus is obsolete, but the pupil remains), and, with few exceptions, a tendency toward strong sexual dimorphism. The genus embraces well over one hundred species that are divided into ten species groups and many subspecies (Stichel 1930–31), with the greatest concentration of species being found in the Amazon Basin. The quantity of undetermined material in museums and the confusion regarding the relationships and matching of the sexes within *Mesosemia* reflect a very real need for a revision of this genus. Members of the genus are found from Mexico throughout Central and South America, and approximately twenty species occur in Central America. Although fourteen species have been reported from our area, this esti-

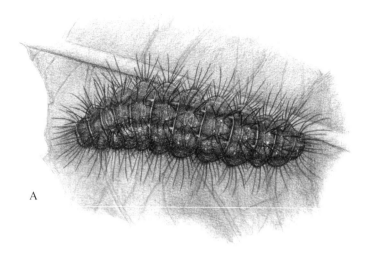

FIGURE 39. (A) *Mesosemia asa* caterpillar. (Drawings by J. Clark)

mate is hampered by not knowing with any degree of certainty the status of various species, subspecies, and forms. For this reason it is likely that *Mesosemia* may eventually prove to contain more species than are presently recognized.

All hostplant records for *Mesosemia* are from the Rubiaceae, of which understory shrubs in the genera *Psychotria, Faramea, Guettarda, Cephalanthus,* and *Cephaelis* seem most important (Beizanko et al. 1978; DeVries et al. 1994). However, considering the number of species in *Mesosemia*, surprisingly few have been reared. As far as is known, the caterpillars tend to be uniformly green in color, bear a sparse covering of medium-length, stiff setae, and when viewed from above show pronounced lateral lobes (or skirts) on all of the segments. The caterpillars bear a striking resemblance to those of the South East Asian genus *Abisara* (see illustration in Johnston and Johnston 1980), and the endemic Malagasy genus *Saribea* (pers. obs.). The early instars may feed constantly, whereas the later instars feed exclusively at night. While on plants, all instars are sufficiently cryptic as to be almost invisible. No caterpillar of this genus is known to associate with ants. The overall shape of the pupae strongly resembles those of the related genus *Leucochimona,* except those of *Mesosemia* are larger.

The butterflies in *Mesosemia* are important components of butterfly species richness in most low- to mid-elevation sites. Due to the habit of walking about on top of the leaves of understory shrubs with characteristic jerky movements (like clockwork toys) *Mesosemia* is one of the most frequently observed genera of all riodinids. However, these butterflies (among other genera) can be a source of frustration in developing authoritative checklists. Many sites throughout the Neotropics are inhabited by species of *Mesosemia* that may be common, but after many years work one generally finds that each site also includes some extremely rare species. In our area this trend is most apparent on the Atlantic slope forests near Braulio Carrillo, where a suite of species shows different activity times and occurs in differing microhabitats within the same forest.

Mesosemia esperanza
Schaus, 1913
FW length: 13.5–15 mm   **Plate 4**
Range: Costa Rica to Panama
Hostplant: Unknown
Early stages: Unknown
• **Adult:** Sexes dimorphic. *Male*—FW upperside ground color pale blue with a broad black distal margin that is set with a thin blue submarginal line, a distinct black postmedial line, and a black spot in the cell that has a distinct white pupil; HW upperside pale blue with a thin black postmedial and submarginal band, and thin black distal margin; underside gray overshot with pale brown, and bears distinct golden brown postmedial and submarginal lines on both wings. *Female*—upperside white with a broad diffusely brown FW apex, and a series of distinct brown transverse lines on

both wings; underside as in the male. *Note.* In some literature this taxon is considered a subspecies of *ephyne,* a species that ranges throughout the Amazon basin to Bolivia. Compare with *coelestis, albipuncta, hesperina.* **Habits:** In our area this butterfly has been recorded in association with a few rain forest habitats ranging from sea level to about 300 m on the Atlantic slope. In Panama, however, G. Small found this butterfly in forest habitats up to an elevation of 1200 m, thus suggesting that it may be found to be more widely distributed in our area. I have never seen this species alive. Rare in Costa Rican collections. **Localities:** [C]: Esperanza [TL]. [L]: Limon (May, September, November).

Mesosemia coelestis
Godman and Salvin, 1885
FW length: 17–17.5 mm   Plate 4
Range: Costa Rica to Colombia
Hostplant: Unknown
Early stages: Unknown
• **Adult:** Sexes slightly dimorphic. *Male*—FW upperside sky blue with the distal margin broadly black and set with a thin blue submarginal line, a distinctly dark postmedial line, and a conspicuous black spot at distal end of cell; HW upperside sky blue with dark margins, and black postmedial and submarginal lines; FW underside warm brown overshot with a violet cast, and a distinct yellow-brown area at the distal margin that encompasses the tornus; HW underside warm brown set with straight violet-white lines across the discal area that run from costa to inner margin. *Female*—upperside similar to male except the HW postmedial and submarginal lines are indistinct, and the distal margin of HW bears a short lobe; underside similar to male. *Note.* The male of this butterfly was described as *cachiana* Schaus, 1913—a synonym that was recognized even in the original description! Compare with *esperanza , albipuncta.* **Habits:** In our area this butterfly has been recorded from sea level to 800 m on the Atlantic slope in association with rain forest habitats. I have twice encountered females of this butterfly. Both times the females were flying low to the ground in shady understory testing the leaves of many understory plants for oviposition sites between 11:00 and 12:00 hrs. Uncommon in Costa Rican collections. **Localities:** [A]: Peñas Blancas (February). [C]: Cachi [TL]. [SJ]: Carrillo (April), La Montura (March, April). [H]: La Selva (January, April, July, August), Plastico (January, February). [L]: Limon, Rio Estrella.

Mesosemia albipuncta
Schaus, 1913
FW length: 16.5–17 mm   Plate 4
Range: Costa Rica and Panama
Hostplant: Unknown
Early stages: Unknown
• **Adult:** Sexes presumably dimorphic. *Male*— FW upperside clear, dark medium blue with a broad black apex and distal margin, and a tiny white dot in the FW cell; HW upperside dark medium blue with black distal margins, and a small black post medial bar that typically runs from costa at subapex almost to end of cell, but may continue as a thinner, indistinct line to inner margin in some specimens; FW underside dark brown with a distinct black eyespot ringed in yellow, and a light postmedial band that has iridescent blue in it; HW underside dark brown with a lighter medial line bordered on either side by dark brown that runs straight from costa to inner margin, and a light, wavy submarginal line set in dark margin. *Female*—unknown, and in need of description. *Note.* Another form exists in our area (which may prove to be a distinct species) that is distinguished by being slightly large (18.5–20.5 mm) and having a postmedial black band on the HW dorsum that extends from the costa to the inner margin in a tapering curve. However, *albipuncta* (both forms) may eventually prove to be a subspecies of the South American butterfly *mehida* Hewitson, 1809. Compare with *M. coelestis.* **Habits:** This butterfly has been recorded in our area from sea level to 800 m on the Atlantic slope in association with rain forest habitats. The few times I have observed it, it was flying low to the ground in shady understory between 11:00 and 13:00 hrs. Solitary males perch on low vegetation and fly out in looping sorties. Uncommon in Costa Rican collections. **Localities:** [A]: Cariblanco (March, June), Esperanza [TL] (February). [C]: Cachi (October). [H]: La Selva (April), Chilamate (March, September), Tirimbina (March). [L]: Cerro Cocori (March). [G]: Volcan Santa Maria.

Mesosemia hesperina
Butler, 1874
FW length: 14–17.5 mm   Plate 4
Range: Costa Rica to Venezuela
Hostplant: Unknown
Early stages: Unknown
• **Adult:** Sexes dimorphic. *Male*—upperside deep blue with two thin black postmedial bands that traverse both wings, a distinct black submarginal band on both wings, and a black eyespot in FW cell set with a distinct white pu-

pil; underside gray-brown with distinct warm brown medial, postmedial, and submarginal bands on both wings. *Female*—upperside gray-brown with a series of lighter gray medial lines (at times overshot with violet) surrounding the eyespots on both wings, an obvious warm brown submarginal band on both wings, and a rounded distal HW margin; underside ground color is similar to upperside, only lighter. *Note.* There appear to be two forms of this butterfly. The males originating from the Atlantic slope are larger and darker blue, and those from the Pacific slope around the Osa Peninsula are smaller with paler blue ground color. Furthermore, the upperside of the Atlantic slope females has a blue-gray cast and a thinner submarginal band on the HW, and the underside pattern is in darker relief. Perhaps further investigation may reveal specific differences. Compare with *hypermegala, ceropia.*

Habits: In our area this butterfly occurs locally in forest areas from sea level to about 1200 m on both slopes. Typically encountered as solitary individuals flying low to the ground in shaded light gaps and trails deep within the forest. The males perch between 11:00 and 13:00 hrs in tiny light gaps (sun flecks) that illuminate the understory plants that are less than half a meter above the ground. Perching males fly out in looping sorties and return to the same perches again and again throughout their activity period. When perching, the males vigorously chase other small butterflies that fly past. This butterfly is infrequently observed, but it is common in most localities.

Localities: [C]: Florencia de San Carlos (March, June, September). [C]: Moravia de Chirripo (April, August), Turrialba (October). [SJ]: Carrillo (May, June, September, November). [H]: La Selva (April), Chilamate (May, June). [P]: Sirena (February, July, August, September). [L]: Guapiles (September), Coen (March), Hacienda Tapezco (August).

Mesosemia zonalis
(Godman and Salvin, 1885)
FW length: 18–19 mm   Plate 4
Range: Honduras to Panama
Hostplant: Unknown
Early stages: Unknown
• **Adult:** Sexes slightly dimorphic. *Male*—FW upperside dirty brown (especially the apex and distal margin) with a distinct black eyespot ringed in yellow bearing white pupils, and perhaps most conspicuous is the white postmedial band that begins narrowly at costa and expands considerably as it extends to meet the inner margin; HW upperside set with many thin brown straight medial lines that run from costa to inner margin, and with the distal half of the wing white. *Female*—upperside similar to male but the white on the HW is reduced and is typically bisected by a brown postmedial band that is variable in its extent. Compare with *Leucochimona* and satyrines in the genus *Cissia* (Nymphalidae).

Habits: In our area this butterfly occurs locally on both slopes from sea level to 600 m in association with lowland rain forest habitats. Typically encountered as solitary individuals between 10:00 and 13:00 hrs in shady forest understory, or along streams and shaded forest edges. While flying, this butterfly can easily be mistaken for a satyrine in the genus *Cissia*. Although seldom (if ever) abundant, this butterfly is generally present in particular habitats throughout the year.

Localities: [C]: Florencia de San Carlos (April, September, October). [C]: Rio Estrella (April), Cachi. [H]: La Selva (April), Chilamate (April), Magsaysay (December), Plastico (August). [P]: Piedras Blancas (August), Llorona (March, April, July), Sirena (February, September, December). [L]: Guapiles (February, March, August), Limon (October), Banana River (March), Cerro Cocori (March), Rio Estrella (April), Petroleo (October).

Mesosemia carissima
Bates, 1866
FW length: 18–19.5 mm   Plate 4
Range: Nicaragua to Panama
Hostplant: *Psychotria elata* (Rubiaceae)
Early stages: *Mature caterpillar*—pale green, and overall very similar to that of *M. asa.*
• **Adult:** Sexes dimorphic. *Male*—upperside dark brown with a distinct black, pupillate eyespot ringed in yellow in the FW cell, and a rounded patch of intense sky blue on the discal area of the HW. *Female*—similar to the male except paler brown, the blue patch on HW upperside is broader and more angular, and the HW distal margin is produced into short tooth. Compare with *grandis, lamachus, telegone, asa.*

Habits: This butterfly has been recorded in our area from sea level to 1200 m on both slopes in association with rain forest habitats. The males are encountered as solitary individuals perching in small, sunny light gaps in the forest or along streams between 07:00 and 08:30 hrs, and occasionally later. When making sorties from a perch located between 2 and 5 m from the ground, I have observed males skyrocket into the canopy to chase other butterflies, and then, like a shot, return to the

same perch. While the butterfly is flying, the blue patch on the HW literally glows in the sunlight. Generally present in most appropriate habitats, but typically in low abundance.
Localities: [A]: San Rafael de Guatuso (July), Cariblanco (January–April, August, September). [C]: Turrialba (March, October, December), Esperanza, Rio Chitaria (March, September), La Suiza (August). [SJ]: Carrillo (September), Escazu. [H]: La Selva (February, March), Chilamate (March), Magsaysay (January), Plastico (September), Tirimbina (February, November). [P]: San Vito (April). [L]: Guapiles (March, September). [G]: Pitilla (May) [L]: Petroleo (April, October), Jimenez (March).

Mesosemia grandis
Druce, 1874
FW length: 24–25 mm   **Plate 5**
Range: Costa Rica to Panama
Hostplant: Unknown
Early stages: Unknown
• **Adult:** Sexes dimorphic. *Male*—upperside black with wide pale blue bands extending from FW costa to HW tornus, where the distal margin is produced into a toothlike lobe. *Female*—upperside warm red-brown with a conspicuous black, pupillate eyespot ringed in yellow in the FW cell, a dark medial line that runs relatively straight from FW costa to middle of HW inner margin, a distinct yellow-brown postmedial line (especially noticeable on FW), and a distinct tooth at distal margin of HW. Compare with *ceropia, hypermegala, gaudiolum.*
Habits: This butterfly occurs in our area from 700 to 2000 m on both slopes, and is typical of cloud forest habitats. The males are encountered individually or in small groups between 08:30 and 10:30 hrs. During this time they perch on vegetation between 1 and 3 m above the ground in small light gaps in the forest or along streams, and frequently in the company of *M. asa.* By sequentially removing or marking individuals at Las Alturas, I found that particular light gaps were used by the same individual males over the course of up to several months. Moreover, these same light gaps were typically used by this butterfly species throughout the year. The females are encountered as uncommon solitary individuals flying low to the ground along streams or in the shaded understory between 09:30 and 11:00 hrs. In my experience this butterfly occurs in virtually all cloud forest habitats in Costa Rica.
Localities: [A]: San Ramon Reserve (March, May, June), Vara Blanca (March, September),

La Cinchona (September). [C]: Tapanti (March), Cachi, Redondo, Orosi (March). [SJ]: La Montura (April, May), Carrillo (March–June, October), Dota (April). [H]: Zurqui (March). [P]: Agua Buena, San Isidro General (July, August), Monte Verde (October), San Vito (June, September, October), Las Alturas (March, April, July, August, September, December). [G]: Miravalles, Volcan Cacao (August), Cerro Hacha (August).

Mesosemia gaudiolum
Bates, 1865
FW length: 22–23.5 mm   **Plate 5**
Range: Mexico to Nicaragua, Costa Rica(?)
Hostplant: Unknown
Early stages: Unknown
• **Adult:** Sexes dimorphic. *Male*—FW upperside black with a wide pale blue band that begins broadly at costa and narrows to tornus; HW upperside black with distal third pale blue, including the toothlike lobe at distal margin. *Female*—upperside brown with a distinct pale blue submarginal band along HW distal margin. Compare with *grandis.*
Habits: In areas north of Costa Rica this butterfly apparently occurs in lowland rain forest. Although Seitz (1916) reported it as occurring in our area, I have been unable to discover the specific locality to which his material refers. Perhaps the most likely habitat would be in north central Costa Rica, along the Nicaraguan border. The presence of this distinctive species requires confirmation in our area.
Localities: Needs to be confirmed for our area.

Mesosemia ceropia
Druce, 1874
FW length: 22–24 mm   **Plate 5**
Range: Costa Rica to Colombia
Hostplant: Unknown
Early stages: Unknown
• **Adult:** Sexes dimorphic. *Male*—upperside dark blue-black with a tiny white spot in the FW cell, and distinct iridescent blue bands on FW base that continue as postmedial and submarginal lines, and then along entire margin of the HW; underside dark brown with straight gray medial lines surrounding the eyespots on both wings, and red-brown margin on FW. *Female*—upperside pale brown with dark brown postmedial bands and margins on both surfaces of both wings; distal margin of HW slightly produced almost into a toothlike lobe. Compare with *grandis, hypermegala.*
Habits: This butterfly has been recorded in our area from sea level to 800 m on both slopes in association with rain forest and cloud forest

habitats. Typically encountered as uncommon, solitary individuals are found between 11:30 and 14:00 hrs perching about 2 to 3 m above the ground in shaded forest understory or along small shaded streams. During this time the males will perch on top of leaves for 2 to 10 min intervals without moving. Uncommon in Costa Rican collections.

Localities: [A]: Reserva San Ramon (May), Bajo de Rodriguez (February), Cariblanco (February, May, September), Florencia de San Carlos (April, June), Esperanza. [C]: Parismina (April), Pejivalle (March). [H]: Magsaysay (July), La Selva (September). [P]: Llorona (April–July). [L]: Guapiles (December), Banana River, Esperanza.

Mesosemia hypermegala
Stichel, 1909
FW length: 18.5–19 mm   **Plate 5**
Range: Costa Rica to Colombia
Hostplant: Unknown
Early stages: Unknown
• **Adult:** Sexes dimorphic. *Male*—upperside blue-black with a shining blue postmedial band that curves gently from FW costa to inner margin, and then continues along distal margin of HW. *Female*—FW upperside gray-brown with prominent FW ocellus set in a yellow-gray medial area, and a distinct red-brown postmedial band that curves gently from costa to inner margin; HW upperside gray-brown with dark brown, relatively straight medial band, a dark brown postmedial band that has a distinctly crenate distal margin, and a distinct dark brown spot in the toothlike lobe on the distal margin; underside with reddish brown submarginal band on FW, and HW ground color white with brown lines. Compare with *ceropia, hesperina, grandis.*
Habits: This butterfly is known in our area from a single specimen that was collected in montane cloud forest on the Atlantic slope between 1000 and 1200 m elevation. I have never seen this species alive. This butterfly is apparently extremely rare throughout its range. However, J. Hall (pers. comm.) suggests that it may simply be a variant of *ceropia.*
Localities: [C]: Moravia de Chirripo.

Mesosemia lamachus
Hewitson, 1857
FW length: 17.5–18 mm   **Plate 5**
Range: Mexico to Colombia
Hostplant: *Psychotria* sp. (Rubiaceae)
Early stages: *Egg*—white, deposited singly on the underside of leaves or in the axils of new leaves.

• **Adult:** Sexes dimorphic. *Male*—FW upperside brown with a light brown postmedial band that runs from the costa straight to the inner margin, and with purplish blue along base and basal half of inner margin; HW upperside brown with a purple-blue iridescence across most of wing, a thin brown medial line, a broad brown postmedial line, a thin brown submarginal line, and a brown distal margin set with isolated blue spots; underside brown with the medial area encompassing the eyespots on both wings, and this area is not filled with filigree patterns. *Female*—upperside similar to male, but with paler blue, brown lines on the HW more distinct, and FW with a red-brown postmedial band. Compare with *telegone, carissima.*
Habits: This butterfly occurs commonly, but locally from sea level to 800 m in association with primary and secondary rain forest on both slopes. Encountered as solitary individuals flying in shady understory from 09:00 to 12:30 hrs. The same perching areas may be used by successive males through time. Females oviposit from 11:30 to 12:30 hrs in shady understory.
Localities: [A]: Pando Azucar 2.5 km N of Rio Grande (August). [C]: Juan Viñas (November), Turrialba (June, August), Colombiana. [H]: La Selva (April, August). [P]: San Vito (May). [L]: Hitoy Cerere (October), Tortuguerro (August), Guapiles.

Mesosemia telegone telegone
(Boisduval, 1836)
FW length: 18–19 mm   **Plate 5**
Range: Mexico to Peru. **Subspecies:** Costa Rica to Colombia
Hostplant: *Palicourea guianensis* (Rubiaceae)
Early stages: *Egg*—small, white, deposited on underside of leaves or in leaf axils. *Mature caterpillar*—pale green with a sparse covering of stiff white setae; overall shape similar to the caterpillar of *asa* but smaller.
• **Adult:** Sexes slightly dimorphic. Distinguished from *lamachus* by a more striking blue upperside, and the postmedial and submarginal bands on the HW upperside are narrower, and both roughly of the same width. Compare with *lamachus, carissima, asa.*
Habits: This butterfly occurs locally on the Pacific slope from sea level to 1400 m in association with primary and secondary rain forest. Typically encountered as solitary individuals flying in shady understory between 08:00 and 11:00 hrs. The males perch in small light gaps and sun flecks in the forest understory between 07:30 and 08:45 hrs, and the same

perching areas may be used through time by successive males. Moreover, males will perch in these areas even in cloudy weather. **Localities:** [A]: Alajuela (January), Carrillos de Poas (March), Atenas. [SJ]: El Rodeo (June, October). [P]: Palmar Norte (August), San Vito (April, August), Sirena (July–September, December), Monte Verde (September, October). [G]: Cañas, Parque Santa Rosa (January, December).

Mesosemia asa asa
Hewitson, 1869
FW length: 20.5–21.5 mm   **Plate 4**
Range: Nicaragua to Colombia. **Subspecies:** Costa Rica to Colombia
Hostplant: *Psychotria macrophylla, Psychotria* spp. (Rubiaceae)
Early stages (Fig. 39): *Egg*—white, laid on the stem of the plant near the ground. Early instars are pale green with a sparse covering of bristlelike setae. *Mature caterpillar*—medium dark green, with the lateral edges of each segment slightly lobed at the venter (best seen from above); abdominal segments with two small white dots located on either side of the dorsal midline; the setae arise in sparse tufts, especially those located laterally near venter. The setae are most noticeable when viewed from above. *Note*—those caterpillars that have been parasitized by tachinid fly larvae turn a dark maroon just prior to the emergence of the tachinid maggot. *Pupa*—dull pale green, with a robust thorax and compacted abdomen whose overall shape and color recalls the pupa of *Metacharis*.
- **Adult:** Sexes dimorphic. *Male*—FW upperside black with metallic royal blue on basal third of wing; HW upperside metallic royal blue with all margins black. *Female*—FW upperside brown with a conspicuous white band running from costa to distal margin anterior to the tornus; HW upperside brown with distinct brown medial, postmedial, and submarginal lines. *Note.* The females from the Pacific slopes have a narrower white band on FW than those originating from the Atlantic slope. Compare with *carissima, telegone, lamachus.*
Habits: This butterfly is found commonly and abundantly in our area from 700 to 2200 m in virtually all types of primary and secondary forest habitats on both slopes. This butterfly is perhaps the most abundant *Mesosemia* species in all of Costa Rica. The males are found scattered, or in small groups, throughout the forest understory along trails, rivers, light gaps, and especially along streams where they maintain perches on understory vegetation. The

males are active between 07:30 and 14:00 hrs, but the main perching times appear to be between 08:30 and 13:00 hrs—a time period that apparently corresponds to the activity times of virgin females. A study done at Monte Verde showed that males arrive at territories between 09:30 and 15:00 hrs; these territories remain occupied for up to 25 days, and mating occurs when a female flies into male territories (Alcock 1988). The females search for oviposition sites in light gaps and the dappled light of the understory between 11:00 and 13:00 hrs when they may be observed to alight frequently on low plants growing in the forest understory. When a plant has been chosen for oviposition, the female tests various leaves, then walks backwards down the stem, then lays a single egg on the stem near the ground. An individual female may lay several eggs on the same plant, but each time she will walk about on the stem before she lays another egg. While flitting about in the forest understory, the females bear a strong resemblance to clear winged ithomiines, particularly species in the genera *Ithomia* and *Oleria.* Both sexes occasionally visit flowers of *Psychotria* and other plants with tiny white flowers.
Localities: [A]: Cariblanco (February, March, August), Florencia de San Carlos (March, June). [C]: Tapanti (July), Navarro (March), Turrialba (January, July), Cartago (April, September), Tuis (October). [SJ]: Carrillo (February, April, June, July, December), San Jose (September, October), 14.3 km N of San Isidro general (April). [H]: Plastico (January–December), Chilamate (April, September), Barva. [P]: Las Alturas (January–December), Monte Verde (January–December), San Vito (March–September). [L]: Madre de Dios (September), Guapiles (March). [G]: Volcan Santa Maria (February, March), plus numerous other localities throughout the country.

Mesosemia harveyi
DeVries and Hall, 1996
FW length: 17.5–20 mm   **Plate 25**
Range: Costa Rica to Panama
Hostplant: Unknown
Early stages: Unknown
- **Adult:** Sexes similar. Upperside dark chocolate brown with prominent black FW ocellus and small HW ocellus. Underside similar to *asa,* but the fine medial lines are yellow, not white. This is the only *Mesosemia* species in Central America that is known to be entirely dark brown in both sexes. Compare with *ceropia, hesperina, hypermegala.*

Habits: This butterfly is known in our area from a single locality on the Atlantic slope at 1600 m. Nothing is known regarding the habits of this distinctive species, but likely to be found in cloud forest habitats. Obviously rare in Costa Rican collections (see DeVries and Hall 1996).

Localities: [C]: Tapanti (February).

Tribe EURYBIINI Reuter, 1897

The butterflies embraced by this tribe are formally characterized by having bristlelike scales on the medial surface of the palpi, and an extraordinarily long proboscis (*Eurybia*). I may also add that all members here have distinct metallic blue-green eyes that, although especially evident in life, nevertheless persist in pinned museum specimens. As currently understood, the Eurybiini embraces three genera: *Eurybia*, *Alesa*, and *Mimocastnia*, of which the latter two are confined to the Amazon Basin of South America. The hostplants reported for the tribe include Marantaceae, Zingiberaceae, and Solanaceae. Judging from *Eurybia* and *Alesa*, the caterpillars are myrmecophilous and are unusual in being able to produce calls without vibratory papillae (DeVries 1991c).

Genus EURYBIA Illiger, 1807

These remarkable butterflies are immediately recognized by the reflective ocellus in the FW cell, an often striking iridescent color on the upperside of the HW, and by their metallic eyes, which are especially noticeable in live specimens. There is a noticeable sexual dimorphism with respect to the eyes—the eyes of the males are much larger than those of the females. Furthermore, members of *Eurybia* have a very unusual characteristic: a proboscis that is typically one and a half times the length of the body, and likely the longest in any group of butterfly. Approximately twenty species are currently placed in *Eurybia*, but taxonomic literature and museum collections suggest that the genus is in desperate need of revision (R. Hanner, in prep.). The butterflies are found from Mexico throughout Central and South America, and there are six species in our area, most of which can be locally common.

The hostplants for *Eurybia* include the Marantaceae and Zingiberaceae, especially the genera *Calathea*, *Ischnosiphon*, *Maranta*, *Costus*, and *Renealmia*. Available evidence indicates that the caterpillars feed exclusively on flower parts, not foliage (DeVries et al. 1994). The eggs of *Eurybia* are flattened, lozenge shaped, bear an uncanny resemblance to the diatom genus *Stephanodiscus* (Fig. 1d), and are typically laid singly on the stems and leaves of the hostplants. The maggotlike caterpillars are without obvious setae or granulations (Fig. 40), and burrow into the inflorescence of the hostplant to feed on the open and unopened flowers. Caterpillars may frequently be found resting in the nests of ant species (e.g., *Wasmannia*, *Pheidole*, *Megalomyrmex*) that commonly inhabit the sheathing stems of the Marantaceae. While resting within the ant nests, walking on the plant, or feeding on the flowers ants are in constant attendance soliciting secretions from the caterpillar's well-developed tentacle nectary organs. The call production of *Eurybia* caterpillars is unusual among riodinids in that they do not possess vibratory papillae or specialized head granulations, thus indicating that *Eurybia* has evolved a distinct and as yet unknown mechanism to produce calls (DeVries 1990, 1991c). Among butterflies, the pupae of *Eurybia* are truly exceptional. To accommodate the exaggerated length of the adult proboscis, the sheath enclosing it may extend a full body length beyond the last abdominal segment (Fig. 40). In nature, the pupae can generally be found inside the sheathing leaf bases amid the profusion of other insect life that is associated with its hostplants.

In the field, these butterflies are seldom found away from thickets of *Calathea* or their other hostplants. When disturbed from under the broad leaves in these thickets, the butterfly's very fast, erratic flight makes them easy to recognize. It is not uncommon to find individuals with bite marks on their wings, almost certainly from the many lizard species in the genera *Anolis* and *Norops* (Iguanidae) that maintain territories in these thickets. It has been my experience that at dusk the males of *lycisca* and *patrona* exhibit a pronounced leklike activity along natural boundaries such as streams, trails, or in forest light gaps. During these times, the males engage in courtship and territorial behaviors, flying in long, sweeping loops around a stand of the hostplant and often remaining airborne for several minutes without stopping. While engaged in these long flights, an individual will interact vigorously with other *Eurybia* butterflies that are also engaged in flight.

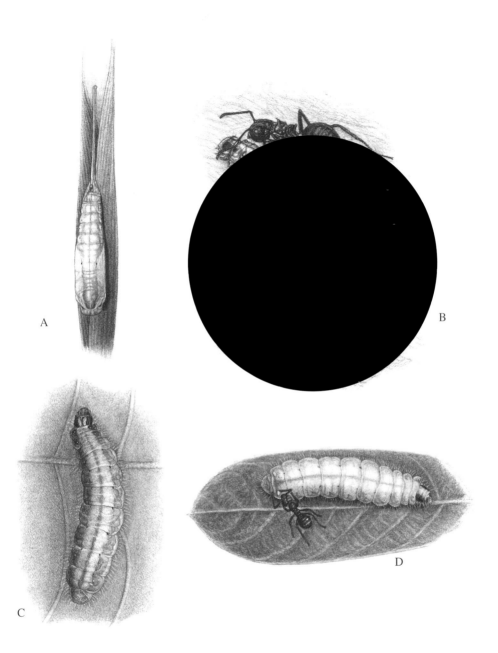

FIGURE 40. (A) *Eurybia lycisca* pupa. (B) *Eurybia lycisca* caterpillar. (C) *Eurybia elvina* caterpillar. (D) *Eurybia patrona* caterpillar. (Drawings by J. Clark)

One consequence of having an exaggerated proboscis length is that it allows these butterflies to drink nectar from flowers that have long corolla tubes, a floral feature that typically excludes other butterflies with a shorter proboscis. In addition to *Cephaelis*, *Psychotria*, and some Asteraceae, the nectar plants of *Eurybia* frequently include various species of *Calathea*, *Costus*, and *Renealmia* that have flowers typically pollinated by euglossine bees or hummingbirds. On several occasions on th̶ ̶C̶ ̶P̶insula, I have found *Eurybia* [obscured]
doscorpions (pr̶[obscured]
attached to th̶[obscured]
spection of̶ [obscured]
at times, ̶[obscured]
in the st̶[obscured]
these p̶[obscured]
with *E*[obscured]
sects (̶[obscured]
mains̶[obscured]

Eurybi[obscured]
Stiche[obscured]
FW leng[obscured]
Range: C̶[obscured]
Hostplant:[obscured]
Early stages:[obscured]
• **Adult:** Sexes[obscured]
brown with some[obscured]
rior portion of the disc̶[obscured]̶nct
white spots at the distal end of the cell near the costa; HW upperside brown with reddish brown on distal margin that is set with a row of black submarginal spots between the radial veins. The males have a slight iridescent sheen to the reddish brown areas, the females do not. Compare with *patrona*, *elvina*.

Habits: In our area this butterfly has been reported only from Atlantic slope rain forest habitats that range in elevation from sea level to 600 m. Once I collected this butterfly in shady understory, thinking it was *E. elvina*. Uncommon.

Localities: [C]: Turrialba (May–August). [H]: La Selva (October). [L]: Guapiles (January, February).

Eurybia caerulescens fulgens
Stichel, 1910
FW length: 24–26 mm   **Plate 6**
Range: Costa Rica to Venezuela, Ecuador. **Subspecies:** Costa Rica to Panama
Hostplant: Unknown
Early stages: Unknown
• **Adult:** Sexes similar. FW upperside brown with two subapical white spots near the costa, and except at the costa and inner margin, the

entire HW is a brilliant iridescent blue. Compare with *lycisca*, *unxia*.

Habits: In our area this butterfly has been reported from Atlantic slope rain forest habitats from sea level to 800 m. There is one record from the central mesa near San Jose suggesting that the butterfly may eventually be found in some habitats on the Pacific slope. Encountered as rare, solitary individuals in old treefall gaps near streams, generally in the company of *elvina* or *lycisca*. Judging from locality data, this butterfly may be present throughout the year. Uncommon in Costa Rican collections.

[Lo]calities: [A]: Cariblanco (January–May, Au̶[gus]t–October), San Ramon Reserve; La Liber-[tad. C]: Juan Viñas, Tuis (September), Tur-[rialba] (June, July, November), Cachi. [SJ]: [...] (February, May, June, October, No-[vember], Zapote. [H]: Plastico (February, Au-[gust], Selva (November), Chilamate (Sep-[tember], Magsaysay (July). [L]: Guapiles [...] March).

[Eurybia] unxia
[Godma]n and Salvin, 1885
[FW len]gth: 22–23.5 mm   **Plate 6**
[Range]: Costa Rica to Brazil, Bolivia. **Subspecies:** [Co]sta Rica and Panama
[H]ostplant: Unknown
Early stages: Unknown
• **Adult:** Sexes dimorphic. *Male*—FW upperside brown with 2 white spots near the subapex near the costa, and a row of submarginal spots; HW upperside brown with an iridescent blue sheen (best seen obliquely) across most of the wing, and a submarginal row of black spots that are ringed in yellow. *Female*—upperside similar to male except the HW appears entirely brown, with but a faint sheen of iridescent violet that can be seen when viewed obliquely. Compare with *lycisca*, *caerulescens*, and *elvina*.

Habits: In our area this butterfly has been reported locally from Atlantic slope rain forest habitats that range in elevation from sea level to 900 m. In my experience, this butterfly is typically confined to thickets of Marantaceae that grow along rivers, streams, or in the shady interior of wet forest. Both sexes visit flowers of *Calathea*, *Ischnosiphon*, and *Cephaelis*.

Localities: [A]: Cariblanco (February, March, September, October, December). [C]: Turrialba (May, July), Upala (November), Tuis (September). [SJ]: Carrillo (February, June). [H]: Plastico (February), La Selva. [P]: San Vito (September, October). [L]: Guapiles (March).

Eurybia patrona persona
Staudinger, 1876
FW length: 30–35 mm   **Plate 6**
Range: Honduras to Panama. **Subspecies:** Costa
Rica to Panama
Hostplant: *Calathea inocephala* (Marantaceae)
Early stages (Fig. 40d): *Egg*—lozenge shaped,
pale green at first, then turning white after a
few days. Laid on the stems, inflorescence, or
at the base of the plant. *Mature caterpillar*—yellow with two brown patches on dorsum of segment T1; head capsule dark brown. All instars
may be found burrowing into the spongy mass
of the hostplant inflorescence. The caterpillars
are typically found associated with a mass of
attending ants, and their slimy frass that adheres to the inflorescence is quite noticeable
when specifically looked for. The caterpillars
are parasitized by *Rogas* sp. (Braconidae: Rogadiinae). *Pupa*—pale brown, generally found
within sheathed leaves below the infloresence,
often amid a temporary ant colony. At Sirena I
found the caterpillars and pupae tended by a
variety of ants, including *Pheidole* sp. *Paratrechina* sp., *Crematogaster* sp., *Wasmannia auropunctata* (Myrmicinae), *Camponotus* sp. (Formicinae), and *Pachycondyla villosa* (Ponerinae).
• **Adult:** Sexes similar. This is the largest Central American species. FW upperside reddish
brown with some indistinct, dark postmedial
and submarginal spots; HW upperside brown
with a conspicuous orange-brown marginal
band set with a row of elongate black postmedial spots, and a row of submarginal spots.
HW underside with a prominent ocellus in the
cell. Compare with *cyclopia* and *elvina*.
Habits: This butterfly occurs locally on both
slopes from sea level to about 400 m in association with rain forest habitats. In my experience this butterfly is typically encountered
during the dry season as uncommon, solitary
individuals in old treefall gaps where the hostplant has become established and is in flower.
I found that marked individual males may remain near the same patch of hostplant for several days. Perhaps due to good variation in
availability of hostplant flowers, parasitism, or
variation of yearly weather patterns, the local
abundance of this butterfly may vary dramatically from year to year at the same site. For
example, during the 1983 dry season at Sirena, caterpillars and adults of this butterfly
were very abundant, yet in subsequent years
this butterfly has been uncommon to rare.
Both sexes visit flowers of *Heliconia, Calathea,
Ischnosiphon,* and *Cephaelis*.
Localities: [A]: Upala (September), La Fortuna
nr Quebrada Piedrita (October), 10 km N of
Florencia de San Carlos (January, March–May,

September–December), Esperanza. [C]: Tur-
rialba. [SJ]: Santa Rosa de Puriscal (January).
[H]: La Selva (April, September). [P]: Rincon
de Osa (January, February), Sirena (February–
April, June, September, October, December),
Llorona (February, March, April), Carrara
(August, October). [L]: Tortuguerro (August),
Sixaola.

Eurybia elvina elvina
Stichel, 1910
FW length: 24–27 mm   **Plate 6**
Range: Mexico to Brazil. **Subspecies:** Costa Rica
and Panama
Hostplant: *Calathea lutea, C. crotalifera, C. inocephala, C. latifolia, Ischnosiphon pruniosus* (Marantaceae)
Early stages (Horvitz et al. 1987): *Egg*—lozenge
shaped, pale green, laid on the stems, inflorescence, or at the base of the plant. *Mature caterpillar* (Fig. 40c)—pale green with two brown
patches on dorsum of segment T1; head capsule brown. All instars may be found amid the
hostplant inflorescence. Two tell-tale signs will
help find them: they are typically found associated with a mass of attending ants, and the
frass that adheres to the inflorescence is quite
noticeable when specifically looked for. In
Costa Rica and Panama, the caterpillars are
parasitized by *Rogas* sp. (Rogadiinae: Braconidae). *Pupae*—pale brown, generally found
within sheathed leaves below the infloresence,
often amid a temporary ant colony. In Costa
Rica and Panama I have found the caterpillars
and pupae tended by a variety of ants, including *Pheidole* sp., *Crematogaster* sp., *Solenopsis* sp.
Wasmannia auropunctata (Myrmicinae), *Camponotus* spp. (Formicinae), *Ectatomma ruidum,
Pachycondyla villosa* (Ponerinae).
• **Adult:** Sexes similar. FW upperside brown
with a postmedial row of small white spots and
a submarginal row of black spots; HW upperside brown with no trace of iridescent blue, a
postmedial row of red-orange spots, and a submarginal row of black spots. Compare with *cyclopia*.
Habits: This butterfly has been reported from
both slopes in association with primary and
secondary forest ranging from sea level to 800 m
and is by far the most common member of the
genus in our area. Typically encountered as
solitary individuals in treefall gaps, streams,
forest edges, or wherever a suitable hostplant
is growing. Horvitz and Schemske (1984)
found that in Mexico the caterpillars have a
strong negative impact upon the seed crop of
individual *Calathea ovandensis* plants—the caterpillars can destroy a large percentage of the
maturing seed. Both sexes feed at flowers of

Cephaelis, Psychotria, Centropogon, Stachytarpheta, Calathea, and *Ischnosiphon.*

Localities: [A]: Cariblanco (August), Aguas Claras (September), La Fortuna nr Quebrada Piedrita (October), 10 km N of Florencia de San Carlos (May), Atenas (January, March, April, December), San Mateo. [C]: Turrialba (January, May–July), Cachi. [SJ]: Desamparados (March, September), El Rodeo (October), Carrillo. [H]: Magsaysay (February), La Selva (April, May, August, July), Chilamate (March, May–July, September), Plastico. [P]: Barranca (September, November), Ujarras de Buenos Aires (September), Avangarez, Sirena, Golfito, Carrara. [L]: Tortuguerro (August), Siquirres (July), Guapiles (March, September), Petroleo (September), Puerto Viejo (September), Limon. [G]: Barranca (August), Santa Rosa (December), Las Juntas de Guanacaste (September), and numerous other localities throughout the country.

Eurybia lycisca
Westwood, 1851
FW length: 24–27.5 mm   Plate 6
Range: Mexico to Ecuador
Hostplant: *Calathea lutea, C. crotalifera, C. inocephala, C. latifolia, C. warsczewisczia, Ischnosiphon pruniosus* (Marantaceae)
Early stages (Figs. 1d, 40a, b): *Egg*—pale blue-green, lozenge shaped, with the convex dorsal surface (with central micropyle) slightly wider than body of the egg that produces a distinct rim with the entire egg surface covered with a slightly raised honeycomb pattern, giving the overall impression of a diatom in the genus *Stephanodiscus.* The egg may be laid singly on stems, bracts, or on dead plant tissue associated with the hostplant. *Mature caterpillar*—pale yellow-green with two brown patches on dorsum of segment T1, with a brown head capsule. All instars may be found amid the hostplant inflorescence, whereas late instars often are found inside the hollow stems during the day and feeding on the flowers at night. The caterpillars are almost always found associated with a mass of attending ants, and often more than one caterpillar will be found on a single inflorescence. The caterpillars are parasitized by nocturnally active *Rogas* sp. (Rogadiinae: Braconidae). *Pupa*—pale brown, generally found within sheathed leaves below the infloresence, often amid a temporary ant colony. In Costa Rica and Panama I have found the caterpillars and pupae tended by a variety of ants, including *Paratrechina* sp., *Pheidole* sp., *Crematogaster* sp., *Aphaenogaster araneoides, Solenopsis* sp. *Wasmannia auropunctata,*

Megalomyrmex foreli (Myrmicinae), *Camponotus* spp. (Formicinae), *Pachycondyla villosa, Pachycondyla* sp. (Ponerinae).

• **Adult:** Sexes similar. FW upperside brown without any white spots at the subapex; HW upperside brown with an obvious metallic blue across the entire discal area. Compare with *caerulescens* and *unxia.*

Habits: This butterfly occurs throughout the year on both slopes in association with primary and secondary forest from sea level to 1400 m. The butterflies are generally encountered in small colonies wherever there is a suitable thicket of hostplant. Both sexes are active from 08:00 to 13:00 hrs, and then later in the day from 16:00 to 18:00 hrs. The males may be observed performing rapid and elaborate "territorial" displays around the hostplants. In these instances a male will commence from under a leaf, then zoom off into the forest understory, then return to the same plant where it started from. I found no evidence that marked individuals remain near the same hostplant on a daily basis, but rather they seem to change locations every day. Oviposition behavior appears to occur at any time from 0900 to 1300 hrs. During oviposition behavior the female lands on a plant, then backs down toward the ground constantly probing the substrate with the end of her abdomen. When a suitable spot on the stem, bract, leaf base, or inflorescence is blundered into, the female lays a single egg. After laying the egg, she flies off a short distance and will habitually rest on top of a leaf that is illuminated by sunshine. After a few moments of basking she will either begin landing on plants in search of other oviposition sites, feed at the open flowers on the hostplant, or she will rest under a leaf. Both sexes feed at the flowers of all their Marantaceae hostplants, plus the flowers of *Psychotria* spp, *Cephaelis* sp., *Stachytarpheta* sp., and *Lantana camara.* While feeding at flowers, the butterflies will occasionally become involved in "territorial disputes" with various species of bees (Apidae: Euglossinae) that also visit the same flowers.

Localities: [A]: Cariblanco (May–August), Bijagua (September), La Tigra de San Carlos (May). [C]: Turrialba (January), Rio Reventazon (September). [SJ]: Santa Rosa de Puriscal (December), Carrillo. [H]: La Selva (February, June, July), Plastico (February), Chilamate (March, June), Santa Clara (September). [P]: San Vito (April–July, September, October), Las Alturas (April–June, August), Carrara (May), Sirena (February, April, September, October, December), Rincon (August), Aguas Claras (September), Guayabo (September), Monte Verde. [L]: Tortuguerro (August), Petroleo (April), Rio Estrella Negro (September), Puerto Viejo (September), Bannanito Sur (September), Guapiles, plus many other localities throughout the country.

Group INCERTAE SEDIS

All the butterflies in this group have five radial veins in FW, but were not included in the Mesosemiini or Eurybiini by Harvey (1987a). Hence, the systematic placement of the members of this group is unresolved and in need of revisionary work. In other words, this group is a catch-all for taxonomic problems, and the closest relatives of the members of this group within the context of the Riodinidae are unknown. Overall the group includes nearly forty species placed in nine genera: *Hermathena*, *Cremna*, *Napaea*, *Voltinia* (in our area) plus the South American genera *Hyphilaria*, *Ithomiola*, *Eunogyra*, *Teratophthalma*, and *Eucorna*.

Host records for *Hermathena*, *Cremna*, *Napaea*, and *Eunogyra* include the monocot plant families Bromeliaceae, Orchidaceae, and Araceae. The caterpillars of these genera are nonmyrmecophilous and bear a dense pile of long setae. There is no information available for the other genera in this group.

Unlike marine shells or the bones of vertebrates, the delicate nature of butterflies does not lend them to fossilization. Thus it follows that the fossil remains of butterflies are extremely rare, often only in small fragments, and make our understanding of the fossil record for butterflies tenuous at best. Nevertheless, some well-preserved fossil butterflies do exist, and available evidence suggests that butterflies in the families Papilionidae, Pieridae, Nymphalidae, Riodinidae, and Lycaenidae existed as long as 48 million years ago (see Durden and Rose 1978; Shields 1976; Emmel et al. 1992).

Through the kindness of D. Grimaldi at the American Museum of Natural History, I am informed that recently a number of riodinid specimens in fossil amber have come to light from the Dominican Republic dated at approximately 25 million years old. Unlike flattened rock fossils where only one aspect of a specimen can be studied, inclusions in fossil amber typically yield specimens preserved in three dimensions (see Grimaldi 1993, 1995, 1996). The preservation of these riodinids in amber is so remarkable that minute morphological details are intact, including the color patterns on some of the specimens, and they were readily determined by D. Harvey at the Smithsonian Institution as being closely related to the genus *Napaea* (Fig. 41).

These exciting fossils permit us to view a fragment of riodinid evolution and make it certain that members of the *Incertae Sedis* group originated at least 25 million years ago. However, Grimaldi points out that the major strengths of these fossils are twofold. First, the facts that the group of genera forming *Incertae Sedis* are extant only in Central and South America and that the only riodinid genus occurring presently on the Antilles (*Dianesia*) belongs to the tribe Emesini show that these fossils represent direct evidence of extinction events in the butterfly fauna of the Antilles. Second, these riodinids in amber, together with other insect fossils from the Dominican Republic, strengthen biogeographical indications that the Antilles were formerly fused with Central America (see Liebherr 1988; Woods 1989).

As scientific interest in fossil amber has increased dramatically in recent years, more riodinid fossils are certain to become available for study. Eventually such future fossils may provide us a better understanding of the riodinids because they permit us to gaze through unique windows in time.

Genus NAPAEA Hübner, 1819

These butterflies are readily recognized by their broad, rounded wings, with a scattering of spots that forms a calico pattern. As currently understood, *Napaea* embraces about a dozen, mainly South American species, although Seitz (1916) considered that most were variable and recognized only seven species. Members of *Napaea* are found from Mexico throughout Central and South America (but see also above and Fig. 41). Three species occur in our area.

Hostplant records from Central and South America indicate that the caterpillars feed on members of the Bromeliaceae and Orchidaceae (Zikán 1953; Beutelspacher 1972; Beizanko et al. 1978; Brevignon 1992; DeVries et al. 1994). The eggs are bluntly conical with a broad base, and the caterpillars are densely covered in long

FIGURE 41. Fossil riodinid in amber. This specimen from Dominican amber is thought to be very close to the extant genus *Napaea*, and the fossil inclusion has been dated as at least 25 million years old.

setae and can easily be mistaken for moth caterpillars. The pupae are robust, angular, and recall the pupa of the satyrine genus *Euptychia* (Nymphalidae).

In Central America, these butterflies are typically found locally in lowland rain forest and are on the whole uncommon. All of our species fly slowly and have a characteristic fluttery flight.

Napaea eucharila
(Bates, 1867)
FW length: 17.5–22 mm   Plate 5
Range: Mexico to Brazil
Hostplant: *Ananas comosus, Aechmaea* spp., *Vriesia* sp., *Guzmania* sp. (Bromeliaceae)
Early stages (Fig. 42): *Egg*—white, deposited singly on leaves or inflorescences of young and mature plants. *Mature caterpillar*—densely covered with long, pale yellow setae in such a manner as to strongly resemble moth larvae in the families Noctuidae and Arctiidae; head capsule brown. When molested by ants or an observer, the caterpillar can reflex the long setae toward the point of stimulus as a defense. The setae, however, do not urticate. The caterpillars graze on the leaf underside and leave the epidermis intact to form a "window" in the leaf. This characteristic feeding damage can indicate the presence of a caterpillar or a leaf that was damaged in the recent past. *Pupa*—in overall shape similar to the pupa of the satyrine genus *Euptychia* (see DeVries 1987); gray-brown with dark brown lateral

spots on abdomen; dorsum of first abdominal segments with a raised keel; cremaster is very stout and flat, and pupation takes place head downward, with the body away from the substrate.

• **Adult:** Sexes dimorphic. *Male*—FW upperside black set with many small white spots; HW upperside black with few or no white spots, and either with a conspicuous red band at distal margin, or without the red distal margin. *Female*—FW upperside gray-black set with many rectangular white or pale yellow spots; HW upperside gray-black with white or pale yellow spots, and an irregular orange-red submarginal band that runs from costa to inner margin. *Note.* Godman and Salvin (1885) first noted that there are two forms of this species, especially noticeable in the males. One form has the red band on the HW very thin or extinct [named *picina* (Stichel, 1910)], and the other form has a wide, conspicuous red HW band [named *rufolimbata* (Stichel, 1910)]. Although C. Callaghan (pers. comm.) is of the opinion that these two forms represent separate species, here I treat them as a single species. Future workers may be able to decide which is correct.

Habits: This butterfly occurs locally in our area on both slopes from sea level to 1400 m in association with primary and secondary forest habitats. The butterfly is generally present throughout the year and not infrequently encountered in small colonies. On the Atlantic slope of Costa Rica, I generally found solitary perching males between 08:00 and 10:30 hrs along forest edges or in light gaps. The perches were located between 2 and 5 m above the ground. In the Canal area of Panama G. Small reported finding the males perching between 13:00 and 14:00 hrs. The females are most active from 11:00 to 1300 hrs, but are occasionally found as early as 08:00 hrs along forest edges or flying high in the subcanopy of the forest. During this time the females may be observed to investigate large epiphytic bromeliads.

Localities: [A]: Peñas Blancas (August). [C]: Turrialba (March, April, June–August), San Francisco. [SJ]: Carrillo (October). [H]: La Selva (February, May–August, October), Santa Clara (April), Chilamate (September), Tirimbina (March). [P]: San Vito (June–September), Sirena (March, July), Rincon (March), Las Alturas (May), Isla del Caño (March, September). [L]: Guapiles (May), Siquirres (March), Germania (September), Sixaola, Rio Estrella.

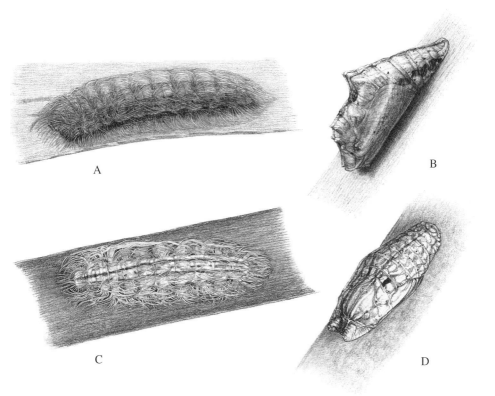

FIGURE 42. (A) *Napaea eucharila* caterpillar. (B) *Napaea eucharila* pupa. (C) *Cremna thasus* caterpillar. (D) *Cremna thasus* pupa. (Drawings by J. Clark)

Napaea theages theages

(Godman and Salvin, 1878)

FW length: 17–18 mm   **Plate 5**

Range: Nicaragua to Colombia, Ecuador. **Subspecies:** Nicaragua to Colombia

Hostplant: *Vriesia* sp. (Bromeliaceae); *Scaphyglottis* sp. (Orchidaceae)

Early stages: *Egg*—tiny, white, laid singly on leaves and stems. *Mature caterpillar*—green with a black band on the dorsum and sparsely covered with short tubercles that bear short tan setae. *Pupa*—similar in overall appearance to *Napaea eucharila*, but entirely pale green.

• **Adult:** Sexes dimorphic. *Male*—FW upperside brown with two conspicuous white spots at end of cell, and a few tiny white spots along costa and submargin; HW upperside brown with a conspicuous white bar that runs from inner margin to end of cell, and a pale blue submarginal area at tornus; tip of abdomen blue. *Female*—upperside similar to male except the white spots in FW are fused into a bar, and the white bar on HW fills the discal area, contains no blue. Compare with *Thisbe irenea* and *Menander laobotas*.

Habits: In our area this butterfly occurs from sea level to 1500 m on both slopes, generally in association with mature forest habitats. Both sexes are active along rivers and streams, roadcuts, and forest edges between 08:00 and 12:30 hrs. The males perch in sunny areas between 5 and 10 m above the ground and chase passing butterflies that are of approximately the same size. The females search for oviposition sites during midday, and they can be found flying outside of the forest along edges or in second growth. For some reason, the females are much more commonly encountered than the males. In the field, the females may be confused with members of the nymphalid genera *Castilia*, *Eresia*, and *Janatella* (Melitaeinae).

Localities: [A]: Cariblanco (March, April, September), Florencia de San Carlos (March). [C]: Peralta (July), Juan Viñas (March), Turrialba (May, July), Volcan Irazu Rd 12.8 km S of summit (October). [SJ]: Carrillo. [H]: Chilamate (August), La Selva. [P]: San Vito (August), Las Alturas (April, August, September). [L]: Tortuguerro (November), Laguna Dabagri (November).

Napaea umbra
(Boisduval, 1870)
FW length: 18.5–19.5 mm   Plate 5
Range: Mexico to Brazil
Hostplant: Unknown
Early stages: Unknown
• **Adult:** Sexes similar. Upperside pale brown with thin, wavy, dark brown basal, medial, and postmedial lines; FW apex produced into a small hook, with a small white spot in the subapex. The underside is paler and has more distinct lines and markings.
Habits: This butterfly has been recorded in our area from sea level to 800 m on both slopes from a wide range of forest habitats. Typically encountered as rare, solitary individuals flying from ground level to approximately 5 m above the ground. As in *theages*, the females are encountered more often than the males. Uncommon.
Localities: [A]: Cariblanco (February–April, June, July, September, October), Rio Macho (September). [C]: Juan Viñas (March), Turrialba (June, August, December), Rio Chitaria (October), 11.5 km E of Tuis (September). [H]: San Miguel (September), La Selva (July). [P]: Sirena. [L]: 20.7 km W of Guapiles (September). [G]: Bagaces, Cañas.

Genus **VOLTINIA** Stichel, 1910

As noted by Seitz (1916), the two species of butterflies included in this genus are very dissimilar and may belong in other genera, yet the butterflies are distinct enough to identify them. However, D'Abrera (1994) relegated one species (*radiata*) to the genus *Esthemopsis*. As considered here members of *Voltinia* are found from Costa Rica to Colombia and Ecuador. There is nothing known of their hostplants or early stages, and in Costa Rica both of the species are quite rare.

Voltinia theata
Stichel, 1910
FW length: 18.5–21 mm   Plate 6

Range: Costa Rica to Colombia and Ecuador
Hostplant: Unknown
Early stages: Unknown
• **Adult:** Sexes dimorphic. *Male*—FW upperside black with reflective blue bands on FW discal area that are basal to end of cell; HW upperside black with a reflective blue discal area that is divided by three to four black lines that cross the cell area. Underside dark gray with fine dark lines that form a pattern not unlike that found on *Napaea umbra*. *Female*—similar to male but with a conspicuous white subapical band on FW on upperside. Compare with *Mesosemia hesperina, M. lamachus, M. telegone.*
Habits: This butterfly is known in Costa Rica on the strength of a single female collected at 600 m from a rain forest locality on the Atlantic slope. I am informed by G. Broom that the butterfly flew between 4 and 7 m above the ground along a forest edge during late morning. In Panama, G. B. Small collected a number of males that were perching between 15:45 and 16:15 hrs, again in a similar habitat. Rare in Costa Rican collections.
Localities: [C]: Tuis (May).

Voltinia radiata
(Godman and Salvin, 1886)
FW length: 21.5–22   Plate 6
Range: Costa Rica to Colombia
Hostplant: Unknown
Early stages: Unknown
• **Adult:** Sexes similar. Recognized by dark blue-black ground color, and by the cuneiform white rays on both wings that begin broadly at the distal margins and terminate narrowly almost to the medial area. This pattern is virtually identical on both wing surfaces. In their original description (holotype being a female, as is the specimen pictured), Godman and Salvin noted that palpi are erect, hairy, and red. The males of this butterfly are very rare in collections, but a close-up photograph of a male from Costa Rica shows pale orange palpi and a small pale orange tuft of setae on either side of the eyes. *Note*: The correct generic placement of this butterfly is open to question. It was provisionally described by Godman and Salvin in the genus *Esthemopsis*, later transferred to *Voltinia* by Stichel, and most recently returned to *Esthemopsis* by D'Abrera (1994), who figured, along with the female, a male specimen that is apparently not of this species (J. Hall, pers. comm.). Compare with *Esthemopsis, Necyria beltiana, Uraneis ucubis, Brachyglenis.*
Habits: This butterfly has been recorded in our area only from two localities on the Atlantic

slope around the Turrialba Valley between 600 and 1000 m elevation. This curious butterfly species is known only from a few specimens, and when our fauna is better known, it may eventually be shown to have a broader distribution. Given the species' extreme rarity and the tattered condition of extant specimens, a redescription of both sexes or any biological information about this butterfly would be worth publishing.

Localities: [A]: Platanar de San Carlos (January). [C]: Turrialba (June), Moravia de Chirripo (April).

Genus **CREMNA** Doubleday, 1847

All the butterflies in this genus are small, quite fragile, and have wings that are covered in intricate patterns of spots and bars. Members of *Cremna* are found from Mexico to the Amazon Basin, and, as currently understood, the genus embraces seven species, one that occurs in our area. In the past, some of the species now considered part of *Napaea* were placed in this genus.

The host records for *Cremna* are in the Orchidaceae and Bromeliaceae (Brevignon 1992; DeVries et al. 1994). The caterpillars are sparsely covered in medium-long setae and superficially resemble moth larvae in the family Pyralidae. The pupae are stoutly and bluntly cylindrical and have a very wide cremaster.

Cremna thasus subrutila
Stichel, 1910
FW length: 15.5–17 mm   **Plate 7**
Range: Mexico to Brazil. **Subspecies:** Costa Rica and Panama
Hostplant: *Oncidium* sp., *Catasetum virdiflavum, Dimerandra emarginata, Caularthron bilamellatum* (Orchidaceae), *Tilandsia bulbosa* (Bromeliaceae)
Early stages (Fig. 42): *Mature caterpillar*—body pale translucent green and sparsely covered with tufts of long, yellowish setae that curve toward the posterior and arise mainly from the lateral areas, leaving the dark midline exposed; the setae on the first thoracic segment are short. The caterpillars feed on the leaves and developing flower buds of their host plants. *Pupa*—pale brown or pale green, bluntly barrel shaped, with two dark brown dorsal spots on thorax that resemble holes; cremaster extremely broad and stout. The pupae are frequently found on their epiphytic

hostplants and look like small, brown flower buds. *Note*: The observations of Brevignon (1992) in French Guyana suggest that the caterpillars associate with *Camponotus* ants. However, my own observations of these caterpillars and ants in Panama and Costa Rica, suggest that the association is not likely to be myrmecophilous. Rather, it is a simple, nonsymbiotic interaction resulting from caterpillars feeding on a plant that is part of the ant colony's territory. Nevertheless, observations demonstrating that the caterpillars are protected by the ants would be very interesting indeed.

• **Adult:** Sexes dimorphic. *Male*—upperside black with white transverse stripes, and overshot entirely with pale iridescent orange-violet. *Female*—upperside black with sharply contrasting white stripes. Compare with *Hermathena candidata* and members of the genus *Leucochimona*.

Habits: This butterfly has been recorded from our area only from lowland Atlantic slope rain forest around the Rio Sarapiqui. In Costa Rica and Panama I have never observed males in the field. The females typically search for oviposition sites between 11:00 and 13:00 hrs, and while doing so they investigate mature and immature epiphytic orchids growing from 1 to 8 m above the ground. Females will also investigate other epiphytic plants that grow into the reaches of the forest canopy. The caterpillars can be fairly common on some local orchid populations, and the presence of pupae attached to the flowering spikes (alive or dead) suggests that some orchids are used as hosts almost throughout the year. Apparently this butterfly is considered rare throughout its range, but it is likely that part of this rarity may be due to the adults spending most of their time in the forest canopy.

Localities: [H]: Chilamate (April, May, July, October), La Selva (March, April, July).

Genus **HERMATHENA** Hewitson, 1874

The butterflies in this genus are recognized by their snow-white ground color that is set with gray spots. There are two species of butterflies in *Hermathena*, and the members of the genus range from Mexico to South America. Both species occur in Central America. As is the case for certain other members of our fauna (e.g., *Synargis nymphidioides, Thisbe lycorias*), members of *Hermathena* may be mistaken for a white species of the Pieridae. At least one species appears to feed on members of the family Bromeliaceae (DeVries et al. 1994).

Hermathena oweni
Schaus, 1913
FW length: 20–26 mm   Plate 6
Range: Mexico to Costa Rica
Hostplant: Unknown
Early stages: Unknown
• **Adult:** Sexes similar. Upperside snowy white. FW distal margin with charcoal gray spots (may be gray-green in specimens originating north of our area) that are mainly concentrated in apex and subapex and then again just above the tornus; two additional spots in FW cell, and base of both wings charcoal gray with a trace of a subbasal line. HW with spots at distal margin between the veins, plus two submarginal spots: one at the costa, the other just below it. Underside similar to upperside. Compare with *candidata.*
Habits: Since its original description, this butterfly has been included in the Costa Rican fauna on the basis of the type specimen that bears the label "Costa Rica." Because many museum collections typically have abundant material from areas north of Nicaragua yet the type was the only specimen reported from our area, the question of whether Schaus described this butterfly based on erroneous locality data had arisen. Recently, however, W. Haber has established it as a member of our fauna, thus lending some validity to the origin of the type specimen. In our area this species is known from a single cloud forest locality but may be found to have a wider distribution as our fauna becomes better known. The observations of Steinhauser from El Salvador (in Emmel et al. 1975) indicate that this butterfly is encountered in small groups, flying at or above the forest canopy level. They perch on both the upper and undersides of leaves. To the untrained eye, the butterfly may be mis-

taken for a member of the Pieridae. Obviously rare in Costa Rican collections.
Localities: Costa Rica [TL]. [P]: Monte Verde (September, October).

Hermathena candidata
(Hewitson, 1874)
FW length: 20.5–21.5 mm   Plate 6
Range: Costa Rica to Colombia, Guianas, and east of the Andes into Bolivia
Hostplant: *Vriesia* sp. (Bromeliaceae)
Early stages: *Egg*—white, laid singly on the emerging inflorescence.
• **Adult:** Sexes similar. Upperside snowy white with distinctly fused gray spots along the apex and distal margins of both wings, and a gray rectangular bar at FW costa that intrudes into the cell. Compare with *H. oweni, Synargis nymphidiodes, S. palaeste.*
Habits: This curious butterfly is encountered locally as rare, solitary individuals from 900 to 1400 m on both slopes in association with primary and secondary montane rain forests. During the few times I have observed this butterfly, both sexes were active from 08:00 until 12:30 hrs. While flying this butterfly can easily be mistaken for a member of the genera *Leptophobia* or *Catasticta* (Pieridae), which fly in the same habitats. Using binoculars, I was able to observe about 5 min of oviposition behavior in this species. On this brilliantly sunny day the female flew high in the forest subcanopy and persistently investigated a variety of epiphytic plants, including members of the Bromeliaceae, Araceae, and Orchidaceae that were growing on one particular tree. During oviposition she repeatedly landed on an emerging flower spike of the bromeliad, backed down the stalk, and deposited several individual eggs where her abdomen contacted bracts. Uncommon in Central American collections.
Localities: [SJ]: La Montura (April, May). [P]: Las Alturas (May), Monte Verde (July).

Tribe **RIODININI** Grote, 1895

This tribe embraces butterflies exhibiting a great diversity of form and size and is divided into two sections: the *Ancyluris* section and the *Riodina* section (Harvey 1987a). The members of this tribe are characterized by the posterior margin of the male tegumen that bears a deep invagination visible in dorsal view; FW R2 originates beyond the cell and arises from a common stalk with R3 and R4 (*Ancyluris* section); ostium bursa of the female is placed asymmetrically on the right side of the abdomen. The tribe contains more than three hundred species placed in over forty genera, well over half of which are represented in our area. The host records for this tribe are very diverse and include the plant families Melastomataceae, Euphorbiaceae, Vochysiaceae, Gesneriaceae, Combretaceae, Hippocrateaceae, Olacaceae, Quiinaceae, Malpighiaceae, Passifloraceae, Flacourtiaceae, Sterculiaceae, Asteraceae, Fabaceae, Ulmaceae, and others. The caterpillars are covered in a dense pile of setae (sometimes very long) and can easily be mistaken for moth caterpillars.

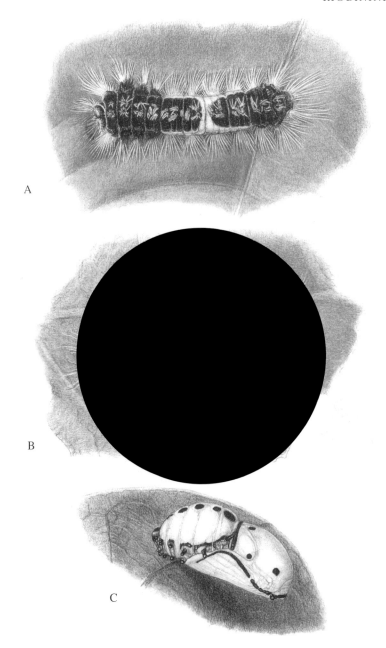

FIGURE 43. (A) *Necyria beltiana* caterpillar. (B) *Chorinea octauius* caterpillar. (C) *Lyropteryx lyra* pupa. (Drawings by J. Clark)

Genus **LYROPTERYX** Westwood, 1851

These medium-large butterflies are recognized by their broad, almost round wing shape with an astounding black, white, and red coloration that gives rise to a prominent ray pattern. Members of *Lyropteryx* are found from Mexico through Central and South America. The genus is thought to embrace about five strongly dimorphic species, three that occur entirely in South America. A revisionary treatment would prove useful in alleviating the confusion in collections and the literature regarding the proper matching of the sexes and the limits of the species. One species enters our area.

The only known host record for *Lyropte*___ in the family Vochysiaceae (DeVries ___ Observations of a single species ___ caterpillars and pupae bear___ blance to those of *Necyria*, ___ *rinea*.

In our area, and in the ___ ica, these butterflies ar___ land rain forest habitat ___ The bright coloratio___ clearly evil arctiid ___ flight behavior sugge___ may be unpalatable to ___

Lyropteryx lyra cleadas
Druce, 1875
FW length: 25.5–28.5 mm
Range: Mexico to Ecuador, B___
Mexico to Panama
Hostplant: *Vochysia guatemalensis* (Voc___
Early stages (Fig. 43): *Mature caterpillar—over___
shape similar to *Necyria beltiana*; head capsule shiny black; body densely covered in a short pile of white setae with the first two segments pale brown and the last two segments black; a conspicuous skirt of pale brown lateral setae. *Pupa*—stocky and flattened ventrally; overall color chalk white with a black dorsal spot on each abdominal segment; each side of abdomen with five short, black blunt lateral spines, and five very short, sublateral wartlike processes, with the area between colored orange-brown; five black spots on dorsum of thorax; wing pads, thorax, and slightly flanged head outlined in black.
• **Adult:** Sexes dimorphic. *Male*—upperside black with broad, blue-green margins that are divided by white between the radial veins, and HW costa with a red spot near base; underside black with white lines radiating from medial

area to distal margins of both wings, and a series of irregular red spots near the base of both wings. *Female*—upperside black with a broad red band on both wing margins that bears black radial veins and overall resembles the nymphalid *Biblis hyperia*. Compare with *Necyria beltiana*, *N. ingaretha*, *Uraneis ucubis*.
Habits: This spectacular butterfly occurs locally from sea level to 1000 m on both slopes in association with wet and rain forest habitats. The butterflies are encountered as rare, solitary individuals along forest edges, rivers, or in light gaps deep in the forest. The color pattern and conspicuous flight behavior of the male resemble the noxious day-flying arctiid moth *Hypocritta aletta*. On the other hand, the female's conspicuous black and red color and slow, ___ ing flight bears strong resemblance to ___ ___alid butterfly *Biblis hyperia* and to ___ ___oths. I once observed a fly- ___ *Tyrannus*: Tyranidae) cap- ___ take it to a perch, manip- ___ ___ents, and then reject the ___ release the butterfly ___ and slowly and con- ___ ___wings. When I exam- ___it unharmed (except ___ wings); upon being ___ ___rgetically and could ___ had I released it. ___est that this species ___redators. Uncommon. ___eo (November, Decem- ___Guacima (September). ___ Puriscal (January). [H]: ___Selva (August, June), Chila- ___er). [P]: Carrara (October, De- ___olfito (February), Sirena (July, Sep- ___er), San Vito (March).

Genus **NECYRIA** Westwood, 1851

The butterflies in this genus are closely related to *Cyrenia* and *Ancyluris* but are distinguished by the lack of tails or lobes on the hindwing, and often have a ray pattern, as seen in members of the genus *Lyropteryx*. In fact, *N. ingaretha* was long placed in the latter genus. There are twelve species in *Necyria*, three of which are Central American; only two occur in our area.

The hostplants for two species of *Necyria* include the Melastomataceae, Gesneriaceae, and Vochysiaceae (DeVries et al. 1994). Such a diversity of hostplant families suggests that the

host range for the genus may be even broader. In general form and ornamentation, the caterpillars and pupae resemble those of *Ancyluris* and *Lyropteryx*.

Necyria beltiana
Hewitson, 1870
FW length: 26–27.5 mm   **Plate 7**
Range: Nicaragua to Panama
Hostplant: *Conostegia xalapensis* (Melastomataceae), *Vochysia guatamalensis* (Vochysiaceae), *Drymonia* sp. (Gesneriaceae)
Early stages: I. Chacon provides the following descriptions: *Egg*—a white, flattened sphere with a reddish central area. Eggs are laid on the underside of leaves at the confluence of major veins or where the petioles join the stem. A female may lay over ten individual eggs on the same branch. *Mature caterpillar* (Fig. 43)—when viewed from above, the entire body is covered in a dense pile of short black setae with a conspicuous saddle of two large white triangles located slightly toward the posterior from the center of the body. The apices of these triangles meet at a black dorsal midline, and their broad bases are at a ventral skirt of longish black setae. Head capsule is unmarked pale brown. *Pupa*—stocky and flattened ventrally; overall yellow; each side of abdomen with five short, black blunt lateral spines, and five very short, sublateral wartlike processes, with the area between colored orange-brown; several black spots on dorsum of thorax; wing pads, thorax, and slightly flanged head outlined in black.
Adult: Sexes dimorphic. *Male*—upperside blue-black with an iridescent blue-green submarginal band on both wings that bears white highlights on the radial veins, and FW apex elongate; underside dark blue with an intense iridescent sheen, a medial red spot near FW inner margin, and sides of abdomen with a reddish lateral line. *Female*—upperside similar to male, but with white ray pattern more pronounced and rounded FW apex; underside blue-black without iridescence and a broad white cuneiform ray pattern along margins of both wings. Both sexes can readily be identified in the field with the aid of binoculars. Compare with *ingaretha, Lyropteryx lyra, Uraneis ucubis, Voltinia radiata.*
Habits: This butterfly has been recorded in our area from 400 to 1300 m on the Atlantic slope in association with wet forest habitats mainly within Parque Braulio Carrillo and the Turrialba Valley. Encountered as rare, solitary individuals along rivers and forest edges. The males perch high in the canopy on top of leaves that are illuminated by sunlight between 11:00 and 13:30 hrs. The males are extremely fast fliers and dart out and chase any dark-colored insects that fly past, and then they generally return to the same leaf they used as a perch. The females are also active at the same time of day, but they have a slow, floppy flight that shows the color patterns on the underside to advantage. Twice I observed females searching for oviposition sites about 5 to 10 m above ground, and both times they persistently investigated the terminal leaves of trees that were growing along a forest edge. I. Chacon informs me that a female may lay single eggs repeatedly on the same plant during an oviposition bout. Uncommon.
Localities: [A]: Cariblanco (June, August, September), Quebrada Honda nr Crucero (February). [C]: Moravia de Chirripo (February, July). [SJ]: Carrillo (July). [H]: Plastico (February–May, July, August, October, December), Tirimbina (February), Magsaysay (January). [L]: Guapiles (March).

Necyria ingaretha
(Hewitson, 1872)
FW length: 25–27.5 mm   **Plate 6**
Range: Nicaragua to Costa Rica.
Hostplant: *Vochysia guatamalensis* (Vochysiaceae)
Early stages: I. Chacon informs me that the mature caterpillar is extremely similar to that of *N. beltiana*, but differs by having the head capsule with a dark ecdysial suture. The pupa differs from that of *N. beltiana* by having a row of black subdorsal spots on the abdomen.
• **Adult:** Sexes presumably dimorphic. *Male* (not illustrated)—similar to that of *beltiana*, but differs by having less distinct blue-green iridescent marginal bands on FW and HW upperside and a red spot (sometimes indistinct) at the HW anal margin; underside differs from *beltiana* by having less iridescent blue-green on both wings, a red spot at the HW anal margin (sometimes indistinct), and an orange lateral band on the sides of the abdomen. *Female*—upperside black with white marginal band composed of elongate triangles; underside blue-black with white marginal ray pattern and a conspicuous red patch at the HW inner margin. *Note*: The history of this butterfly is interesting. For many years it was known only from a handful of female specimens; in addition to its placement by some authors in the genus *Lyropteryx*, the male has always been assumed to be unknown. However, recent work (J. Hall, pers. comm.) indicates that the male has been represented abundantly in most collections for many years, but specimens have been con-

founded under *N. beltiana*. Compare with *beltiana, Lyropteryx lyra, Uraneis ucubis, Hades noctula, Voltinia radiata,* and the lycaenid *Eumaeus godartii.*

Habits: This rare butterfly, until recently known from only a few female specimens (all but one originating from Costa Rica), was an enduring enigma. At present, the problem of getting a better understanding of its distribution depends upon sorting out the males from series of *beltiana,* something that will occur too late for inclusion here. In our area the butterfly has been positively recorded from the Atlantic slope in montane forest habitats from 700 to 1000 m elevation. Although I have never seen the female of this butterfly in the field, its form and pattern suggest that it could be confused with the common species *Hades noctula* or the aposematic lycaenid genus *Eumaeus,* whereas the male certainly resembles *Necyria beltiana.* Given the peculiar history of this spectacular butterfly, careful observations on its natural history would be worthy of publication.

Localities: [C]: Moravia de Chirripo (July), La Suiza (September), Orosi. [H]: Plastico (February, March).

Genus **CYRENIA** Westwood, 1851

These butterflies have a robust body, a small head, and red on the abdomen, as seen in *Ancyluris* and *Necyria.* But butterflies in the genus *Cyrenia* do not have iridescent or metallic colors, and the hindwing is without a pronounced tail (although the female has an incipient one). The single species of *Cyrenia* ranges from Costa Rica to the Amazon Basin. In Central America this butterfly is very rare, but it apparently can be abundant in some areas of South America. Although there is nothing known of its hostplants or early stages, it is probable that they will resemble those of *Ancyluris* and *Necyria.*

Cyrenia martia pyrippe
Godman and Salvin, 1878
FW length: 20.5–21.5 mm   **Plate 6**
Range: Costa Rica to Peru, Brazil. **Subspecies:** Costa Rica and Panama
Hostplant: Unknown
Early stages: Unknown
• **Adult:** Sexes slightly dimorphic. *Male*—upperside black with a blue-gray cast at the base of the wings; FW with oblong white medial band; HW with two conspicuous red spots—one at

costa, one at inner margin, and a white spot in medial area. *Female*—more gray in ground color; HW distal margin with a distinct lobe. Cannot be confused with anything else from our fauna.

Habits: This unusual butterfly has been recorded in our area from two adjacent lowland Atlantic rain forest localities. On a single occasion in 1978 at approximately 10:30 hrs, I observed a small aggregation of males and females visiting flowers of an *Inga* sp. tree that was growing along a forest edge. The butterflies flew quite rapidly and literally buzzed around the flowers in a manner reminiscent of *Ancyluris.* Given the proclivity of collectors through the years, it seems odd that such a conspicuous butterfly can be so rare in Central America. However, this is a quintessential trait of many riodinids; inexplicable rarity. G. Austin informs me that in Rondonia, Brazil, this species is apparently most frequently seen in the canopy.

Localities: [H]: Puerto Viejo (August), Chilamate (September).

Genus **ANCYLURIS** Hübner, 1819

It is definitely a memorable experience to observe an *Ancyluris* butterfly at close quarters for the first time. These distinctive butterflies are immediately recognized by their black upperside set with orange, scarlet, or white bands, and long tails on the hindwing, appearing as miniature swallowtails (Papilionidae). Generally, if not always, the sexes are dimorphic; the males bear a gleaming iridescence on the underside, and the females are more somberly colored. In older literature these butterflies have been referred to under the name *Erycina.* The only revisionary study of this spectacular group was that of Saunders (1859). Members of *Ancyluris* are found from Mexico throughout Central and South America, and the genus embraces twenty-seven mostly South American species. There are two, perhaps three Central American species, two that definitely occur in our area.

The known hostplants reported for *Ancyluris* are in the Melastomataceae and Euphorbiaceae (DeVries et al. 1994). The caterpillars are covered with a short pile of setae and bear long lateral tufts of setae that make them look like larvae in the moth families Arctiidae and Lymantriidae. The caterpillars are docile, and at least in *A. inca* they may be encountered in sizable groups composed of all instars.

During the early morning, these butterflies (especially males) are frequently met with visiting wet soil along road-cuts and streams. Both sexes may be observed flying high in the canopy visiting trees bearing small white or yellow flowers. In Costa Rica the genus may be found from sea level to well over 2000 m in virtually all habitats. Although present in a wide range of habitats, in Costa Rica the adults are rarely observed in large numbers, even at sites where the caterpillars may be abundant.

Ancyluris inca inca
(Saunders, 1850)

FW length: 21–25.5 mm   **Plate 7**
Range: Mexico to Colombia **Subspecies:** Mexico to Panama
Hostplant: *Miconia argentea, M. elata, M.* spp (Melastomataceae)
Early stages (Fig. 44): *Egg*—white, highly sculptured, laid singly in leaf axils or in fissures on stems and branches of the hostplant. *Caterpillars*—early instars eat the shell and are pale orange with short tufts of black setae. *Mature caterpillar*—body orange, densely piled with short setae; wide orange dorsal band bearing erect tufts of dorsal setae runs the length of body; bordered by wide black subdorsal bands set with white spots on all abdominal segments except the sixth (which is an orange band) and last two which are also orange. Long tufts of orange lateral setae on all segments are motile, and twitch when caterpillar is disturbed; head capsule pale brown. All instars feed by chewing holes in the leaf underside but not destroying the many leaf veins. The feeding damage, and the fact that caterpillars frequently become dusted with the leaf pubescence after feeding, makes them very cryptic. The caterpillars are frequently encountered in groups composed of various instars (first through fifth) within a semirolled leaf. However, they are somewhat cannibalistic, and in times of stress the smaller instars may provide food for the larger ones. Several times I have observed fourth and fifth instar caterpillars eaten by medium-sized jumping spiders (Salticidae). *Pupa*—overall pale green, stocky, and flattened ventrally; each side of abdomen with six medium-sized, black blunt lateral spines, and four very short, sublateral spines; two black spots on dorsum at interface of thorax and abdomen; wing pads outlined in black, and two very short, black laterally projecting spines on head.

• **Adult:** Sexes dimorphic. *Male*—FW black with a conspicuous orange band running from costa, across cell, to inner margin near tornus; HW with iridescent blue at base of tail. Underside overshot entirely with deep, iridescent blue; FW with orange spot on inner margin near tornus; HW with orange spot near inner margin and a white spot in tornus. *Female*—FW upperside with broad orange band that runs from costa, across cell, ending in a curve just before the tornus; HW with iridescent blue near tornus, and an orange triangular spot on costa. FW underside black with white spots in FW apex, and an orange band from costa to tornus; HW with an orange band running from costa to inner margin, and distal margin set with white spots. Both sexes are easily identified in the field with the aid of binoculars. Cannot be confused with any other riodinid species, although when flying the female might be confounded with the genus *Callicore* (Nymphalidae).

Habits: This butterfly occurs in our area from sea level to 1400 m on both slopes in association with all types of forested habitats. Generally encountered as solitary individuals along forest edges, rivers, and in large light gaps, but occasionally found in small concentrated populations. The males perch on the undersides of leaves of high forest subcanopy trees to low second-growth vegetation from 08:00 to 10:00 hrs, and during these times they chase other insects in rapid, erratic sorties. The females actively search for oviposition sites between 11:00 and 13:30 hrs. When a female finds a suitable plant, she slowly walks down the main stem (often backwards), probing crevices in the bark with her ovipositor. When an appropriate place is found, a single egg is deposited in a fissure in the bark, and she flies a short distance and suns herself. A single individual may return to the same plant and oviposit numerous times. Acceptable plants for oviposition range from small saplings to trees over 6 m tall. Both sexes visit flowers of *Lantana, Alibertia, Tetrathylacium, Cordia, Croton, Mikania,* and various Asteraceae.

Localities: [A]: Cariblanco (June), Atenas (January, December). [C]: Tapanti (March), Turrialba (August–October). [SJ]: Santa Anna (February), Hacienda El Rodeo (August–October), San Jose (September), Santa Rosa de Puriscal (January, September), Carrillo. [H]: Magsaysay (July), La Selva (September, October), Chilamate (July–October), Plastico (June, September, October). [P]: San Vito (April–September), Sirena (March), and many other localities throughout the country.

Ancyluris jurgensenii jurgensenii
(Saunders, 1850)
FW length: 22–25 mm   **Plate 8**
Range: Mexico to Colombia. **Subspecies:** Mexico to Panama
Hostplant: *Hyeronima oblonga* (Euphorbiaceae)
Early stages: *Egg*—laid singly on twigs, stems, and inflated stipules of saplings and small trees. I have watched individual females oviposit in bouts of three, rest for a few minutes in a sunny spot, and then repeat the performance. In this way a single plant may receive a dozen or so eggs. *Early instars*—first-second instars have an entirely yellowish body with long white lateral setae. The larvae initially feed on the inflated stipules near the petioles, and then switch to feeding on underside of young leaves, making irregular-shaped holes on the leaves. *Mature caterpillars*—overall covered in a dense, short pile of white setae with two conspicuous black rectangles on the dorsum (one on the anterior third, the other on the posterior third), a conspicuous black dorsal line, and a lateral skirt of longer black setae; posterior segment with long tufts of black lateral setae, with the dorsal segments colored brown; head capsule shiny brown. *Pupa*—in general shape and color similar to that of *A. inca* but with the dorsum of the abdomen colored reddish brown; the six larger lateral spines on the abdomen are yellow except for the anteriormost pair, which is black.
• **Adult:** Sexes dimorphic. *Male*—FW upperside black with a crimson medial band running from costa to inner margin, and a faint iridescent blue postmedial band; HW upperside with a crimson band running from costa almost to tornus, distal margin with iridescent blue band. FW underside black overshot with intense, iridescent blue, and a crimson medial spot at inner margin; HW underside with iridescent blue bands at margin and base, a crimson spot at inner margin, and a white spot at base of tail. *Female*—FW upperside black with broad white medial band that contains a distinct crimson spot at costa and a thin white postmedial band; HW upperside black with a broad white medial band running from costa almost to tornus, a broad, curved crimson band running from inner margin to posterior end of white medial band, base of tail with an isolated crimson spot next to a white spot at anal margin. Underside with same pattern. Compare with *Rhetus periander, R. dysonii*.
Habits: This butterfly is recorded in our area from sea level to 1400 m on both slopes in association with wet forest habitats. Typically encountered as solitary individuals in local populations along forest edges, rivers, and in large light gaps, or in second growth surrounded by primary forest. The males perch on the undersides of leaves from approximately 07:00 to 09:00 hrs, between 5 and 10 m above the ground, and chase other insects in rapid, erratic sorties. The females are active during midday. Both sexes visit flowers of *Inga, Croton, Serjania, Cordia*, and various Asteraceae. Uncommon.
Localities: [A]: San Mateo (July, October), Florencia de San Carlos (June). [C]: Turrialba (April, June–September), Juan Viñas (September, October), La Florida [H]: Plastico (June), La Selva (February), Chilamate (July). [P]: Sirena (March, June, November), Llorona (March), San Vito (April, July, October). [L]: Limon.

Ancyluris cacica cacica
(Felder and Felder, 1865)
FW length: 21–24 mm   **Not illustrated**
Range: Nicaragua(?) to Peru. **Subspecies:** Nicaragua(?), Colombia, and Peru
Hostplant: Unknown
Early stages: Unknown
• **Adult:** Sexes dimorphic. *Male*—FW upperside black with a broad red to magenta band running from costa, across cell, and terminating at inner margin near tornus; HW upperside with similar red band running from costa into or across the cell, and with a distal patch of iridescent blue near the tornus; underside overshot with blue iridescence; a red patch at the FW and HW inner margins. *Female*—apparently undescribed, but likely to be similar to that of *jurgensenii*. Compare with *jurgensenii*.
Habits: This butterfly has been reported from Central America on the basis of a single specimen in the collection of Boisduval (see Godman and Salvin 1885, pp. 394–395). However, no other specimens have been seen thus far, and its presence in Central America remains unconfirmed; it seems unlikely to be part of our fauna. It is possible the specimen in question (which I have not seen) may have been a misidentified specimen of *jurgensenii*. This butterfly is included here as a possible member of our fauna, and certainly this is a record that requires confirmation.
Localities: "Nicaragua"—specimen in British Museum of Natural History.

Genus **RHETUS** Swainson, 1829

The members of this genus all have long tails and in general form resemble the members of

Ancyluris. However, *Rhetus* butterflies are recognized by their noticeably long palpi and lack of iridescence on the underside of the wings as in *Ancyluris.* There are no problems separating the species, although it is apparent that size, shape, and color of certain spots and bands in these butterflies are quite variable, often within the same population (perhaps making some of the subspecies names of little utility). In older literature, the butterflies here have been referred to under the name *Diorina.* Although out of date, the revision by Saunders (1859) remains a useful taxonomic reference. The genus *Rhetus* contains four species, three of which are wide ranging and occur in our area.

The hostplant records for these butterflies include the Combretaceae and Euphorbiaceae (DeVries et al. 1994). The caterpillar of *Rhetus* is covered in a dense pile of setae, bears tufts of elongate lateral setae, and in general appears much like a tiny caterpillar of the genus *Battus* (Papilionidae). In overall form, the early stages show clear affinities to *Ancyluris, Necyria, Lyropteryx,* and *Chorinea.*

In Costa Rica these butterflies are found in a wide range of habitats from sea level to 2000 m. They are fast flying, generally found as solitary individuals, and may be found visiting wet soil along roadcuts and streams during the early mornings; later in the morning both sexes may visit flowers high in the forest canopy.

Rhetus arcius castigatus
Stichel, 1909
FW length: 18–18.5 mm   Plate 8
Range: Mexico to Brazil, Bolivia. **Subspecies:** Mexico to Costa Rica
Hostplant: *Terminalia amazonica* (Combretaceae), *Mabea occidentalis* (Euphorbiaceae)
Early stages (Fig. 44): *Egg*—white, laid singly on stems or in leaf axils. *Mature caterpillar*—head shiny black with a white transverse line on epicranium; body dull, velvety black with subdorsal tufts of short red setae on either side of the dorsal line; each segment bears a lateral tuft of long white setae, of which the anterior and posterior-most setae are longest; two tufts of long black setae on the first thoracic segment that articulate back and forth while the caterpillar walks, not unlike the motile larval tubercles of the nymphalid genera *Melinea* or *Danaus*; abdominal segments 5 and 6 each with an obvious half-moon-shaped patch of short, cream-colored setae. In overall appearance, the caterpillar appears quite similar to a small *Battus* caterpillar (Papilionidae)—perhaps a diminutive form of mimicry. The caterpillars feed on soft young leaves. *Pupa*—over-

all lime green color with five short black lateral spines, and three very short black sublateral spines on each side of abdomen; a black dorsal spot on first abdominal segment; wing pads and the slight flange on head outlined in black. The general shape is very similar to the pupa of *Ancyluris.*
• **Adult:** Sexes slightly dimorphic. *Male*—FW upperside black with a broad white basal band, and a thin postmedial band running from costa to tornus; HW upperside with a white medial band that runs from costa, across cell, then becomes pale metallic blue and continues to the end to the HW tail, red spot (or spots) at base of tail, and thorax pale metallic blue; underside similar except a red spot at base of FW costa, and no metallic blue except for a few areas near base of tail. *Female*—similar to male except without metallic blue, and red spots at base of tail typically more pronounced. Compare with *dysonii.*
Habits: This butterfly is widespread in our area, found from sea level to 1400 m on both slopes in association with all forest types. Typically encountered as solitary individuals along forest edges, rivers, and in large light gaps, or in second-growth vegetation that is surrounded by forest; occasionally in pastures or in cities (migrating?). In montane habitats I found that the males perch on the undersides of leaves from approximately 06:30 to 08:30 hrs from 3 to 8 m above the ground. While perching, these butterflies chase other insects in rapid, erratic sorties, often returning to the same perch. In lowland habitats in Panama, G. Small found the males perching between 09:00 and 09:30 hrs. The females are active during late morning until midday. Both sexes are often found with other species of Lepidoptera visiting a variety of small, white-flowered plants including *Inga, Croton, Serjania, Cordia,* and various herbaceous Asteraceae.
Localities: [A]: Cariblanco (June), Alajuela (September), San Mateo (October). [C]: Turrialba (June, August), Desamparados (April, August, September), Cachi, Guatili. [SJ]: Curridibat (April), El Rodeo (March), San Jose (September, October), Desamparados (August), Patarra (December), Santana (July, August), Guatuso, Carrillo. [H]: Tibas (February), La Selva (October). [P]: San Vito (July, September, December), San Luis at Rio Guacimal (August). [G]: Santa Rosa (July), Volcan Santa Maria.

Rhetus dysonii caligosus
Stichel, 1929
FW length: 20.5–22 mm   Plate 8

Range: Costa Rica to Peru, Brazil. **Subspecies:** Costa Rica to Colombia
Hostplant: Unknown
Early stages: Unknown
• **Adult:** Sexes dimorphic. *Male*—FW upperside black with dark reflective blue medial area, white postbasal and postmedial bands, both that may be indistinct; HW upperside dark blue with indistinct white bands, a conspicuous scarlet crescent running from inner margin to tornus, and a short, broad-based tail; underside similar to upperside but with red at the base of costa. *Female*—similar to male except without reflective blue, and the medial bands are wider and more distinct. *Note:* Specimens from Guanacaste may have wider white bands and a more intense blue. Compare with *arcius* and *periander.*
Habits: This butterfly is found locally on both slopes in association with rain forest habitats between 1000 and 1500 m elevation. The males are encountered as solitary individuals between 08:30 and 11:30 hrs along forest edges and rivers where they perch between 3 and 5 m above the ground. While perching, they chase other insects in rapid, erratic sorties, often returning to the same perch. During extended periods of dry weather, the males may be found visiting fresh bird droppings on the rocks and boulders in montane rivers and streams. The females fly from 10:00 to 12:00 hrs in shaded light gaps, forest edges, and along rivers. Both sexes visit flowers of *Ocotea, Conostegia, Croton,* and other trees with small white flowers. Uncommon in Costa Rican collections.
Localities: [A]: Guacima (September). [C]: Moravia de Chirripo (February), Juan Viñas. [SJ]: Desamparados (April, September). [P]: Las Alturas (March, September, November, December), San Vito (January, March, June, July). [G]: Volcan Cacao (February).

Rhetus periander naevianus
Stichel, 1910
FW length: 21.5–24.5 mm   **Plate 8**
Range: Mexico to Brazil, Argentina. **Subspecies:** Honduras to Costa Rica
Hostplant: Unknown
Early stages: Unknown
• **Adult:** Sexes dimorphic. *Male*—FW upperside deep reflective blue with an indistinct, white postmedial band, and broad black apex; HW upperside with a white medial band that may be indistinct in some specimens but conspicuous in others, and two conspicuous crimson spots along inner margin and one at base of tail; underside dull gray-black; distinct white medial bands, FW costal margin red from base to cell, and the crimson spots on inner margin and base of tail overshot with reflective blue. *Female*—similar to male except without reflective blue on the upperside, the white postbasal and postmedial bands are conspicuous, and the HW tail is very broad. Compare with *dysonii, arcius, Ancyluris jurgensenii, Rodinia calpharnia.*
Habits: This butterfly is found locally in association with wet forest habitats on both slopes from sea level to 1400 m. The males perch on the underside of leaves in the subcanopy of the forest along forest edges, streams, and in large light gaps from 07:30 to 09:30 hrs during sunny weather. Typically, perching areas seldom contain more than two males at a time. When making sorties the males chase many other types of insects with a fast erratic flight. Individuals do not appear to return to the same perches after a sortie, but rather perch at various places along a particular edge. The females are active between 08:00 and 11:00 hrs in the forest understory, and along ridge-top trails. Both sexes visit the small white flowers of various Melastomataceae and *Croton* spp. Uncommon in Costa Rican collections.
Localities: [SJ]: Carrillo (September). [C]: Turrialba (June). [H]: La Selva (January, April, June–August), Chilamate (July). [P]: San Vito (June, July), Las Alturas (August, November). [L]: Guapiles.

Genus **CHORINEA** Gray, 1832

The butterflies in this distinct genus are immediately recognized by looking like diminutive, transparent, winged swallowtails. In fact, members of *Chorinea* are reminiscent of the Southeast Asian genus *Lamproptera* (Papilionidae). Closely allied to *Rhetus,* the butterflies in *Chorinea* are distinct by having palpi that are reduced into a very short cone. As currently understood, the genus embraces about seven mainly South American species, including one that occurs in our area. In older literature these butterflies have been referred to under the generic name *Zeonia.*

The hostplant families reported for *Chorinea* include Aquifoliaceae, Celastraceae, Flacourtiaceae (Beizanko et al. 1978), and Hippocrateaceae (DeVries et al. 1994). The caterpillars have a wonderful dense pile of short setae, possess tufts of long lateral setae, and bear an overall similarity to those of *Ancyluris.* The pupa strongly resembles that of *Rhetus.*

Range: Costa Rica to Venezuela. **Subspecies:** Costa Rica and Panama

Hostplant: *Heisteria* sp. (Olacaceae)

Early stages: *Egg*—pink, flattened disks with a scalloped rim and two concentric circles around the micropyle. Laid cluster of forty-five to fifty, with rims touching on the upperside of old leaves.

• **Adult:** Sexes similar. Immediately recognized by the elongate black FW with elongate white submarginal spots; HW discal area reddish with white spots set in black margins; abdomen orange with a black dorsal line. Both sexes vary with regards to the amount of reddish and black on the HW. Compare with *Hyposcada virginiana* (Nymphalidae: Ithomiinae).

Habits: This striking butterfly occurs locally from 700 to 1400 m on both slopes in association with wet forest habitats, encountered as solitary individuals flying in the forest understory or in shady light gaps and trails. Judging from collections, and my own experience with it, this butterfly is apparently rather seasonal, appearing only during the drier portions of the year. The males are active in shady forest understory from 08:30 to 09:30 hrs when they perch on the upperside of vegetation about 0.5 m above the ground. An individual male will walk about on the top of a leaf and pulse its wings open and shut for a few minutes, then fly around in an erratic circle and re-perch in the same general vicinity. The flight behavior is remarkably like the ithomiine *Hyposcada virginiana* (which flies in the same areas), including the habit of soaring for short distances on air currents with the wings held open at about a 145-degree angle. During flight, and even in collections, this butterfly may be mistaken for members of the nymphalid genera *Heliconius*, *Eueides*, *Eresia*, or *Hyposcada*. In addition to deceiving vertebrates, the mimetic appearance of this butterfly may also deceive insects. On one occasion I observed a male *Heliconius hecalesia* persistently court a perched *Ithomeis* male for over 10 min! The females may be observed actively searching for oviposition sites along forest edges and in the forest understory between 10:00 and 12:30 hrs. Although I have never observed this butterfly visiting flowers, I have repeatedly observed individual males visiting and feeding on pellets of fresh Lepidoptera larval frass that had fallen to rest on top of the leaves of understory plants, and on pellets that were scattered on the forest floor. Uncommon.

Localities: [A]: Cariblanco. [C]: Navarro (January), Tres Rios (October), Juan Viñas (February, June, August, October), San Geronimo, Cachi. [P]: San Vito (March, April, September), Monte Verde (September, November).

Genus **BRACHYGLENIS** Felder, 1862

The members of *Brachyglenis* are recognized by their short white palpi that are appressed to the face, and by a forewing cell that is particularly short. Members of the genus are found from Mexico throughout Central and South America and have been referred to in older literature under *Tmetoglene*. As currently understood, *Brachyglenis* encompasses seven species, although the limits of these taxa are unclear. There are four species in our area (one of which may be misplaced here), all of which are uncommon. There is nothing known of the hostplants or early stages for any species.

The butterflies in this genus have hyaline wings and are involved in mimicry complexes that embrace geometrid, arctiid, and notodontid moths, ithomiine butterflies, and members of the riodinid genera *Lepricornis* and *Esthemopsis*.

Brachyglenis esthema
Felder and Felder, 1862

FW length: 21.5–23 mm   **Plate 25**

Range: Costa Rica to Colombia, Ecuador

Hostplant: Unknown

Early stages: Unknown

• **Adult:** Sexes similar. FW upperside dark blue-black with indistinct white lines between the veins that radiate outward from base to the submargin; apex entirely blue-black, an indistinct subapical bar fuses with a distinct, broad white subapical band that begins at the costa and curves toward the tornus at the distal margin. HW upperside with indistinct white lines radiating out from base to blue-black margin. The radial pattern is more distinct when viewed from the underside. The abdomen is blue-black on dorsum and ventrally orange from its base to the posterior end. Compare with *dinora*, *Esthemopsis colaxes*, *Lepricornis strigosa*.

Habits: This butterfly has been found from sea level to 1400 m on the Pacific slope in association with primary forest habitats, with one record from a lowland rain forest on the Atlantic slope. Encountered as rare, solitary individuals during the early morning flying low to the ground along forest edges and rivers. The clumsy flight behavior gives the impression that the butterflies are weak fliers. However, when alarmed these butterflies are swift, agile fliers. Uncommon.

Localities: [A]: Upala (November). [SJ]: Santa Rosa de Puriscal (November). [P]: San Vito (March–May, July, September), Las Alturas (September), Rincon de Osa (July). [G]: Pitilla (April).

Brachyglenis dinora
(Bates, 1866)
FW length: 21.5–23 mm   Plate 8
Range: Nicaragua to Colombia
Hostplant: Unknown
Early stages: Unknown
• **Adult:** Sexes similar. Upperside with transparent medial areas of both wings (which may have a sprinkling of white scales), thorax and all distal margins reflective blue-black; FW with a distinct, dark medial band that curves slightly from costa to distal margin almost at tornus; HW tornus produced into a rounded tooth, and the sides of abdomen orange-red. Compare with *esthema*, *Esthemopsis colaxes*, and *Lepricornis strigosa*.
Habits: This butterfly occurs locally in our area from 400 to 1400 m on both slopes in association with rain forest habitats. Encountered as rare, solitary individuals along forest edges and in light gaps. Uncommon.
Localities: [A]: Florencia de San Carlos (March). [C]: Rio Chitaria (December), La Suiza (September). [SJ]: Carrillo (February–April). [L]: Guapiles (February). [G]: Volcan Santa Maria (June).

Brachyglenis dodone
(Godman and Salvin, 1886)
FW length: 21–21.5 mm   Plate 8
Range: Mexico to Panama. **Subspecies:** Costa Rica and Panama
Hostplant: Unknown
Early stages: Unknown
• **Adult:** Sexes similar. FW upperside dark blue-black with well-defined white lines between the veins that radiate outward from base and terminate at a distinct blue-black subapical bar that runs almost straight from costa to just above the tornus, and a conspicuous, elliptical white subapical band that begins at the costa and runs to the distal margin well above the tornus. HW upperside with well-defined white lines radiating out from base to thin blue-black margin, and a tornus that is slightly elongated. The abdomen is blue-black on dorsum and bright orange ventrally. Compare with *dinora*, *Esthemopsis colaxes*, *E. clonia*, *Lepricornis strigosa*.

Habits: This butterfly has been recorded in our area from two localities: one from a site in lowland rain forest on the Atlantic slope at 400 m, and the other from montane rainforest at 1400 m on the Pacific slope. I encountered this butterfly twice at Las Alturas, both times between 08:30 and 09:30 hrs along a trail deep in the forest. In Panama, G. Small found males perching between 12:00 and 12:45 hrs. Rare in Costa Rican collections.
Localities: [P]: Las Alturas (September). [L]: Guapiles (August).

Brachyglenis nr dodone
FW length: 21–21.5 mm   Plate 25
Range: Costa Rica and Panama
Hostplant: Unknown
Early stages: Unknown
• **Adult:** Sexes similar. Upperside ground color blue-gray with gray bands between the veins that radiate out from the base to the distal margins (especially prominent on HW); no gray in the FW cell. A conspicuous white FW postmedial band runs from costa to tornus but terminates before reaching the distal tornal margin. The area surrounding the head, the palpi, the frons, and the forelegs (males only) are orange; lateral areas of abdomen gray, with a dark band on the venter. *Note:* The possession of the orange palpi and "neck" is similar to features found on *Lepricornis* or *Esthemopsis* and the butterfly is provisionally placed here until further study reveals its true relationships. Compare with *Brachyglenis esthema*, *B. dinora*, *Lepricornis strigosa*, *Esthemopsis colaxes*.
Habits: This butterfly has been reported from our area in forest habitats at approximately 400 m elevation on the Atlantic slope, and from 1000 to 1400 m on the Pacific slope. Again, I am uncertain as to the proper generic placement of this butterfly (which is likely undescribed), but include it as one of the many mysteries of our riodinid fauna worth pursuing. Rare in Costa Rican collections.
Localities: [P]: San Vito (August), Las Alturas (September). [L]: Guapiles (August).

Genus **MONETHE** Westwood, 1851

The butterflies in this genus are recognized by their black and yellow coloration, the sharp angle at the interface of the inner margin and the tornus of the forewing, and their stout body. Members of this genus are found from Nicaragua south to the Guianas and the Amazon Basin and are a component of mimicry complexes

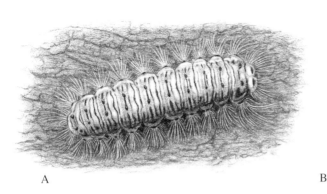

FIGURE 45. (A) *Melanis pixie* caterpillar. (B) *Melanis pixie* pupa. (Drawings by J. Clark)

that include other riodinid genera as well as geometrid, notodontid, and arctiid moths (Fig. 19). As currently understood, *Monethe* contains four species, although Seitz (1917) recognized only two. Most of the taxa occur only in South America, and one occurs in our area. There is nothing known of the hostplants or early stages for any species. In Ecuador I found these butterflies visiting mammal dung along river banks.

Monethe rudolphus rudolphus
Godman and Salvin, 1885
FW length: 18–19 mm   **Plate 7**
Range: Nicaragua to Guyana. **Subspecies:** Nicaragua to Colombia
Hostplant: Unknown
Early stages: Unknown
• **Adult:** Sexes similar. Upperside dull black set with a flat yellow ellipse in the FW medial area, a small yellow bar in the subapex; HW medial area entirely flat yellow with broad black margins. Underside with more extensive flat yellow areas and a conspicuous row of white spots set in the black HW margin. Compare with *Pachythone gigas*, *Setabis cleomedes*, *Chamaelimnas villagomes*.
Habits: This curious little butterfly is known only from rain forest habitats on the Atlantic slope between sea level and 1200 m elevation. I. Chacon informs me that the single specimen taken by him was flying along a forest edge. In the Darien Peninsula of Panama, G. Small found that this butterfly was common from early to late morning along forest edges. I have never seen it alive in Costa Rica.

Localities: [A]: Cariblanco (October). [C]: Moravia de Chirripo (August). [L]: Cunabri (July), Limon (July).

Genus **MELANIS** Hübner, 1819

In Central America, these butterflies may be recognized by the black ground color with bright yellow and/or red on the wings, a small head, long antennae, and a robust abdomen. Members of *Melanis* are found from the southwestern USA south to Argentina, and the genus is thought to embrace nearly forty, mostly South American species plus as many subspecies—a reliable indication that the genus needs revision. Three species occur in our area; none pose any problems in identification. In a large percentage of the literature, these butterflies have been referred to under the synonym *Lymnas*.

Available records indicate that the hostplants of *Melanis* are trees in the family Fabaceae (Kaye 1921; Jorgensen 1932; Hayward 1973; Scott 1986; DeVries et al. 1994). The caterpillars are covered in a dense pile of short setae, form no association with ants, and may be gregarious as caterpillars and pupae.

In Costa Rica, members of *Melanis* are found in virtually all lowland habitats below about 1200 m. These butterflies may show seasonally marked population explosions at the local level, during which they may literally swarm over trees that are in flower. In overall appearance and behavior these butterflies have a decidedly aposematic demeanor that calls to mind moths in the families Arctiidae, Geometridae, and Notodontidae and the riodinid genera *Xenandra* and *Pterographium.* Although I have no direct evidence, I would not be surprised to find that these butterflies are unpalatable to vertebrate predators.

Melanis pixie sanguinea
(Stichel, 1910)
FW length: 21–24 mm   **Plate 9**
Range: Texas to Brazil **Subspecies:** Costa Rica to Panama
Hostplant: *Albizia caribea, Inga* sp., *Pithecellobium* spp. (Fabaceae)
Early stages (Fig. 45): *Egg*—pale green, deposited in small clusters of ten to thirty on underside of leaves, stems, or the bark of the plant. Hatching is synchronous, and all of the caterpillar instars are gregarious. The first instar may eat a portion of the egg, but generally the egg shell is left relatively intact. *Mature caterpillar*—body cream colored with trace of green; each segment with a thin black dorsal line, and a black spot on either end bearing a short rosette of setae; lateral parts of each segment with a thin black line, often with an indistinct black line to either side of central line; the sublateral portion of each segment lobed outward, bearing a distinct, central black spot, and tufts of white setae project outward; the second thoracic segment bears a tuft of lateral setae that are directed forward; head shiny black with a sparse covering of short, white setae. *Pupa*—body may range from pale green to tan; a conspicuous black line runs from the first abdominal segment, widening as it terminates at anterior portion of thorax, and at this terminus it curves to either side to form an anchor shape; a thick black dorsal bar on first abdominal segment (which may cover entire segment); thorax with three pairs of black subdorsal protuberances and a single pair of lateral black protuberances; all abdominal segments with two raised black subdorsal bumps, which may appear as short black lines in some specimens. Overall appearance not unlike the pupae of *Lepricornis* or the nymphalid genus *Chlosyne.* Pupation may take place in large aggregations on the trunk of the host tree. The caterpillars are attacked by tachinid flies; fresh pupae are attacked by the parasitic wasp, *Spilochalcis* sp. (Chalcididae).
• **Adult:** Sexes similar. Upperside black with orange-yellow FW apex, one or two red spots in the FW tornus, a red spot near the base of each wing, and red along the distal margin of HW. *Note:* Some of the spots may vary from partly to entirely yellow-orange. Compare with *electron.*
Habits: This butterfly occurs from sea level to about 1400 m on both slopes in a wide variety of habitats, but it is most frequently found in disturbed forest or in open second growth, especially on the Pacific slope. Generally encountered during the dry seasons as small colonies (reflecting the synchronous, gregarious habits) around host trees or plants that bear abundant white flowers, including coffee plants. The slow and fluttery flight renders these butterflies very conspicuous, strongly suggesting that they are aposematic. However, like most butterflies when alarmed, they can fly very fast. On occasion, many hundreds of caterpillars, pupae, and eggs will festoon the leaves, branches, and trunk of individual trees, plus large groups of adults may fly about the tree and emerge from the pupae on the trunk. In these instances, the adults form spectacular spiraling clouds of individuals swirling around the crown, all involved in frenetic male-male and male-female interactions. The butterflies visit flowers of *Albizia, Inga, Pithecellobium, Coffea, Cordia, Citrus, Lantana camara,* and various herbaceous Asteraceae. Common and widespread.
Localities: [A]: Atenas (August, December), Grecia (December), Cariblanco (February), San Antonio de Belen (January, April). [SJ]: El Rodeo (June, August–October), San Jose (January, March, May, December), San Pedro Mts. de Oca (June), Tibas (December), Santana (August), Patarra (August, October, November), Paso Ancho. [H]: Chilamate (March, September), La Selva (July). [P]: Volcan Arenal (March), Sirena (February), Monte Verde (August, September). [L]: Siquirres (March), Germania (September). [G]: Cañas (March), Santa Rosa (July).

Melanis cephise
(Menetries, 1855)
FW length: 22.5–24 mm   **Plate 9**
Range: Mexico to Costa Rica
Hostplant: Unknown
Early stages: Unknown
• **Adult:** Sexes similar. Upperside black with the radial wing veins off-white, a red spot near the base of both wings, fringe on FW black, and fringe on HW white. Cannot be confused with any other riodinid in Costa Rica.
Habits: This butterfly is recorded in our area from sea level to 300 m on the Pacific slope, only in association with deciduous forest habitats, and it is here where the butterfly appears to terminate its southernmost range. Encoun-

tered as rare, solitary individuals flying in open scrubby areas. The butterfly visits flowers of *Cordia, Lantana,* and various Asteraceae. Uncommon in Costa Rican collections.

Localities: [P]: Las Juntas (September). [G]: Playas del Coco (July), Cañas (July), Bagaces (July, August), La Pacifica (July, August), Santa Rosa (June).

Melanis electron melantho
(Menetries, 1855)
FW length: 21–23 mm   **Plate 9**
Range: Guatemala to Venezuela, Trinidad. **Subspecies:** Guatemala to Panama
Hostplant: *Pithecellobium samman* (Fabaceae)
Early stages: Guppy [in Kaye (1921)] reported finding caterpillars and pupae on the host tree in Trinidad, but did not describe the caterpillars or pupae.
• **Adult:** Sexes similar. Upperside black with a conspicuous transverse yellow-orange band across the end of the FW cell, a red spot near the base of both wings, and red-orange on HW distal margin. *Note:* In older literature, this species was widely known under *iarbas,* a preoccupied name (C. Callaghan, pers. comm.). Compare with *pixie.*
Habits: This butterfly occurs in our area from sea level to 600 m on both slopes, but it is decidedly more common on the Atlantic slope. Found mainly in association with rain forest habitats, it also occurs in second-growth forest within the Meseta Central. Most frequently encountered as solitary individuals flying along forest edges, rivers, and in large light gaps between 08:30 and 11:00 hrs. Occasionally found in small, local populations. Both sexes visit flowers of *Inga, Cordia, Lantana, Coffea,* and various weedy Asteraceae.
Localities: [A]: Cariblanco (February, April–July, September, October), San Mateo (December), Arenal (February). [C]: Turrialba (August). [H]: Chilamate (August). [SJ]: Desamparados (September), Santa Rosa de Puriscal (September, December), Carrillo. [L]: Tortuguerro (August), Guapiles (July), Siquirres (February, March), Banana River (March), Coen (March), Madre de Dios (September), Rio Victoria (April).

Genus **ISAPIS** Doubleday, 1847

The butterflies in this genus are considered to represent a single species that may be recognized by its black, orange, and yellow colora-

tion, long legs, broad head, short palpi, and thick antennae that end in distinct clubs. *Isapis* is found from Mexico south to Bolivia and Brazil. However, its broad range and the various subspecies suggest that *Isapis* may contain more than one species. As in *Melanis,* these butterflies appear to be aposematic and bear strong resemblance to moths in the families Arctiidae, Notodontidae, and Geometridae.

Apparently nothing is known about the hostplants or early stages of *Isapis.* Seitz (1917) indicated that in South America the butterfly is very local but not rare at particular sites, and that individual butterflies perch on the tips of bare branches in clearings. Again, such a description is reminiscent of the habits of *Melanis.*

Isapis agyrtus hera
Godman and Salvin, 1886
FW length: 14.5–15.5 mm   **Plate 9**
Range: Mexico to Bolivia, Brazil. **Subspecies:** Mexico to Panama
Hostplant: Unknown
Early stages: Unknown
• **Adult:** Sexes similar. Upperside entirely black with an orange band on the FW that extends from near the costal margin almost to the tornus. Underside black with the FW band pale orange, and a distinct yellow band that extends from the FW costa near base across the base of HW to the inner margin. Compare with *Xenandra, Pterographium.*
Habits: This butterfly is reported in our area only from a single locality in the Meseta Central. Once I collected this butterfly along an old second-growth forest edge in the early afternoon where it was perched about 3 m above the ground on the branches of a tree. This remnant tract of forest was destroyed some years ago for a housing development and for the expansion of the Pan-American highway.
Localities: [SJ]: Curridibat (January).

Genus **NOTHEME** Westwood, 1851

The small and unassuming butterflies in this genus are recognized by their black ground color with distinct white medial bands, and a robust head, thorax, and abdomen, as in *Lyropteryx.* As currently understood, *Notheme* contains two species, one that is confined to South America and the other ranging widely throughout the Neotropics. However, it may be that the butterflies referred to under *Notheme* represent a single wide-ranging species (Seitz 1916), or

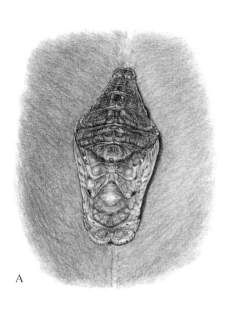

FIGURE 46. (A) *Metacharis victrix* pupa. (B) *Lepricornis strigosa* pupa.
(Drawings by J. Clark)

that there are a number of closely related species. Nothing definite is known of its early stages. These butterflies can be abundant in South America, but in our area they are rare.

Notheme erota diadema
Stichel, 1910

FW length: 16–16.5 mm   **Plate 7**
Range: Mexico to Colombia, Argentina. **Subspecies:** Mexico to Peru
Hostplant: *Olyra latifolia* (Poaceae)?
Early stages: *Egg*—small, white, deposited singly.
• **Adult:** Sexes similar. Immediately recognized by the black ground color set with a distinct white medial band that runs from FW costa, across both wings, and terminates at the HW inner margin near the tornus in a roughly triangular orange spot, and by the presence of an orange spot on the HW costa where the white medial band begins. *Note:* This taxon was known for many years under the specific epithet *eumeus*, apparently a preoccupied name (Hemming 1967).
Habits: This peculiar little butterfly has been reported only from Atlantic slope habitats between 200 and 800 m elevation. I. Chacon observed females showing distinct oviposition

behavior in very tall thickets of *Olyra* in the forest between 13:00 and 14:00 hrs. Rare in Costa Rican collections.
Localities: [H]: Plastico (August), Magsaysay (April).

Genus **METACHARIS** Butler, 1867

The butterflies in this genus are recognized by their elongate forewings, the silvered streaks at the ends of the radial veins, and males that often have velvety blue or gray monochrome undersides. Members of *Metacharis* are found from Nicaragua to the Amazon Basin. As currently understood, the genus embraces at least ten sexually dimorphic species. However, the quantities of undetermined and/or mismatched material in museum collections makes it probable that this number will increase when *Metacharis* is revised. Two species occur in our area.

The only hostplant record for *Metacharis* is from the Olacaceae (Callaghan 1991; DeVries et al. 1994). The caterpillars bear long setae, and the pupa has a blocky form that recalls that

PLATES

PLATE 1 · CORRACHIA, HADES, METHONE, EUSELASIA

1. **Corrachia leucoplaga** ♂: D, Costa Rica, 12 to 18 mi N of San Isidro General

2. **Hades noctula** ♂: D, Panama, Barro Colorado Island

3. **Hades noctula** ♀: V, Panama, Barro Colorado Island

4. **Methone cecilia** ♂: D, Costa Rica, Agua Buena

5. **Methone cecilia** ♀: D, Costa Rica, San Vito

6. **Euselasia bettina** ♂: D, Costa Rica, Cariblanco

7. **Euselasia bettina** ♀: V, Panama, Cana

8. **Euselasia aurantia** ♂: D, Costa Rica, San Vito

9. **Euselasia aurantia** ♀: D, Costa Rica, Agua Buena

10. **Euselasia chrysippe** ♂: D, Costa Rica, Cariblanco

11. **Euselasia chrysippe** ♀: V, Costa Rica, La Selva

12. **Euselasia chrysippe** ♀: D, Costa Rica, La Selva

13. **Euselasia matuta** ♂: D, Costa Rica, Juan Viñas [HT]

14. **Euselasia matuta** ♂: V, Costa Rica "no data"

15. **Euselasia leucophryna** ♂: D, Costa Rica, Cachi [HT]

16. **Euselasia corduena** ♂: D, Costa Rica, San Vito

17. **Euselasia corduena** ♂: V, Costa Rica, Las Alturas

18. **Euselasia corduena** ♀: D, Costa Rica, Fila Las Cruces

PLATE 2 · EUSELASIA

1. **Euselasia labdacus** ♂: D, Panama, Colon

2. **Euselasia labdacus** ♂: V, Panama, Colon

3. **Euselasia labdacus** ♀: D, Panama, Colon

4. **Euselasia mystica** ♂: D, Costa Rica, San Mateo

5. **Euselasia mystica** ♀: V, Panama, Rio Taracuna

6. **Euselasia mystica** ♀: D, Panama, Cana

7. **Euselasia hieronymi** ♂: D, Costa Rica, Las Alturas

8. **Euselasia hieronymi** ♂: V, Costa Rica, Las Alturas

9. **Euselasia hieronymi** ♀: D, Costa Rica, Las Alturas

10. **Euselasia eubule** ♂: Costa Rica, San Mateo

11. **Euselasia eubule** ♂: V, Costa Rica, San Mateo

12. **Euselasia eubule** ♀: D, Panama, Potrerillos

13. **Euselasia eucrates** ♂: Panama, Potrerillos

14. **Euselasia eucrates** ♂: V, Costa Rica, Tabarcla

15. **Euselasia eucrates** ♀: D, Panama, Potrerillos

16. **Euselasia inconspicua** ♂: D, Costa Rica, Las Cruces

17. **Euselasia inconspicua** ♂: V, Panama, Potrerillos

18. **Euselasia inconspicua** ♀: D, Panama, Potrerillos

19. **Euselasia amphidecta** ♂: D, Panama, Rio Guache

20. **Euselasia amphidecta** ♂: V, Panama, Isla Coiba

21. **Euselasia amphidecta** ♀: D, Colombia, Victoria

22. **Euselasia gyda** ♂: D, Costa Rica, Las Alturas

23. **Euselasia gyda** ♂: V, Costa Rica, Las Alturas

24. **Euselasia gyda** ♀: D, Costa Rica, Las Alturas

25. **Euselasia leucon** ♂: D, Panama, Cerro Colorado

26. **Euselasia leucon** ♀: V, Costa Rica, Turrialba [PT]

27. **Euselasia argentea** ♂: V, Costa Rica, Las Alturas

28. **Euselasia argentea** ♂: D, Costa Rica, Las Alturas

PLATE 3 · EUSELASIA, PEROPTHALMA

1. **Euselasia midas** ♂: D, Panama, Cana

2. **Euselasia midas** ♂: V, Costa Rica, Moravia de Chirripo

3. **Euselasia midas** ♀: D, Panama, Bugaba

4. **Euselasia rhodogyne** ♂: D, Panama, Gatun

5. **Euselasia rhodogyne** ♂: V, Costa Rica, Turrialba

6. **Euselasia rhodogyne** ♀: D, Panama, Gatun

7. **Euselasia subargentea** ♂: D, Costa Rica, Moravia de Chirripo

8. **Euselasia subargentea** ♂: V, "Colombia"

9. **Euselasia regipennis** ♂: D, Panama, Colon

10. **Euselasia regipennis** ♂: V, Costa Rica, Turrialba

11. **Euselasia regipennis** ♀: D, Costa Rica, La Selva

12. **Euselasia regipennis** ♀: D, Panama, Colon

13. **Euselasia aurantiaca** ♂: D, Guatemala, Cayuga

14. **Euselasia aurantiaca** ♀: D, Panama, Colon

15. **Peropthalma lasus** ♂: D, Panama, Fort Clayton

16. **Peropthalma lasus** ♀: V, Panama, Cocoli

17. **Peropthalma tullius** ♀: D, Costa Rica, Guapiles

18. **Peropthalma tullius** ♀: V, Costa Rica, Golfito

19. **Euselasia angulata** ♂: V: Costa Rica, Turrialba

20. **Euselasia onorata** ♂: V, Costa Rica, Carrillo

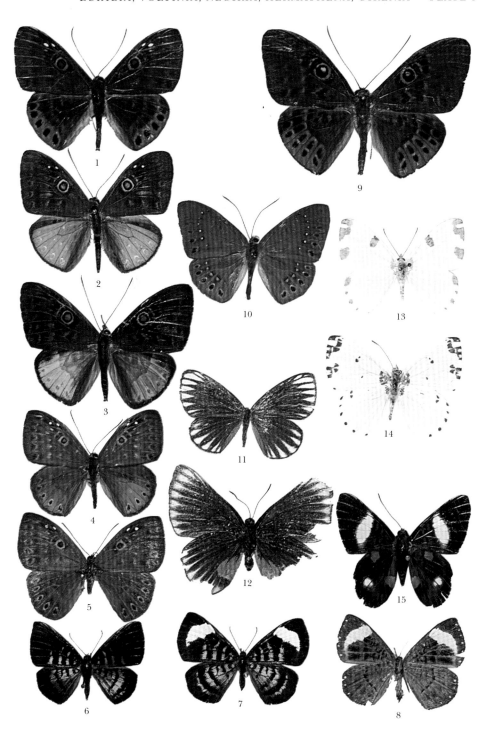

PLATE 7

1. **Lyropteryx lyra cleadas** ♂: D, Panama, Bugaba

2. **Lyropteryx lyra cleadas** ♂: V, Panama, Cocoli

3. **Lyropteryx lyra cleadas** ♀: D, Panama, Cocoli

4. **Chorinea octauius** ♂: D, Panama, Cerro Campana

5. **Ithomeis eulema** ♂: D, Costa Rica, San Vito

6. **Necyria beltiana** ♂: D, Costa Rica, Carrillo

7. **Necyria beltiana** ♂: V, Costa Rica, Carrillo

8. **Necyria beltiana** ♀: D, Costa Rica, Moravia de Chirripo

9. **Necyria beltiana** ♀: V, Costa Rica, Carrillo

10. **Monethe rudolphus** ♀: D, Costa Rica, Moravia de Chirripo

11. **Monethe rudolphus** ♀: V, Costa Rica, Moravia de Chirripo

12. **Cremna thasus** ♂: D, Trinidad

13. **Cremna thasus** ♀: D, Panama, Gamboa

14. **Notheme erota** ♂: D, Panama, Cerro Pirre

15. **Ancyluris inca** ♂: V, Panama, Barro Colorado Island

16. **Ancyluris inca** ♀: D, Panama, Barro Colorado Island

PLATE 9

1. **Cariomothis poeciloptera** ♂: D, Panama, Colon

2. **Cariomothis poeciloptera** ♂: V, Panama, Cerro Pirre

3. **Cariomothis poeciloptera** ♀: D, Panama, Colon

4. **Cariomothis poeciloptera** ♀: V, Panama, Gatun

5. **Syrmatia nyx** ♂: D, Costa Rica, Chilamate

6. **Syrmatia aethiops** ♂: D, Costa Rica, Turrialba

7. **Chamaelimnas villagomes** ♂: D, Panama, Summit

8. **Chamaelimnas villagomes** ♀: D, Panama, Bayano

9. **Exoplisia cadmeis** ♂: D, Ecuador, Limoncocha

10. **Exoplisia cadmeis** ♂: V, Ecuador, Limoncocha

11. **Exoplisia hypochalbe** ♂: V, Colombia, Caquita

12. **Pterographium elegans** ♂: D, Costa Rica, Carrillo

13. **Pterographium elegans** ♀: D, Panama, El Llano

14. **Isapis agyrtus** ♂: D, Panama, La Pita

15. **Isapis agyrtus** ♂: V, Panama, Cocoli

16. **Melanis pixie** ♂: D, Costa Rica, Cañas

17. **Melanis electron** ♂: D, Costa Rica, Madre de Dios

18. **Melanis cephise** ♂: D, Costa Rica, Cañas

19. **Xenandra desora** ♂: D, Panama, Piña

20. **Xenandra helius** ♀: D, Panama, Gatun

21. **Xenandra caeruleata** ♂: D, Costa Rica, La Selva

22. **Xenandra caeruleata** ♀: V, Costa Rica, La Selva

PLATE 9

PLATE 10

1. **Metacharis victrix** ♂: D, Costa Rica, Las Alturas

2. **Metacharis victrix** ♂: V, Costa Rica, Las Alturas

3. **Metacharis victrix** ♀: D, Costa Rica, Las Alturas

4. **Metacharis victrix** ♀: V, Costa Rica, Sirena

5. **Caria rhacotis** ♂: D, Ecuador,

6. **Caria rhacotis** ♂: V, Pana

7. **Caria rhacotis** ♀: D, P

8. **Caria rhacotis** ♀: V,

9. **Esthemopsis clonia** ♂

10. **Esthemopsis clonia** ♀

11. **Esthemopsis colaxes** ♂

12. **Esthemopsis colaxes** ♀: V, Pa

13. **Caria lampeto** ♂: D, Panama, Farfan

14. **Caria lampeto** ♂: V, Costa Rica, La Florida

15. **Caria lampeto** ♀: D, Panama, Farfan

16. **Caria lampeto** ♀: V, Panama, Farfan

17. **Caria domitianus** ♂: D, Costa Rica, San Mateo

18. **Caria domitianus** ♂: V, Costa Rica, Sam Mateo

19. **Caria domitianus** ♀: D, Guatemala, Zacapa

20. **Baeotis nesaea** ♂: D, Panama, El Llano

21. **Baeotis nesaea** ♀: D, Panama, Cerro Campana

22. **Baeotis zonata** ♂: D, Costa Rica, San Vito

23. **Baeotis macularia** ♂: D, Costa Rica, La Florida

24. **Baeotis macularia** ♀: V, Costa Rica, La Florida

25. **Argyrogrammana holosticta** ♂: D, Panama, Gatun

26. **Argyrogrammana holosticta** ♀: V, Panama, Farfan

27. **Parcella amarynthina** ♂: D, Panama, Bayano

28. **Parcella amarynthina** ♀: V, Panama, Gamboa

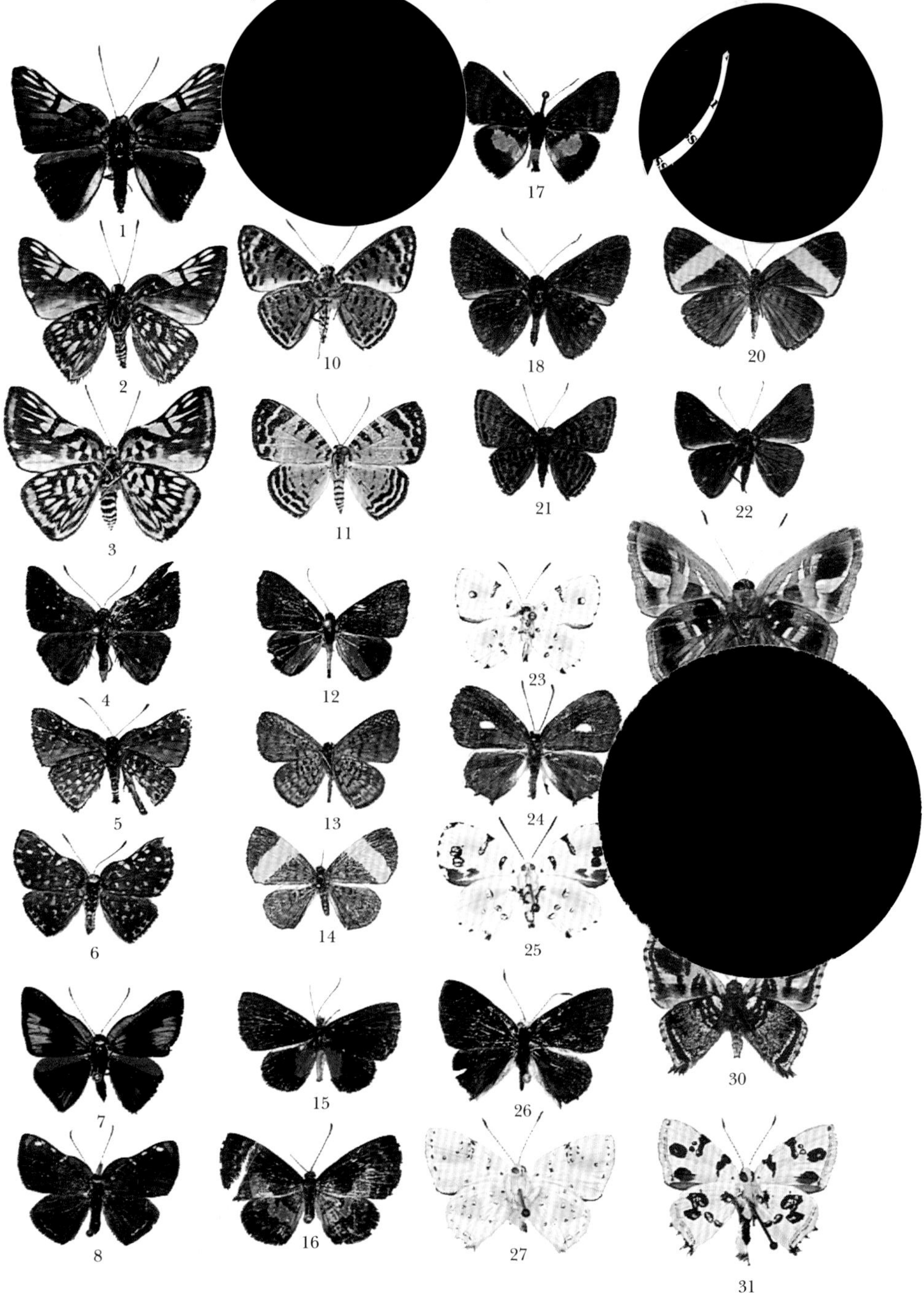
1
17
10
18
20
2
3
11
21
22
4
12
23
5
13
24
6
14
25
7
15
26
30
8
16
27
31

PLATE 15 · ANTEROS, SAROTA, CHALODETA, CHARIS

cupris ♂: V, Panama, Gatun

is ♀: D, Panama, Pot

ellata ♂: D, Panama

sellata ♂: V, Costa Ric

tessellata ♀: V, Panama, Cer

rota turrialbensis ♂: V, Costa Rica, Turrialba [HT]

7. **Sarota chrysus** ♂: V, Panama, Bayano

8. **Sarota chrysus** ♀: V, Panama, Canal Zone

9. **Sarota myrtea** ♂: V, Panama, Cerro Campana

10. **Sarota gamelia** ♂: V, Panama, Cerro Jefe

11. **Sarota spicata** ♂: V, Costa Rica, Madre de Dios

12. **Sarota estrada** ♂: V, Mexico, Chiapas

13. **Sarota estrada** ♀: V, Costa Rica, Carrillo

14. **Sarota psaros** ♂: V, Panama, Potrerillos

15. **Sarota gyas** ♂: V, Panama, Bayano

16. **Sarota acantus** ♂: V, Costa Rica, Las Alturas

lia ♂: V, Costa Rica, Las Alturas

♀: V, Costa Rica, Las Alturas

♂: D, Costa Rica, Juan Viñas

: D, Panama, Altos de Pacora

♀: V, Panama, Piña

tis ♂: D, Costa Rica, Guapiles

onitis ♂: V, Panama, Cocli

eta candiope ♂: D, Costa Rica, Las Alturas

25. **Chalodeta candiope** ♂: V, Costa Rica, Las Alturas

26. **Chalodeta candiope** ♀: D, Costa Rica, Las Alturas

27. **Charis iris** ♂: D, Costa Rica, Turrialba

28. **Charis iris** ♂: V, Costa Rica, San Vito

29. **Charis iris** ♀: D, Panama, Cerro Campana

PLATE 17 · EMESIS

1. **Emesis lacrines** ♂: D, Panama, El Valle
2. **Emesis lacrines** ♂: V, Costa Rica, Moravia de Chirripo
3. **Emesis lacrines** ♀: D, Costa Rica, Uvita
4. **Emesis lucinda** ♂: D, Panama, Gatun
5. **Emesis lucinda** ♂: V, Panama, La Pita
6. **Emesis lucinda** ♀: D, Panama, Farfan
7. **Emesis mandana** ♂: D, Panama, Cerro Pirre
8. **Emesis mandana** ♂: V, Panama, Madden Forest
9. **Emesis mandana** ♀: D, Panama, Paraiso
10. **Emesis fatimella** ♂: D, Panama, Cocoli
11. **Emesis fatimella** ♀: D, Panama, Madden Forest
12. **Emesis cypria** ♂: D, Panama, Cerro Campana
13. **Emesis tenedia** ♂: D, Costa Rica, Las Alturas
14. **Emesis tenedia** ♂: V, Costa Rica, Las Alturas
15. **Emesis tenedia** ♀: D, Costa Rica, Las Alturas
16. **Emesis tenedia** ♀: V, Costa Rica, Las Alturas
17. **Emesis tegula** ♂: D, Panama, Cocoli
18. **Emesis tegula** ♂: V, Panama, Cocoli
19. **Emesis tegula** ♀: D, Panama, Rodman

PLATE 18

1. **Thisbe irenea** ♂: D, Panama, Barro Colorado Island
2. **Thisbe irenea** ♀: D, Panama, Barro Colorado Island
3. **Thisbe lycorias** ♀: D, Panama, Chiriqui
4. **Uraneis ucubis** ♂: D, Panama, Alto Pacora
5. **Uraneis ucubis** ♀: V, Panama, Cerro Campana
6. **Juditha dorilas** ♀: D, Panama, Gatun
7. **Lemonias agave** ♂: D, Panama, Gatun
8. **Lemonias agave** ♂: V, Panama, Gatun
9. **Lemonias agave** ♀: D, Panama, Gatun
10. **Juditha molpe** ♂: D, Panama, Cocoli
11. **Juditha molpe** ♀: V, Costa Rica, Sirena
12. **Juditha dorilas** ♂: D, Panama, Llano
13. **Juditha dorilas** ♀: V, Costa Rica, Rio Tuis
14. **Catocyclotis aemulius** ♂: D, Panama, Potrerillos
15. **Catocyclotis aemulius** ♀: D, Panama, Potrerillos
16. **Synargis mycone** ♂: D, Costa Rica, Carrillo
17. **Synargis mycone** ♂: V, Panama, Paraiso
18. **Synargis mycone** ♀: D, Costa Rica, El Rodeo
19. **⌐ ⌐ s ochra sicyon** ♂: D, Panama, Cocoli
20. **ochra sicyon** ♀: V, Panama, Cocoli

PLATE 22 · SETABIS, PIXUS ███████ IUM, PSEUDONYMPHIDIA

1. **Setabis lagus** ♂ ███
2. **Setabis lagus** ███
3. **Setabis lagu** ███
4. **Setabis alcm** ███
5. **Setabis alcma** ███ a
6. **Setabis alcmae** ███ ince
7. **Setabis cleomedes** ███ on de Osa
8. **Setabis cleomedes** ♀: D, Panama, Gatun
9. **Setabis cleomedes** ♀: V, Costa Rica, La Vacita
10. **Pixus corculum** ♂: D, Costa Rica, Limon
11. **Pixus corculum** ♂: V, Panama, Gatun
12. **Pixus corculum** ♀: D, Panama, Ojo de Agua
13. **Nymphidium mantus** ♂: D, Panama, Barro Colorado Island
14. **Nymphidium lenocinium** ♂: D, Panama, El Llano
15. **Nymphidium lenocinium** ███ rrialba
16. **Nymphidium oli** ███
17. **Pseudonymp** ███
18. **Nymphidi** ███ o
19. **Nymphi** ███
20. **Nymphi** ███
21. **Nymphi** ███
22. **Nymphi** ███
23. **Nymphidi** ███

PLATE 23 · THEOPE

Theope virgilius ♂: D, Panama, Los Rios

♂: V, Panama, Los Rios

♀: D, Panama, Piña

♂: D, "no data" [HT]

♂: V, Guatemala, Esquintla

♀: D, Guatemala, Esquintla

♂: D, Panama, Los Rios

♂: V, Panama, Los Rios

♀: D, Panama, Los Rios

♂: D, Panama, Cocoli

♂: V, Panama, Madden Forest

♀: D, Panama, Gatun

♂: D, Panama, Gatun

♂: V, Panama, Cocoli

15. **Theope basilea** ♀: D, Panama, Gatun

16. **Theope cratylus** ♂: D, Panama, Madden Dam

17. **Theope cratylus** ♂: V, Panama, Cocoli

18. **Theope cratylus** ♀: D, Panama, Cerro Campana

of *Leucochimona*, except that the cremaster is more slender. In Costa Rica these butterflies occur on both slopes and are encountered typically in local, seasonal populations along well-shaded streams or trails. Their flight behavior is rather frantic and reminiscent of a small *Eurybia*.

Metacharis victrix
Hewitson, 1870
FW length: 24–25.5 mm   **Plate 10**
Range: Nicaragua to Colombia and western Ecuador
Hostplant: *Heisteria* sp. (Olacaceae)
Early stages (Fig. 46a): *Mature caterpillar*—pale green and sparsely covered in long yellow setae. *Pupa*—pale gray-green overshot with white flecks that impart the appearance of a dull, epiphyll covered leaf surface; overall form similar to *Leucochimona* but more flattened ventrally, with the abdomen tapering to a small cremaster.
• **Adult:** Sexes dimorphic. *Male*—upperside dark red-brown with broken black medial lines, margins of both wings with brick-red spots between veins each set with a black spot, and distal ends of radial veins covered with a silvered streak; underside entirely black, overshot with a deep iridescent blue. *Female*—upperside orange-brown medial lines and marginal patterns similar to male; underside dull yellow-orange set with a scattering of distinct black spots across entire surface of both wings. Compare with *umbrata, Emesis fatimella*.
Habits: In our area this butterfly has been reported from sea level to 1600 m on both slopes in association with rain forest habitats. Encountered in the forest understory as solitary individuals in shady light gaps, or more commonly along streams or swampy places. However, at times this butterfly may be found locally in small groups, occasionally very abundantly. The flight is rapid, erratic, and not unlike that of members of the genus *Eurybia*. The males perch 3 m or less above the ground between 11:30 and 14:30 hrs. Generally, the males perch on the underside of leaves, but in bright sunshine they will occasionally perch on top of leaves. Depending on the locality, abundance, and weather, the males may then have another activity period from 16:00 hrs until dark. During these afternoon displays, the male-male interactions can extend for several minutes and result in wild parading flights back and forth along a stream or other landmark. The females are active in the forest understory between 11:30 and 15:00 hrs when they search for oviposition sites. Both sexes are not infrequently found with bird beak and *Anolis* lizard jaw marks on the wings. In Corcovado and at Las Alturas I found that this butterfly underwent periodic population explosions followed by long periods of either low abundance or total absence.
Localities: [A]: Reserva San Ramon (May), Dos Rios (May), San Carlos (February). [C]: Turrialba. [SJ]: Carrillo (May). [P]: San Vito (March–May, September, October), Sirena (February–April, July, September–December), Llorona (March, April, June, August), Rincon (March), Palmar Norte (September), Monte Verde (January, July, November), Las Alturas (August, September, November), Rincon de Osa. [G]: Rincon de la Vieja (September), Miravalles.

Metacharis umbrata
Stichel, 1929
FW length: 17.5–21 mm   **Plate 25**
Range: Costa Rica to western Ecuador
Hostplant: Unknown
Early stages: Unknown
• **Adult:** Sexes presumably dimorphic. *Male*—upperside black overcast with a deep iridescent purple that tends to obscure the medial markings; underside dull velvet-blue with little iridescence. **Female** (not illustrated)—judging from an Ecuadorian specimen, the upperside is a washed-out orange-fawn with medial lines and marginal patterns similar to that of *victrix* but with the postmedial line more distinct, and a dark area in the FW subapex that extends to the tornus as a broad but indistinct submarginal line; underside dull yellow-fawn set with distinct black spots across entire surface of both wings that mirrors that of the upperside. Compare with *victrix*.
Habits: This butterfly has been recorded in our area only from a few Atlantic lowland rain forest localities. On one occasion I collected this butterfly at 12:25 hrs along a shaded trail through primary rain forest at La Selva. I have not seen any female specimens from our area. Rare.
Localities: [H]: Chilamate (April), La Selva (May). [L]: Guapiles (December), Limon (February).

Genus LEPRICORNIS Felder, 1865

These butterflies bear a strong resemblance to those in the genera *Brachyglenis* and *Esthemopsis* and have often been confused with them. Aside from overall appearance, *Lepricornis* may be recognized by the short orange palpi, traces of orange around the cervical area behind the head, and their densely scaled antennae that give the appearance of lumpy and thickened antennae. Members of *Lepricornis* are found from Mexico through Central and South America, and the genus is thought to contain about eight species. These butterflies form mimicry complexes involving various riodinid genera (e.g., *Brachyglenis, Esthemopsis, Voltinia, Uraneis*), and members of the Ithomiinae, Arctiidae, Geometridae and Notodontidae. Because they are variable mimetic species (Seitz 1916), a number of *Lepricornis* species may, in reality, be forms. Two species occur in our area, one of which is quite rare and should probably be placed in another genus.

The only hostplant record available for *Lepricornis* is from the Malpighiaceae (DeVries et al. 1994). The caterpillars are covered in a dense pile of setae, and in general form recall those of *Ancyluris, Lyropteryx,* and *Necyria.*

Lepricornis strigosa strigosa
(Staudinger, 1876)

FW length: 21–22.5 mm   **Plate 8**
Range: Costa Rica to Peru. **Subspecies:** Costa Rica to Colombia
Hostplant: *Heteropteris laurifolia* (Malpighiaceae)
Early stages (Fig. 46b): *Mature caterpillar*—body densely covered mostly in short dark brown to black setae with the head, entire underside, first thoracic segment, and last abdominal segment dull orange-brown; each segment with longer, paired tufts of black dorsal and lateral setae; the second thoracic segment has very long lateral tufts that curve slightly forward, and these tufts are raised and lowered as the caterpillar walks. *Pupa*—a pale brown cylinder with all segments bearing a series of dorsal and lateral black spots, five pairs of short, blunt black-tipped lateral abdominal spines (as seen on *Ancyluris* and relatives), and wing pads whose veins are marked with black lines. Overall, this pupa recalls those of *Melanis* or nymphalids in the subfamily Melitaeinae (e.g., *Eresia, Chlosyne*).
• **Adult:** Sexes slightly dimorphic. *Male*—upperside dull black with a sprinkling of white scales over otherwise hyaline areas between the radial veins that are located as five elongate subapical FW spots, the FW disco-basal area posterior to cell, and across most of the HW. *Female*—similar to male but often duller black, and the extent of the white areas is often more

pronounced. The pattern of both sexes varies with respect to the amount of black covering the white radial bands. *Note:* Some specimens from the Atlantic slope, especially the females, may have an orange tinge on the white areas. These have been named *trichroma* (Seitz 1920) and were originally described as a full species in the genus *Brachyglenis*. Compare with *Esthemopsis, Brachyglenis.*
Habits: This butterfly has been recorded in our area from sea level to 600 m on both slopes in association with rain forest habitats. The species occurs as uncommon, solitary individuals along forest edges, rivers, and in light gaps. Typically, the females are encountered more frequently than males. I have found specimens of both sexes on the Osa Peninsula that were carrying orchid pollinaria on the proboscis, suggesting that they are involved in orchid pollination. Infrequent in Costa Rican collections.
Localities: [A]: San Carlos (December). [C]: Turrialba (June, September). [H]: La Selva (July, August), Chilamate (March, May, July). [P]: Sirena (February, March, June), Rincon de Osa (February). [L]: Hacienda Tapezco (August), Germania (April, October, September).

Lepricornis bicolor
Godman and Salvin, 1886

FW length: Not measured   **Not illustrated**
Range: Costa Rica(?), Panama
Hostplant: Unknown
Early stages: Unknown
• **Adult:** *Male* (based on the illustration in D'Abrera 1994)—ground color yellow with broad black margins on both wings; the FW apex is broadly black with a prominent yellow spot in the subapex. Bears an overall similarity to members of the genus *Chamaelimnas. Female*—apparently unknown. *Note:* This butterfly is something of an enigma in that it was described from a unique specimen collected in Bugaba, Panama (near the Osa Peninsula), the only specimen known. J. Hall informs me that the antennae of the type do not show the characteristic scaling of the genus *Lepricornis*, but that they have been glued onto the type specimen. Thus, without more material, and genitalic dissection we cannot be certain of the proper placement of this taxon. Compare with *Chamaelimnas poeciloptera.*
Habits: Unknown
Localities: Not reported from our area, but should be looked for in lowland rain forest areas around the Osa Peninsula.

Genus CARIOMOTHIS Stichel 1910

The butterflies in this genus bear a resemblance to certain members of the genus *Calospila* but are immediately separated by having a silvered submarginal line. Members of *Cariomothis* are found from Costa Rica to the Amazon Basin, and the genus is composed of three strongly dimorphic species. In older literature these butterflies are referred to under the genus *Metacharis*. Only one species enters our area.

The only information available regarding hostplants suggests that the South American species *C. erythromelas* feeds on *Viscum verticellatum* (Loranthaceae), and that the caterpillars and pupae are densely clothed in long white setae (Sepp 1828–48).

Cariomothis poeciloptera poeciloptera
(Godman and Salvin, 1878)
FW length: 13.5–14.5 mm   Plate 9
Range: Costa Rica to Colombia. **Subspecies:** Costa Rica and Panama
Hostplant: Unknown
Early stages: Unknown
• **Adult:** Sexes dimorphic. *Male*—upperside jet black with the discal areas of both wings rich orange, and a broken silvered submarginal line; FW underside white with broad, dark postmedial areas, and a yellow medial patch posterior to cell; HW underside white with a series of five to six broken black lines across entire wing that follow the contour of the distal margin. *Female*—upperside brown broken by a complicated series of yellow spots, apical region black, and a broken silvered submarginal line; underside as in male except the FW is pale yellow, and the black lines on the HW are less distinct. Compare with *Calospila asteria*, *Setabis cleomedes*.
Habits: In our area this butterfly has been recorded only from the Atlantic slope between sea level and 600 m in association with rain forest habitats. I have never seen it alive. Rare in Costa Rican collections.
Localities: [C]: Turrialba (July). [H]: La Selva. [L]: La Florida.

Genus SYRMATIA Hübner, 1819

The peculiar and utterly distinct wing shape of these butterflies make it almost impossible not to recognize this genus. Members of *Syrmatia* are found from Costa Rica through the Amazon Basin, and the genus is considered to embrace four species, although Seitz (1917) was of the opinion that the genus contained a single variable species. Two apparently sympatric species occur in our area.

The only hostplant record for *Syrmatia* is that of Barcant (1970), who indicates that in Trinidad the caterpillars feed on a terrestrial lily that is likely to be in the genus *Hedychium* (Liliaceae). There are, however, no descriptions of the early stages, and it would be desirable to verify the hostplant.

In Costa Rica these butterflies are rarely encountered, and all available reports indicate that they are local and seasonal.

Syrmatia nyx
(Hübner, 1817)
FW length: 13–14.5 mm   Plate 9
Range: Costa Rica to Colombia, Venezuela, Trinidad, and Brazil
Hostplant: Unknown
Early stages: Unknown
• **Adult:** Sexes similar. Upperside black with prominent medial white spot on FW, a red spot near base of FW, and a white band on HW from base to inner margin. *Note:* This taxon was known for many years under *dorilas* (Cramer, 1775), which, according to C. Callaghan (pers. comm.), is apparently a preoccupied name. Compare with *aethiops*.
Habits: This butterfly has been recorded in our area from sea level to 600 m only in Atlantic slope rain forest habitats. P. Knudsen informs me that in Chilamate the butterfly is found occasionally in local populations near streams. There he notes that both sexes are active and visit flowers of weedy Asteraceae during the morning. In Trinidad, Barcant (1970) remarked that this butterfly is found in local populations during the early morning, and that it avoids flying in sunshine. Rare in Costa Rican collections.
Localities: [H]: La Selva (July), Turrialba (December), Chilamate (July). [L]: Hacienda Tapezco (August).

Syrmatia aethiops
Staudinger, 1888
FW length: 13–14.5 mm   Plate 9
Range: Costa Rica to Colombia and Brazil
Hostplant: *Hedychium* (Liliaceae) (Barcant 1970)
Early stages: Undescribed
• **Adult:** Sexes similar. Distinguished from its

congener by having an entirely black upperside. Compare with *S. nyx.*
Habits: This butterfly is recorded in our area from 300 to 700 m only on Atlantic slope rain forest habitats. In Trinidad, Barcant (1970) indicated that this butterfly was found in local populations along shaded rivers, and that they were active between 07:00 and 08:00 hrs. He also noted that the butterflies perch between 2 to 5 m above the ground on the tips of branches with their wings open, and that all activity ceased when the perching area became illuminated by sunlight. Rare in Costa Rican collections.
Localities: [C]: Turrialba (May, June, July). [SJ]: Carrillo (March). [H]: Plastico (July), La Selva (June, July).

Genus CHAMAELIMNAS Felder, 1865

The butterflies in this genus are recognized by their elongated wings, very short palpi, and bright yellow and black colors. These butterflies bear a strong resemblance to the genera *Mesenopsis* and *Monethe*, and members of the day-flying notodontid moths in the subfamily Dioptinae, especially the genus *Josia* (see J. Miller 1996). Seitz (1916) noted that some Brazilian *Chamaelimnas* species were found to fly exclusively with their model day-flying moths. Members of *Chamaelimnas* are found from Panama throughout the Amazon Basin, and most likely occur in Costa Rica. The genus is considered to contain about twelve variable and sexually dimorphic species, one that occurs in Central America. The hostplants and early stages of these butterflies are apparently unknown.

Chamaelimnas villagomes xanthotaenia
Stichel, 1910
FW length: 17–17.5 mm   **Plate 9**
Range: Costa Rica(?) to Colombia and Ecuador.
Subspecies: Costa Rica(?), Panama
Hostplant: Unknown
Early stages: Unknown
• **Adult:** Sexes slightly dimorphic. *Male*—FW upperside black with an elongate yellow postmedial bar and a thin yellow line at base that runs into the cell. HW upperside black with the discal area and costal margin yellow. *Female*—FW upperside similar to male except the yellow areas are much more extensive. HW upperside yellow with black margins. Compare

with *Monethe rudolphus* and *Mesenopsis melanochlora.*
Habits: This butterfly has not been recorded from our area. However, its presence in Panama suggests that this species will eventually turn up as our fauna becomes better known. In Ecuador I observed several species of *Chamaelimnas* all of which flew low to the ground deep within the rain forest understory and were active between 11:00 and 13:00 hrs.
Localities: Not yet recorded for Costa Rica

Genus BAEOTIS Hübner, 1819

The butterflies in this genus are recognized by their yellow and black coloration, their extraordinarily short hindwing cell, and a submarginal silvered line. Members of *Baeotis* are found from Mexico through Central and South America, and the genus is considered to contain about twelve species, most which are entirely South American. Three species enter our area. However, it is evident from collections that the taxonomic limits of the members of this genus are poorly understood, and the genus is in need of revision.

In Costa Rica these delicate butterflies are typically found flying in bright sunshine. They may be found from sea level to about 1200 m and are seldom, if ever, common. There is apparently nothing known of the hostplants or early stages of any species.

Baeotis nesaea
Godman and Salvin, 1889
FW length: 14.5–15.5 mm   **Plate 10**
Range: Costa Rica to Ecuador and Peru
Hostplant: Unknown
Early stages: Unknown
• **Adult:** Sexes slightly dimorphic. *Male*—upperside cream-yellow with broad black costa and margins, a black postbasal band that runs from FW costa to HW inner margin, FW with a yellow submarginal band (width and extent variable), a black postmedial band on HW bearing a silvered line, and another silvered line in submargin. *Female*—similar to male except with a dull orange medial spot at the FW costa, and often with the postmedial silvered line extinct. Compare with *zonata.*
Habits: This butterfly is recorded in our area from 800 to 1,600 m on both slopes, generally in association with cloud forest habitats. Typically encountered as uncommon, solitary individuals perching under leaves from 1 to 3 m

above the ground along forest edges, roadcuts, and rivers. Both sexes are active between 10:30 and 13:00 hrs. Uncommon in Costa Rican collections.
Localities: [A]: Cariblanco. [SJ]: San Pedro (March). [C]: Turrialba (June), Tuis (March), Cachi. [P]: San Vito (April, June, December), Las Alturas (August, September). [G]: Volcan Santa Maria (May).

Baeotis zonata zonata
Felder, 1869
FW length: 12.5–13 mm   **Plate 10**
Range: Mexico to Venezuela, Trinidad. **Subspecies:** Mexico to Venezuela, Ecuador
Hostplant: Unknown
Early stages: Unknown
• **Adult:** Sexes similar. Upperside pale yellow with broad black wing margins, two yellow submarginal spots in the black FW margin (one at the tornus), a black medial line that runs from FW costa almost to HW inner margin, a black postmedial spot on HW costa, and another black spot in HW tornus at inner margin that bears a yellow spot. *Note:* Some specimens may have a slight orange cast, a characteristic that becomes more prominent as this species enters South America. Compare with *nesaea*.
Habits: In our area this butterfly has been recorded from 400 to 1700 m in association with all forest areas, although it is apparently absent in the Guanacaste dry forest. Encountered on brilliantly sunny days as rare, solitary individuals along forest edges, roadcuts, and rivers. This butterfly has a fast zigzag flight that is reminiscent of many lycaenids. Both sexes are active between 09:30 and 14:00 hrs.
Localities: [A]: Atenas (December), San Mateo (December), Guacima (September), Alajuela. [C]: Turrialba (May, August), Cachi. [H]: Chilamate (March, August). [SJ]: San Jose (July), San Pedro (July), Patarra (September), Santa Ana (July), Paso Ancho (March), Desamparados (March). [P]: San Vito (April), Las Alturas (April).

Baeotis sulphurea macularia
(Boisduval, 1870)
FW length: 13.5–14 mm   **Plate 10**
Range: Mexico to Colombia, Ecuador. **Subspecies:** Guatemala to Colombia
Hostplant: Unknown
Early stages: Unknown
• **Adult:** Sexes similar. Upperside pale yellow ground color set with conspicuous irregular black spots along costa, margin, and discal areas. *Note:* Both D. Harvey and C. Callaghan (pers. comms.) indicate that this butterfly was

long misplaced under the genus *Argyrogrammana*. Compare with *Argyrogrammana holosticta, leptographia, venilia*.
Habits: This butterfly has been recorded in our area from sea level to 1200 m on both slopes in association with habitats that range from second growth to mature forest. Encountered as solitary individuals along forest edges, roadcuts, and rivers. Both sexes visit flowers of various weedy Asteraceae.
Localities: [A]: San Mateo (September), Cariblanco (June). [C]: Turrialba (August), Orosi (December), Cachi (October). [SJ]: Curridibat (October), Pattara (May, August). [P]: San Vito (April, September), Rio Coton (September). [L]: La Florida (March, May), Guapiles (February).

Genus **CARIA** Hübner, 1823

The butterflies in this genus are recognized by the conspicuous metallic iridescence on the upperside of the wings and the bowed forewing costa as seen in the genus *Symmachia*. The sexes of *Caria* are dimorphic, where the females are colored more somberly. Members of the genus are found from the southwestern USA throughout Central and South America. As currently understood, the genus embraces about twelve species, three that occur in our area.

The hostplants reported for *Caria* are in the Ulmaceae and Bromeliaceae (Beutelspacher 1972; DeVries et al. 1994; Kendall 1976). The caterpillars are densely covered with long, fine setae and feed on the underside of semirolled leaves. The egg of one species has been illustrated by Downey and Allyn (1980).

The males of these butterflies are most commonly observed with their wings open on bright, sunny days visiting wet sand along water courses or mud in roads. The butterflies are nervous, fast flying, and typically difficult to observe or capture.

Caria rhacotis
(Godman and Salvin, 1878)
FW length: 14–16 mm   **Plate 10**
Range: Guatemala to Colombia, Peru
Hostplant: *Celtis iguanae* (Ulmaceae)
Early stages: *Egg*—deposited singly on the underside of old or young leaves. *Mature caterpillar* (Fig. 47a)—body covered entirely in short white setae, except for the lateral setae which are long and capable of being deflected toward a stimulus; the head is pale yellow. The caterpillar makes a crude tube out of young

leaves by tying two leaf edges together with silk. It then rests and feeds inside the tube. After a tube is mostly eaten away, the caterpillar then moves to another shoot and builds a new shelter.

• **Adult:** Sexes dimorphic. *Male*—FW upperside dark brown with iridescent green along FW costa and through medial area, and iridescent blue at base of costa; HW upperside dark brown with iridescent green along tornus and inner margin; FW underside red-brown with a few black discal spots; HW underside dull gray-brown with a little red-brown near costa, or sometimes entirely red-brown. *Female*—upperside similar to male except with many broken lines across discal areas, and a short red-brown submarginal band in FW apex; costa only slightly bowed; underside pale orange with many black spots on both wings. Compare with *C. domitianus, C. lampeto, Emesis fatimella.*

Habits: This butterfly occurs from sea level to 1400 m on both slopes in association with a variety of forest habitats. Typically encountered as solitary individuals along forest edges, roadcuts, and rivers. The males are most frequently observed visiting wet soil between late morning and early afternoon. The females are generally closely associated with a dense tangle of the hostplant, where they oviposit between 09:00 and 11:00 hrs. Oviposition generally consists of four to five single oviposition events per plant, then the female rests in the sun on the upperside of a leaf for a few minutes and the process is repeated. Both sexes visit the small white flowers of *Cordia, Croton,* and various Asteraceae. Uncommon.

Localities: [A]: Esperanza. [C]: Turrialba (June, July). [H]: La Selva (December). [P]: San Vito (July), Carrara (June). [G]: Tilaran.

Caria domitianus domitianus
(Fabricius, 1793)
FW length: 12.5–13 mm   Plate 10
Range: Texas to Venezuela, Trinidad. **Subspecies:** Mexico to Colombia
Hostplant: *Tillandsia* (Bromeliaceae) in Mexico (Beutelspacher 1972)
Early stages: Apparently undescribed.
• **Adult:** Sexes slightly dimorphic. *Male*—upperside pale brown with an ill-defined iridescent green running from FW costa into the cell, and a thin straight iridescent green postmedial band on HW that borders a red-brown submarginal band; underside red-brown overshot with pink-violet iridescence. *Female*—upperside similar to male but without iridescent green on the FW, and the iridescent green line on HW follows the contour of the distal margin. Compare with *C. lampeto, Chalodeta candiope.*

Habits: This butterfly is recorded in our area from sea level to 1000 m on both slopes in association with primary and secondary forest habitats. My only experience with this butterfly is confined to observing individual males visiting wet sand along rivers at midday. Uncommon in Costa Rican collections.

Localities: [A]: San Mateo (February, October–December). [C]: Turrialba (June). [P]: Carrara (September, October). [L]: Guapiles (January).

Caria lampeto
Godman and Salvin, 1886
FW length: 14.5–16 mm   Plate 10
Range: Mexico to Ecuador, Bolivia
Hostplant: Unknown
Early stages: Unknown
• **Adult:** Sexes dimorphic. *Male*—FW upperside dark brown with iridescent green on FW costa, medial area, and base, and a distinct silvered postmedial line; HW upperside with iridescent green at base and as a submarginal band. FW underside dark blue-black with a distinct crimson spot in the cell; HW underside blue-black with gray highlights. *Female*—upperside as in male but with only a sparse scattering of iridescent green scales. FW underside dirty brown with dull orange on the anterior one-third, and set with silvered spots; HW underside dirty brown with broken lines across the discal area. Compare with *C. rhacotis,* and *Chalodeta candiope.*

Habits: This butterfly has been recorded in our area from sea level to 800 m on the Atlantic slope in association with primary and secondary forest habitats. Encountered as solitary individuals along rivers and forest edges from midmorning until early afternoon during brilliantly sunny days. Both sexes visit the flowers of *Cordia, Croton, Serjania, Warscewiczia,* and *Mikania.*

Localities: [A]: Aguas Claras (September). [C]: Juan Viñas (January), Turrialba (June–August). [SJ]: Carrillo (February). [H]: La Selva (March, August, November, December). [L]: La Florida (March), Guapiles (May).

Genus **CHALODETA** Stichel, 1910

The butterflies in this genus are quite similar to members of *Charis* but have short setae arising from between the facets of the eyes and are of-

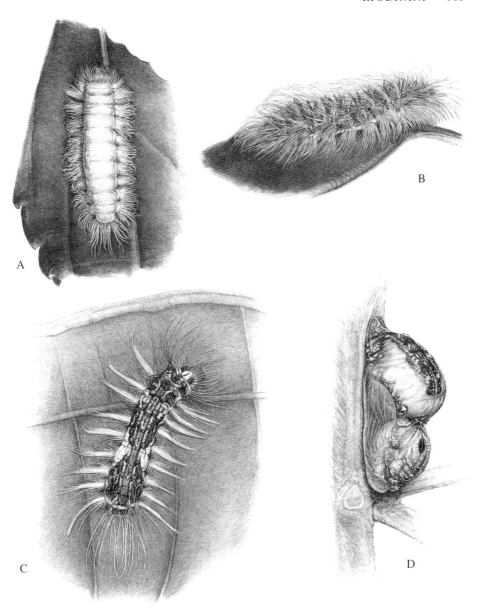

FIGURE 47. (A) *Caria rhacotis* caterpillar. (B) *Charis auius* caterpillar. (C) *Chalodeta chaonitis* caterpillar. (D) *Chalodeta chaonitis* pupa. (Drawings by J. Clark)

ten larger. The genus contains about eight species, and members are found from Mexico throughout Central and South America. Three species occur in our area.

The hostplants reported for *Chalodeta* include the Sterculiaceae, Passifloraceae, and Melastomataceae (DeVries et al. 1994; Kirkpatrick 1953). The caterpillars are covered in a short, dense pile of setae and bear long tufts of lateral setae, and in overall appearance they resemble a cross between a caterpillar of *Emesis* and *Rhetus*. The pupa is roundly squat with an extended cremaster, and except for the cremaster, it gives the impression of belonging to the Lycaenidae.

In Costa Rica, all of the species are apparently quite local, rare, and poorly represented in collections. However, it is likely that *Chalodeta* butterflies are mistaken for *Charis* in the field and hence easily ignored or overlooked.

Chalodeta chaonitis
(Hewitson, 1866)
FW length: 12–14.5 mm   **Plate 15**
Range: Mexico to Brazil, Trinidad
Hostplant: Flowers of *Miconia longifolia* (Melastomataceae)
Early stages: *Mature caterpillar* (Fig. 47c)—head capsule pale yellow with short white setae on face; body maroon overall mottled by tiny white flecks; a wide pale maroon dorsal line bordered in yellow from which arise eleven pairs of short tubercles composed of orange setae (one each per segment, except for the last three abdominal ones) from which arise some longer dark setae that curve toward the posterior; each abdominal segment with long tufts of white lateral setae (best seen when viewed from above); thoracic segments with tufts of pale brown lateral setae; a white band on abdominal segment 9 that begins at venter (as the tuft) and rings the entire dorsal portion of the segment; a large white lateral triangle on most abdominal segments, except the first abdominal segment which bears an irregular white patch; anterior edge of first thoracic segment bears short tufts of white setae. While on the inflorescence of the hostplant, both in nature and in captivity, the caterpillars feed on the developing flower buds and rest amid them, rendering them very cryptic. *Pupa* (Fig. 47d)—very rounded and lycaenid-like, appearing as though two globes were fused together; overall color green (paler on abdomen) with reddish brown areas on dorsum of thorax and abdomen; a round black spot in the middle of the thorax that appears to be a hole; the cremaster is extended and broad.

• **Adult:** Sexes slightly dimorphic. *Male*—upperside dark brown with the discal areas of both wings velvet-black, a medium silver-blue postmedial line and thin submarginal lines bordering a red-brown submarginal band; HW with a wide golden-brown margin; underside gray with a dark, iridescent blue cast that allows the medial and margin spotting to show through. *Female*—upperside similar to the male; underside yellow-brown set with many medial and marginal black spots but without any trace of blue iridescence. Compare with *lypera, Charis iris, auius*.

Habits: This butterfly has been recorded in our area from a few Atlantic lowland rain forest localities around the Sarapiqui area, and a single rain forest locality on the Pacific slope near the Osa Peninsula. In flight behavior and habitat this butterfly is similar to a large *Charis*, and thus it is likely to be mistaken for that genus while on the wing. The two times I have seen this species alive in Costa Rica occurred at the interface of primary forest and second growth during midday. In Ecuador, I frequently observed small aggregations of males perching along forest edges and in light gaps from 0.5 to 1 m above the ground between 15:00 and 15:30 hrs. In Ecuador these butterflies were typically found perching with several species of *Charis*. Rare in Costa Rican collections.

Localities: [H]: La Selva (June, July). [L]: Guapiles (November). [P]: Palmar Norte (July).

Chalodeta lypera
(Bates 1868)
FW length: 13.5–15 mm   **Plate 15**
Range: Guatemala to Brazil
Hostplant: *Theobroma cacao* (Sterculiaceae), *Passiflora* sp. (Passifloraceae)
Early stages: Kirkpatrick (1953) reports that in Trinidad the caterpillars feed on young leaves. *Mature caterpillar*—brown with grayish white at sides, and a lateral fringe of long, white hairs; a pinkish brown dorsal stripe with a pair of verrucae on each segment, each with five to seven stiff setae. The entire body when viewed from above is covered thickly with minute, spherical drops of "exudatory matter," most which are white, but some are pink or brown. *Pupa*—bright green.

• **Adult:** Sexes slightly dimorphic. *Male*—upperside dark gray-brown with a thin, angular and broken black medial line beginning near FW costa and terminating near HW inner margin, and a black submarginal line that bears some silver-blue spots across both wings; underside gray-brown overshot with some blue iridescence; fringe of both wings alternately white and brown. *Female*—upperside similar to male with margin of HW paler; underside dull gray-brown without any blue iridescence. *Note*: The female of this butterfly was described as *speusippa* Schaus, 1928, a junior synonym. Compare with *Exoplisia*.

Habits: This butterfly has been recorded in our area on the strength of a few specimens taken at two localities: one in the Atlantic lowlands, the other in the Pacific lowlands. I have never seen this insect alive, but assume its habits are similar to those described for *C. candiope*. Very rare in Costa Rican collections.

Localities: [C]: Juan Viñas (November). [P]: Cerro de Oro (January).

Chalodeta candiope
(Druce, 1904)
FW length: 13.5–15 mm   **Plate 15**
Range: Costa Rica to Colombia
Hostplant: Unknown
Early stages: Unknown
• **Adult:** Sexes dimorphic. *Male*—upperside rich dark brown with a red-brown submarginal band with black spots between the veins that is bordered on either side by thin, broken, silvered lines; fringe of both wings dark; underside distinctive red-brown overshot with iridescent violet when viewed obliquely, and set with distinct broken medial lines. *Female*—upperside lighter brown than male, with discal markings more distinct; underside rich red-brown without any iridescent violet cast, the black submarginal spots appearing to be isolated, not contained in a submarginal band. Compare with *hermodora, gynaea, auius*.
Habits: In Costa Rica this butterfly is known from two montane forest localities between 1100 and 1600 m: one locality on the Atlantic slope, and the other on the Pacific slope. Encountered typically as local solitary individuals along forest edges, streams, and occasionally in light gaps. The males perch in direct sunshine on top of leaves approximately 1 to 5 m above the ground between 06:30 and 08:00 hrs. While perching, an individual male will frantically chase other darkly colored insects of the same size and, more often than not, return to the same perch. The females fly low to the ground along forest edges between 09:00 and 12:30 hrs. Both sexes visit flowers of *Phoebe, Ocotea, Nectandra, Dendropanax, Lantana camara*, and various weedy Asteraceae that grow along sunlit forest edges. Rare in Costa Rican collections.
Localities: [SJ]: La Montura (July). [P]: Las Alturas (March–May, August–October).

Genus **PARCELLA** Stichel, 1910

This genus contains a single species that ranges from Panama to Argentina. The butterfly is recognized by being black with an orange medial band traversing both wings. In older literature this butterfly has been placed under the genera *Amblygonia, Charis*, and *Baeotis*. There is apparently nothing known of its hostplants or the early stages.

Parcella amarynthina amarynthina
(Felder and Felder, 1865)
FW length: 13 mm   **Plate 10**
Range: Costa Rica(?) to Argentina. **Subspecies:** Costa Rica(?), Panama to eastern Brazil
Hostplant: Unknown
Early stages: Unknown
• **Adult:** Sexes slightly dimorphic. *Male*—upperside black with a pale orange medial band running almost straight from FW costa to HW inner margin; underside black with the medial band much wider than on upperside. *Female*—similar to the male except with one or more yellow spots in the middle of the distal margins of both wings. Compare with *Isapis agyrtus* and *Notheme erota*.
Habits: This butterfly has not been recorded from Costa Rica. However, its presence in Panama at several localities and its enormous geographical range suggest that the butterfly may eventually be found in our area as the fauna becomes better known. In Ecuador I have observed individuals of this butterfly flying low to the ground along shaded trails, streams, and in large light gaps in the forest. G. Austin informs me that in Rondonia, Brazil, this butterfly frequently visits mud.
Localities: Not yet recorded for our area.

Genus **CHARIS** Hübner, 1819

All of the butterflies in this genus are small, generally somberly patterned on the upperside, and bear metallic markings on both sides of the wings. The butterflies in *Charis* are separated from their close allies in the genera *Calephelis* and *Chalodeta* by characteristics of the eyes and venation. Members of *Charis* are found from Mexico throughout Central and South America. Perhaps as a result of their tendency to fly low to the ground and to inhabit sunny areas, these butterflies are well represented in museums. However, most collections typically contain a great deal of jumbled and unidentified material, much of which does not associate the sexes properly. Given the current taxonomic resources, these butterflies are difficult to identify, and there is little doubt that the genus could use a proper revision. Five species are reported from our area.

For a group of butterflies that has many abundant species, surprisingly little is known about the hostplants of *Charis* (DeVries et al. 1994). In Central and South America I have not infrequently observed that on sunny days following a period of cloudy weather, the females oviposit single eggs on a variety of dead leaves that litter the forest floor. The only requirement appears to be that the leaves be moist and in a state of decay. The caterpillars of several species feed on dead leaves and are covered with long, densely packed setae (Fig. 47b), giving the impression of a tiny member of the Megalopygidae. In my experience, the caterpillars grow very slowly and are rather difficult to rear to adulthood.

In Costa Rica these butterflies are commonly, and often abundantly, found in second growth or sunny areas within forests ranging from sea level to well over 1200 m elevation. At any particular site there are typically several species that fly together.

Charis auius
(Cramer, 1776)
FW length: 12–14 mm   **Plate 11**
Range: Costa Rica to Brazil
Hostplant: Dead leaves
Early stages: *Egg*—tiny, white, lozenge-shaped, typically deposited on the confluence of the veins on dead leaves. *Mature caterpillar*—extremely hirsute and effectively looks like a small brown ambulatory puff-ball.
• **Adult:** Sexes dimorphic. *Male*—upperside dark brown with a red-brown submarginal band on both wings that is bordered on either side by broken silver-blue lines, and in many specimens a submarginal band that contains black spots between the radial veins that are pushed toward the distal margin, not centered; underside dark gray to black, overshot entirely with a magnificent deep blue iridescence through which may be seen thin, broken, black medial lines on both wings; fringe of both wings black and white. *Female*—upperside similar to male except warmer brown, and the broken discal lines and black spots in postmedial band are more distinct; underside dull dark gray without any blue iridescence, and the two submarginal silver-blue lines are distinct. Compare with *iris, velutina, hermodora, gynaea, Chalodeta candiope.*

Habits: This common butterfly has been reported in our area from 200 to 1500 m on both slopes in all habitats except the Guanacaste dry forest, although it is decidedly more abundant in montane areas. Typically encountered in local populations in open areas along forest edges or along streams between 08:30 and 13:00 hrs. Both sexes fly close to the ground. During courtship the male hovers above the female while they are flying, extending his iridescent blue forelegs. Courtship may last for up to 30 sec as the pair steadily ascends higher into the air, then both will rocket off in a fast and furious flight. Individual males may remain faithful to particular perching leaves for a few days. Common.
Localities: [C]: Turrialba. [H]: Chilamate (September, November, December), Tirimbina (February, September). [P]: San Vito (October), Piedras Blancas (June), Sirena (March), Las Alturas (January–December), and without doubt many more localities.

Charis velutina
Godman and Salvin, 1878
FW length: 13–14 mm   **Not illustrated**
Range: Mexico to Colombia
Hostplant: Unknown
Early stages: Unknown
• **Adult:** Sexes dimorphic. *Male*—upperside similar to *auius*; underside with a deep iridescent violet cast almost as in *gynaea*, with a silvered marginal line extends from the acute FW costa to HW inner margin; fringe on the both wings checkered black and white. *Female*—unknown to me, but judging from the illustration in D'Abrera (1994), the upperside is pale brown with two silvered submarginal lines, and an acute FW apex. Compare with *auius, gynaea, iris, Chalodeta candiope.*
Habits: This butterfly has been reported in our area from a single mid-elevation locality on the Atlantic slope.
Localities: Cachi.

Charis iris
Staudinger, 1876
FW length: 13–15 mm   **Plate 15**
Range: Guatemala to Colombia
Hostplant: Unknown
Early stages: Unknown
• **Adult:** Sexes dimorphic. *Male*—upperside dark brown with a wavy silver-blue postmedial line that runs from FW costa to HW inner margin, and a silver-blue submarginal line that smoothly follows the contour of the distal margins, the FW with distinct white fringe (sometimes interspersed with some brown) and HW

with pure white fringe; underside dull, deep blue with some iridescence, and a distinct, silver-blue submarginal line that smoothly follows the distal margins of both wings. *Female*— upperside dark red-brown with the silver-blue postmedial and submarginal lines and fringe of both wings as in the male; FW apex slightly falcate; underside red-brown with a broken, black medial line that traces from end of FW cell to HW inner margin; broken silver postmedial and marginal lines run from FW costa to HW inner margin; fringe on both wings distinctly white. Compare with *hermodora, gynaea, auius, velutina, Chalodeta candiope,* and *chaonitis* **Habits:** This butterfly occurs in our area from sea level to 1000 m on both slopes in association with rain forest habitats. Typically encountered as infrequent solitary individuals or in very small local populations along overgrown streams between 08:30 to 15:00 hrs. The males often perch on the upperside of low vegetation that extends over the water and engage in aerial interactions with other males, including those of *C. auius*. During these interactions, the two males face each other while flying in place, project their conspicuous blue forelegs, and slowly ascend into the air for about a meter or so. Between 5 and 10 seconds later they break off the interaction and each will return to its individual perch. Both sexes visit flowers of weedy Asteraceae.
Localities: [A]: San Gabriel Dos Rios (May), Cariblanco (May, June). [C]: Turrialba (March), Juan Viñas, Tuis. [SJ]: Carrillo (September). [H]: La Selva (April), Chilamate (May), Plastico (August). [P]: Rincon (February), Sirena (March), San Vito (August, September), Palmar Norte (July). [L]: Rio Bannano. [G]: Tilaran.

Charis hermodora
Felder and Felder, 1861
FW length: 12–13 mm   **Plate 11**
Range: Costa Rica to Venezuela, Trinidad
Hostplant: Unknown
Early stages: Unknown
• **Adult:** Sexes dimorphic. *Male*—upperside rich, dark brown with a red brown submarginal band on both wings, with the black spots centered between the radial veins; underside brown with no iridescence, discal areas with a series of fine, broken lines, and a single silver-blue submarginal line that smoothly follows the distal margins. *Female*—upperside medium brown, but otherwise patterned as the male; underside red-brown and patterned as in male. Compare with *velutina, iris, auius, gynaea, Adelotypa eudocia, Chalodeta candiope.*

Habits: This butterfly has been reported in our area from a single lowland Atlantic locality. In Panama, G. Small found this butterfly abundant in a variety of localities around the canal. I presume that its habits are similar to other species in the genus, and it is likely that this butterfly has simply been overlooked in our area.
Localities: [L]: Limon.

Charis gynaea
(Godart, 1824)
FW length: 12–14 mm   **Plate 11**
Range: Costa Rica to Brazil
Hostplant: Dead, slightly decayed leaves
Early stages: *Egg*—lozenge-shaped, pale green deposited on the confluence of the veins on dead leaves. *Early instar caterpillars*—very densely covered in long brown setae. The caterpillars feed on the epidermis of dead leaves, and they may be found wandering across the forest floor.
• **Adult:** Sexes dimorphic. *Male*—upperside dark brown with a red-brown submarginal band set with dark spots centered between radial veins, and the band bordered on either side by smooth silver-blue lines; underside reddish brown overshot with a faint violet iridescence and a single silver-blue submarginal line on HW. *Female*—upperside patterned as in male; underside warm brown without iridescence, a smooth silver-blue submarginal line across both wings, and conspicuous broken lines on discal areas. Compare with *hermodora, auius, iris, velutina, Adelotypa eudocia, Chalodeta candiope.*
Habits: This butterfly occurs commonly from sea level to 800 m on both slopes in all forest types, including the Guanacaste dry forest. Typically encountered in local populations along forest edges, light gaps, and even in pastures flying with *Calephelis* species. In my experience, this common butterfly is active from midmorning until early afternoon, it is present throughout the year, and it is the most abundant species of the genus in our area. Both sexes avidly visit flowers of various weedy Asteraceae.
Localities: [A]: Cariblanco (June), San Gabriel Dos Rios (May). [C]: Tres Rios (December), Turrialba (May, June, August), Juan Viñas, Tuis. [SJ]: Carrillo (June), El Rodeo (June, July). [H]: La Selva (April–September, December), Chilamate (May, July), Tirimbina (February, March, June). [P]: San Vito (July), Piedras Blancas (June, July), Sirena (March, April), San Luis at Rio Guacimal (June). [L]: Guapiles (March), Rio Bannano. [G]: Santa Rose (December), Tilaran.

Genus **CALEPHELIS** Grote and Robinson, 1869
by George T. Austin

Members of *Calephelis* are small, drab, and usually inconspicuous butterflies that are difficult to identify. The genus is readily recognized by the brown to red-brown upperside with series of usually broken, concentric lines on the basal portion of the wings, and two narrow marginal series of silvery, metallic bars. The outer black line is often shaded proximally and forms an irregular dark medial band across both wings on some species. The underside varies from pale yellow-brown to pale red-brown, with the markings of the upperside repeated but usually more distinct. Females usually have more rounded wings than males. The genus is distinguished from *Charis* and *Chalodeta* by the absence of setae on the compound eyes and a usually paler underside. Difficulty in determining the species is due to the external similarity of many taxa and the occurrence of seasonal forms. Clues to identity include wing shape, presence and intensity of a median dark band across the upperside of the wings, and either a single or double outer black line on the underside. The genitalia of both sexes often need to be examined for definite determination; even then it is useful to have series of several species for comparison (see Table 11). The female genitalia are very fragile, and it is often easiest to identify this sex by their associated males. Members of *Calephelis* are found from southern Canada to Argentina, and the genus has its greatest diversity in Central America.

So little is known of the biology and local distribution of this genus that the exact number of species in *Calephelis* is unknown. The revision by McAlpine (1971), who recognized thirty-seven species, must be the starting point for future studies; additional species have recently been described by de la Maza et al. (1977) and Austin (1993). The utility of McAlpine's revision, however, is hampered by poor figures, incomplete descriptions, and few comparative notes. Further study may well show that the genus is oversplit at the specific level. For example, Scott (1986) lumped a number of McAlpine's (1971) species mainly on the basis of wing shape and female genitalia. For the present purpose, however, the taxonomy of McAlpine will be followed, and the reader should be aware that undescribed or misplaced species may be involved.

The early stages are known only for some of the North American taxa (Comstock 1928; Comstock and Dammers 1932; dos Passos 1936; McAlpine 1938; de la Maza and de la Maza 1976). The eggs are turban shaped, usually reddish, often with white ridges, and turn shiny white before hatching. They are laid singly on the hostplant, often on the lower surface of leaves or in leaf axils. The larvae eat leaves, or the epidermis of stems, build no nests, and have no symbiotic associations with ants. The larvae vary from pale green to gray, have long and thick whitish dorsal and lateral setae, and are often spotted black dorsally. The hostplants include Asteraceae and Ranunculaceae. The pupae are suspended by a silken girdle and vary from pale green to yellow, brown, and gray with dark spots. Often the pupal abdomen is a different shade than the rest of the body. The pupae are covered with the setae of the last larval instar.

Calephelis fly in sunny places and avoid shaded habitats. Adults visit flowers and occasionally mud, bask with their wings open, and rest in the same position beneath leaves. Males usually perch to wait for passing females, and the males of some species evidently also actively patrol in search of females.

In Costa Rica, *Calephelis* butterflies are found throughout the country in open areas from sea level to over 2000 m elevation. The butterflies are also common sights in scrubby second growth and in weedy situations, including banana and coffee plantations, gardens, and abandoned lots in towns, and along roadsides.

Calephelis sixaola
McAlpine, 1971
FW length: 13–14 mm   **Plate 12**
Range: Costa Rica
Hostplant: Unknown
Early stages: Unknown
• **Adult:** Sexes slightly dimorphic. This species is the largest and easiest to identify. Both sexes have a sinuous outer margin to the FW that terminates in a falcate apex; upperside brown with a darker band across the median area; two large, dark brown spots between the indistinct silvery lines at the FW apex; there may be one or two additional ones toward the FW tornus. Dry season (March, April) individuals are pale brown; wet season individuals (September, October) are dark brown, and both forms tend to be paler distally than basally. Underside bright yellow-brown (dry season) to red-brown (wet season) with the inner silvered and outer black lines the most prominent. Compare with *fulmen*.

Table 11
Characters for Distinguishing the Costa Rican *Calephelis*

	sixaola	fulmen	schausi	browni	sodalis	costaricicola	exiguus	argyrodines	inca	laverna
Wings										
Size	Large	Large	Medium	Medium	Medium	Medium	Small	Medium	Small	Small
FW apex	Falcate	Falcate	Not falcate	Not falcate	Not falcate	Not falcate	Not falcate	Not falcate	Not falcate	Not falcate
Upperside										
Color	Dark brown	Medium brown	Red-brown	Dark gray-brown	Dark gray-brown	Medium red-brown	Dark red-brown	Dark red-brown	Orange-brown	Pale red-brown
Median band	Prominent broad	Prominent broad	Very faint broad	Faint broad	Faint broad	Prominent narrow	Prominent narrow	Prominent broad	Absent	Faint broad
Silver lines	Prominent	Faint	Prominent	Prominent	Prominent	Faint	Faint	Faint	Prominent	Prominent
Between silver lines	Dark spots	Dark apical spots	Red-brown	Distinctly dark	Distinctly dark	Indistinctly dark	Indistinctly dark	Indistinctly dark	Pale	Brown
Underside										
Color	Dark red-brown to ochraceous	Red-brown to ochraceous	Red-brown	Red-brown	Red-brown	Ochraceous	Ochraceous	Ochraceous	Ochraceous	Bright red-brown
Prominent lines	Inner silver, outer black	Inner silver, outer black	Outer black	Inner silver	Inner silver	Outer black	Inner silver	Inner silver, outer black	Inner silver	Inner silver, outer black
Male genitalia										
Ventral view of valvae	Robust, straight	Robust, straight	Robust, straight	Robust, straight	Robust, straight	Thin, rounded	Thin, rounded	Thin, straight	Thin, straight	Short, stout
Transtilla in relation to valvae	Longer	Longer	Longer	Shorter	Longer	Shorter	Equal	Shorter	Longer	Longer

Habits: This species appears to be restricted to the Atlantic slope in Costa Rica, where it is not uncommon from sea level to about 1000 m in disturbed areas along roads and cacao plantations. It visits flowers along forest edges, and is occasionally seen along forest trails.
Localities: [A]: Cariblanco (June). [C]: Bajo Pacuare (October), Rio Chitaria (September), Rio Reventazon (June), Turrialba (April, July), Juan Viñas. [H]: Finca La Lola (September), Chilamate (March, May), La Selva (May). [L]: Banana River (March), Puerto Viejo (April), Germania (March, April), Rio Blanco (March), Guapiles (August), Rio Victoria (April, October), Rio Hondo (September), Sixaola River [TL] (September).

Calephelis fulmen
(Stichel, 1910)
FW length: 12–14 mm   Plate 12
Range: Mexico to Panama
Hostplant: Unknown
Early stages: Unknown
• **Adult:** Sexes slightly dimorphic. Similar to *sixaola*, but usually paler, FW margin less sinuous, and the apex less falcate. Wings are similarly crossed by a dark band in medial area, but the basal and distal areas are nearly of the same color (basal area appears slightly darker than the distal area on *sixaola*). The dark spots between the silvered lines on FW similar to *sixaola* but less contrasting, and the posterior ones are more often absent. Wet season individuals tend to be darker than those of the dry season (which are a rich tan—not dull brown as in *sixaola*). The median band of the dry season form extends more distally than on the wet season form. The outer black line which defines the distal limits of this band in the wet season form occurs in the middle of the dark area on dry season individuals. This line is nearly continuous and clearly discernible on *fulmen*, but on *sixaola* it is generally blurred into the dark band. Underside duller than that of *sixaola*. Note: Male genitalia of *sixaola* and *fulmen* clearly separate them from other Costa Rican congeners: their anterior lateral processes of the transtilla extend beyond the posterior lateral processes (shorter on congeners). In *sixaola* the processes do not extend to the tip of the valva, whereas on *fulmen* they extend to the tips or beyond. Compare with *sixaola*.
Habits: This species appears to be uncommon, and it is known only from the central Pacific slope along roadsides between 600 and 1000 m elevation.
Localities: [A]: Atenas (March, December), Rio

Colorado (October), Alajuela (March), San Carlos [TL]. [SJ]: Villa Colon (September), Finca El Rodeo (March, June), Puriscal (September), Carrillo de Poas (April), San Jose (August). [P]: San Luis at Rio Guacimal (December).

Calephelis schausi
McAlpine, 1971
FW length: 10–12 mm   Plate 12
Range: Honduras to Panama
Hostplant: Unknown
Early stages: Unknown
• **Adult:** Sexes dimorphic. *Male*—upperside pale brown to dark red-brown with a faint dark band across FW median area (often absent on HW). Silvered lines are usually broad, distinct, and the inner one bends outward at its center on the FW. Between the silvered lines is a series of distinct black points encircled with a rich red-brown. A similar, more prominent series is on the HW. The basal lines are usually indistinct and lost in the ground color. Dry season individuals seem paler than wet season ones. Underside pale red-brown (more ochraceous in dry season), with a basal portion of the wings lightly marked with disconnected black lines. Silver lines prominent, equal in their intensity, and the inner one is distinctly broken at the veins. Male genitalia have a long thin transtilla that clearly exceeds the length of the valva, and the tip is strongly recurved dorsally. The smaller and brighter *inca* has a broader transtilla. *Female*—paler red-brown than the male, with rounded wings. The darker medial band ranges from faint to obsolete, the series of black-centered red-brown dots between the silvered lines are similar to the male but less contrasting, and the black basal lines are more distinct. Underside ochraceous to almost orange and paler than in males. Compare with *browni, laverna*.
Habits: This species is relatively common over the length of the Pacific slope from sea level to 3300 m, with a single record from the Atlantic slope. The butterflies visit flowers along forest edges and are found occasionally in forest openings.
Localities: [A]: San Mateo [TL] (October, September), La Balsa (August), Atenas (March, September), Guacima (September), Monte Verde Road (September), Rio Colorado (October), San Antonio de Belen (September). [SJ]: Finca El Rodeo (June, October), Villa Colon (September), Puriscal (September), Orotina (December), Cerro de la Muerte. [H]: Chilamate (May). [P]: Monte Verde (July), Rio Pita (September), Barranca (Au-

gust, September), Quepos (September), Buenos Aires (September), Osa Peninsula (January), Rio Cacao (September), Rio Catarata (October), Palmar Norte (June). [G]: Cañas (February, December), Bijagua (September), El Coco (September), Parque Santa Rosa (March), Avangarez (July), Finca Comelco (June, August, September, November, December), Pitilla (March).

Calephelis browni
McAlpine, 1971
FW length: 10–12 mm   **Plate 12**
Range: Guatemala to Panama
Hostplant: Unknown
Early stages: Unknown
• **Adult:** Sexes dimorphic. *Male*—upperside dark, gray-brown with a distinct band in the median area, and black basal lines poorly defined. The outer silver line is prominent, and the inner one is less prominent and irregular. The area between the silver lines is usually as dark as the median band and bears a series of black points. There is no apparent seasonal dimorphism. Underside dull red-brown to pale yellow, red-brown; basal lines are distinct, with the outer one often partially doubled. The genitalia are comparable to *costaricicola*, *exiguus*, and *argyrodines* in that the transtilla does not exceed the length of the valvae. However, the valvae of *browni* are robust and straight in ventral view. *Female*—upperside similar to male but with broader wings and with basal lines more distinct; FW slightly concave below the apex. Underside brighter than male, and silver line very distinct. Distinguished from *schausi* by the gray-brown upperside, distinct median band, area between silver lines without red-brown spots, males with produced FW, and females with undulating distal margins. Compare with *schausi*, *sodalis*, *costaricicola*, *exiguus*, *argyrodines*.
Habits: This is the most common and widespread species in our area and was originally described from Turrialba. There are records from sea level to over 2000 m on both slopes, in all habitats except Guanacaste. Typically found along roadsides and forest edges.
Localities: [A]: Atenas (January, September, December), Guacima (September), Reserva San Ramon (September), Mt. Poas (June). [C]: Turrialba [TL] (May–August), Cartago (February), Casamata (September), Rio Chitaria (March, September), La Suiza (September), Juan Viñas (March). [SJ]: Finca El Rodeo (June, September, October), Villa Colon (September), Desamparados (August, September), Monte Claro (September), San Ger-

onimo (September), Copey (September), Orotina (December). [H]: La Virgin (March), Chilamate (September), Puerto Viejo (March), Cariblanco (March, June). [L]: Germania (March), Guapiles (August, November), Perla de Siquirres (April), Siquirres (February, July). [P]: Rio Cacao (September), Rio Catarata (September), Rio Coto (September), Villa Neily (July), Buenos Aires (January, September), Palmar Norte (March).

Calephelis sodalis
Austin, 1993
FW length: 11–13 mm   **Plate 12**
Range: Costa Rica, Panama(?)
Hostplant: Unknown
Early stages: Unknown
• **Adult:** Sexes slightly dimorphic. Strongly resembles *browni*, but the male genitalia have shorter valvae, and transtilla are longer than the valvae. Compare with *schausi*, *browni*, *laverna*, *inca*.
Habits: Known only from 1400 to 1600 m on the Pacific slope in the Valle de Coton rain shadow near the Panamanian border. However, it is certain that this species will be found to have a broader range as the Central American fauna becomes better known. Both sexes are encountered between 10:00 and 13:30 hrs in open pastures where there is water seepage, or along rivers with wide banks covered in herbaceous second growth. Adults fly low to the ground in direct sunshine and frequently visit flowers of various weedy Asteraceae. These butterflies may be common in the appropriate habitat.
Localities: [P]: Las Alturas [TL] (May, June, August, September).

Calephelis costaricicola
Strand, 1916
FW length: 9–11 mm   **Plate 12**
Range: Mexico(?), Honduras to Panama
Hostplant: Unknown
Early stages: Unknown
• **Adult:** Sexes dimorphic. *Male*—similar to *browni* but smaller and with FW apex distinctly pointed. Upperside pale, gray-brown with a dark but indistinct medial band with black basal lines narrow and prominently defined; silver lines are barely discernible, the area proximal to them without gray, and the area between these lines not very dark. The anterior portion of the outer basal line is sharply angled. Underside ranges from ochraceous to ochraceous-red and does not have prominent silver lines; black basal lines well developed (the outer one often doubled) and are the

most prominent. The transtilla of the genitalia are short and similar to *browni*, but rounded in ventral view, and have the appearance of a toilet seat. *Female*—broader wings than the male. Compare with *browni, exiguus, argyrodines*. **Habits:** This species, originally described from Costa Rica, is known from 600 to 1200 m on the Pacific slope. It has been taken in disturbed areas along roadsides and in weed lots in towns and villages. The main flight period appears to be during the dry season. **Localities:** [A]: Atenas (January, March, December), Orotina (September). [C]: Cartago (March, September, December), Volcan Irazu (April). [SJ]: Paso Ancho (March), San Jose (April, July, August), Villa Colon (September), Desamparados (February, March, November), Patarra (November), San Pedro (July), Monte Redondo (March). [P]: Buenos Aires (September).

Calephelis exiguus
Austin, 1993
FW length: 10–11 mm   Plate 12
Range: Costa Rica
Hostplant: Unknown
Early stages: Unknown
• **Adult:** Sexes slightly dimorphic. Upperside dark red-brown with a faint medial band, silver lines indistinct. Underside dull orange-brown, with very fine black basal lines, the outer one of which is not doubled or shaded. Resembles a small *costaricicola* but with medial band less well developed, underside more orange than ochraceous, and the outer basal black line not doubled or very prominent. Male genitalia not broadly rounded, and transtilla short but narrower than *costaricicola*. Compare with *costaricicola, inca, laverna*. **Habits:** This recently described species is known only from the lowland Atlantic slope southeast of Limon, and perhaps two specimens collected near the Sarapiqui may be of this species. It may be found to have a broader range as our fauna becomes better known. Adults occur in second growth, open areas. **Localities:** [H]: Magsaysay (June), Chilamate (May). [L]: Paraiso (September), Bribri (September), La Bomba (September), Rio Victoria (October), Madre de Dios (July).

Calephelis argyrodines
(Bates, 1866)
FW length: 10–12 mm   Plate 12
Range: Guatemala to Costa Rica
Hostplant: Unknown
Early stages: Unknown
• **Adult:** Sexes slightly dimorphic. Confusingly

similar to *browni* and *costaricicola*, and some specimens defy determination. The placement of this phenotype here is tentative, but it appears closest to this species than any other. Slightly larger than *costaricicola* with both outer black line and inner silver line on underside of HW prominent. The FW in *browni* is more pointed. Male genitalia are similar to *browni* but with the valvae slimmer. Compare with *browni* and *costaricicola*. **Habits:** This species occurs from near sea level to 1200 m on both slopes. It is found at many of the same localities and elevations as *costaricicola*, but appears to have a longer flight period—from end of wet season through dry season, and into beginning of wet season. **Localities:** [A]: Balsa (August), Vera Blanca (March), Atenas (April), Alajuela (February). [C]: Orosi (August), Cartago (December). [SJ]: Desamparados (February–May, September, November, December), Geronimo (December), Patarra (March, November), Paso Ancho (March), Escazu (May), Univ. de Costa Rica (July). [H]: Santo Domingo de Heredia (February). [P]: Buenos Aires (September). [L]: Siquirres (April).

Calephelis inca
McAlpine, 1971
FW length: 9–10 mm   Plate 12
Range: Costa Rica to northern Brazil
Hostplant: Unknown
Early stages: Unknown
• **Adult:** Sexes slightly dimorphic. *Male*—upperside bright orange-brown with black basal lines, and no dark band across medial area; underside bright ochraceous orange; black basal lines very fine, the outer one not doubled, and inner silver line very bold, especially on females. *Female*—wings more rounded than the males. Distinguished from all other Costa Rican species by the small size, and the paler and brighter upperside. The male genitalia resemble those of *schausi*. Compare with *laverna*. **Habits:** In our area this species is apparently very locally distributed and known only from two localities between sea level and 1000 m on the Pacific slope. Uncommon. **Localities:** [A]: Atenas (March). [P]: Mata Limon (March).

Calephelis laverna parva
Austin, 1993
FW length: 9–10 mm   Plate 12
Range: Costa Rica, Trinidad to northern Brazil.
  Subspecies: Costa Rica
Hostplant: Unknown
Early stages: Unknown

• **Adult:** Sexes slightly dimorphic. Upperside red-brown, basal black line very broad and slightly shaded proximally; inner silver line on both wings notably sinuous, and often distinctly offset basally toward hind margin of FW. Underside pale red-brown, with the silver lines well defined, and the outer black line not doubled. Male genitalia with distinctive transtilla that extend posterior to the valvae; the tip of transtilla is thin and not curved dorsally. The valvae are short, stout, and broadly joined anteriorly. The red-brown underside, genitalia, and small size distinguish this species from other Costa Rican congeners. Compare with *schausi, sodalis, browni, laverna.*

Habits: This species is reported from below 200 m on the Pacific slope in southern Costa Rica from areas around the Osa Peninsula.

Localities: [P]: Sirena (March), La Vacita (March), Rincon (March), Paso Canoa (July), 20 km N of Palmar Sur (July).

Acknowledgments—The author of this treatment of Costa Rican *Calephelis* (G. Austin) thanks the Allyn Museum of Entomology (L. Miller, J. Miller), the Carnegie Museum (J. Rawlins), the Milwaukee Public Museum (S. Borkin), the American Museum of Natural History (F. Rindge, the late G. E. Martinez), P. J. DeVries, and J. Brock for the loan of material.

Genus **LASAIA** Bates, 1868

The butterflies in this genus generally have a metallic blue upperside set with fine black spots, and a cryptic underside covered with broken lines and spots. In appearance, these butterflies resemble members of the genera *Apodemia, Calydna,* and *Exoplisia.* Members of *Lasaia* are found from the southern USA to Argentina, and the most recent revision (Clench 1972) recognized twelve species that are distributed almost equally between Mexico and Central America on one hand, and South America on the other. Five species occur in our area.

The only hostplant record available for *Lasaia* is from the Fabaceae (DeVries et al. 1994). The flattened egg of *Lasaia* is highly unusual in its resemblance to two stacked pies (Downey and Allyn 1980). The caterpillars are covered in dense setae much like those in the genus *Melanis.*

These butterflies are most commonly encountered flying in bright sunshine or visiting damp sand along streams and river crossings.

However, *Lasaia* butterflies are extremely skittish, and their fast, erratic flight makes them difficult to capture or observe. In our area these butterflies are typically found most frequently in Pacific lowland habitats. Apparently some of the species can be abundant in other countries, but not in our area.

Lasaia agesilas
(Latreille, 1809)
FW length: 15–17 mm   Plate 16
Range: Mexico to Colombia
Hostplant: Unknown
Early stages: Unknown
• **Adult:** Sexes dimorphic. *Male*—FW upperside dark, shining blue with distinct black bands in the cell; HW upperside almost entirely blue with only a few black spots near costa and base; underside variable, but typically mottled gray and white with many dark spots (some specimens may be marked distinctly with gray-white areas at FW tornus and HW costa). *Female*—upperside dirty gray-brown with the basal half of both wings darker; underside white mottled with many black spots and zig-zag lines on both wings. *Note:* Two recognized subspecies occur in Costa Rica: *agesilas* (Latreille, 1809) which ranges from the Meseta Central south to Brazil, and *callaina* Clench, 1972, which ranges from Mexico to approximately the Meseta Central in Costa Rica. Compare with *sula, pseudomeris.*

Habits: This butterfly occurs locally and sporadically in our area on both slopes from sea level to 1600 m in association with all forest habitats. Encountered as solitary individuals during midday along forest edges visiting small white flowers, or wet sand. The flight is very fast and erratic, thus making visual identification and capture difficult. Although there is abundant material of this species from areas north and south of Costa Rica, it is uncommon in Costa Rican collections.

Localities: [A]: San Antonio de Belen (April), Atenas (June). [SJ]: El Rodeo (June, September). [C]: La Suiza (September). [P]: Las Alturas (April), Palmar Sur, Palmar Norte (June). [L]: Guapiles. [G]: Santa Rosa (December), Cañas (May–July, October), Bagaces.

Lasaia sessilis
Schaus, 1890
FW length: 13–16 mm   Plate 16
Range: Mexico to Costa Rica
Hostplant: Unknown
Early stages: Unknown
• **Adult:** Sexes similar. Upperside dull, dark blue-gray with a profusion of short black lines

on the discal area of both wings; underside an almost uniform gray with a scattering of small, black crescent marks in the medial area. Some specimens may have a yellowish cast at the FW base and inner margin. Compare with *sula* and *agesilas*.

Habits: In our area this butterfly has been recorded from two Pacific slope localities that range from sea level to 1400 m. In the Guanacaste dry forest, the butterfly appears to be present throughout most of the year, but in the Talamancas it appears to fly in the drier periods. Both sexes visit small white flowered trees, shrubs, and vines for nectar. Uncommon in Costa Rican collections.

Localities: [P]: Las Alturas (April–July). [G]: Cañas (February–June, August, September, November, December).

Lasaia sula sula
Staudinger, 1888
FW length: 14.5–15.5 mm   **Plate 16**
Range: South Texas to Costa Rica. **Subspecies:** Western Mexico to Costa Rica
Hostplant: *Albizia* sp. (Fabaceae)
Early stages: *Egg*—highly unusual; appears as two stacked pies. The eggs have been well illustrated by Downey and Allyn (1980), who muse that the egg looks like a flying saucer complete with illuminated windows. It does! *Mature caterpillar*—similar in overall appearance to *Melanis pixie*, but gray with black bands along each segment, covered in a fine pile of setae, and with a series of long lateral setae that obscure the legs.
• **Adult:** Sexes dimorphic. *Male*—upperside pale metallic blue with distinct black markings at FW apex, costa, and a submarginal row of black spots on both wings; underside mottled pale brown and gray with pearly gray areas along distal half of FW and HW. *Female*—upperside gray checkered with black and white, the latter color forming a broken postmedial band; underside similar to upperside, but with more extensive white areas. Compare with *agesilas*, *pseudomeris*.
Habits: This butterfly is recorded mainly from the Pacific slope in association with dry forest and agricultural habitats between sea level and 1200 m, and is apparently absent from the wetter forest habitats south of San Mateo. On the Atlantic slope it has been reported from forest habitats between 200 and 600 m. Uncommon in Costa Rican collections.
Localities: [SJ]: San Jose (November). [C]: Turrialba (June). [H]: Magsaysay (August). [G]: Bagaces (May), Santa Rosa (June, August), Cañas (June, July), Taboga (February).

Lasaia oileus
Godman, 1903
FW length: 10–13 mm   **Plate 16**
Range: Honduras to Peru, Brazil
Hostplant: Unknown
Early stages: Unknown
• **Adult:** Sexes dimorphic. *Male*—upperside almost black with pale gray-blue areas along distal margins of both wings (especially noticeable on HW) and a white spot at costal margin near end of FW cell; underside white with a dense marbling of brown, especially in the medial areas. *Female*—upperside marbled dark brown with a scattering of bluish white patches at base and distal margins of both wings; underside washed extensively with white. This is the smallest of our *Lasaia* species. Compare with *Calydna hiria*, *Apodemia walkeri*.
Habits: This tiny butterfly is apparently rare throughout its entire range. In Costa Rica it is known from a few specimens taken by W. Schaus at a single lowland Atlantic slope locality that presumably had, at the time, much greater expanses of rain forest than are present today. The apparent rarity of this butterfly in collections is likely to be explained, in part, by its diminutive size.
Localities: [L]: Sixaola (March).

Lasaia pseudomeris
Clench, 1972
FW length: 13.5–14.5 mm   **Plate 16**
Range: Costa Rica to Colombia, Venezuela, Peru
Hostplant: Unknown
Early stages: Unknown
• **Adult:** Sexes presumably dimorphic. *Male*—upperside shining blue-green with a few small white spots at FW costa near end of cell, and a black HW apex; underside marbled pale brown and blue-gray, the latter color especially noticeable on the postmedial areas of both wings. *Female*—apparently unknown and in need of description. Compare with *sula* and *agesilas*.
Habits: This butterfly is recorded in our area from sea level to 900 m on the Pacific slope. Rare in Costa Rican collections.
Localities: [A]: San Antonio de Belen. [G]: Cañas (May–October), Santa Rosa.

Genus **EXOPLISIA** Godman and Salvin, 1886

In overall appearance, the butterflies in *Exoplisia* superficially resemble some members of the genus *Emesis*, but they may be separated by the iridescent blue sheen on the underside of the wings. In older literature these butterflies have been placed in the genera *Charis*, *Amarynthis*, and *Nelone*. Members of *Exoplisia* are found from Honduras through Central and South America, and the genus is considered to embrace four species. There is decidedly one species in our area, and a second that is attributed to our fauna on the strength of what may be an erroneous record.

In contrast to many areas of South America, these butterflies appear to be very rare in our area. In Ecuador, I frequently found individual males of *E. cadmeis* in forest light gaps and along small shaded streams visiting wet sand or mud. When disturbed from the ground, these extremely skittish butterflies fly away with a rapid, erratic flight and perch under leaves between 1 and 3 m from the ground. After a few minutes, the same individuals will generally return to patches of wet ground. The only host record I have found is that of G. Onore, who reared *E. cadmeis* on *Ochroma pyramidale* (Bombacaceae) in Ecuador.

Exoplisia cadmeis
(Hewitson, 1866)
FW length: 17–17.5 mm   Plate 9
Range: Honduras to Peru
Hostplant: *Ochroma pyramidale* (Bombacaceae)
Early stages: Undescribed
• **Adult:** Sexes dimorphic. *Male*—upperside sooty brown with some gray areas along submargin of both wings; underside dark gray with many indistinct black transverse stripes, and completely overshot with an imposing blue iridescence; FW margin with alternating white and dark fringe, whereas HW fringe entirely white. *Female*—upper and undersides entirely brown; HW distal margin more rounded

than the male. Compare with *hypochalbe*, *Emesis ocypore*, *Lasaia*.
Habits: In our area this butterfly is known only from the Atlantic slope in montane forests in the Turrialba and Estrella valleys at 800 to 1200 m. In Panama, however, G. Small found this butterfly on the Pacific slope at sea level. In Ecuador I frequently found the skittish males of this species visiting damp soil along streams and trails deep in the forest. Rare in Costa Rican collections.
Localities: [C]: Moravia de Chirripo (June), Cachio. [L]: Coen (March).

Exoplisia hypochalbe
(Felder and Felder, 1861)
FW length: 22 mm   Plate 9
Range: Nicaragua(?), Peru, and Bolivia
Hostplant: Unknown
Early stages: Unknown
• **Adult:** Sexes dimorphic(?). *Male*—upperside dark brown; underside overshot with iridescent light blue and dark blue bands running across the medial area of both wings. *Female*—apparently undescribed. Compare with *cadmeis*.
Habits: This butterfly has been reported as occurring in Central America on the basis of a single specimen in the collection of Boisduval (see Godman and Salvin 1886), and subsequently listed as a species whose range includes Central America. However, it apparently has never been observed subsequently to occur outside of South America. Thus it seems likely that the historical inclusion of this butterfly as a member of the Nicaraguan fauna is based upon an erroneous record.
Localities: Not recorded for our area, nor the western Andes, and thus in need of confirmation as a member of the Central American fauna.

Tribe SYMMACHIINI Bates, 1859

The members placed in this tribe are characterized by having males with androconial scales on the anterior margins of abdominal tergites 4 through 7. The group embraces upwards of 130 species placed in nearly a dozen genera: *Mesene*, *Mesenopsis*, *Xenandra*, *Esthemopsis*, *Chimastrum*, *Symmachia*, *Phaenochitonia*, *Pterographium*, *Stichelia*, and the South American genus *Lucillella* and the genus *Xynias* that was recently sunk by D'Abrera (1994). Hostplant families reported for this tribe include Melastomataceae, Sapindaceae, Fabaceae, Ulmaceae, and Violaceae. The caterpillars are densely covered in a short pile of setae and often make shelters by rolling leaf edges.

Genus MESENE Doubleday, 1847

Brilliant crimson, orange, or yellow with black markings is the typical coloration of the small

and fragile butterflies embraced by *Mesene*, and they are readily recognized by these illustrious colors. Rather than bearing a similarity to other riodinids, overall these butterflies have an uncanny resemblance to day-flying moths in the families Arctiidae, Geometridae, and Notodontidae. Members of *Mesene* are found from Mexico throughout Central and South America, and many species are notoriously variable, forming local color morphs across relatively short geographical distances (Seitz 1917). The genus embraces over fifty described taxa (many are subspecies), and certainly would benefit from a taxonomic revision. Five species occur in our area.

The hostplants for *Mesene* include members of the Violaceae, Melastomataceae, and Sapindaceae (DeVries et al. 1994; Harvey 1987a). The caterpillars are covered in a dense pile of long setae, form no associations with ants, and in overall form resemble those of *Anteros*, except they do not bear tufts of bladderlike setae on the first thoracic segment. The pupae are flattened ventrally and bear a dorsal row of long, erect setae.

In Costa Rica these butterflies are encountered but occasionally, and in my experience never in abundance. Some of our *Mesene* species (*phareus, margaretta, mygdon, croceella*) are extremely good mimics of moths in the Geometridae (*Eudulophasia* and *Eubaphe*), and Arctiidae (*Holomelina*)—moths that are rejected by a variety of spiders as prey items (L. E. Gilbert, pers. comm.). However, no experiments have been attempted offering any *Mesene* species to predators to test whether they too are unpalatable.

Mesene phareus rubella
Bates, 1865
FW length: 13–14 mm   **Plate 13**
Range: Mexico to Brazil, Peru. **Subspecies:** Guatemala to Colombia
Hostplant: Various reports—Sepp (1824–48) described a fluffy white caterpillar (as *nigrocinctus*) on *Paullinia pinata* (Sapindaceae) from Surinam. This description was repeated by Kaye (1921) from Trinidad (as *phareus*). In Panama I found a caterpillar feeding on a sapling of *Inga* sp. (Fabaceae). Together this information suggests at least three interpretations: both Sapindaceae and Fabaceae are used as hostplants, the plants have been misidentified, and/or there are two species of butterflies.
Early stages (Fig. 48a): *Mature caterpillar*—pale green, flattened with segments produced in lateral lobes; overall with a sparse covering of white setae, and a conspicuous crest of very long white dorsal setae. The caterpillar grazes the epidermis of old leaves. *Pupa*—light brown, flattened ventrally; entire body has a

marked dorsal ridge that gives the pupa the impression of being almost triangular in cross-section; a dorsal ridge with a row of long dorsal setae, and abdomen with flattened lateral lobes.
• **Adult:** Sexes dimorphic. *Male*—upperside crimson, FW costa and both margins evenly black, two or three small black bars intrude into the FW cell from the costa, and abdomen crimson; underside with the FW entirely dusty black, HW crimson with dusty-black costa and margins, and abdomen black. *Female*—upperside entirely crimson with thin black FW costa and wing margins; underside similar, with a small black bar that intrudes into the FW cell from the costa. Compare with *mygdon*.
Habits: This butterfly has been recorded in our area from sea level to 700 m on both slopes in association with rain forest habitats. Typically encountered as uncommon, solitary individuals flying along forest edges, rivers, and in light gaps between 12:30 and 16:00 hrs. Their flight is slow, fluttery, and generally unidirectional. In Panama, G. Small found the males perching between 14:00 and 16:00 hrs. Both sexes visit flowers of various Asteraceae.
Localities: [A]: Poco Sol (February), Cariblanco. [SJ]: Carrillo. [H]: La Selva (May), Magsaysay (August), Plastico (July, August). [P]: Quepos (February, July, September), Sirena (January, March, July), Rio Catarata (September). [L]: Guapiles (June), Tuis (June). [G]: Taboga (September).

Mesene mygdon
Schaus, 1913
FW length: 14–16 mm   **Plate 13**
Range: Costa Rica and Panama
Hostplant: Unknown
Early stages: *Mature caterpillar* (wandering phase)—similar to that described for *phareus*, but with a few dorsal black bars between the abdominal segments. *Pupa*—similar to that described for *phareus*, but with two erect subdorsal tufts of plumose setae on the first thoracic segment that curve forward.
• **Adult:** Sexes similar. Upperside deep crimson with broad black distal margins on both wings, FW base black, joining the costa and extending broadly to the apex. The abdomen is black. Underside is similar to upperside except the crimson is duller. Compare with *phareus*.
Habits: This butterfly is known to occur in our area from sea level to 700 m in association with Atlantic slope rain forest habitats. Encountered as rare, solitary individuals along forest edges, rivers, and in light gaps. As in

phareus, their flight is slow, fluttery, and generally unidirectional. In Panama, G. Small noted that the males perch between 14:45 and 15:15 hrs. Uncommon.

Localities: [A]: Cariblanco (March), La Tigra de San Carlos (February). [C]: Rio Azul (September), Pejivalle (March). [SJ]: Carrillo (February). [H]: Magsaysay (August), Plastico (March). [L]: Guapiles (June).

Mesene croceella
Bates, 1865

FW length: 13–14 mm   **Plate 13**
Range: Mexico to Costa Rica, Panama(?)
Hostplant: Unknown
Early stages: Unknown
• **Adult:** Sexes similar. Both the upper and underside of the wings are bright yellow-orange, and both wings have thin, evenly black margins, although the black margins may be somewhat wider in the female. Compare with *phareus*, *silaris*.
Habits: This butterfly has been recorded from our area at two localities: one in the Atlantic lowlands in association with rain forest, and the other from Pacific montane rain shadow habitat in the Coton Valley. My experience with this butterfly is limited to the single occasion where I found a male and a female between 08:20 and 08:40 hrs along a sunny forest edge at Las Alturas. The male was visiting the white flowers of an undetermined subcanopy vine in the Asteraceae. The female was perched under a leaf about 3 m above the ground. When flying, the butterfly reminded me of a frenetic *Tegosa anieta* (Nymphalidae), a species that is common to most montane areas. Godman and Salvin (1886) originally noted that this species strongly resembles the common geometrid moth, *Eudulophasia invaria* (often placed under the generic name, *Eudule*). Recently L. Gilbert (pers. comm.) showed that *Eudulophasia invaria* can be locally abundant in Parque Corcovado, and that this moth is unpalatable to spiders. Given the uncanny mimetic similarity between the butterfly and moth, Gilbert's observations raise the distinct possibility that *M. croceella* may eventually be found at sea level on the Pacific slope when our fauna becomes better known. Rare in Costa Rican collections.
Localities: [H]: La Selva (July). [P]: Las Alturas (December).

Mesene silaris
Godman and Salvin, 1878

FW length: 12–13.5 mm   **Plate 13**

Range: Nicaragua to Venezuela, Guianas, Ecuador, and Peru
Hostplant: *Rinorea squamata* (Violaceae)
Early stages: *Egg*—tiny, white, laid in the terminal leaf axils of emerging leaves
• **Adult:** Sexes similar. Both wing surfaces with a deep yellow ground color, and thick black borders on both wings. *Note*: Specimens with white instead of yellow legs from Guatemala were originally described as a distinct species, *leucopus* Godman and Salvin, 1886, and may eventually be found in our area. Compare with *Pachythone gigas*, *Setabis cleomedes*.
Habits: This butterfly is known to occur in our area from sea level to 700 m on both slopes in association with wet and rain forest habitats. Encountered as rare, solitary individuals along forest edges, rivers, and in shaded light gaps. I found both sexes to be active between 09:00 and 14:00 hrs, and once observed an ovipositing female lay five individual eggs on a plant growing in direct sunlight at about 11:30 hrs. In Panama, G. Small noted that the males perched between 14:00 and 15:15 hrs. Both sexes visit flowers of *Croton*, and probably other plants with small white flowers as well. Uncommon in our area.
Localities: [A]: San Mateo (October). [C]: Turrialba (July). [H]: La Selva (April, July). [L]: Guapiles (May, June).

Mesene margaretta semiradiata
Felder and Felder, 1865

FW length: 13.5–14.5 mm   **Plate 13**
Range: Mexico to Colombia
Hostplant: Unknown
Early stages: Unknown
• **Adult:** Sexes similar. Both wing surfaces red-orange ground, FW apex broadly black with white lines between the radial veins, and the HW distal margin with elongate black triangles between the radial veins. The coloration varies in this species (especially when it enters Panama), but it cannot be confused with any other riodinid. *Note*: The black ray pattern on this species is variable, and in some Mexican and South American specimens it may be completely absent (see illustration in de la Maza and de la Maza 1980). Such specimens would thus be properly called nominate *margaretta* (White, 1843), and suggest that both forms may occur together. However, I have never seen any Costa Rican specimens without the black ray pattern.
Habits: This curious little butterfly is recorded in our area from sea level to 1200 m on both slopes in association with wet and rain forest habitats. Encountered as rare, solitary individ-

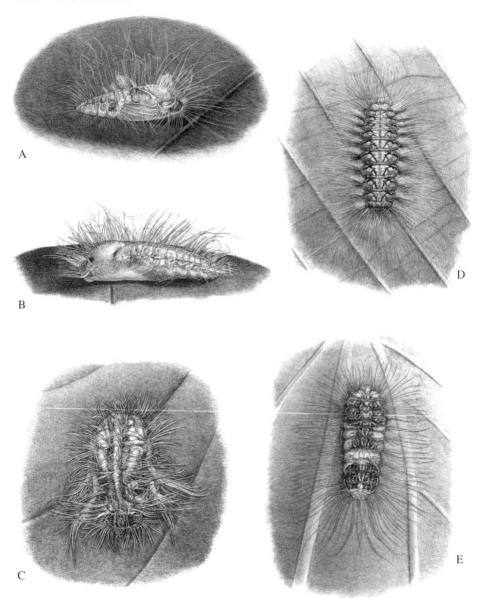

FIGURE 48. (A) *Mesene phareus* pupa. (B) *Mesenopsis melanochlora* pupa. (C) *Symmachia rubina* pupa. (D) *Mesenopsis melanochlora* caterpillar. (E) *Symmachia rubina* caterpillar. (Drawings by J. Clark)

uals along forest edges, rivers, and in shaded light gaps. In my experience both sexes are active between 09:00 and 11:00 hrs. The fluttery flight behavior and color pattern of this butterfly strongly resemble a common day-flying moth in the genus *Eudulophasia* sp. (Geometridae). Of interest is that as this butterfly ranges into eastern Panama, the radiating lines become wider, most likely following a similar change in appearance of the model species of *Eudulophasia*. I have found this butterfly visiting flowers of *Croton* and the extrafloral nectaries of *Heliocarpus*. Uncommon in our area.

Localities: [C]: Tuis (June). [SJ]: San Jose (July), Desamparados (August). [H]: La Selva (July, April). [P]: Palmar Norte (August), San Vito, (July). [L]: Guapiles (May, June).

Genus **MESENOPSIS** Godman and Salvin, 1866

The butterflies in this genus may be distinguished by their elongate wing shape set with long yellow and black patterns. Members of *Mesenopsis* are found from Mexico to the Amazon Basin, and the genus contains at least five described species. Here are treated what I believe to be two species in our area that have been placed by some authors under the single taxon, *bryaxis*.

The only hostplant record for *Mesenopsis* are from the family Melastomataceae (DeVries et al. 1994). The caterpillars are covered in a dense pile of long setae, and hide and feed inside the rolled edges of leaves.

In Costa Rica these butterflies are typically rare, although their hostplant is certainly common and widespread. Perhaps one of the more extraordinary things about these butterflies is that they are excellent mimics of several unpalatable day-flying moths (see Miller 1996), including *Josia ligata* (Notodontidae: Dioptinae), *Eudulophasia* sp., *Eubaphe* sp., *Flavinia* spp. (Geometridae), and the clearly toxic *Josiamorpha* (Arctiidae).

Mesenopsis melanochlora
Godman and Salvin, 1878
FW length: 15–18 mm　　　　**Plate 13**
Range: Nicaragua to Peru and Bolivia
Hostplant: *Miconia argentea* (Melastomataceae)
Early stages (Fig. 48b, d): *Egg*—white, deposited singly in the leaf axils or in fissures in the bark along the main stem. *Mature caterpillar*—

overall dull green-white (like the underside of the hostplant leaves); the flattened dorsum is naked and has a pebbled surface (Fig. 48d), but in nature it appears to be covered in tufts of long white setae that project outward in all directions. These setae all arise laterally, but can be moved upwards to cover the body, as well as projected forward and downward. The setae bear fine filaments on the shafts that are likely to adhere to ants if the caterpillar is molested (Fig. 5e, f). The caterpillars are typically found on sapling plants and have the habit of folding the edge of a leaf into an irregular tube, and feeding inside the tube (the underside of the leaf). When the leaf shelter has been eaten away, the caterpillar moves to another portion of the leaf and begins again. These tubelike shelters are tell-tales for finding plants with caterpillars on them. *Pupa*—pale brown, flattened ventrally and dorsally (except for thorax); abdominal segments with slight lateral lobes; head with dark spots over the eyes; entire pupa with a sparse covering of long dorsal and lateral setae, where those on the head and thorax curve forward, and those on the abdomen curve to posterior. Pupation takes place inside the leaf shelter amid a crude cocoon of loosely spun silk.
• **Adult:** Sexes dimorphic. *Male*—both upper and underside of the wings are black with a wide, rectangular orange band in the middle of each wing that runs from the base to the distal margin. *Female*—the orange bands are paler and may swell slightly in the discal areas but do not terminate roundly in the subapex. Compare with *bryaxis*.
Habits: This butterfly is recorded in our area from sea level to 900 m on the Pacific slope in association with wet and rain forest habitats. Encountered as rare, solitary individuals along forest edges and in large shaded light gaps. The males perch in light gaps on the upperside of leaves from approximately 2 to 5 m above the ground between 09:00 and 11:00 hrs. Courtship and male-male interactions consist of a fast and prolonged circular flight around the perimeter of a particular male's light gap. The females oviposit on sapling plants that grow along forest edges, shaded light gaps, or in the understory of well-lit forest between 10:00 and 13:00 hrs, generally on brilliantly sunny days. Both sexes visit flowers of *Croton*, *Cordia*, *Casearia*, and various herbaceous Asteraceae. This butterfly is an extremely good mimic of the day-flying moths *Josia ligata* (Notodontidae: Dioptinae), and *Josiamorpha* spp (Arctiidae). Uncommon in our area.

Localities: [P]: Agua Buena (August), Sirena (June), Chacarita (September). [G]: Pitilla (March).

Mesenopsis bryaxis
(Hewitson, 1870)
FW length: 17–23 mm   **Plate 13**
Range: Nicaragua to Panama, Colombia
Hostplant: Unknown
Early stages: Unknown
• **Adult:** Sexes dimorphic. *Male*—both upper and underside of wings are black with a wide yellow-orange band in the middle of each wing that runs from the base, expanding in the discal area, and then terminating more narrowly at the submargin. *Female*—the yellow bands are paler and broader than in the male, and terminate roundly and broadly at the submargin. Compare with *melanochroa*.
Habits: This butterfly is recorded in our area from sea level to 900 m on the Atlantic slope in association with rain forest habitats between Parque Braulio Carrillo and the Turrialba Valley. Typically encountered as rare, solitary individuals along forest edges and in large shaded light gaps between 09:00 and 11:00 hrs. This butterfly is a mimic of the day-flying moths *Flavinia laeta* (Geometridae: Sterrhinae) and *Josiamorpha* spp (Arctiidae). Uncommon in our area.
Localities: [C]: Juan Viñas. [SJ]: Carrillo (March, April). [H]: Chilamate (July), Plastico (June, September). [L]: Hacienda Tapezco (August).

Genus **XENANDRA** Felder, 1865

The butterflies placed in this genus are recognized by their short robust bodies, narrowed wing shape, and black ground color, often with red or orange bands. In older literature, some of the species now contained in *Xenandra* were placed under *Esthemopsis* and *Melanis*. Members of *Xenandra* are found from Costa Rica throughout the Amazon Basin, and the genus is considered to contain about ten, mainly rare, species. However, the generic placement of these butterflies was, and is, problematic. For example, Godman and Salvin (1887), noting the morphological characteristics similar to the genera *Esthemopsis*, *Melanis*, and *Panara*, were uncertain as to the placement of what we now call *Xenandra caeruleata*. The present-day situation seems little better. Overall, the taxonomic limitations of *Xenandra* itself, the species con-

tained therein, how the sexes match up, and even the nomenclature of the few species found in our area alone is a complete muddle. Hence, there is every indication that the genus is in need of a thorough revision.

In our area there appear to be three species, two with taxonomic problems that center on butterflies that have males that are black with red on or near the HW discal area: the wide-ranging and apparently variable South American species *Xenandra helius* (Cramer, 1779), the Colombian taxon *vulcanalis* Stichel, 1910, and the Costa Rican taxa *nigrivenata* Schaus, 1913, and *desora* Schaus, 1928. Basically, the problem is that there is abundant material of *helius*, but few specimens available of *vulcanalis*, *nigrivenata*, or *desora*, and the sexes of the latter three taxa are not matched in any reliable way. Until more material becomes available for study, and our understanding of *Xenandra* increases substantially (hopefully in the form of a taxonomic revision), I treat *desora* and *helius* as members of our fauna and suggest that *nigrivenata* may be a synonym of *helius*.

Nothing is known about the hostplants or early stages for any species of *Xenandra*. The aposematic coloration, flight behavior, and the habit of "playing dead" when handled strongly suggests that at least some of the species may be unpalatable to predators.

Xenandra caeruleata
(Godman and Salvin, 1878)
FW length: 18.5–20 mm   **Plate 9**
Range: Costa Rica and Panama
Hostplant: Unknown
Early stages: Unknown
• **Adult:** Sexes similar. Upperside blue-black with a yellow-orange band extending from near FW costa to tornus; HW with a trace of gray-blue between the radial veins. Underside similar to upperside but with the gray-blue on HW distinct, and face and palpi yellow-orange. The forelegs of the male are yellow-orange, whereas they are brown in the female. Compare with *helius*, *vulcanalis*, and *Isapis agyrtus*.
Habits: This butterfly has been recorded in our area from 200 to 1000 m on the Atlantic slope (with one record from the Meseta Central), mainly in rain forest habitats. I collected this species once while it was visiting flowers of *Inga* during late morning. Uncommon in Costa Rican collections.
Localities: [C]: Turrialba (August). [SJ]: Carrillo (February), Curridibat (October). [H]: La Selva (May, August, September). [L]: Bribri (August), Sixaola (March).

Xenandra desora
Schaus, 1928
FW length: 16–20 mm **Plate 9**
Range: Costa Rica and Panama
Hostplant: Unknown
Early stages: Unknown
• **Adult:** Sexes dimorphic. *Male*—upperside black with a slight cast of gray-green between the radial veins of both wings; HW with a conspicuous red oval extending from base to costa, and this oval may overlap onto FW inner margin (but see below); underside has a more pronounced gray-green between the radial veins, and red patch is much duller. *Female*—upperside black with a red band on FW that is roughly square (not rectangular) in outline, and runs from near costa almost to tornal margin. *Note:* It is important to compare this account with that of with *helius*.
Habits: This butterfly is recorded in our area from three lowland rain forest localities: two on the Atlantic slope in the Sarapiqui region, and the other on the Pacific slope near the Panama border. I once collected a female of this species that was flying along the interface of open second growth and forest edge during early afternoon. This butterfly is rare.
Localities: [H]: Magsaysay (January), La Selva (March).

Xenandra helius
(Cramer, 1779)
FW length: 15 mm **Plate 9**
Range: Costa Rica south through the Amazon Basin
Hostplant: Unknown
Early stages: Unknown
• **Adult:** Sexes dimorphic. *Male*—Variable. FW upperside black. Some specimens may have the distal half of wing gray-green with the radial veins black (as the type of *nigrivenata*). HW upperside black with similar gray-green between the radial veins, and a red patch in the discal area that extends narrowly from base, along costa to near the end of the cell, and then straight along posterior margin of cell. The red does not extend to the FW. The underside has the gray-green between radial veins more conspicuous (pronounced in the type specimen). *Female*—upperside black with a red-orange rectangular (not square) band on the FW that extends from costa to the tornus, and the HW is entirely black. *Note:* It is important to compare this to the account of *desora*.
Habits: This butterfly is recorded in our area from a single locality on the Atlantic slope at 1300 m (the type locality of *nigrivenata*), and a

single lowland locality on the Pacific slope. More material and observations are desperately needed on this butterfly.
Localities: [C]: [TL] Juan Viñas (September). [P]: Villa Neily (July).

Genus ESTHEMOPSIS
Felder, 1865

These butterflies are recognized by their blue-black ground color, the white cuneiform bars between the radial veins, and the red-orange palpi and prothorax. The genus appears to contain a heterogeneous mixture of species, some of which have in the past been placed under *Melanis*, *Lepricornis*, *Xenandra*, and *Brachyglenis*. Seitz (1917) commented that every person who has treated these butterflies disagrees about how many species there are, and what the generic limitations of *Esthemopsis* may be. Indeed, it is not at all clear from material in museums how the species are separated. A taxonomic revision of the genus would be welcome. Members of *Esthemopsis* are found from Mexico to southern Brazil, and the genus is considered to contain about twelve species. Two species occur in our area, and perhaps another that has been misplaced in the genus *Brachyglenis*.
There is nothing known of the hostplants or early stages for any *Esthemopsis* species. In the field these butterflies are easily mistaken for members of the riodinid genera *Brachyglenis*, *Uraneis*, *Voltinia*, and *Lepricornis*, and some of the species are very good mimics of unpalatable moths in the family Arctiidae.

Esthemopsis clonia
Felder and Felder, 1865
FW length: 21–23.5 mm **Plate 10**
Range: Mexico to Colombia
Hostplant: Unknown
Early stages: Unknown
• **Adult:** Sexes similar. Upperside and underside blue-black; conspicuous white bands on the FW subapex and HW distal margin that are formed by cuneiform spots between the radial veins; the palpi, face, and prothorax are distinctly red-orange. Compare with *colaxes*, *Uraneis ucubis*, *Brachyglenis dinora*, *Voltinia radiata*, and *Lepricornis strigosa*.
Habits: This butterfly has been recorded in our area from sea level to 600 m on both slopes in association with primary rain forest habitats. Encountered as rare solitary individuals along

forest edges, shaded light gaps, or in open forest understory during the late morning. **Localities:** [SJ]: Carrillo. [H]: Magsaysay (February), La Selva (March). [P]: Sirena (July), Llorona (February, May). [L]: Tortuguerro (January), Guapiles (May, June), Hacienda Tapezco (March), Cerro Cocori.

Esthemopsis colaxes
Hewitson, 1870
FW length: 22.5–23.5 mm   **Plate 10**
Range: Costa Rica to western Ecuador
Hostplant: Unknown
Early stages: Unknown
• **Adult:** Sexes similar. The area surrounding the head, the frons, and palpi are crimson. Ground color blue-black with discal areas of both wings, and FW submarginal band with a thin covering of white scales, but almost transparent. *Note:* This butterfly has been misidentified in many Costa Rican collections as *Esthemopsis sericina* (Bates, 1867), a South American species. Compare with *clonia, Brachyglenis dinora, B. dodone, Lepricornis strigosa.*
Habits: This butterfly has been reported from sea level to 700 m from a few rain forest localities on both slopes. I have only encountered it during the late morning as rare solitary individuals along forest edges and in shaded light gaps.
Localities: [SJ]: Rio Chirripo Pacifico, 5 km N of Rivas (September). [H]: La Selva (March). [L]: Sixaola (March), Guapiles (June). [G]: Volcan Santa Maria (June).

Genus CHIMASTRUM Godman and Salvin, 1865

The butterflies in this genus are recognized by their delicate, almost translucent white wings. Members of *Chimastrum* are found from Mexico to Colombia and Ecuador, and the genus is considered to embrace two species. One species is found in Central America and Colombia, and the other is found elsewhere in South America. Nothing is known of the hostplants or early stages.

In our area *Chimastrum* may be found in most lowland rain forest habitats, although the butterflies are seldom if ever abundant. Their delicate appearance and slow flight resembles various day-flying moths in the family Geometridae.

Chimastrum argenteum argenteum
(Bates, 1866)
FW length: 14.5–17.5 mm   **Plate 13**

Range: Mexico to Colombia. **Subspecies:** Mexico to Panama
Hostplant: Unknown
Early stages: Unknown
• **Adult:** Sexes similar. Upper and underside of both wings is shiny, off-white with thin gray-black along all margins, and some yellow-orange at the base of both wings. The female has paler markings along the margins. *Note:* In eastern Panama, radial veins may be overlaid with black, giving the butterfly a ray pattern, in appearance approaching the South American species (or perhaps subspecies) *carnutes* Hewitson, 1875. Compare with female *Euselasia gyda.*
Habits: This butterfly has been recorded in our area from sea level to 1200 m on both slopes in association with rain forest habitats. Typically encountered as uncommon, solitary individuals along forest edges, trails, streams, and in shaded light gaps between 08:00 and 12:30 hrs. Their flight is slow and fluttery, but the butterflies can fly rapidly when alarmed. Both sexes rest under leaves less than 1 m above the ground. I have never observed males engage in noticeable perching activity, although G. Small suggests that, in Panama, the males perch between 15:00 and 16:00 hrs. I have, however, observed the females searching low vegetation for oviposition sites between 10:30 and 12:30 hrs in shaded forest understory. The coloration and feeble flight give this butterfly the appearance of the day-flying moth *Eubaphe* (Geometridae).
Localities: [A]: Cariblanco (June), La Tigra de San Carlos (March, June). [C]: Turrialba (January, May–August). [H]: La Selva (August, September). [P]: Llorona (March), Sirena (April, July), Carrara (October), San Vito (July). [L]: Guapiles (February, March, May, June), Siquirres (April, December), Zent, Esperanza.

Genus SYMMACHIA Hübner, 1819

These butterflies may be recognized by the peculiar bulge of the FW costa found in many species (especially in the males), the almost triangular-shaped hindwing, and festive colors. In these respects *Symmachia* butterflies resemble members of *Caria*, except that they have no iridescent green on the wings. Members of *Symmachia* are found from Mexico to Argentina, and the genus may contain over forty mainly South American species. In Central America there are nine species, seven that occur in our area.

It is surprising that for a genus as large as *Symmachia* so little early stage information is available. Based on two species from our fauna, the only hostplant records include the Melastomataceae and the Ulmaceae (DeVries et al. 1994). The caterpillars are covered in a dense pile of setae and bear long lateral setae, and may roll leaf edges into a shelter to hide in during the day. The caterpillars do not have vibratory papillae, do not produce calls, and are not known to form associations with ants. However, the caterpillar of *S. rubina* has paired depressions ringed with tubercles on the eighth abdominal segment that correspond to the position where the tentacle nectary organs are found on typically myrmecophilous species (see p. 23). The pupa is flattened ventrally and bears conspicuous and stiff setae along the lateral edges. The overall shape and the habit of maintaining the cast larval skin attached to the cremaster create the impression of an irregular mass of plant material.

These butterflies are fast, agile fliers, and are most often encountered in light gaps or along forest edges. During their activity periods (generally in the early morning), interacting individuals of several *Symmachia* species may be observed to engage in long swirling dogfights, and their rapidly beating wings makes an audible whirring sound. It appears that throughout their range *Symmachia* butterflies are found almost exclusively in the lowlands. As noted by Godman and Salvin (1886), the genus seems to be composed of mainly rare species that seldom make their way into museums.

Symmachia rubina rubina
Bates, 1866
FW length: 13–15.5 mm   **Plate 13**
Range: Mexico to Colombia, Ecuador. **Subspecies:** Mexico to Colombia
Hostplant: *Trema micrantha* (Ulmaceae)
Early stages: *Mature caterpillar* (Fig. 48e)—body pale, almost translucent green, especially along the lateral areas of the abdominal segments and anal plate; each segment bears a rounded lateral lobe from which arise tufts of pale brown lateral setae that are as long as the body is wide; dorsum covered in a red-brown pile of setae that is interspersed with tiny white tubercles that are similar to those found on myrmecophilous species (e.g., *Thisbe irenea*); the third and fifth abdominal segments have a conspicuous pale yellow dorsal band, especially on the fifth segment. The caterpillar feeds from the underside of the leaf and chews irregular holes in the margin of mature leaves. While at rest, the caterpillar may silk down the edge of a leaf to form a simple shel-

ter to hide in, or simply rest on the leaf underside. *Note*: Of great interest are two tiny orifices covered in white tubercles found on the eighth abdominal segment that correspond to the location of the tentacle nectary organs. These organs are characteristic of riodinid caterpillars that are typically myrmecophilous, a phenomenon unknown in the tribe Symmachiini. *Pupa*—overall color pale brown with a few darker areas on abdomen and wing pads, conspicuously flattened ventrally, a prominent dorsal ridge, and conspicuous stiff lateral setae radiating outward along the body. The lateral setae, along with the cast larval skin that remains attached to the cremaster, creates the impression of a bit of plant detritus on the top of a leaf.
• **Adult:** Sexes slightly dimorphic. *Male*—FW upperside red-orange with the anterior half of the wing black, set with short cream-colored bars; HW upperside red-orange with black apex; abdomen orange. *Female*—upperside pattern similar to the male but paler orange with wider cream-colored FW bars, and abdomen ringed white, black, and orange; thorax black with white highlights that form a tiny "death's head" pattern. Compare with *xypete*.
Habits: This butterfly has been recorded locally in our area from sea level to 1200 m on both slopes in association with rain forest habitats. Typically encountered between 08:00 and 13:00 hrs as rare, fast-flying, solitary individuals that land under leaves along forest edges, trails, and rivers. Both sexes visit the small white flowers of *Heliocarpus* (Tiliaceae) and various Asteraceae. Uncommon in Costa Rican collections.
Localities: [A]: Atenas (December), San Mateo. [C]: Moravia de Chirripo (August). [H]: La Selva (April, August, September). [P]: Sirena (December). [L]: Guapiles (October), Hitoy Cerere (October).

Symmachia threissa
Hewitson, 1870
FW length: 16–16.5 mm   **Plate 13**
Range: Nicaragua to Colombia
Hostplant: Unknown
Early stages: Unknown
• **Adult:** Sexes presumably dimorphic. *Male*—upperside blue-black with a medial transparent triangle at costa that intrudes into the cell, and orange-red on the discal area of HW and sides of abdomen; underside dull black with small, indistinct light spots scattered on HW. *Female*—apparently unknown and in need of description. Compare with *accusatrix*, *probetor*, and *Phaenochitonia sagaris*.
Habits: This butterfly has not been officially re-

corded for our area. However, its presence in Nicaragua and Panama indicate that this butterfly will be found when our fauna becomes better known. On two separate occasions in the canal area of Panama, I observed males perching and patrolling on a hilltop covered in second-growth vegetation between 09:30 and 12:30 hrs. Individuals perched on the undersides of sunlit leaves that were less than half a meter above the ground. When flying off the perch, the butterflies patrolled back and forth in irregular circles and vigorously interacted with other riodinid species.
Localities: Not yet recorded for our area.

Symmachia accusatrix
Westwood, 1851
FW length: 16–17 mm   **Plate 14**
Range: Mexico to Colombia, Ecuador, Brazil
Hostplant: Unknown
Early stages: Unknown
• **Adult:** Sexes dimorphic. *Male*—FW upperside blue-black with a series of large triangular transparent spots along the costa; HW upperside blue-black with a distinct red costa. Underside dark brown with a profusion of elongate off-white spots on both wings. *Female*—FW upperside brown with a blue base that is set with a few red spots, a series of transparent triangular spots along costa, and a short red bar in the apex; HW upperside almost entirely brown. Underside similar in pattern to male except the elongate spots are yellowish, and both wings with orange-red submargins. Compare with *threissa, probetor.*
Habits: This butterfly has been recorded in our area from 600 to 1200 m on the Atlantic slope in association with rain forest habitats. In Panama between 11:40 and 13:30 hrs I typically found small groups of three to five males perching under leaves in large light gaps. The perches were no higher than 4 m above the ground. The flight of these butterflies is very fast and erratic, and two males will engage in long swooping, circular flights that may wind upwards of 20 m into the air. Uncommon in Costa Rican collections.
Localities: [A]: Florencia de San Carlos (June). [C]: Turrialba (April, June, July), Moravia de Chirripo (April, July, August). [SJ]: Carrillo (February). [H]: Plastico (September).

Symmachia leena leena
Hewitson, 1870
FW length: 11.5–12.5 mm   **Plate 14**
Range: Nicaragua to Colombia. **Subspecies:** Nicaragua to Panama
Hostplant: Unknown

Early stages: Unknown
• **Adult:** Sexes dimorphic. *Male*—FW upperside dark brown with a camouflage pattern of dull red-brown on posterior half of the wing; HW upperside dull red-brown with black apex and margins, a few black spots in the discal area, and the inner margin with a conspicuous tuft of long black androconial hairs; underside dark brown with many blue-gray spots, especially on the HW. *Female*—upperside dark brown with whitish spots along the FW costa, pale orange spots scattered across medial areas of both wings, and orange along submargin of both wings that is set with brown spots between radial veins. Compare with *probetor, Phaenochitonia phoenicura.*
Habits: This butterfly has been recorded in our area from sea level to 1000 m in association with Atlantic slope rain forest habitats. I have never seen it alive. Rare in Costa Rican collections.
Localities: [C]: Moravia de Chirripo (June). [H]: La Selva (August). [L]: Guapiles (June), Limon.

Symmachia probetor belti
Godman and Salvin, 1886
FW length: 12–13 mm   **Plate 14**
Range: Mexico to Brazil. **Subspecies:** Nicaragua to Colombia
Hostplant: Unknown
Early stages: Unknown
• **Adult:** Sexes dimorphic. *Male*—FW upperside black with iridescent royal blue at base, costa, and margins; HW upperside black with iridescent blue at inner margin and bright crimson along the entire costa; underside dull black with a slight orange-brown iridescent sheen when viewed obliquely. *Female*—upperside dark brown with some iridescent blue at base, a few white spots along costa, a few red spots near base, and a small orange-red band in subapex; HW upperside dark brown with a thin, white, sometimes indistinct submarginal line. Compare with *accusatrix, leena.*
Habits: This butterfly is recorded from 400 to 1200 m on both slopes in association with habitats ranging from rain forest to semideciduous forest. Not infrequently along the canal area in Panama, I observed males perching and patrolling large light gaps. All activity took place between 09:30 and 12:00 hrs, their fast and erratic flight was generally low to the ground (6–20 cm), and they perched on the underside of leaves. On occasion, however, two or more males would engage in long, swooping flights that sometimes ascended more than 10 m into the air. At these sites I typically

found this butterfly in the company of other *Symmachia* species. Rare in Costa Rican collections. **Localities:** [A]: Cariblanco (June), Atenas (December). [C]: Moravia de Chirripo (July), Turrialba (June). [SJ]: Puriscal nr Santiago (September).

Symmachia tricolor hedemanni
(Felder, 1869)
FW length: 12–13 mm   **Plate 13**
Range: Mexico to Colombia. **Subspecies:** Mexico to Panama
Hostplant: *Miconia argentea* (Melastomataceae)
Early stages: *Egg* (Fig. 1e)—round, base narrower than dorsum, highly sculptured with eight dorsal lobed ridges radiating from micropyle to margins; micropyle a slightly recessed dome with pores around the perimeter. The egg is pale blue-green when first laid, turning white after about 24 hours. Deposited in damaged portions of mature leaves (often feeding holes made by a first instar), in leaf axils, and stems. *First instar* (Fig. 5c, d)—dorsally flattened with a row of short, blunt subdorsal setae on all segments; all segments with lateral setae that are confined to the "perimeter" of the caterpillar, all which are extremely long and gently twisted. *Mature caterpillar*—body translucent green densely covered in long white setae, and similar to the caterpillar of *Mesenopsis bryaxis*. The caterpillars roll leaf margins into a crude tube and rest and feed inside this tube. When the tube has been mostly consumed, the caterpillar moves to another portion of the leaf, or to another leaf and builds another shelter. These shelters make excellent tell-tales as to the presence of caterpillars and are typically filled with the scaly underside of the leaf, and some pellets of frass. *Pupa*—light brown, flattened dorsoventrally with long dorsal and lateral setae, and in overall appearance very similar to *Mesenopsis bryaxis*.
• **Adult:** Sexes slightly dimorphic. Distinguished by the yellow-orange bands on both wings set in a black ground color. The female's dorsum of the abdomen is banded yellow and black, whereas in the male it is black. Compare with *Mesenopsis bryaxis*.
Habits: In our area this butterfly is recorded from rain forest habitats ranging from sea level to 1200 m elevation. However, except for one record from the Pacific slope, it has been found only on the Atlantic slope. In Panama I typically encountered this butterfly as solitary individuals along forest trails, in the forest understory, and in light gaps. Depending on the circumstances, the flight of both sexes may be fast and erratic: at times I found it flying low to the ground, and other times flying up to 5 m above the ground. The males perch from 1 to 5 m above the ground on the undersides of leaves between 11:00 and 13:00 hrs. Ovipositing females are active in shaded understory or forest edges between 12:30 and 13:30 hrs. Typically, the ovipositing female flits about an individual plant, lands on it, then walks to the underside of a leaf. While walking, she drags her abdomen along the underside until the tip of the abdomen drops into a pit or damaged portion of the leaf. She then deposits an egg at the edge of the damaged leaf fraction. Occasionally eggs are laid in fissures in a stem. Uncommon in Costa Rican collections.
Localities: [A]: La Tigra de San Carlos (January). [C]: Juan Viñas (March), Turrialba (June, July), Moravia de Chirripo (April, June–September), Cachi. [SJ]: Carrillo (February, March), La Selva (May), Chilamate (July), Monte Redondo. [H]: Plastico (August, September). [P]: San Vito (July).

Symmachia xypete
(Hewitson, 1870)
FW length: 11.5–13 mm   **Plate 14**
Range: Nicaragua to Panama
Hostplant: Unknown
Early stages: Unknown
• **Adult:** Sexes slightly dimorphic. *Male*—distinguished from all other species by the red-orange ground color; FW upperside with four to five short black costal bars that intrude into the cell; distal margins of both wings may have black spots; underside duller orange with black spotting more prominent. *Female*—more pale in color and less distinct black spots. *Note*: In some literature this butterfly is considered as a subspecies of *asclepia* Hewitson, 1870. Compare with *rubina, Argyrogrammana venilia*.
Note: Godman and Salvin (1886) placed this species in the genus *Cricosoma* (Felder and Felder, 1865) and noted that this and several other South American species close to *Symmachia* and *Mesene* that do not have a bowed forewing costa form a recognizable group. They also noted that *xypete* possesses unique intersegmental tufts of bulbous scales that arise laterally from between abdominal segments 2 and 3, and then again between segments 3 and 4. Seitz (1917) reiterated that the butterflies form a recognizable group. It seems to me that a revisionary study, or a study of the early stages, will be necessary to determine whether the butterflies are properly placed in

Cricosoma or whether they belong to *Symmachia* or *Mesene*.
Habits: In our area this butterfly has been recorded from two Atlantic lowland sites. However, its occurrence at a number of localities in Nicaragua and Panama suggests that it will be found to be more widespread in Costa Rica as our fauna becomes better known. On a deforested hilltop in the canal area of Panama, I found groups of five to ten individual males of this butterfly perching between 10:30 and 12:30 hrs on vegetation less than half a meter tall. In these instances the males perched on either the upper or underside of leaves, and were found in the company of other *Symmachia* species. Rare in Costa Rican collections.
Localities: [A]: La Tigra de San Carlos (January). [H]: Chilamate (March).

Genus PTEROGRAPHIUM
Stichel, 1910

This genus embraces a mixture of butterflies that were at one time placed in *Mesene* or *Symmachia*, but were separated on the basis of venation and the presence of long androconial scales in the cell of the HW. These androconia are connected to a fold in the wing membrane, and can be erected when the wing membrane is stretched. Some of the butterflies currently placed here have, in the past, been referred to under the genera *Panara* and *Lymnas*, including the single species that enters our area (Callaghan, pers. comm.). Members of *Pterographium* are found from Mexico to Brazil, and as currently understood the genus embraces about twelve mainly South American species (C. Callaghan, pers. comm.).

In coloration and flight behavior members of *Pterographium* may be mistaken in nature for members of the riodinid genera *Symmachia*, *Stichelia*, *Melanis*, *Emesis*, and *Isapis*, as well as moths in the families Arctiidae, Geometridae, and Notodontidae. The single hostplant record for *Pterographium* is from the family Melastomataceae.

Pterographium elegans
(Schaus, 1913)
FW length: 19–22.5 mm   **Plate 9**
Range: Guatemala to Panama
Hostplant: Unknown
Early stages: Unknown
• **Adult:** Sexes dimorphic. *Male*—FW upperside

black with a faint purple iridescent cast, and a yellow-orange band that runs from costa to tornus, underside similar; HW upperside black with broad metallic blue on distal third of wing, underside entirely black; black fringe. *Female*—FW upperside dark brown to black with a conspicuous yellow-orange band that runs from costa to tornus; HW upperside dark brown to black with distinct white fringe. *Note:* This butterfly was long known as *Panara elegans*. Compare with *Xenandra caeruleata*, *Emesis cypria*, *Setabis lagus*.
Habits: This butterfly occurs locally on both slopes from sea level to 800 m in association with rain forest habitats. Typically it is encountered as solitary individuals along forest edges, trails, streams, and in shaded light gaps between 08:00 and 12:30 hrs. On the Osa Peninsula I have, on occasion, found this butterfly in local populations of five to six individuals. The butterflies typically perch between 2 and 5 m above the ground under the leaves of a tree that is relatively isolated from the surrounding vegetation. Their flight is very fast, erratic, and not unlike that of the nymphalid genus *Callicore*. On the Pacific slope, both sexes visit flowers of *Terminalia* and *Croton*. Although uncommon in Costa Rica collections, this butterfly may be present regularly at particular localities for periods of several weeks.
Localities: [SJ]: Carrillo [TL] (September, June). [P]: Piedras Blancas (June), Llorona (March, April, August), Golfito (April).

Genus STICHELIA Zíkan, 1949

This genus embraces a mixture of butterflies that were at one time placed in *Mesene*, *Phaenochitonia*, *Pterographium*, or *Symmachia*, but were separated by Zíkan (1949) on the basis of the male androconia, and in the case of some species, the presence or absence of black markings on the wings. The butterflies in *Stichelia* are separated from those in *Pterographium* by possessing a dispersed patch of elongate androconia on the HW of the males that cannot be erected. Members of *Stichelia* are found from Mexico throughout Central and South America. As currently understood, the genus embraces over fourteen species of mainly South American species, two that occur in our area.

There are no host records for the genus. However, interpolating from the description and photos by Callaghan (1989), *Stichelia* hosts might include members of the Melastomataceae, and the caterpillars are likely to be similar to those in the genera *Mesenopsis* and *Symmachia*. In Costa Rica these butterflies appear to be confined to lowland rain forests and are uncommon. Seitz (1917) notes that in Brazil some of the species are found locally abundant, or as he describes it, "swarming," and that the butterflies use traditional perches for long periods of time. The observations by Barcant (1970) in Trinidad also suggest that *P. sagaris* can be locally abundant.

Stichelia sagaris tyriotes
(Godman and Salvin, 1878)
FW length: 11–13 mm   **Plate 14**
Range: Mexico to Brazil, Trinidad. **Subspecies:** Costa Rica and Panama
Hostplant: Melastomataceae (undetermined genus)
Early stages: In a partial life history, Callaghan (1989) reported that a female deposited five eggs on the inside of a rolled leaf of an undetermined Melastomataceae. Upon hatching, the gregarious caterpillars fed on the tissues inside of the tube, or a folded leaf, and would fold leaves when presented with new leaf material. The pale green, slightly hirsute caterpillars remained inside the rolled leaf at all times. The frass of each caterpillar was bound together with silk, forming a long chain behind the caterpillar. Reading between the lines, the description of the caterpillar sounds similar to that of *Mesenopsis melanochlora* and *Symmachia tricolor*.
• **Adult:** Sexes dimorphic. *Male*—FW upperside black; HW upperside black with a broad red-orange medial band that extends from near costal margin across discal area to inner margin; dorsal portion of the abdomen red-orange with the distal portion black; underside uniformly black. *Female*—FW upperside black with a broad traverse orange-yellow band extending from costal margin to the tornus; abdomen and HW upperside black; underside as in male. Compare with *Phaenochitonia ignipicta*, *Calospila cilissa*, *Symmachia threissa*.
Habits: This butterfly is recorded in our area from three lowland Atlantic slope localities near the Braulio Carrillo area. In Panama, I found males perching on low vegetation approximately 1 m above the ground and vigorously chasing other passing insects in wild, erratic flights. These males did not return to the same perch after a chase, but rather tended to perch on adjacent vegetation or even in a completely different area. Rare in Costa Rican collections.
Localities: [SJ]: Carrillo. [C]: Turrialba (Au-

gust). [H]: Chilamate (June, July), Plastico (March).

Stichelia phoenicura
(Godman and Salvin, 1886)
FW length: 11–12 mm   **Plate 14**
Range: Nicaragua [TL] to Colombia
Hostplant: Unknown
Early stages: Unknown
• **Adult:** Sexes presumably dimorphic. *Male*—upperside dirty brown ground with small, darker brown transverse stripes in discal area, and a dark submarginal line; terminal half of abdomen red-orange on dorsal surface; underside entirely deep reflective blue. *Female*—apparently unknown. However, type photographs of the unique female of *Symmachia histrica* Stichel, 1910, from Bugaba, Panama (a habitat that was similar to the area around the Osa Peninsula), suggest that it may belong to this species. In general appearance *histrica* has a warm brown ground color on both surfaces with both wings set with a series of broken yellow-brown transverse stripes. *Note*: In the canal area of Panama, I collected male specimens that were flying with *phoenicura* and that agree superficially in all respects with that species except that their abdomen is entirely brown. It is likely that these individuals indicate the occurrence in Panama of the South American species *arbuscula* Möschler, 1883, and that this taxon should be looked for in our area. Compare with *Chalodeta, Charis.*
Habits: This butterfly has not been recorded for Costa Rica to date. However, as its type locality is in Nicaragua and it occurs regularly in Panama, we may expect to find this butterfly as our fauna becomes better known. In the canal area of Panama during the dry season, I found that males perch approximately 1 m above the ground between 10:00 and 12:00 hrs, and vigorously chase other insects that fly past their perch.
Localities: Not yet recorded for our area.

Genus PHAENOCHITONIA
Stichel, 1910

This genus embraces a mixture of butterflies that were at one time placed in *Mesene* or *Symmachia* but separated by Stichel on the basis of venation. The butterflies considered here under *Phaenochitonia* are all sexually dimorphic, typically recognized by their black ground color set with red patches on the wings or abdomen, and do not possess elongate androconia on the male HW. Members of *Phaenochitonia* are found from Mexico throughout Central and South America. As currently understood, the genus embraces about ten mainly South American species. At least two species occur in our area.

There are no hostplant records for the genus. In Costa Rica these butterflies appear to be entirely confined to the humid lowland rain forests where the males may be found perching in light gaps. These butterflies are uncommon to rare in Costa Rican collections.

Phaenochitonia ignicauda
(Godman and Salvin, 1878)
FW length: 12–13.5 mm   **Plate 14**
Range: Costa Rica, Panama(?)
Hostplant: Unknown
Early stages: Unknown
• **Adult:** Sexes dimorphic. *Male*—FW upperside entirely black; HW upperside black with an irregular red patch that runs from base, along inner margin, and encompasses the cell but does not extend to tornus; dorsum of abdomen red; underside gray-brown with a scattering of black and gray spots across the discal area of both wings. *Female*—FW upperside black with a red medial band that extends from posterior of the cell to inner margin; HW upperside black with an irregular red medial band extending from costa to inner margin; dorsum of abdomen black; underside similar to male except the black and gray spots more distinct, and FW bears orange medial band plus some traces of orange on median of HW. Compare with *ignipicta*.
Habits: This butterfly is recorded only from the Pacific slope in lowland rain forest areas around the Osa Peninsula, and it is apparently endemic to our fauna. Although this species was not collected by G. B. Small in Panama, it

may enter that country along the Peninsula de Burica, if any suitable habitat has escaped destruction. The males fly in bright sunshine along forest edges and rivers, and they perch on the underside of leaves from 1 to 3 m above the ground between 10:00 to 12:30 hrs. The females have been collected in open areas during midday visiting flowers of *Lantana*. Rare.
Localities: [P]: Llorona (February–May), Sirena (March, August, December).

Phaenochitonia ignipicta
Schaus, 1913
FW length: 10.5–11.5 mm   **Plate 14**
Range: Costa Rica to Panama
Hostplant: Unknown
Early stages: Unknown
• **Adult:** Sexes dimorphic. *Male*—FW upperside black; HW upperside black with a distinct red band that begins broadly at base near the costa, runs along inner margin, and tapers toward the tornus; dorsum of abdomen red; underside gray-brown set with black and white spots in the discal areas of both wings. *Female*—FW upperside brown with a broad transverse yellow band that runs from costa to tornus; abdomen brown; underside as in male except for the yellow band on FW. Compare with *ignicauda, Calospila cilissa*.
Habits: In our area this butterfly is recorded only from Atlantic slope rain forest habitats around Guapiles and the Rio Sarapiqui. Interestingly, the distribution seems to mirror that of its close relative *ignicauda*, which occurs only on the Pacific slope. I have never seen it alive. Rare in collections.
Localities: [C]: Peralta (August). [H]: Chilamate (March). [L]: Guapiles [TL] (January–March, May, July, October), La Florida.

Tribe **CHARITIINI** Stichel, 1911

The butterflies embraced by this tribe are united on the basis of the females bearing spatulate scales surrounding the ovipositor lobes. The tribe contains at least thirty species (some undescribed) placed within three genera: *Sarota, Anteros,* and *Ourocnemis,* the latter of which is entirely South American. Host associations reported for members of this group include Euphorbiaceae, Vochysiacae, Melastomataceae, and Lejuniaceae, and the caterpillars are all densely covered in long, downy setae.

Genus **ANTEROS** Hübner, 1819

The peculiar butterflies in this genus are easily recognized by the dense covering of setae on their legs (as if they were sheathed in tasseled

leggings), and the noticeable metallic spots that appear as raised drops of gold or silver on the underside of the wings. Members of *Anteros* are found from Mexico throughout Central and South America. As currently understood, the genus embraces approximately fifteen species and a considerable number of subspecies. Seven species occur in our area.

Hostplant records for *Anteros* include the Euphorbiaceae, Vochysiaceae, and Melastomataceae (DeVries et al. 1994). The caterpillars are covered with a long, fluffy down of white setae and bear a topknot of reddish bladderlike setae on the dorsum of the first thoracic segment. These spectacular caterpillars make nonsense out of the conventional wisdom of how to tell a moth from a butterfly caterpillar. In fact, they resemble moth caterpillars so strongly that when I have shown photographs to experts, they identified *Anteros* caterpillars as members of the families Lymantriidae, Megalopygidae, or Noctuidae. The caterpillars typically construct shelters by webbing leaves together or curling the edge of a leaf and forming a tube. When not feeding, the caterpillars hide inside these shelters. The pupa is an elongate, rounded cylinder and morphologically rather simple. However, prior to pupation the caterpillar envelops itself in a cocoon composed of its long setae that are loosely webbed together with abundant quantities of silk. Pupation typically takes place inside the shelter of a folded leaf. In general appearance and in habits, the caterpillars strongly resemble those of the entirely South American genus *Helicopis* (which probably belongs in the Charitini).

In Costa Rica these butterflies are found in forested habitats from sea level to about 1500 m meters elevation, and they are typically very local. In the field, many *Anteros* species recall members of the family Lycaenidae because the males patrol back and forth along linear landmarks (like a forest edge) and settle abruptly on a particular perch. The butterflies are very fast fliers, rather easily damaged when netted, and as a rule have short and discrete activity periods during each day.

Anteros allectus
Westwood, 1851
FW length: 10.5–12 mm   **Plate 14**
Range: Costa Rica to Colombia, Ecuador
Hostplant: Unknown
Early stages: Unknown
• **Adult:** Sexes slightly dimorphic. *Male*—upperside dark brown; FW underside pale yellow with darker yellow in the discal area, a metallic blue-green costal bar that enters the cell, one near cell, and a single metallic blue-green submarginal spot at distal end of cell; HW underside pale yellow with darker yellow in the discal area. There are five conspicuous metallic blue-green spots on the HW: three that form a straight medial line, one located basally to the

medial line, and one located distally to this line; often a few metallic spots at extreme edge of distal margin. *Female*—upperside of FW often, but not always, with an oblong white spot located posterior to the cell; underside as in male, but with two fused metallic blue-green submarginal spots on FW and a black area near tornus. Compare with *cumulatus*.
Habits: This butterfly has been recorded in our area from sea level to 600 m on both slopes in association with rain forest habitats. Even though it has been known to be a part of our fauna for many years, this butterfly is less well represented in Costa Rican collections than its close relative *cumulatus*. I have never seen this butterfly alive. Uncommon in collections.
Localities: [A]: San Mateo (December). [C]: Juan Viñas (September). [P]: Rincon de Osa (December).

Anteros cumulatus
Stichel, 1909
FW length: 13–15 mm   **Not illustrated**
Range: Costa Rica to Ecuador
Hostplant: Unknown
Early stages: Unknown
• **Adult:** Sexes slightly dimorphic. *Male*—upperside black with a thin white fringe on HW; underside similar to *allectus*, but the metallic spots almost black with only a trace of metallic blue-green, and only four conspicuous spots on the HW: three that form a medial line, and one at base. *Female*—upperside with a large oblong medial patch on FW that may range in color from yellowish to white; underside as in male except the FW has two fused submarginal metallic spots and a dark area in the tornus. *Note:* Stichel noted in his original description of a single specimen, that with more material available this butterfly might be found to be of specific or subspecific rank. Compare with *allectus*.
Habits: This butterfly has been reported locally from sea level to 800 m on the Atlantic slope in association with rain forest habitats. The males perch on the undersides of leaves from 3 to 5 m above the ground along rivers and in light gaps between 08:00 and 11:30 hrs during periods of bright sunlight. This butterfly is typically more common than *allectus* in Costa Rican collections.
Localities: [C]: Rio Chitaria (March). [SJ]: Carrillo. [H]: Cariblanco (February, June), Plastico (January). [L]: Sixaola [TL].

Anteros chrysoprastus roratus
Godman and Salvin, 1886
FW length: 13.5–14 mm   **Plate 14**

Range: Guatemala to Peru, Brazil. **Subspecies:** Guatemala to Panama
Hostplant: Unknown
Early stages: Unknown
• **Adult:** Sexes similar. Upperside jet black; underside pale yellow with darker yellow on the medial area of both wings, and a scattering of small, metallic silver-green spots on the basal, medial, and marginal areas of both wings. Compare with *cumulatus* and *allectus*.
Habits: This butterfly occurs in our area locally from sea level to 800 m on the Atlantic slope in association with rain forest habitats. The males are encountered during periods of bright sunlight as small, local aggregations along rivers and in light gaps between 10:00 to 11:30 hrs. Individual males typically perch on the undersides of leaves about 3 to 5 m above the ground. At Cariblanco I frequently observed small aggregations of four to ten males engaged in rapid, agonistic flights that moved back and forth in a pulsating, sinuous line. Typically these diminutive clouds of males used the edge of an isolated shrub, a fallen tree trunk, or a bridge as a focal landmark. Periodically, individual males would leave this small whirling cloud, perch on the underside of a leaf for several minutes, then return to the fracas. Unfortunately, this traditional perching arena was destroyed for construction of a hydroelectric project. Uncommon.
Localities: [C]: Cachi, Chitaria. [SJ]: Carrillo. [H]: Cariblanco (June–October), Plastico (February).

Anteros formosus micon
Druce, 1875
FW length: 13.5–14 mm   **Plate 14**
Range: Honduras to Colombia, Peru. **Subspecies:** Honduras to Panama
Hostplant: *Miconia lacera, M. impetiolaris, M. argentea* (Melastomataceae), *Vochysia* sp. (Vochysiaceae)
Early stages (Fig. 49a): *Mature caterpillar*—body covered in long, downy white setae that measure at least twice the width of the body. The longest setae are those projecting laterally and anteriorly; the anterior edge of the first thoracic segment is covered with a topknot of obvious red-orange, bladderlike setae that almost cover the head capsule. The caterpillar folds the leaf edge over to make a crude tube, feeds on the underside of the leaves (or interior of the tube), and rests inside. The frass is expelled at one end of the tube. *Pupa*—the long larval setae are spun around the prepupa as in *Sarota*, making a cocoon inside a rolled leaf.

• **Adult:** Sexes similar. Upperside black with a white medial spot just posterior to the FW cell; underside pale yellow with metallic green medial and submarginal spots set in irregular maroon patches. Compare with *allectus*, *cumulatus*.
Habits: This butterfly occurs commonly from sea level to 1100 m on both slopes in association with all forest habitats. Although it has not been recorded from the lowland Guanacaste dry forest, it is likely to occur there. Typically encountered as solitary individuals along forest edges, streams, secondary vegetation, and in large forest light gaps. The males perch on the upper or underside of leaves from 2 to 4 m above the ground between 11:30 to 13:30 hrs. Even though the adults may be uncommon during a particular time of year, at most localities the caterpillars may be abundant on hostplants that grow along forest edges. Common.
Localities: [A]: Cariblanco (July), San Mateo (February). [SJ]: Patarra (September). [H]: Chilamate (September, November, December), La Selva (September, December), Plastico (June, September). [P]: San Luis at Rio Guacimal (December). [L]: Limon (July), Sixaola (September), La Florida, Madre de Dios.

Anteros kupris kupris
Hewitson, 1875
FW length: 20–23 mm   **Plate 15**
Range: Costa Rica to Peru, Bolivia. **Subspecies:** Costa Rica to Colombia
Hostplant: Unknown
Early stages: Unknown
• **Adult:** Sexes dimorphic. *Male*—FW upperside dark brown with a large cream patch posterior to cell; HW upperside dark brown; FW underside pale yellow with various irregular maroon medial and submarginal squares set with metallic spots; HW underside pale yellow with an even greater number of maroon squares set with metallic spots than on the FW. *Female*—FW upperside as in male; HW upperside cream colored with a dark brown costal band that enters the cell, and a thin brown submarginal band at distal margin. This butterfly can be distinguished from all other congeners by its very large size.
Habits: This spectacular butterfly has been reported in our area from 700 to 1600 m on both slopes in association with all forest habitats. Encountered as solitary individuals along forest edges, streams, and in light gaps. I have twice observed males perching high in the forest canopy during late morning. This butterfly will, without doubt, have a spectacular downy

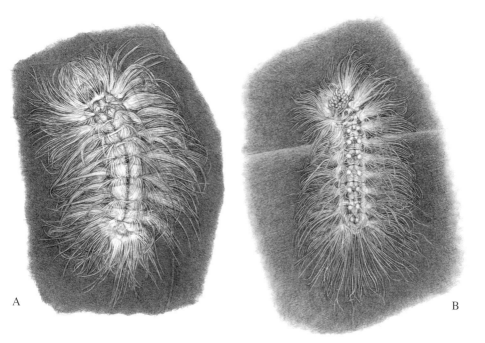

A

B

FIGURE 49. (A) *Anteros formosus* caterpillar. (B) *Sarota gyas* caterpillar. (Drawings by J. Clark)

caterpillar. Uncommon in Costa Rican collections.
Localities: [A]: Cariblanco (March, September). [C]: Tres Rios (December), Turrialba (June), Cachi. [SJ]: Patarra (September). [P]: San Vito (August, September), Monte Verde (February).

Anteros carausius carausius
Westwood, 1851
FW length: 14–14.5 mm   **Plate 14**
Range: Mexico to Venezuela, Bolivia. **Subspecies:** Mexico to Panama
Hostplant: Unknown
Early stages: Unknown
• **Adult:** Sexes similar. FW upperside black set with two elliptical, almost transparent postmedial spots (one in cell, one distal to it); HW upperside brown with light metallic blue on medial area. FW underside maroon, with the costa, apex, and distal margin yellow; HW underside maroon with medial area suffused with violet-brown, distal margin yellow. Compare with *renaldus*.
Habits: This butterfly has been reported in our

area from 100 to 1200 m on both slopes in association with a wide variety of habitat types, including agricultural areas and cities. For example, the first individual of this butterfly I observed was perched on a wall at the Museo Nacional, and subsequently I observed them in the streets of San Jose. In a more natural setting these butterflies are typically encountered as solitary individuals along forest edges, streams, in light gaps, and occasionally in old second growth. The males perch from 3 to 5 m from the ground during midmorning. Both sexes visit flowers of *Cordia*, *Terminalia*, *Citrus*, and herbaceous Asteraceae.
Localities: [A]: Avangarez (July), San Mateo (October), Guacima (September). [C]: Juan Viñas (October), Turrialba. [SJ]: Santana (July), San Jose (August). [P]: Rio Pita (September). [G]: La Pacifica (May, July), Santa Rosa (June–August, November), Cerro Hacha (November), Rio Piedras (December).

Anteros renaldus indigator
Stichel, 1911
FW length: 17–17.5 mm   **Plate 14**

Range: Nicaragua to Brazil. **Subspecies:** Nicaragua to Panama
Hostplant: Unknown
Early stages: Unknown
• **Adult:** Sexes similar. FW upperside metallic blue with costa, apex, and distal margin broadly black, and two medial transparent spots (one at end of cell, one distal and posterior to cell). HW upperside metallic blue with black costa. Entire underside olive-yellow with a dark, irregular submarginal band, pale iridescent blue on medial areas, and distinctly pink "furry" legs and HW inner margin. Compare with *carausius*.
Habits: This butterfly has been reported in our area from sea level to 800 m on both slopes in association with rain forest and cloud forest habitats. Encountered as rare, solitary individuals along forest edges, streams, and in light gaps. With the aid of binoculars I have observed males perching during midmorning high in the forest canopy. Uncommon.
Localities: [C]: Cachi (August), Moravia de Chirripo (September), Turrialba (January, July, October). [SJ]: Moravia (April). [P]: Marenco (March). [L]: Guapiles.

Genus **SAROTA** Westwood, 1851

The butterflies in this genus are recognized by their brown upperside and the complex patterns and metallic spots on the undersides of the wings. At various times these butterflies have been placed in the genera *Charis, Anteros,* and *Helicopis.* However, members of *Sarota* are separated from those genera on the basis of leg morphology, wing venation, and the configuration of the genitalia. There are two groups of butterflies within *Sarota*: those species that are tiny, uniformly brown on the upperside, typically have entire HW margins (as in *S. gyas*), and those that are medium sized bear white spots on the upperside and typically several "tails" on the HW margin (as in *S. chrysus*).

Members of *Sarota* are found from Mexico throughout Central and South America. The quantity of undetermined material in museums is a fairly clear indication that the total number of species embraced by *Sarota* is unknown. In fact, the Costa Rican fauna alone argues that the total number of *Sarota* species is underestimated. For example, the catalog of Bridges (1988) indicates that nine species and seven subspecies are embraced by *Sarota.* My best estimate is that there are at least eleven, and likely twelve, species in Costa Rica alone, most of which are rare, and every museum collection has many specimens that are clearly undescribed. In short, it is evident that the genus needs revision.

A number of characteristics contribute to why our understanding of *Sarota* is poor. One is that they are inconspicuous in the field and easily overlooked. Second, the species appear to have short and discrete activity periods. Third, these butterflies are hellishly fragile, and hence the investigator is typically confronted with specimens damaged in the normal course of the butterfly's life (as evidenced by finding them in the field), or damaged in the process of preparation. Finally, even with a series of good specimens, the similarity and confusing color patterns of many of the *Sarota* species make them difficult to identify. When using this field guide, pay close attention to the form and color of the fringe, the color and form of the distal margins, and the color of the legs.

Available evidence suggests that for *Sarota,* leafy liverworts and mosses that grow on top of old leaves are important hostplants (DeVries et al. 1994). As in *Anteros,* the caterpillars are covered with a long down of setae and bear a dorsal topknot of bladderlike setae on the first thoracic segment. Pupation takes place inside a rolled leaf, and the long setae of the caterpillar surround the pupa to form a loose cocoon.

In Costa Rica members of *Sarota* are found from sea level to 1200 m elevation, occasionally as high as 2000 m. Curiously, no records have been available to me from the lowland Guanacaste dry forest, suggesting that these butterflies are restricted to wet and rain forest habitats. As in the related genus *Anteros,* butterflies in *Sarota* may be mistaken by the casual entomologist as members of the Lycaenidae. This is likely to be due to the metallic spots on the underside and the presence of filamentous tails on the HW of some species. This similarity is further enhanced in the field by the males who have the habit of patrolling back and forth along vegetation with a fast erratic flight, and then settling abruptly on a perch. However, in the field most of the *Sarota* perch under leaves, and I have never observed members of our fauna rubbing the hindwings together as do the lycaenids (but see Robbins 1985). Observations at Las Alturas on several species suggest that these butterflies are active early in the morning, and very local. Furthermore, I found that those at Las Alturas were active during short windows of time and did not overlap those of other species occurring at the same locality.

Sarota gyas
(Cramer, 1775)
FW length: 10–10.5 mm **Plate 15**
Range: Honduras to Colombia, Brazil
Hostplant: Mosses and liverworts (Lejuniaceae)
Early stages (Figs. 1f, 49b): *Egg*—a tiny white globe entirely covered with irregular ellipsoid holes that gives the impression of a sponge; dorsum slightly depressed with a vaguely conical micropyle. The egg is laid singly. *Mature caterpillar* (DeVries 1988a)—covered in long, downy white setae that arise in dorsolateral tufts and project outward in all directions; the longest setae are directed laterally; anterior edge of the first thoracic segment has a dorsal tuft of whitish bladderlike setae. The caterpillars graze mosses and liverworts that grow as epiphyls on old leaves. While resting, the head capsule is held down flat against the substrate. If molested by ants, the caterpillars deflex their setae toward the stimulus to keep the ant away from the body. When molested by an ant, the long setae will break off, get stuck in the mandibles of the ant, and cause the ant to groom itself rather than bother the caterpillar.
• **Adult:** Sexes similar. Upperside dull brown, with even brown fringe on distal margins of both wings. Underside reddish medial area set with blue lines; FW costa yellow; distal margins of both wings yellow; two dark medial spots on both wings: posterior to FW cell, and inside HW cell; the legs are cream colored. Compare with *acantus, gamelia, myrtea*.
Habits: This butterfly occurs from sea level to 800 m on both slopes in association with rain forest habitats. Generally encountered between 10:00 to 12:30 hrs as solitary individuals (occasionally two or three) along forest edges, streams, and in light gaps where they perch at 3 to 5 m above the ground on the underside of leaves. The females oviposit during midday on epiphyll-encrusted leaves of many plants growing in the forest understory. Not uncommon, but difficult to spot in the field.
Localities: [A]: Cariblanco (October). [C]: Turrialba (May, June), Paraiso (September), Peralta. [SJ]: Carrillo. [H]: Magsaysay (August), La Selva (March, April, June, July, November), Chilamate (September), Tirimbina (February, March). [P]: Carrara (October), Rio Catarata (September), Chacarita de Osa (September), Rincon (February, March), Llorona. [L]: Sixaola (September), Hacienda Tapezco (August), Esperanza, Limon, Guapiles.

Sarota myrtea
Godman and Salvin, 1886
FW length: 11–11.5 mm **Plate 15**
Range: Mexico to Brazil
Hostplant: Unknown
Early stages: Unknown
• **Adult:** Sexes similar. Upperside dull brown; fringe on distal margins of both wings composed of irregular, sparse, short black tufts that arise at the veins; FW distal margin bowed outward slightly just above the tornus. Underside with pale metallic blue medial lines on both wings; FW subcosta and distal margin with a thin yellow-orange band, three to four dark postmedial spots, two metallic blue lines in subapex run parallel to the costa, and two metallic blue submarginal spots (that may be fused) run parallel to the distal margin; HW medial area with three dull red chains with black centers in each link, and distal margin with black fringe. The legs are dark brown with white tibia and black tarsi (male forelegs entirely black). Compare with *gamelia, spicata, psaros, gyas*.
Habits: This butterfly has been recorded in our area from 500 to 800 m on both slopes from both rain forest and deciduous forest habitats. The males are encountered as solitary individuals perching from 2 to 3 m above the ground along forest edges between 10:00 and 11:30 hrs. Uncommon in Costa Rican collections.
Localities: [A]: San Mateo. [C]: Turrialba (May—July), Peralta, Cachi. [SJ]: Santa Rosa de Puriscal (January). [H]: La Selva (May), Plastico (March), Magsaysay (March).

Sarota gamelia
Godman and Salvin, 1886
FW length: 10.5–11.5 mm **Plate 15**
Range: Guatemala to Panama
Hostplant: Unknown
Early stages: Unknown
• **Adult:** Sexes similar. Upperside dull brown. When viewed from underside many specimens have a bright yellow fringe on distal margins of both wings and a long tuft of black at HW tornus. In other specimens this fringe may be a more subdued yellow, but it is distinct. Underside red set with pale metallic blue lines, a distinct medial yellow triangle at FW costa, and another submarginal yellow patch near the tornus, medial area on HW with three red chains that have black centers in each link, and distal margin of tornus with a black tuft. The legs are entirely yellow. *Note:* Populations from the Pacific slope from 1100 to 1600 m associated with premontane wet forest habitats in the Coto Brus area may represent a different species from *gamelia*. These individuals are distinguished as follows: upperside dark brown; underside with two elongate metallic

green bands near FW apex and two short ones distal to the cell, both parallel to the costa; an indistinct yellowish medial mark at the FW costa; three black spots on FW: one in subapex, one in tornus, and a third much larger medial one between tornus and posterior margin of the cell; distal margins of both wings with a thin band of dull yellow; HW with a distinct tuft of long black fringe at tornus and inner margin, another shorter tuft at tornus and distal margin, and often less distinct medial tufts at distal margin. The legs are dark brown with cream-yellow tibia and tarsi, and the male forelegs are entirely cream-yellow. Compare with *myrtea, acantus, psaros, gyas.*

Habits: This butterfly has been recorded in our area from 400 to 1600 m on both slopes in association with rain forest, deciduous forest, and premontane wet forest habitats. In populations found below 1000 m, both sexes may be encountered as solitary individuals between 10:00 and 12:30 hrs along forest edges and light gaps where they perch from 2 to 5 m above the ground. In the populations from the Coto Brus area I found that the males are encountered very locally in small groups of two to six individuals between 7:30 and 8 A.M. During this brief window of time, they are found perching along forest edges from 3 to 5 m above the ground only on particular trees. The flight is very fast and erratic, and individuals often engage in whirling aerial dogfights that typically last for a few seconds. After a dogfight, each individual returns abruptly to a particular perch, which may change during the course of the daily activity period. The butterflies may perch either on the upper or underside of leaves, but always in a position that is illuminated by direct sunshine. At Las Alturas, I noted that this species was often in the company of *Euselasia hieronymi, E. argentea,* and *Sarota acantus.* Again, it may be that there are two species covered in this account. Uncommon in Costa Rican collections.

Localities: [C]: Turrialba (August), Juan Viñas (February, March). [SJ]: El Rodeo (July), Carrillo (February). [H]: La Selva (April, May), Plastico (March). [P]: Carrara (October, November), Buenos Aires (March), Rincon de Osa (February), Las Cruces (June), Las Alturas (August, September). [L]: Guapiles (September), La Florida (March). [G]: Pitilla (October).

Sarota estrada
Schaus, 1928
FW length: 14.5–15.5 mm   **Plate 15**
Range: Mexico to Costa Rica, Panama(?)

Hostplant: Unknown
Early stages: Unknown
• **Adult:** Sexes similar. This butterfly is distinguished from similar species by its large size. The entire underside has conspicuous pale metallic blue-green spots set into a rich, reddish brown (almost brick red) ground color. HW underside with three distinct brick-red chains that bear small black centers in each link, a thin orange-yellow distal margin, and the radial veins with a series of conspicuous, black tufts at distal margin giving the appearance of short, bristly tails, a trait that is especially noticeable in the female. Compare with *gamelia, myrtea.*

Habits: This butterfly is rare in our area, and has been recorded from only two Atlantic slope localities between 600 and 1200 m, both of which are rain forest habitats in the Parque Braulio Carrillo area.

Localities: [SJ]: [TL] Carrillo (July), [L]: Madre de Dios (July).

Sarota spicata
(Staudinger, 1888)
FW length: 10.5 mm   **Plate 15**
Range: Costa Rica to Peru, western Brazil
Hostplant: Unknown
Early stages: Unknown
• **Adult:** Sexes similar. Upperside brown with reddish overcast. Underside pattern slightly resembles that of *gamelia,* but with three distinct tails on the HW distal margin, and two elongate medial white spots on FW near inner margin. The male forelegs are cream white. *Note:* This butterfly was originally described by Staudinger as a variety of *acanthoides* (Herrich-Schäffer, 1853), but given its very distinctive appearance I treat it here as a full species. Compare with *myrtea, gamelia, psaros, acantus.*

Habits: This butterfly has been recorded from only two localities in our area, both of which are Atlantic slope rain forest habitats between sea level and 300 m. Rare in collections.

Localities: [H]: Finca la Selva. [L]: Madre de Dios (July).

Sarota acantus
(Stoll, 1782)
FW length: 11.5–12 mm   **Plate 15**
Range: Costa Rica to Amazonas
Hostplant: Unknown
Early stages: Unknown
• **Adult:** Sexes similar. Upperside entirely black. Underside pattern reminiscent of *myrtea,* but distinguished from it by being overall somberly colored; FW with two short rectangular, metallic blue subapical bars that parallel the

costa and that are set in an ill-defined amber patch, a small medial amber patch at costa. Almost the entire area posterior to FW cell is charcoal-gray with three to four indistinct black bands, the distal margins of both wings dull orange-brown, the fringe of both wings is short and black, with a few tufts of white on FW where it bows outward slightly just above the tornus, and the underside of the abdomen is gray (not white). The legs are black (male forelegs entirely so), with the distal portion of the tibia slightly cream colored, and black tarsi. Compare with *gyas*, *gamelia*, *myrtea*, *spicata*.

Habits: This butterfly is known from a single Costa Rican locality on the Pacific slope between 1200 and 1600 m in premontane wet rain forest in the Coto Brus area. The males are encountered very locally as solitary individuals between 07:30 to 08:00 hrs (rarely later) perching along forest edges from 3 to 5 m above the ground, always in bright sunshine. The flight is fast and erratic, and individuals often engage in whirling aerial "dogfights" with other small butterflies. I found this butterfly in the company of *Sarota gamelia* and *Euselasia argentea*, but never as abundant as those species. Uncommon in Costa Rican collections, but may be locally abundant.
Localities: [P]: Las Alturas (August, September).

Sarota psaros psaros
(Godman and Salvin, 1886)
FW length: 11–11.5 mm   Plate 15
Range: Guatemala to Brazil. **Subspecies:** Guatemala to Colombia
Hostplant: Unknown
Early stages: Unknown
• **Adult:** Sexes similar. Upperside dark gray with black submarginal crescents at the HW margin. FW underside white suffused with red-brown at base apex and margin interspersed with a few silver-blue lines, and three distinct black bars at inner margin. FW distal margin with a distinct lobe just above tornus. HW underside white, suffused with indistinct red-brown patterns and interspersed with silver-blue submarginal lines. HW distal margin scalloped, and with tiny spiked tails at each radial vein. The legs are white. Compare with *spicata*.
Habits: This butterfly has been recorded in our area from 600 to 1400 m on both slopes in association with rain forest and cloud forest habitats. In my experience the males are encountered as rare, solitary individuals perching from 3 to 5 m above the ground on isolated trees or shrubs between 12:00 and 12:30

hrs, in the company of other *Sarota* species. At Finca la Selva, N. Greig found an individual male that had been attracted to a black light at night. Uncommon.
Localities: [SJ]: Carrillo. [H]: La Selva (January), Finca la Lola. [P]: Las Alturas (August). [L]: Madre de Dios (July).

Sarota chrysus
(Stoll, 1781)
FW length: 14.5–15 mm   Plate 15
Range: Mexico to Colombia, Peru, Bolivia
Hostplant: Most likely mosses and liverworts that grow as epiphyls
Early stages: *Egg*—tiny, white, laid singly on upper or underside of old leaves covered in epiphyls (DeVries 1988a)
• **Adult:** Sexes slightly dimorphic. *Male*—upperside dark brown with three to four white spots (two subcostal near apex, one in cell, and the largest one postmedial and below cell), distal third of HW with a faint gold-gray iridescence, especially at base of the two tails, and two black spots at margin between tails; FW underside white, set with red-brown medial bands that are divided by thin black lines (especially in cell), a pale metallic blue subcostal line that expands in the apex and continues as a thin submarginal line that divides a red-brown submarginal band, and a separate metallic line in tornus located basal to the submarginal band; HW underside white at base and discal area, with red-brown chains bearing black centers in each link, distal half of wing obscured with a dull buff color (extent variable), a broad olive-buff submarginal band that has one or two black spots between tails and bordered on either side with distinct silver-blue lines (the distal-most is edged in black), and the tails are cream colored with black borders. The forelegs are buff, and the remaining legs are black with the long setae cream, and tarsi ringed in black and white. *Female*—FW upperside dark brown, gray at base, and with four to six white spots (variable); HW upperside gray with a slight iridescent cast when viewed obliquely, anterior quarter light gray to white, often with some dark spots at costa, two conspicuous distal tails trimmed in black with a short spike between them, tornus produced into a tooth, and a thin submarginal line along distal margin at base of tails. FW underside as in male except the pale metallic blue lines at the subcosta, apex, and submargin are more obvious; HW underside similar to male except silver-blue lines more pronounced, and olive buff area more extensive. The forelegs are buff with the tarsi ringed in black and white, the

remaining legs are black with the long setae cream, and tarsi ringed in black and white. Compare with *turrialbensis*, *dematria*, *subtessellata*.

Habits: This butterfly has been recorded in Costa Rica between sea level and 1000 m from Atlantic slope rain forest and cloud forest habitats. In Panama I observed females ovipositing on old leaves of understory woody shrubs that were covered in epiphyls. Oviposition took place during midday. Both sexes visit flowers of *Croton* and *Alibertia*. Infrequent in Costa Rican collections.

Localities: [A]: Reserva de San Ramon (May). [C]: La Florida (March), Turrialba (June). [H]: Chilamate (March), Magsaysay (September), La Selva (June, July), Plastico (March). [P]: Sirena (May).

Sarota subtessellata
(Schaus, 1913)
FW length: 17–18.5 mm   **Plate 15**
Range: Costa Rica to Panama
Hostplant: Unknown
Early stages: Unknown
• **Adult:** Sexes dimorphic. *Male*—Upperside varies from black to dark brown, generally with four white spots on the FW: two in subapex, one in cell, and the largest one at end of cell. FW underside rich red-brown interspersed with white patches, a broad red-brown marginal band set with a thin metallic blue line, costa with a distinct white triangle that is outlined in thin black, and little or no metallic sheen when viewed obliquely. HW underside with discal area white with five to six red-brown link shapes, distal third of wing brownish with a metallic green cast in tornus that is seen when viewed obliquely, two pronounced buff-colored tails (that are easily broken) that bear two black spots at their base, and a produced buff-colored lobe on the tornus. The long setae on the legs have a distinctly orange cast (especially the forelegs), with the tarsi ringed alternately in black and white. *Female*—FW upperside dark brown to gray set with four to six white spots of variable size; HW upperside gray with a slight olive cast on medial area when viewed obliquely. FW underside similar to male except without red-brown ground color, and metallic blue line dividing the red-brown marginal band is wider; HW underside similar to male (including the metallic green cast at tornus, and two black spots at base of tails) but with distal half of wing a buff-cream color. Compare with *chrysus*, *dematria*, *turrialbensis*.

Habits: This butterfly has been reported in our

area from 100 to 900 m on the Atlantic slope in association with rainforest habitats. The males are encountered as solitary individuals perching from 2 to 5 m above the ground along forest edges and in light gaps between 12:30 and 13:30 hrs. The females are most frequently found in the shaded forest understory between 12:00 and 14:00 hrs. Uncommon.

Localities: [A]: Cariblanco (June). [SJ]: [TL] Carrillo (April, May). [H]: La Selva (June, July, September), Chilamate (September). [L]: Hacienda Tapezco (August).

Sarota dematria
(Westwood, 1851)
FW length: 14.5–15 mm   **Not illustrated**
Range: Costa Rica to Colombia
Hostplant: Unknown
Early stages: Unknown
• **Adult:** Sexes dimorphic. *Male*—upperside dark brown with four white spots on the FW: two in subapex, one in cell, and the largest one at end of cell, and a gray band at distal submargin of the HW that is set with several dark spots. HW distal margin with two distinct tails, a spike between them, and a lobed tornus. FW underside rich red-brown with a distinct white subcostal triangle bordered in silver-blue that enters the cell, and buff colored as it meets the costa; three white discal bands that run to the inner margin, the two basal-most are silver-blue bordered in black in or near the cell; subapex with two well-defined white spots that are bordered in silver-blue; a broad red-brown submarginal band bordered in silver-blue, with a yellow-brown distal margin. HW underside red-brown set with silver-blue bands in discal area (basal-most is white), a very broad, dull, buff-colored submarginal band with an irregular silver-blue distal border, distal margin with an olive-buff band set with two black spots between base of tails, and bordered distally by a silver-blue line. Legs and palpi yellow-buff with tarsi ringed in black and white. *Female*—upperside similar to male but with four to six white spots in the FW (variable), and HW with a distinct buff-colored postmedial band; underside similar to male but silver-blue lines more distinct, and often with the buff-colored postmedial band in HW more defined. *Note*: This distinctive taxon is considered by some authors to be a synonym of *chrysus*. However, based on consistent differences in patterns it seems plausible that the two taxa are distinct species. Sexes slightly dimorphic. Compare with *turrialbensis*, *chrysus*, *subtessellata*.

Habits: This butterfly has been recorded in our

area from sea level to 1400 m, mainly from Pacific slope rain forest in the southwest of the country. There are, however, a few records from Atlantic slope rain forest near the Rio Sarapiqui. My experience with this butterfly on the Osa Peninsula and in Panama has been that the females are found as rare, solitary individuals along trails and light gaps in the forest understory during late morning and midday. I have never observed the male in the field, and, interestingly, the females are decidedly more common in collections than the males, perhaps indicating the males perch high in the forest canopy. Uncommon. **Localities:** [H]: Chilamate (June, September), La Selva (July). [P]: Rincon (November), Sirena (June, November), Llorona (May), Las Alturas (September).

Sarota turrialbensis
(Schaus, 1913)
FW length: 13.7 mm   Plate 15
Range: Costa Rican endemic(?)
Hostplant: Unknown
Early stages: Unknown
• **Adult:** *Note*: This description is based on the unique type. Sexes presumably similar. *Male*—upperside dark brown with a gray band at distal submargin of the HW that is set with several dark spots. FW underside orange-red, a distinct cream triangular spot at costa that in-

trudes into cell and is bordered by silver-blue, a black postmedial line bordered on either side by orange-red, a broad orange-red marginal band that is divided by a thin silver-blue line, and three conspicuous triangular white shapes at inner margin with the two basal shapes set in black. HW underside with three orange-red chains in discal area that are separated by silver-blue lines and have black centers in each link, distal quarter broadly cream colored with black fringe bearing two distinct tails (also with black fringe), and a distinct black spot near the base of the anterior-most tail. The forelegs are cream colored, and the remaining legs are dark gray with tibia and tarsi cream colored. *Female*—apparently unknown and in need of description. Compare with *dematria, chrysus, subtessellata*.
Habits: This butterfly is known only from the unique type specimen in the U.S. National Museum that forms part of the W. Schaus collection. The specimen bears the locality data "Turrialba, 5800 ft," suggesting that perhaps the butterfly originated from Volcan Turrialba. The apparent rarity of this species suggests that it may only occur in montane forests within the Turrialba Valley. Any information on the biology, the female, or its rediscovery after so many years would be worth publishing.
Localities: [C]: Turrialba [TL].

Tribe EMESINI Stichel, 1911

The butterflies that have been placed in this group bear unresolved affinities: they represent all riodinid butterflies with four radial veins, but do not share any apomorphic characters with other tribes. Thus, this grouping is composed of a variety of taxa with uncertain relationships and is not monophyletic (Harvey 1987a). The group contains over one hundred species placed in thirteen genera, seven of which occur in our area: *Argyrogrammana, Calydna, Emesis, Pachythone, Roeberella, Pixus*, and *Apodemia*. Host records for members of this group include Olacaceae, Flacourtiaceae, Ranunculaceae, Combretaceae, Aquifoliaceae, Euphorbiaceae, Clusiaceae, Rosaceae, and Fabaceae, and the caterpillars are covered with a dense pile of setae. *Note*: The currently employed family group name Emesini (Stichel 1911) (type-genus *Emesis* Fabricius) is unavailable as it is preoccupied by the senior name Emesini Amyot and Serville (1843) (Heteroptera, Reduviidae; type-genus *Emesa* Fabricius).

Genus ARGYROGRAMMANA Strand, 1932

These delicate little butterflies are recognized by their yellow or orange (sometimes blue) coloration that is speckled with dark spots, and typically with a silvered line on the outer margin. Members of *Argyrogrammana* are found from Mexico throughout Central and South America, and the genus is considered to embrace about twenty species. In older literature, these butterflies have been referred to under *Charis* and *Argyrogramma* Stichel, 1910, a junior homonym. There are at least four species that occur in our area.

The hostplants reported for *Argyrogrammana* are members of the Clusiaceae (DeVries et al. 1994). The caterpillars bear a sparse covering of long setae and have the behavior of folding the edges of leaves into a tube where the caterpillars hide and feed.

In Costa Rica these butterflies are found from lowland to mid-elevation forest habitats, and are typically local and uncommon.

Argyrogrammana holosticta
(Godman and Salvin, 1878)
FW length: 12–14 mm   **Plate 13**
Range: Mexico to Ecuador, Peru
Hostplant: Unknown
Early stages: Unknown
• **Adult:** Sexes similar. Upperside canary yellow (when fresh) set with many fine black spots, and a silvered submarginal line composed of broken segments of the same length. Underside yellow with the black spots more prominent, and the silvered line somewhat expanded in the FW apex. Compare with *leptographia, venilia, Baeotis sulphuria*.
Habits: This butterfly has been recorded in our area from sea level to 600 m on both slopes. Encountered on bright sunny days as solitary, weak-flying individuals along forest edges, roadcuts, and second growth. Judging from museum collections, this butterfly may be common in areas to the north and south of Costa Rica. However, it is uncommon in our area.
Localities: [A]: San Mateo (September, December). [SJ]: Villa Colon (September). [P]: Rio Catarata (September), Coyolar (July). [L]: Guapiles (February).

Argyrogrammana venilia crocea
(Godman and Salvin, 1878)
FW length: 12–13 mm   **Plate 13**
Range: Costa Rica to Colombia, Brazil. **Subspecies:** Costa Rica to Panama
Hostplant: *Rheedia edulis* (Clusiaceae)
Early stages: In Panama, Robbins and Aiello (1982) report, "a flat, orange-brown larva between two overlapping leaves . . . that fed by scraping the leaf surface without disturbing the veins. . . . The pupa resembled the larva in color and pattern."
• **Adult:** Sexes slightly dimorphic. *Male*—FW upperside orange with black bars along costal margin of which the distal-most forms a conspicuous black rectangle, a row of transverse postbasal and submarginal black spots, and a broken silvered submarginal line; HW upperside orange with a scattering of small black spots. Underside similar to upperside except the black spots are more prominent, and the silvered submarginal line is expanded in the FW apex. The fringe of both wings is black. *Female*—upperside and underside ground

color pale orange and similar to male except the black spots on the discal areas and margin of FW are less prominent. The abdomen of both sexes is orange and ringed distinctly in black. Compare with *holosticta, sulphurea, leptographia, barine.*
Habits: This butterfly has been recorded in our area from sea level to 1400 m on both slopes in association with montane forest habitats. Encountered as solitary individuals along forest edges, roadcuts, and rivers flying in bright sunshine. My observations suggest that the males are active between 07:30 and 09:00 hrs, and the females are active between 08:00 and 11:30 hrs. At a single localized site at Las Alturas, I regularly found individuals of this butterfly perched from 1 to 3 m above the ground on the underside of the leaves of plants that received early morning sunshine. Furthermore, I found this species perching on vegetation at this same focal site throughout the year, but not on any of the adjacent vegetation. Uncommon.
Localities: [C]: Valle Escondido de Cartago (March), Moravia de Chirripo (April). [SJ]: La Montura (April). [P]: Las Alturas (April, May, August, September, December).

Argyrogrammana leptographia
(Stichel, 1911)
FW length: 12.5–14 mm   **Plate 13**
Range: Costa Rica to Colombia
Hostplant: *Tovomitopsis* sp., *Garcinia* sp. (Clusiaceae)
Early stages: D. Murray (pers. comm.) provides the following information on the close relative *trochilia* from Ecuador. *Mature caterpillar*—pale yellow, flattened, with marked lateral indentations between the segments, and each segment has long lateral setae projecting outwards. The caterpillars hide inside two leaves that have been fastened together with silk, and feed only on the upper epidermis of the leaf within the shelter (perhaps to avoid the latex of the plant). *Pupa*—rust colored, dorsolaterally flattened, a weak thoracic keel, and a lateral and dorsal fringe of short setae.
• **Adult:** Sexes dimorphic. *Male*—upperside a striking sky-blue with a conspicuous orange subapical band on FW, margins of both wings are orange (may be mixed with black of FW apex), and a broken silver-blue submarginal line; underside yellow-orange with irregular black spots on discal areas of both wings, a conspicuous submarginal line composed of angular black marks, and the silver-blue submarginal line is expanded in the FW apex; fringe of both wings dark brown interspersed

with small white patches. *Female*—upperside dull, pale yellow with a scattering of small black spots across both wings; underside similar to male but with the black spots somewhat blurred. The abdomen in both sexes bears a black dorsal line. *Note*: *Leptographia* has in the past been considered a subspecies of the South American species *trochilia* Westwood, 1851. Compare with *venilia, holosticta, sulphurea, barine*.

Habits: This butterfly has been recorded in our area between 1200 and 1600 m on the Pacific slope in association with cloud forest habitats in the Coton Valley. Generally encountered as solitary individuals along forest edges, roadcuts, and rivers between 10:00 and 12:00 hrs. However, at Las Alturas I found a few local sites along a forest edge where the females congregated under leaves in the morning between 06:30 and 08:00 hrs. I also found the females visiting flowers of an unidentified woody vine (Asteraceae) with white flowers that was growing near these local sites. D. Murray informs me that in Ecuador the ovipositing females of *trochilia* selectively lay eggs on the margins of leaves that are overlapped; either the leaves were fastened together with silk by previous caterpillars, or they had been webbed together by spider silk. Rare in Central American collections.

Localities: [P]: San Vito (July, September), Las Alturas (March–June, September, October).

Argyrogrammana barine
(Staudinger, 1887)
FW length: 13.5–14 mm   **Plate 15**
Range: Costa Rica to Colombia
Hostplant: Unknown
Early stages: Unknown
• **Adult:** Sexes dimorphic. *Male*—FW upperside dirty gray with a large pale blue medial patch on the discal area of FW that runs from inside cell to inner margin, and a broken silvered submarginal line that curves basally in the apex; HW upperside dirty gray with many broken lines in the discal area, and a broken silvered submarginal line that follows the contour of the distal margin. *Female*—FW upperside pale yellow with a scattering of short black bars at base; apex and distal margin broadly black with two conspicuous pale blue subapical spots, and silvered submarginal line as in male; HW upperside pale yellow with many short black bars in the discal and postmedial areas, and submarginal line as in male. Compare with *leptographia, venilia*.
Habits: This butterfly has been recorded in our area from a few specimens taken on the Atlan-

tic slope in the forest associated with Parque Braulio Carrillo. Obviously rare in Costa Rican collections, and little known.
Localities: [SJ]: Carrillo (June).

Genus **CALYDNA** Doubleday, 1847

The butterflies in this genus are small, patterned with a dense covering of small spots, and the wings often bear small transparent spots. Members of *Calydna* are found from Mexico to Argentina, and the genus is considered to contain about twenty-five species. Only two species occur in our area, while the remainder occur entirely in South America. The Central American members of *Calydna* superficially resemble some species of *Cremna, Caria*, and *Apodemia*.

Nothing is known about the hostplant relationships or the early stages of any species. Although some of the South American species have robust bodies and are very agile fliers, those in our area are not remarkable in this respect. The adults of some South American species visit wet sand along rivers and streams, and everywhere they visit plants with small white flowers. In Costa Rica these butterflies appear to be confined to the Pacific slope in dry or disturbed habitats.

Calydna venusta
Godman and Salvin, 1886
FW length: 14.5–15 mm   **Plate 16**
Range: Mexico to Panama
Hostplant: Unknown
Early stages: Unknown
• **Adult:** Sexes similar. Upperside dark red-brown with a complicated and variable calico pattern of various shades of red-brown and light brown; several small transparent medial spots that have a whitish cast near the end of the FW cell and in the HW cell; a distinct postbasal band of black squares crosses both wings; a distinct black postmedial band composed of irregular rectangular shapes bordered on either side by red-orange runs from the FW costa to HW inner margin; a thin white submarginal line runs from FW costa to HW inner margin; the distal margins at the subapex and near the tornus of both wings have conspicuous scalloped excavations. The male tends to have a darker and more contrasting coloration than the female. Compare with *sturnula*.
Habits: This butterfly has been reported in our area only from lowland Pacific forest habitats, mainly from Guanacaste Province. Encoun-

tered as uncommon, solitary individuals flying low to the ground in open areas. Most records indicate that this butterfly is active throughout the year, but mainly during the dry season. Rare in Costa Rican collections. Compare with *sturnula.*
Localities: [P]: Villa Neily. [G]: La Pacifica (January, March, October, November), Santa Rosa (July, August).

Calydna sturnula hegius
Felder, 1869
FW length: 12–13 mm   **Plate 16**
Range: Mexico to Brazil. **Subspecies:** Mexico to Panama
Hostplant: Unknown
Early stages: Unknown
• **Adult:** Sexes dimorphic. *Male*—upperside black with a thin, white, sinuous submarginal line, each wing with a distinct transparent medial spot that has a white cast (the spot in the HW is irregularly shaped), and the distal margins of both wings have scalloped excavations; extreme tip of the abdomen red-orange. *Female*—upperside ground color a complicated calico pattern of various shades of red-brown and light brown, a distinct broken black postmedial band is thinly bordered on either side by red-orange, and postbasal area of both wings with an irregular band of transparent spots. Compare with *venusta.*
Habits: This butterfly has been recorded in our area only from the Pacific slope in association with lowland deciduous forest habitats. Judging from locality data, it is present throughout the year, including the driest months. Typically found flying low to the ground along forest and riparian edges in bright sunshine. P. Opler found this butterfly between 08:00 and 14:00 hrs visiting flowers of *Cordia* and *Croton.* Uncommon in Costa Rican collections.
Localities: [P]: Barranca (March). [G]: Parque Santa Rosa (January, December), Cañas (January, May–December).

Genus EMESIS Fabricius, 1807

The butterflies in this genus are typically recognized by their subtle checkered patterns that are set in a drab brown or gray ground color, and by their stout bodies. When observed in the field, virtually all species of these butterflies all perched on the underside of leaves, and they hold their long antennae close together almost directly in line with the body. I have noticed that when the *Emesis* species are alive, the eyes of many of them are distinctly green and appear to have a tiny black central pupil. As a group, these butterflies range from being monomorphic to exhibiting strong sexual dimorphism. Members of *Emesis* are found from the southern USA throughout Central and South America, and as currently understood the genus contains between thirty and forty mostly South American species. The jumble of material in most museum collections makes it evident that *Emesis* is in need of a taxonomic revision, especially in the *mandana* group. Eleven species have been recorded from our area.

Despite its large geographic range and the number of species contained within *Emesis*, only a few of these butterflies have been reared. Nevertheless, host records indicate that these butterflies use a diverse array of hostplants that include the Fabaceae, Aquifoliaceae, Anacardiaceae, Combretaceae, Moraceae, Euphorbiaceae, Flacourtiaceae, Styracaceae, Ranunculaceae, and Nyctaginaceae (DeVries et al. 1994; see also summary in Harvey 1987a). These records suggest that *Emesis* will be found to utilize an even greater diversity of hostplant families. The caterpillars are covered in a dense, short, often colorful pile of setae, and they may either be solitary or gregarious. The pupae are squat, unadorned by spines, and resemble those of *Lepricornis* and *Theope.* Depending on the species, pupation may take place gregariously or as solitary individuals.

In Costa Rica, members of *Emesis* are found from sea level to the highest mountain peaks. Some of the species occur across broad ranges of elevation and habitats (*lucinda*), while others appear to be restricted to thin bands of elevation in restricted areas (*lacrines*). Most of our species are common, but a few are very rare indeed. The butterflies tend to make rapid zigzag flights, and seldom perch for very long in one place. However, one of our species (*lucinda*) may fly slowly and obviously, perhaps indicating it is unpalatable.

Emesis tenedia tenedia
Felder and Felder, 1861
FW length: 18–20 mm   **Plate 17**
Range: Mexico to Brazil. **Subspecies:** Mexico to Ecuador
Hostplant: *Clematis haenkeana* (Ranunculaceae)
Early stages (Fig. 2b): *Egg*—white, highly sculptured such that it gives the impression of a cactus; bears setae arising from spinelike sculpturing, and a large recessed central micropyle. The eggs are deposited singly or in pairs on the underside of leaves along the leaf

A

FIGURE 50. (A) *Emesis lucinda* caterpillars. (Drawing by J. Clark)

margin or near but not touching the central midvein. Upon hatching, the caterpillars do not eat the egg shell, but leave a clean exit hole around the micropyle. *Caterpillars*—first through third instars are entirely pale green (including the head), with two rows of subdorsal setae and two rows of lateral setae that are slightly curved toward the posterior and run from the thoracic segments to the penultimate abdominal segment. *Mature caterpillar*—body pale green with two prominent purple bands running from the first thoracic segment to the anal plate, and a thin purple dorsal line; the first and second thoracic segments plus abdominal segment 10 bear peglike protuberances that are orange, yellow, and light green, respectively. Both sides of the dorsal line have a raised knob on every segment that bears a few setae. In dorsal view, all body segments have obvious triangular lateral lobes that have yellow tips adorned with four to six short, dark setae. Head capsule pale green with a wavy purple line across the face. All instar caterpillars chew circular holes in the leaf away from the margin creating small holes distributed across an entire leaf, not unlike the feeding damage associated with beetles in the family Chrysomelidae. *Pupa*—roundly elongate without protuberances, obvious setae, or projections; abdomen pale green, wing pads very pale green and sufficiently transparent to show the wing veins, the eyes a contrasting yellow-green, and the cremaster very broad.

Pupation takes place in a semicurled leaf on or off the hostplant.
• **Adult:** Sexes dimorphic. *Male*—upperside dirty, dark brown with a scattering of indistinct medial lines; underside reddish brown with distinct, broken discal lines on both wings. *Female*—upperside varies from dark brown to red-brown; underside varies from red-brown to yellow-brown, but it is readily distinguished by the wide postmedial band on FW that runs from the costa to beyond the cell (the band color varies from white to cream). Compare with *ocypore* and *lucinda*.
Habits: Although decidedly more common in montane regions, this butterfly may occur from 300 to 2500 m on both slopes in virtually any habitat that has some adjacent forest. The males are active along forest edges and in large light gaps between 07:30 and 09:30 hrs, and perch either on top of or under leaves ranging from 0.5 to 5 m above the ground. I never found that males maintained fixed perches. Rather, I found that they will stay on a perch and chase other butterflies for about 5 min, then move to another perch or descend to the ground to visit wet soil or flowers. The females search actively for oviposition sites along forest edges and in light gaps between 11:30 and 13:00 hrs. The eggs are deposited on the underside of new or old leaves or on the stem of the plant. After each oviposition, the female will bask for a few moments in a sunny spot with the wings open and then con-

tinue searching for oviposition sites. Both sexes visit flowers of *Lantana, Asclepias, Diodia, Croton,* and other plants with small white flowers.
Localities: [A]: Cariblanco (March), Atenas. [C]: Tapanti (December), Irazu, Cachi, Azahar de Cartago, Juan Viñas. [SJ]: Desamparados (September), Carpintera (March), San Pedro (July), Patarra (April, December), Santana (June), Colon (January), Copey. [P]: San Vito (July, September), Las Alturas (March–September, November, December), Monte Verde (May, July, October).

Emesis lacrines
Hewitson, 1870
FW length: 23–26 mm   Plate 17
Range: Nicaragua to Panama
Hostplant: *Hyeronima oblonga* (Euphorbiaceae), *Casearia arborea* (Flacourtiaceae), *Pterocarpus hayesii* (Fabaceae)
Early stages: *Mature caterpillar*—body yellow-red with three rows of short, red-brown tufts of setae on each segment; head capsule shiny black. *Pupa*—yellow with black spots on abdomen and thorax, the wing pads are pale yellow trimmed in black, and the cremaster is black.
• **Adult:** Sexes dimorphic. *Male*—upperside a rich red-brown with an iridescent violet cast, and a yolk-colored FW submarginal band that runs from costa across end of cell; underside dull, warm brown with many black spots. *Female*—upperside ground color typically lighter and more orange than the male, and the FW band is pale yellow to white and broader than in male; underside similar to male. Compare with *cypria, lucinda.*
Habits: In our area, this butterfly has been recorded mainly from the Atlantic slope between 400 and 800 m in association with montane forest near Braulio Carrillo. However, there is one record from Pacific lowland forest near the Osa Peninsula. The few times I have met with this butterfly it was along a forest edge in bright sunlight. There I found both sexes perching under leaves between 10:00 and 13:00 hrs. This uncommon and beautiful butterfly appears to have a very restricted range and thus may be a useful indicator species for studies concerned with conservation of particular habitats.
Localities: [A]: Cariblanco (March, June, August, October). [C]: Turrialba (February), Moravia de Chirripo (April). [H]: Plastico (March, July, August), Chilamate (July). [P]: Punta Uvita (August).

Emesis cypria paphia
Felder, 1869

FW length: 20–22 mm   Plate 17
Range: Mexico to Bolivia. **Subspecies:** Mexico to Colombia
Hostplant: Unknown
Early stages: Unknown
• **Adult:** Sexes similar. Upperside dark brown with a conspicuous orange FW band that runs from costa to the tornus; underside red-brown with an orange cast to FW around the transverse band, and discal area of both wings is set with a few dark lines. This species resembles members of the nymphalid genus *Adelpha* (e.g., *boreas, salmoneus, zalmona*) in appearance and habits, and they fly together. Compare with *tenedia, ocypore, Euselasia rhodogyne.*
Habits: This butterfly occurs commonly in our area from 600 to 2100 m on both slopes in association with montane forest habitats. Typically encountered as solitary individuals (or sometimes in small groups) along forest edges, streams, and in light gaps between 09:00 and 11:30 hrs. The males perch from 1 to 5 m above the ground on the upperside of leaves, and vigorously chase insects that are flying past the perch. In general, these butterflies are quite tame and often will alight on an observer who stands near them. The females are rare in Costa Rican collections. Both sexes visit plants with small white flowers.
Localities: [A]: Reserva San Ramon (March), Cariblanco (January–April, July, October, November), Avangarez. [C]: La Estrella (March), Tapanti (January, October), Juan Viñas (October), Turrialba (March), Tuis, Cachi, Orosi. [P]: Las Alturas (March, September–December), San Vito (April, June, July, September, October).

Emesis ocypore aethalia
Bates, 1868
FW length: 17.5–20 mm   Plate 16
Range: Mexico to Ecuador, Bolivia. **Subspecies:** Mexico to Colombia
Hostplant: Unknown
Early stages: Unknown
• **Adult:** Sexes dimorphic. *Male*—upperside dark brown with faint marbling of darker lines on the discal areas, and the FW apex and HW tornus are produced; underside dirty light brown with wavy, dark brown lines on both wings. *Female*—upperside dirty brown to warm brown set with many wavy dark brown lines across both wings; underside gray-brown with many dark brown lines. The FW apex and HW tornus are rounded. Compare with *mandana, lucinda, tenedia.*
Habits: In our area this butterfly occurs commonly from 300 to 1500 m on both slopes in association with habitats that range from semi-

deciduous forest to rain forest. Generally encountered as solitary individuals, occasionally in small colonies, along forest edges, streams, and in light gaps between 10:00 to 12:30 hrs. Both sexes visit flowers of *Lantana, Croton,* various Asteraceae, and many plants with small white flowers. At Turrialba, I collected a female of this butterfly that had a tiny orchid pollinaria attached to its proboscis, suggesting that these butterflies may pollinate some species of orchids.

Localities: [A]: Reserva San Ramon (May), San Mateo (September), Cariblanco (February), Peñas Blancas (September), Atenas. [C]: Moravia de Chirripo (April), Turrialba (February, May–July), Juan Viñas. [SJ]: Finca El Rodeo (March, August, November), Carrillo (June, October). [H]: La Selva (April), Chilamate (March). [P]: Monte Verde (November), Carrara (October), Puriscal. [L]: Guapiles (October). [G]: Rincon de la Vieja (May).

Emesis lupina
Godman and Salvin, 1886
FW length: 17.5–18.5 mm   **Plate 16**
Range: Mexico to Venezuela
Hostplant: Unknown
Early stages: Unknown
• **Adult:** Sexes slightly dimorphic. *Male*—upperside a dirty red-brown with dark gray lines across discal areas, a faint, broad grayish postmedial band in subapex of FW, and FW apex elongate and often with a slight hook; underside orange-brown with a marbling of wavy dark brown discal lines. *Female*—upperside dull red-brown with many wavy lines across both wings, and the distal margins of both wings distinctly bowed outward; underside dull orange-brown with a distinct staggered yellow postmedial band, and a yellowish abdomen. Compare with *mandana, fatimella, tegula.*
Habits: This butterfly has been reported in our area from 200 to 1200 m on both slopes in a wide variety of forest habitats. This butterfly appears to have a broader habitat range than *tegula,* but it is not at all clear that the two are distinct.
Localities: [A]: San Mateo. [C]: Irazu [TL], Redondo, Juan Viñas, Cachi. [SJ]: San Jose, Rio Hondura. [P]: San Luis at Rio Guacimal (February), Villa Neily (February). [G]: Cañas (February), Santa Rosa (March, November).

Emesis tegula
Godman and Salvin, 1886
FW length: 18.5–19 mm   **Plate 17**
Range: Mexico to Colombia
Hostplant: *Pisonia aculeata* (Nyctaginaceae)
Early stages: The eggs are deposited in leaf axils, and the caterpillar may partially fold the leaf and pupate inside the leaf shelter (Kendall 1976). An illustration of the egg is provided in Downey and Allyn (1980).
• **Adult:** Sexes slightly dimorphic. *Male*—upperside dull red-brown with a pale, indistinct gray-brown postmedial band; underside with a brighter orange cast with thin, staggered medial lines, and margins darker than the discal area. *Female*—upperside dull brown-orange with an indistinct, dull yellow-brown postmedial band; underside dull brown with orange-brown postmedial band, and orange-brown abdomen. The distal margins of both wings are distinctly bowed outward. *Note:* In some literature this butterfly has often been considered a subspecies of *mandana.* Compare with *lucinda, lupina, tenedia, mandana.*
Habits: This butterfly has been reported in our area from 300 to 600 m on both slopes in association with a range of forest habitats. This butterfly appears to have a distribution overlapping that of *mandana,* but it is not clear that the two taxa are distinct. Uncommon in Costa Rican collections.
Localities: [A]: San Mateo (September), Turrialba (June). [L]: Guapiles (October).

Emesis mandana mandana
(Cramer, 1780)
FW length: 20–25 mm   **Plate 17**
Range: Mexico to Brazil. **Subspecies:** Costa Rica to Colombia
Hostplant: A variety of records—*Conceveiba pleiostemona* (Euphorbiaceae) in Costa Rica, *Rhizophora mangle* (Rhizophoraceae) in Panama, *Theobroma cacao* (Sterculiaceae), and *Anacardium occidentale* (Anacardiaceae) in Trinidad
Early stages: There are a variety descriptions that apparently apply to the early stages of this butterfly. In Costa Rica, I. Chacon (pers. comm.) found that the mature caterpillar was reddish orange with four rows of short, black rosettes of setae on each segment. The caterpillar is solitary and rests in a folded leaf when not feeding. In Panama, A. Aiello (pers. comm.) found that the mature caterpillar was yellowish beige with star-shaped clusters of black setae. The caterpillars rest in a folded leaf when not feeding. In Trinidad, Kirkpatrick (1953) reported that the mature caterpillar body is red with each segment bearing two pairs of scarlet verrucae that bear a rosette of fifteen to twenty-five stiff setae; the head capsule is black with W-shaped yellow lines, and Kirkpatrick stated that the caterpillar fed on young leaves. In early instars, the body is yellowish orange at sides, black on the

dorsum, and the verrucae are black. *Pupa*—yellow, boldly marked with black spots and longitudinal stripes, and is inside a slight cocoon. Kendall (1976) notes that the pupa appears more similar to that of the nymphalid *Chlosyne* rather than to other species of *Emesis*.
• **Adult:** Sexes slightly dimorphic. An apparently wide-ranging, highly variable species that has had many subspecific names applied to the various forms. In our area it may be recognized by its comparatively large size, the warm, reddish brown upperside (almost as in *lacrines*), and the reddish brown underside, both surfaces of which are set with distinct wavy, broken lines. The female has the distal margin of both wings distinctly bowed outward. *Note:* The subspecies *furor* (Butler and Druce) is applied to specimens with a more acute FW apex, and *tegula* (which I have treated as a separate species) is applied to specimens with a reddish cast to the distal margins of the upperside—both occur in Costa Rica. Compare with *lucinda, tenedia, tegula, lupina, ocypore.*
Habits: Butterflies which are tentatively identified as this species have been reported in our area from sea level to 2100 m on both slopes in a wide range of habitats. However, as noted above, this butterfly is either highly variable with several subspecies in our area, or there are a variety of species confused under the name *mandana*. A great many more careful observations and taxonomic work are needed to begin to understand this butterfly.
Localities: [C]: Turrialba (July). [SJ]: San Pedro (October, November), San Jose (October), Curridibat (May), Santa Ana (June, July), El Rodeo (August), Copey (February). [H]: Plastico (August), La Selva (December). [P]: Monte Verde (February), Punta Banco (August). [G]: Santa Rosa (November).

Emesis fatimella nobilata
Stichel, 1910
FW length: 19.5–20.5 mm   Plate 17
Range: Costa Rica to Bolivia. **Subspecies:** Costa Rica to Colombia
Hostplant: Unknown
Early stages: Unknown
• **Adult:** Sexes slightly dimorphic. *Male*—upperside an almost pumpkin-orange with a profusion of dark, angled lines across both wings, a submarginal row of black spots, and a straight distal margin of FW. *Female*—upperside bright yellow-orange with the dark markings very distinct, and the FW margin bowed outward. *Note:* This species was known for many years under the apparently preoccupied name, *fatima* (C. Callaghan, pers. comm.). Compare with *lupina, mandana, Metacharis victrix.*

Habits: This butterfly occurs in our area from sea level to 600 m in association with rain forest habitats. Typically encountered as rare, solitary individuals along forest edges and streams flying from 1 to 5 m above the ground between 11:30 and 13:00 hrs. In Panama, G. Small noted that the males perch around 09:00 hrs. Both sexes visit flowers of *Casearia, Croton,* and other plants with small white flowers. Uncommon in Costa Rican collections.
Localities: [SJ]: Carrillo. [H]: La Selva (August, September). [P]: Rio Catarata (September), Sirena (March–May). [L]: Guapiles (June), Suretka Talamanca (September).

Emesis lucinda aurimna
(Boisduval 1870)
FW length: 24–25.5 mm   Plate 17
Range: Mexico to Bolivia, Brazil. **Subspecies:** Guatemala to Colombia
Hostplant: *Neea laetevirens, N. amplifolia* (Nyctaginaceae)
Early stages: (Fig. 50): *Egg*—white, highly sculptured, echinoid shaped, laid in clusters of twelve to thirty on stems and petioles of hostplant. *Mature caterpillar*—body dull blackish purple with head and thoracic segments dull orange, and the distal edges of the last three abdominal segments white. The entire body of the caterpillar (regardless of color) is covered with a dense velvety pile of setae that appears to obscure any detailed features; two pairs of short, knobbed tubercles arise from each segment each with tufts of stiff setae—one subdorsal pair of tubercles, and one ventrolateral pair. When viewed from above, the "scalloped" outline enhances the conspicuous lateral projections on each segment. The caterpillars are gregarious and processional throughout life, feed on leaves of all ages, and live inside a rolled leaf when not feeding, not infrequently with several instars sharing the same rolled leaf. *Pupa*—light brown with eyes almost white, smooth and robustly squat, first three abdominal segments bulging and then tapering abruptly to cremaster, and somewhat flattened ventrally. Pupation is typically gregarious (within a cohort of caterpillars) and occurs within the rolled leaf shelter on the hostplant. Occasionally individuals may pupate in isolation off the hostplant on stems or excavations in bark, and frequently these individuals are parasitized.
• **Adult:** Sexes dimorphic. *Male*—upperside dark gray with a lighter area in the FW apex (a characteristic that can be pronounced in some specimens), and a profusion of angled black lines on medial area of both wings; underside

orange-brown with dark medial and post-medial lines, and the FW apical area may be darkened in some specimens. *Female*—upperside dark gray with a conspicuous white patch at the subapex and costa of the FW; underside varies from yellow-brown to straw yellow, and FW apex and medial areas may vary from dark to light. Compare with *mandana* and *tegula*.
Habits: This common butterfly occurs on both slopes in association with all second growth and rain forest habitats from sea level to 600 m, and less commonly above 1000 m, although it has apparently not been recorded from the lowland Guanacaste dry forest. Typically encountered in small colonies along forest edges and streams flying from 1 to 5 m above the ground. At any particular site the abundance of this species may fluctuate dramatically from year to year—sometimes the butterflies may be extremely abundant, at other times they are rare. The males perch under leaves along forest edges between 08:00 and 11:00 hrs and will chase a variety of butterfly species that fly past, often returning to the same perch. The females are generally active between 11:00 and 14:00 hrs along forest edges or in open understory. Both sexes visit flowers of *Lantana, Hamelia, Casearia, Croton,* and other species of plants with small white flowers.
Localities: [A]: Cariblanco (June). [C]: Turrialba (March, June, August), Juan Viñas, Esperanza. [SJ]: El Rodeo (October), Carrillo. [H]: La Selva (May, July, August, October–December), Chilamate (March, October, December), Tirimbina (March), Plastico (November), Magsaysay (July, September). [P]: Las Alturas (November), San Vito (July), Sirena (February), Llorona (March–May), Puriscal. [L]: Guapiles (June), Tortuguerro (February, August), La Florida. [G]: Rincon de la Vieja (September).

Genus **PACHYTHONE** Bates, 1868

The butterflies in this genus are recognized by their corpulent body, stout head, and very short antennae that bear pronounced terminal clubs. Members of *Pachythone* resemble some members of the genera *Mesene* and *Symmachia,* and are excellent mimics of moths in the families Arctiidae, dioptine Notodontidae, and Arctiidae. The genus is found from Mexico throughout Central and South America and is considered to contain about twelve species, most of which are South American. Even though there are relatively few taxa recorded from Central America,

it is unclear how many species actually occur in our area due to apparent variation and the small number of specimens in collections. Our understanding of the butterflies in *Pachythone* would benefit from a systematic revision.
According to Seitz (1917) the butterflies are apparently rare wherever they occur, and certainly I have seldom observed them in Costa Rica, Panama, or Ecuador. Barcant (1970) provides some interesting observations on *P. barcanti* from the island of Trinidad. There he found the males at a single spot where they were active about one hour before dusk. Perhaps the apparent rarity of *Pachythone* is because they are crepuscular. Nothing is known about the hostplants or early stages for any member of the genus.

Pachythone gigas
(Godman and Salvin, 1878)
FW length: 12.5–18 mm   Plate 21
Range: Costa Rica to Panama
Hostplant: Unknown
Early stages: Unknown
• **Adult:** Sexes dimorphic. *Male*—overall red-orange with thin black on the costa, margins, and the transverse bar in the FW cell. *Female*—overall bright lemon yellow with distinct black margins and a transverse bar in the FW cell. *Note:* The name *ignifer* (Stichel, 1911) refers to yellow-orange butterflies that were originally described from Colombia, and indeed some specimens from our fauna do show this yellow-orange color form. Compare with *nigriciliata, Setabis cleomedes.*
Habits: This butterfly has been reported from sea level to 600 m on the Pacific slope in association with dry to rain forest habitats. Label data suggest that the butterflies fly during the wet season. I have found these butterflies flying along rivers and streams at the ground level or at the subcanopy level of trees growing along a ridge top. While in flight their bright coloration is very obvious, and they strongly resemble the day flying moth genera *Eudulophasia* and *Josia.*
Localities: [P]: Villa Neily (August), Llorona (January), Isla del Caño (April), San Luis (June). [G]: Santa Rosa (June, July, November), Cañas (October, November), San Luis (June), Cerro Hacha (January).

Pachythone nigriciliata
Schaus, 1913
FW length: Not measured   Not illustrated
Range: Nicaragua to Panama
Hostplant: Unknown
Early stages: Unknown
• **Adult:** Similar to *gigas* but with the black

markings on the margins and FW almost extinct. Compare with *P. gigas.*
Habits: This butterfly is known in our area from a single collection by William Schaus from Carrillo on the Atlantic slope. The unique holotype is in the U.S. National Museum. It remains to be demonstrated whether this taxon is a separate species, or more likely, simply a color variant of *gigas.* With reservation I maintain it here as a species because it is the only *Pachythone* I have seen reported from the Atlantic slope.
Localities: [SJ]: Carrillo [TL].

Genus **ROBERELLA** Strand, 1932

The somber butterflies in this genus are all are colored dull gray or brown on the upperside, and off-white on the undersides. Some of these butterflies have enjoyed an active generic history. Placed initially in the genus *Lemonias* they were separated out and placed in the *Drepanula* by Röber and then, as the latter genus was a junior homonym, transferred to the genus *Roeberella.* Furthermore, Central American specimens of *lencates* have been placed by some authors in the genus *Adelotypa.* In butterfly systematics, such an itinerary generally indicates that the genus needs revising to place it within the context of other genera.

As currently understood, members of *Roeberella* are found in Central and South America and the island of Trinidad. The genus is comprised of three species, one of which occurs in our area. Nothing is known of the hostplants or early stages for any members of the genus.

Roberella lencates
(Hewitson, 1875)
FW length: 11–12.5 mm   **Plate 11**
Range: Costa Rica to Amazon Basin and Trinidad
Hostplant: Unknown
Early stages: Unknown
• **Adult:** Sexes dimorphic. *Male*—FW upperside entirely brown; HW upperside brown with a broad white band running from the costa near the apex, across medial area, and terminating broadly at inner margin; underside pale brown with a distinctly reddish cast. *Note:* Central American specimens of this butterfly has been referred to previously under the synonym *petronia* Schaus, 1913, and placed in the genera *Echenais* or *Adelotypa.* Compare with *Lemonias agave, Calospila trotschi.*

Habits: This odd little butterfly has been recorded in our area only from the Pacific slope at about 500 m. In Panama, G. Small found the males perching between 15:30 and 16:00 hrs. Rare in Central American collections.
Localities: [A]: San Mateo (November, December). [H]: La Selva (April).

Genus **PIXUS** Callaghan, 1982

Only a single species is currently placed here, and the butterflies in this genus are recognized by the flat, spoon-shaped clubs of the antennae recalling members of the Nymphalidae. Due to their outward similarities, *Pixus* has long been confused in museum collections with members of *Nymphidium* and *Juditha.* Although its true taxonomic relationships are unknown, Callaghan (1982b) tentatively suggested that *Pixus* had affinities with *Pachythone,* and on the strength of this I include it here with members of the tribe Emesini. The genus is found from Mexico to Colombia. Nothing is known of its early stages.

Pixus corculum
(Stichel, 1929)
FW length: 12–20.5 mm   **Plate 22**
Range: Mexico to Colombia
Hostplant: Unknown
Early stages: Unknown
• **Adult:** Sexes strongly dimorphic in size, with the male considerably smaller. *Male*—upperside white with broad, dark brown FW costa, apex, and distal margins; an indistinct reddish band runs from FW costa into cell; a reddish submarginal band may begin narrowly on FW (variable) but is conspicuously wide on HW; distal margin of HW with black, blunt squares. Underside washed out, and all dark markings less distinct. *Female*—much larger, but patterned as in the male. Compare with *Juditha molpe, Nymphidium onaeum, ascolia, azanoides.*
Habits: This butterfly has been reported in our area from rain forest habitats on both slopes ranging in elevation from sea level to 600 m. In Panama, G. Small (in Callaghan 1982) indicated that this butterfly can be locally common, that it is active from 14:00 to 15:00 hrs, and its behavior resembles members of the genus *Nymphidium.* Rare in Costa Rica collections, and almost certainly easily overlooked.
Localities: [C]: Turrialba (May, June). [P]: Rio Catarata (September). [L]: Limon (January).

Genus APODEMIA Felder and Felder, 1865

In general appearance, the butterflies in this genus recall *Lasaia*, *Emesis*, and members of the nymphalid subfamily Phyciodinae (*Tritanassa*, *Phyciodes*), but they are recognized by the configuration of the legs and peculiarities of the venation. The genus is considered to embrace about twelve species, and members of *Apodemia* are found from the southwestern USA to southwestern Costa Rica, then reappear in southeastern Brazil. The greatest number of species of *Apodemia* occur between the southwest of North America and Mexico. Two species occur in our area, both which are restricted to the Guanacaste dry forest in the northwest and are quite rare.

The hostplants reported for *Apodemia* include Euphorbiaceae, Rosaceae, Krameriaceae, Polygonaceae, and Fabaceae (see summary in Scott 1986). The caterpillars are densely covered with long setae, and superficially resemble those of the genera *Charis* and *Calephelis*.

Apodemia multiplaga
Schaus, 1902
FW length: 15.5–17 mm   **Plate 16**
Range: South Texas, Mexico to northwest Costa Rica
Hostplant: Unknown
Early stages: Unknown
• **Adult:** Sexes similar. Upperside black with conspicuous white spots, FW with apex slightly produced and the distal margin excavated. Underside of FW pale brown with white spots, and the cell area surrounding it distinctly yellow; HW distal area extensively white, with the distal margins brown, set with black spots between the radial veins. Compare with *A. walkeri*.
Habits: This butterfly is recorded from sea level to 200 m from two localities on the Pacific slope in the Guanacaste deciduous forest. P. Opler found this butterfly visiting flowers of *Cordia* during bright midday sunshine. Rare in Costa Rican collections.
Localities: [G]: Cañas (May, September, October), Santa Rosa.

Apodemia walkeri
Godman and Salvin, 1886
FW length: 11.5–12.5 mm   **Not illustrated**
Range: South Texas, Mexico to northwest Costa Rica
Hostplant: Unknown
Early stages: Unknown
• **Adult:** Sexes similar. Upperside gray-brown with white submarginal bands on both wings that are composed of indistinct, somewhat smeary squares, red-brown distal margins of both wings. Underside with discal area with the white bands more prominently highlighted with short black borders (reminiscent of *Lasaia* or *Emesis*), and distal margins are red-brown set with black spots between the veins. Overall much smaller than its other congener in our area. Compare with *A. multiplaga*, *Lasaia oileus*.
Habits: In our area this butterfly has been recorded only from a single site on the Pacific slope in association with deciduous forest. There, P. Opler found it visiting flowers of *Cordia* in bright sunshine at about 11:00 hrs. Although fairly abundant in areas to the north, especially Mexico, this species is obviously rare in Costa Rica.
Localities: [G]: Cañas (May).

Tribe LEMONIINI Kirby, 1871

The butterflies embraced by this tribe are characterized technically by the males possessing bifurcate rami that underlie the valvae of the genitalia. As currently conceived, there are over seventy species in eleven genera placed here: *Lemonias*, *Thisbe*, *Uraneis*, *Catocyclotis*, *Juditha*, *Synargis*, *Audre*, *Thysanota*, *Ematurgina*, *Aricoris*, and *Eiseleia*, the latter four genera found only in South America. Available evidence suggests that these butterflies use a wide range of hostplants, their caterpillars are myrmecophilous, they have well developed ant organs, and they may associate as a group with a wide variety of ant taxa.

Genus THISBE Hübner, 1819

The butterflies in this genus are recognized by their broad white discal bands on both wings, and a white band in the FW subapex; the head and the palpi recall members of the Nymphalidae. Members of the genus are found from Mexico through Central and South America,

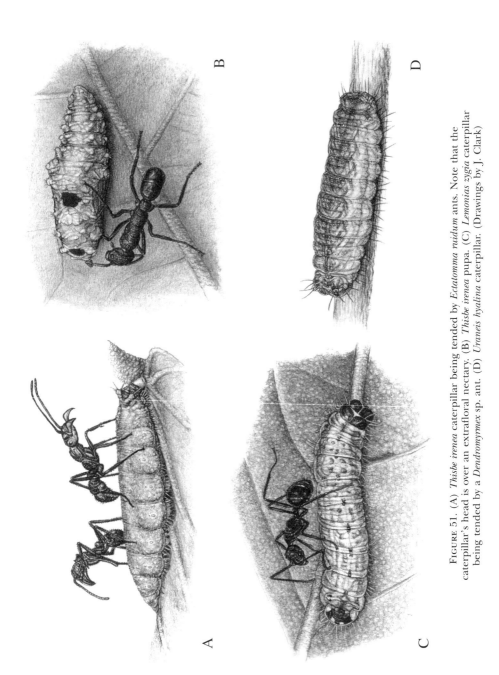

FIGURE 51. (A) *Thisbe irenea* caterpillar being tended by *Ectatomma ruidum* ants. Note that the caterpillar's head is over an extrafloral nectary. (B) *Thisbe irenea* pupa. (C) *Lemonias zygia* caterpillar being tended by a *Dendromymex* sp. ant. (D) *Uraneis hyalina* caterpillar. (Drawings by J. Clark)

and, as presently understood, *Thisbe* contains four species. Two species occur in our area.

The hostplants of *Thisbe* include members of the Euphorbiaceae and Fabaceae (DeVries et al. 1994). The caterpillars are myrmecophilous, bear a full compliment of ant organs, and may associate with a variety of ant genera in the subfamilies Myrmicinae, Formicinae, and Ponerinae. The pupae are covered in fine granules, and at least in one species (*irenea*), they bear two flat black areas on the dorsum that give the appearance of holes.

In Costa Rica, members of *Thisbe* are found from sea level to 1400 m on both slopes in association with a variety of habitats, including second-growth and agricultural lands. Studies on *Thisbe irenea* have amplified our understanding of riodinid-ant symbioses, their interactions with plants, and the evolution of caterpillar-ant communication systems (see DeVries 1988b, 1990, 1991b, c, 1992; DeVries and Baker 1989). Although the adults are seldom, if ever, common, typically *T. irenea* caterpillars may be abundant throughout the year at particular sites, even if the adults are rarely observed.

Thisbe irenea
(Stoll, 1780)
FW length: 18–21 mm   **Plate 18**
Range: Mexico to Brazil
Hostplant: Saplings and young trees of *Croton* spp (Euphorbiaceae) (DeVries et al. 1994)
Early stages (Figs. 2c, 11, 15, 51a,b) (DeVries 1988b): *Egg*—greenish white and smooth with a netlike sculpturing of pentagrams on all areas except the micropylar area; the micropyle consists of a circular, recessed, nipplelike structure. The egg is deposited singly in a variety of places, including dorsal and ventral surfaces of leaves, leaf axils and petioles of live and dead leaf tissue, bark fissures, and stems and plant material adjacent to the hostplant. *Caterpillars*—all instars are gray-green and covered in granules (including head capsule) that allow them to blend in with the scabrous underside of the hostplant leaves. The caterpillars typically feed on the ventral leaf surfaces. Early instars must feed on young leaves, and although older instars prefer new growth they are able to feed on old leaves. The feeding damage of the caterpillars creates distinct oblong or round windows between the main veins of the leaves. All instars are typically encountered with their heads at the extrafloral nectaries, where they drink the extrafloral nectar and derive substantial growth benefits from it (DeVries and Baker 1989). During the day, late fourth and fifth instar caterpillars hide in dead leaves attached to the plant with caterpillar silk, in cuplike structures that result from the young terminal leaves being webbed together, or in the detritus at the base of the plant. The mature instars typically feed at night. The caterpillars are most frequently found in association with *Ectatomma ruidum* or *E. tuberculatum* (Ponerinae) ants, but depending on the location of the hostplant, the caterpillars may associate with other ant genera (e.g., *Solenopsis*, *Camponotus*, *Hypoclinea*, *Wasmannia*, *Tapinoma*). Caterpillars are attacked by several species of tachinid flies that emerge from late fifth instars or fresh pupae. Some of these flies oviposit directly on the caterpillar, others lay minute eggs on the leaves that are ingested by the caterpillar. Parasitic wasps in the braconid genus *Rogas* (Rogadiinae) also attack young caterpillars, leaving the mummified remains of third and fourth instars on the hostplant. *Pupa*—dirty gray-brown; overall the pupa has many tiny knobs and projections that give it the appearance of tree bark, and there are two conspicuous flat black spots (one at head, one at thorax) giving the impression that the pupa has parasitoid exit holes in it! However, I have never seen a parasite exit hole in the pupae that even remotely resembles these spots. Pupation usually occurs off the hostplant, but pupae may be found in fissures in the bark, at the base of the plant, or in dead leaves attached to the plant. Often pupae that are found on the hostplant are dead or parasitized. Ants will attend pupae for a few days after pupation is completed. The adults emerge during the early morning.
• **Adult:** Sexes dimorphic. The species may be distinguished by the conspicuous white medial band running across both wings that is bordered by dull reddish bands on the ventral surfaces. *Male*—upperside brown with a broad white medial band across both wings that is conspicuously bordered at distal margin with pale blue and a little blue along the proximal margin; FW with a small band in the subapex. On the underside, the medial band and FW costa are bordered in dull orange. The tornus of the HW is slightly elongate. *Female*—upperside brown with broad white medial band, but without a trace of the blue border. The tornus of the HW is rounded. In the field the females may be mistaken for several nymphalid species, most notably *Dynamine* spp. and *Janatella leucodesma* (see DeVries 1987). *Note:* Females from Costa Rica typically and consistently have wider dark brown margins on the HW (thus constricting the medial band) than specimens originating from the north or south, and

Costa Rican populations have been given the name *belides* Stichel, 1910. Compare with *Thisbe lycorias, Synargis velabrum, S. mycone, Menander laobotas, Nymphidium azanoides.*

Habits: In our area, this butterfly occurs in all forest types from sea level to 800 m on both slopes, but it is either absent or very rare in the deciduous forest of lowland Guanacaste. Adults are generally present throughout the year, but they appear to be most abundant during the early wet season or early dry season. However, even in areas where caterpillars are abundant, the adults are seldom encountered, and rarely in groups of more than three individuals. Males are typically encountered as solitary individuals perching on top of leaves from 2 to 15 m above the ground between 09:00 and 11:00 hrs. Perching males vigorously interact with other butterflies of approximately the same size during these times. Observing male perching behavior without the aid of binoculars is difficult because they tend to perch high in the canopy. The females generally oviposit from 10:30 to 13:30 hrs on sapling and seedling plants that grow in light gaps and along forest edges that receive direct sunshine. The females will often descend from the canopy into a light gap, investigate a sunlit patch of hostplants, perhaps oviposit, and then fly quickly into the canopy to rest. The plants that they oviposit on may or may not be occupied by ants. After laying an egg, the female rests in direct sunshine with the wings open. After a few moments she may return to the same light gap, oviposit on the same plant (or nearby plants), or simply fly away in search of another light gap. Both sexes visit flowers of *Croton, Cordia, Lantana, Palicourea, Alibertia, Randia, Serjania,* and various herbaceous Asteraceae during the mornings, and then again at midafternoon.

Localities: [A]: Atenas (December), Florencia de San Carlos (December). [C]: Turrialba (January–April, June, August, October), Juan Viñas (September, November), Navarro (April), 4.5 km E de Tuis (September). [SJ]: Patarra (November, December), Desamparados (June, December), Paso Ancho (March). [H]: Chilamate (May–September), Plastico (August, September), La Selva (July), La Virgen (March), Santa Clara (September). [P]: Carrara (October), Sirena (April, December), Rincon (February), Rio Catarata (September). [L]: Florida (March), Siquirres (January), Rio Hondo (September), Banana River.

Thisbe lycorias lycorias
(Hewitson 1853)
FW length: 22.5–26 mm   **Plate 18**

Range: Mexico to Colombia and Amazonas.
Subspecies: Mexico to Panama
Hostplant: *Cassia alata* (Fabaceae)
Early stages: *Mature caterpillar*—my recollection of a caterpillar found years ago feeding on a stump sprout was that the body was green with prominent brown head horns and had the general aspect of a large *Juditha molpe* caterpillar.

• **Adult:** Sexes similar. Upperside brown with a prominent white medial band running across both wings, and short white bands at FW subapex and HW submargin; small reddish brown patches in FW cell and the tornus of both wings; distal margin of HW tornus with a noticeable tooth. Compare with *T. irenea, Nymphidium azanoides.*

Habits: This butterfly is widespread in our area and found in virtually all forest types from sea level to 1200 m on both slopes. Records suggest that adults are present throughout the year, including the deciduous forest of Guanacaste. Encountered as solitary individuals along forest edges, in light gaps, second growth, and coffee plantations. The males perch along forest edges from midday until about 14:30 hrs, and the females are also active at this time. For a riodinid, these butterflies have a moderately slow, fluttery flight that recalls a species of Nymphalidae or Pieridae. Both sexes may be found visiting flowers of *Lantana, Hamelia, Citrus, Coffea, Inga,* and *Cordia* from midday until late afternoon.

Localities: [A]: San Antonio de Belen (June), Atenas (March, December). [C]: Turrialba (June, September). [SJ]: San Pedro (February, June, August), San Jose (January, July, August), Escazu (May, September), Patarra (April, November, December), Colon (January), Paso Ancho (March), Desamparados (June, September, December). [H]: Santo Domingo de Heredia (April, November), Tirimbina (February), La Selva (March, August, September), Chilamate (August). [P]: San Vito (August, September). [L]: Guapiles (March). [G]: Santa Rosa (May–July), Cañas (February–May).

Genus **LEMONIAS** Hübner, 1807

The butterflies in this genus generally are brown on the upperside with white bands and spots, and resemble members of *Nymphidium, Thisbe, Adelotypa,* or *Synargis.* The butterflies are closely related to the genus *Thisbe,* and their resemblance is especially marked in the early stages (Figs. 7b,c,d, 8b, 51c; see also Ross 1964, 1966). In older literature the butterflies now placed here were referred to under *Anatole*. There are six species in *Lemonias*, one that occurs in our area.

There are hostplant records for only two *Lemonias* species, both on *Croton* (Euphorbiaceae): *caliginea* (Butler, 1867) from pine barren habitats in Mexico, and *zygia egaensis* (Butler, 1867) from the Napo region of Ecuador, the latter of which appears to have ant-mediated oviposition (Ross 1964; DeVries et al. 1994). The caterpillars of *Lemonias* have been found associated with *Camponotus* and *Dendromyrmex* (Formicinae) ants. The study of Ross (1964, 1966) on Mexican *Lemonias caliginea* (as *Anatole rossi*) was a benchmark for riodinid ecology and early-stage morphology. Ross's work showed that *caliginea* is seasonal, dependent on ants for survival, and that the species has a very restricted habitat and geographical range. Although we can certainly expect them to be here, these butterflies have not been recorded in our area.

Lemonias agave
Godman and Salvin, 1886
FW length: 15.5–17.5 mm   **Plate 18**
Range: Mexico to Colombia
Hostplant: Unknown
Early stages: Unknown
• **Adult:** Sexes dimorphic. *Male*—upperside reddish brown with a small white spot just posterior to the cell, and HW with anal margin and tornus pure white; underside mottled light brown and white with an irregular medial line on the FW that angles basally as it passes the end of the cell, then straight to inner margin; both wings have rows of irregular, black marginal spots. *Female*—upperside extensively reddish brown with a large white patch just posterior to FW cell, a smaller spot at FW costa, and a conspicuous white spot on the HW in the area distal to the cell. Compare with *Roberella lencates* and *Calospila trotschi*.
Habits: Despite its known geographic range, this species is unrecorded from our area. However, the butterfly was originally described from David, Panama, where it was stated to occur in "the thinly wooded savanna-region of the low country" (Godman and Salvin 1886, p. 462). Because the type locality is almost at the Costa Rican–Panamanian border, it is likely that this butterfly will be found in areas near Villa Neily and Punta Burica. In Panama, G. Small found males perching between 14:30 and 15:45 hrs. Rare in Central American collections, and if its biology is similar to the species worked on by Ross (1966), this butterfly

may be of interest to those concerned with conservation biology.
Localities: Not yet recorded for our area.

Genus URANEIS Bates, 1868

The butterflies in this genus resemble *Lyropteryx* and *Voltinia* but are separated from those genera by having large eyes and slender terminal segments of the palpi. These butterflies quite clearly mimic the toxic, day-flying arctiid moths in the genus *Hypocritta*, as do the riodinid genera *Esthemopsis*, *Lyropteryx*, *Necyria*, *Voltinia*, and *Lepricornis*. There are three members of *Uraneis*, one that occurs in our area.

In Ecuador, I found *Uraneis hyalina* Butler, 1867, using *Phoradendron* sp. (Loranthaceae) as a hostplant. The eggs were deposited in loose clusters of three to six eggs where the mistletoe attaches to the host tree, or directly on the bark of the tree acting as a host for the mistletoe. The caterpillars were semigregarious and fed on the leaves and inflorescence of the *Phoradendron*. The caterpillars have all three sets of ant organs, and strongly resemble the caterpillars of *Thisbe* but have a slightly more developed anal plate (Fig. 51d). During the late fourth and fifth instars, the caterpillars construct a pseudo-cocoon of frass and tiny fragments of chewed tree bark. During the day they hide inside, feed at night, and eventually pupate inside this structure. The pseudo-cocoon is remarkably similar to a true cocoon of a saturniid or arctiid moth, except that it is flimsy and bears a large hole in the center where the butterflies emerge to dry their wings. Furthermore, while sitting on the pseudo-cocoon, these butterflies pulsate their wings open and closed, a behavior that serves to reinforce their appearance to an unpalatable moth.

Uraneis ucubis
Hewitson, 1870
FW length: 25–27 mm   **Plate 18**
Range: Costa Rica to Colombia
Hostplant: Unknown
Early stages: Unknown
• **Adult:** Sexes slightly dimorphic. *Male*—upper and underside ground color blue-black with marginal band composed of white bars between the veins beginning at FW costa and running along distal margins of both wings, most pronounced on the underside; HW tornus bears a slight tooth. *Female*—color pattern same as in the male, but HW tornus broadly rounded, and blue is darker. Compare

with *Esthemopsis, Lyropteryx, Necyria, Voltinia, Lepricornis.*
Habits: This butterfly has been recorded in our area from 400 to 1200 m on the Atlantic slope in association with the rain forest habitats found within the Carrillo Belt. Judging from its appearance, and my experience with *U. hyalina* in Ecuador, the male of our species will almost certainly behave like the day-flying moth *Hypocritta alleta* (Arctiidae) while flying and resting. I have never seen this butterfly alive. Uncommon in Costa Rican collections.
Localities: [A]: La Tigra de San Carlos (January, May). [C]: Moravia de Chirripo (May, August–October), Turrialba (April, May). [H]: Cariblanco (May).

Genus JUDITHA Hemming, 1934

These butterflies resemble members of *Nymphidium* or *Synargis* in coloration (where they were placed in much of the older literature) but are separated on the basis of the genitalia and early stages. Generally, *Juditha* butterflies may be recognized by the chainlike row of marginal spots on the underside of both wings, and typically the sexes are not strongly dimorphic as in *Synargis*. Members of *Juditha* are found from Mexico through Central and South America, and, as currently understood, the genus contains about four species, two that occur in our area.

The hostplant records from *Juditha* in Central America include a broad range of families, and there is even suspicion of a carnivorous habit in one species (DeVries et al. 1994). The caterpillars bear all three sets of ant organs, and have pronounced, stout "horns" arising from the thoracic shield (Fig. 52d). In Central America, these butterflies appear to have an obligate association with ants in the genus *Dolichoderus*, and it is likely that female butterflies use *Dolichoderus* ants as oviposition stimuli rather than the plant. In other words, a female is attracted to plants with *Dolichoderus* ants on it, and then, after alighting on the plant, may lay eggs on it, no matter what plant family it belongs to. The caterpillars of all instars drink extrafloral nectar when not feeding on leaf tissue, and also drink the honeydew produced by Homoptera. An account of Brazilian *Juditha molpe* is found in Callaghan (1982c).

Juditha molpe
(Hübner, 1808)
FW length: 16.5–19 mm   **Plate 18**

Range: Mexico to Colombia, Brazil
Hostplant: *Cassia fruticosa, Pithecellobium* spp., *Inga* spp., *Lonchocarpus* sp., *Acacia* sp., *Calyandra* sp. (Fabaceae), *Tetracera* sp., *Doliocarpus* sp. (Dilleniaceae), *Passiflora vitafolia, P. adenopoda* (Passifloraceae), *Picramnia* sp., *Simaba cedron* (Simaroubaceae), *Serjania mexicana, Paullinia bracteosa, Cardiospermum* sp. (Sapindaceae), *Stigmaphyllon* spp. (Malpighiaceae).
Early stages (Fig. 52b,d): *Egg*—white, laid on or off the hostplant. In fact, a single female may lay eggs on many different hostplants within a small area, providing *Dolichoderus* ants are present. *Mature caterpillars*—dark green with a scattering of white granules over the dorsum (when viewed under magnification), the first thoracic segment is dull brown, produced forward and into two stout horns that create a shield over the head; head capsule is dull brown and obviously granulate. All instars rest with their heads over extrafloral nectaries and are always vigorously attended by *Dolichoderus* ants, generally *D. bispinosus*. The caterpillars produce strong, chirplike calls. They are parasitized by *Apanteles* spp. (Braconidae) and are prey to wasps in the family Vespidae. *Pupa*—cylindrical and resembling a compact splinter of wood.
• **Adult:** Sexes similar. Broad white medial bands on both wings with broad, brown margins and FW costa and apex. The interface where the white bands meet the brown borders is irregular and wavy, and the configuration of this interface (especially on the FW) separates this species from similar ones. Compare with *Synargis mycone, Nymphidium onaeum, Pixus corculum.*
Habits: This butterfly is widespread throughout our area, occurring from sea level to 1200 m on both slopes in association with virtually all vegetation types, from second-growth pasture to primary rain forest. The butterfly is most commonly observed during sunny and dry periods, although the adults are present throughout the year in most lowland habitats. Encountered as solitary individuals along forest edges, streams, and light gaps where there are tangles of vigorously growing vegetation. The females typically search for oviposition sites from 10:00 to 13:00 hrs along forest edges, when they flutter about a new shoot that is occupied with *Dolichoderus* ants. Once such a shoot is found, the female will often repeatedly leave and return to the site before depositing an egg. In fact, one can predict from a considerable distance where the foraging areas of *Dolichoderus* ants are by simply watching an ovipositing female. Although *Dolichoderus bispinosus* is a notably belligerent ant,

I have not observed them behave aggressively toward the butterfly during oviposition. Both sexes visit flowers of *Lantana, Hamelia, Croton, Serjania, Cordia,* and various herbaceous Asteraceae. **Localities:** [A]: San Mateo. [C]: Avangarez. [SJ]: Santa Rosa de Puriscal (August), Carrillo, Desamparados. [H]: La Selva (February, March), Chilamate (April, May, June). [P]: Isla del Caño (March), Golfito (July), Llorona (March, August), Sirena (February–April, June, July, September), Rio Catarata (April, September), Brujo de Buenos Aires (September), Quepos (July, September), Monte Verde (September), Carrara (February). [L]: Tortuguerro (April), Siquirres (April). [G]: Santa Rosa, Bagaces.

Juditha dorilis dorilis
(Bates, 1866)
FW length: 18–21.5 mm   **Plate 18**
Range: Costa Rica to Colombia. **Subspecies:** Costa Rica to Panama
Hostplant: *Ochroma lagapus* (Bombacaceae) infested with nymphs of Membracidae and Coccidae that are tended by *Dolichoderus validus* ants (DeVries et al. 1994)
Early stages (Fig. 2d): *Egg*—a slightly compressed pale yellow sphere with a netlike sculpturing consisting of elongate rectangles that cover the egg except on the flattened dorsum; except for the dorsum, the entire egg is honeycombed with tiny pores; the micropyle consists of punctures that compose a circle whose diameter is about one-quarter the width of the egg. The egg is unusual for a riodinid in that it has clearly demarcated plastrons. It is deposited singly on leaves, stems, and stipules of the plant, in addition to being laid directly on membracids.
• **Adult:** Sexes slightly dimorphic. *Male*—upperside brown with a broad yellow-orange medial band on both wings, and a red-brown, chainlike submarginal band with black centers set into the brown distal margins. *Female*—similar to the male but with the medial band pale yellow and noticeably broader. Compare with *Synargis gela, S. ochra, S. mycone, Nymphidium cachrus.*
Habits: This butterfly has been recorded in our area from sea level to 700 m on both slopes in association with rain forest habitats. In the Atlantic lowlands I found males active between 07:30 and 09:00 hrs along forest edges and streams, while in Panama, G. Small found males active between 15:30 and 16:15 hrs. This suggests that, when considered throughout their range, the butterflies may be found to have midmorning-midafternoon perching cy-

cles. I have observed females on two occasions. At Turrialba I observed a female between 10:15 and 10:30 hrs repeatedly oviposit on the stipules of a mature *Ochroma* tree that was infested with membracids and scales (Homoptera) that were being tended by a large number of *Dolichoderus validus* ants. With binoculars I noted that the ants did not bother the female while she was on the plant or ovipositing, but rather they antennated her body and then moved away. The second instance was at La Vacita, where I collected a female while she was flying low to the ground along a forest edge at 08:15 hrs. Uncommon in Costa Rican collections.
Localities: [C]: Turrialba (April), Tuis (April). [H]: La Selva (May), Chilamate (May). [P]: La Vacita (March). [L]: Limon (May), Guapiles (September).

Genus **CATOCYCLOTIS** Stichel, 1910

These butterflies have an elongate FW recalling members of *Calociasma*; however, they may be recognized by the spidery, chainlike patterns set along the FW costa, and, unlike *Calociasma,* the sexes are dimorphic. *Catocyclotis* is considered to contain a single species that ranges from Costa Rica to Colombia, Ecuador, and Brazil. Nothing is known about the biology of this species. Of interest, however, is that D'Abrera (1994) mentions that this butterfly is said to produce a clicking sound while in flight. An interesting observation, indeed, and clearly worth investigating.

Catocyclotis aemulius adelina
(Butler, 1872)
FW length: 18.5–20.5 mm   **Plate 18**
Range: Costa Rica to Colombia, Brazil. **Subspecies:** Costa Rica to Ecuador
Hostplant: Unknown
Early stages: Unknown
• **Adult:** Sexes dimorphic. *Male*—FW upperside dark brown set with spidery blue lines along costal margins with the tornus and distal portion of inner margin orange; HW upperside orange with dark brown at the base; abdomen distinctly orange; HW underside pearly white with orange fringe, and dark areas at base. *Female*—FW upperside similar to male but paler brown; HW upperside and abdomen pale yellow. Compare with *Calociasma icterica.*
Habits: This butterfly has been recorded in our area principally from montane areas in the

Meseta Central and Turrialba Valley from 800 to 1600 m. However, as it also occurs to the south in the Talamancas, this species will probably be found to be more widespread than presently known. The butterflies occur locally in small populations that may persist for a few weeks at a time. Both sexes are encountered as solitary individuals along sunny forest edges between 08:00 and 10:00 hrs. The males generally fly low to the ground for a short distance, and then perch under leaves a few meters above the ground. However, occasionally males will perch in light gaps and along forest edges between 5 and 10 m above the ground. At Las Alturas I found both sexes visiting flowers of *Dendropanax* sp. (Araliaceae) and small white-flowered vines in the Asteraceae. Infrequently collected, but not rare.

Localities: [C]: Juan Viñas (March, August, September, November), Cachi (July, October), El Alto (October, November), Moravia de Chirripo (April), Las Concovas (December). [SJ]: Patarra (November), Carrillo (May), San Jose (August), Curridibat (March, August), San Pedro (February), Escazu (July). [H]: San Miguel (February), San Josecito (August), Getsemani (July). [P]: Las Alturas (April–June), Monte Verde (November).

Genus **SYNARGIS** Hübner, 1819

The butterflies in this genus typically have strongly dimorphic sexes, and this characteristic has led to not a few instances where males and females were described as separate species or even genera. For example, some of our species have in the past been confused with members of the genera *Nymphidium* and *Juditha*, or referred to under *Nymula* and *Peplia*. For our purposes, the butterflies in *Synargis* may be recognized by their stout bodies, long antennae, distinct palpi, and the tendency to have small dark spots at the HW apex. Given the diversity and heterogeneity of the genus as currently understood, a taxonomic revision of the group would be very useful. Most of the twenty or so *Synargis* species occur in South America. Eight species are reported from our area, although one record (*gela*) seems dubious.

Although only a few species have been reared, available evidence suggests that some of the species use a wide range of hostplants, including Fabaceae, Sapindaceae, Dilleniaceae, Bignoniaceae, Polygonaceae, Euphorbiaceae, Loranthaceae, and others (DeVries et al. 1994).

The caterpillars of some species may be found feeding on the foliage of various plant families, all at the same site. For example, I found *S. mycone* feeding on five hostplant families at one site in Panama, and *S. abaris* caterpillars on four hostplant families at one site in Ecuador. *Synargis* caterpillars have all three sets of ant organs and two well developed horns on the first thoracic segment that project forward of the head. The caterpillars produce strong calls and are typically observed in the presence of many individual ants. The pupae are reminiscent of *Thisbe*, but with dorsolateral projections on the abdomen and a flattened keel on the anteriormost abdominal segments. The caterpillars and pupae of some of our species associate with various ant genera. An account on the life history of *Synargis brennus* from Brazil is provided by Callaghan (1986b).

In Costa Rica, members of *Synargis* are found in a wide variety of habitats from sea level to over 1400 m. In Central and South America, particular sites seem to be used by perching males with a great regularity through time. For example, in Panama I had occasion to observe the condition of individual males of *S. mycone* erode from fresh to very battered over the course of several weeks. Also, observations made from the forest canopy indicate that these butterflies visit flowers of canopy trees and vines. Our fauna contains some common and widespread species, as well as one that may be endemic to Costa Rica and Panama.

Synargis phylleus praeclara

(Bates, 1866)
FW length: 23.5–29 mm   **Plate 19**
Range: Costa Rica to Venezuela, Peru. **Subspecies:** Costa Rica to Colombia
Hostplant: Females have been observed to oviposit on *Heisteria cocinna* (Olacaceae), *Pseudobombax septenatum* (Bombacaceae), and *Ficus* sp. (Moraceae) near Homoptera that are tended by *Dolichoderus bispinosus* ants (DeVries et al. 1994)
Early stages (Figs. 2e,f, 5b): *Egg*—white, round, broadest at base, slightly depressed on dorsum, and entirely covered with a fine net of knobbed sculpturing; micropyle deeply recessed and surrounded with a distinct, erect nipplelike ring. I found eggs laid singly or in pairs on buds or shoots near aggregations of Membracids tended by *Dolichoderus bispinosus* ants. *First instar*—whitish green, the prothoracic shield is well developed and bears six long setae that project over the head; anal plate well developed with long prominent setae projecting along perimeter of anal plate;

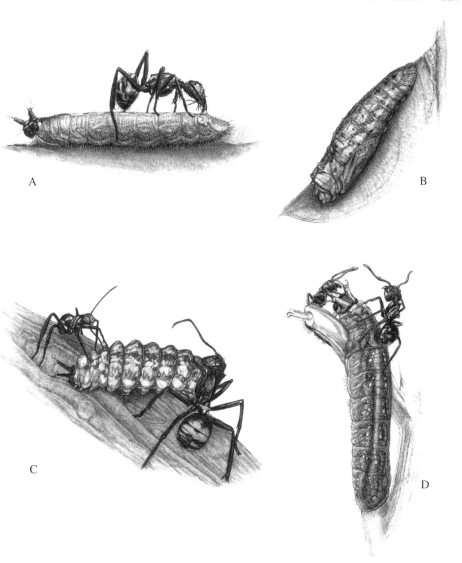

FIGURE 52. (A) *Synargis mycone* caterpillar being tended by a *Camponotus sericeiventris* ant. (B) *Juditha molpe* pupa. (C) *Synargis palaeste* caterpillar being tended by *Camponotus sericeiventris* ants. (D) *Juditha molpe* caterpillar being tended by *Dolichoderus bispinosus* ants. (Drawings by J. Clark)

the subdorsal and lateral setae are prominent and highly unusual by being short, flattened triangles—a condition thus far unknown in other riodinid caterpillars.

• **Adult:** Sexes dimorphic. *Male*—upperside ground color yellow-orange with red-brown FW apex and base, HW with a pale brown band that runs from costa near apex to inner margin; underside washed with pale yellow, with indistinct brownish gray patterns. *Female*—upperside pale yellow or yellowish white with the FW apex and base of both wings brown, and the HW with a conspicuous brown band running parallel to the distal margin; underside almost white with prominent brown apex, margins, and bands. *Note:* Stichel (1911) considered *praeclara* a full species. See *S. nymphidioides, S. palaeste,* and *Juditha dorilis.*

Habits: In Costa Rica this butterfly is recorded only from Pacific lowland rain forest localities around the Osa Peninsula. In Panama, G. Small found males perching between 10:30 and 11:00 A.M. Also in Panama I observed females between 11:30 and 12:30 hrs ovipositing in full sunshine on flower buds or young shoots infested with nymphs of Membracidae that were tended by large numbers of *D. bispinosus* ants. The females laid eggs directly on or near the membracid aggregations. These observations suggest that the caterpillars may be carnivorous on membracids, or in some way have membracids intimately involved in their life histories. Both sexes visit plants with small white flowers, the red flowers of *Lantana,* and *Croton,* and the males drink at extrafloral nectaries of *Croton* and *Inga.* Rare in Costa Rican collections.

Localities: [P]: Llorona (August), Sirena (August), Rincon (August).

Synargis mycone
(Hewitson, 1865)
FW length: 18–22 mm   **Plate 18**
Range: Mexico to Colombia
Hostplant: *Tetracera* sp., *Doliocarpus* sp. (Dilleniaceae); *Cassia* spp., *Inga minutula, I. quaternata, I. ruiziana, Inga* sp. (Fabaceae); *Paullinia fibrigera* (Sapindaceae); *Omphalea diandra* (Euphorbiaceae); *Securidaca diversifolia* (Polygalaceae), *Coccoloba manzillensis* (Polygonaceae); *Pachyptera kere* (Bignoniaceae); *Turnera ulmnifolia* (Turneraceae); *Heteropteris laurifolia, Stigmaphyllon* sp. (Malpighiaceae); flowers of *Gustavia superba* (Lecythidaceae)
Early stages (Figs. 3a, 4c,d, 5a, 52a): *Egg*—round, white, with surface of egg smooth and covered in a raised net of five- to seven-sided polygons that appear as though they were ap-

plied with a tube of toothpaste; dorsum very slightly flattened, without raised polygons and with the micropyle consisting of a wide honeycombed ring that is slightly recessed below the surface. The egg is deposited singly in the axils of new shoots or in bark crevices. *Caterpillars*—typically the body of all instars is entirely dull green but may be colored by the type of food being eaten—purplish, reddish brown, or even grayish. *First instar*—entire body with a pebbled texture; obvious prothoracic shield that bears eight long setae along anterior edge that project well in front of head; conspicuous anal shield narrower than body bears six setae along posterior margin that are longer than the anal shield; each segment bears three to four lateral setae; the subdorsal setae are short and shaped like blunt-ended pine cones; the tentacle nectary organ orifices on abdominal segment 8 are marked by a slightly recessed peglike structure. *Mature caterpillar*—body green with a pebbled epidermis and a rough-textured, brown dorsal midline that is especially noticeable on the thorax; tentacle nectary organ areas are brown and have a roughened texture; thoracic segment 1 is produced into two stout, dark brown horns; head capsule black or dark brown, rough, especially on the lower half. The caterpillars are cryptic while on the plant, but are typically found with the head over an extrafloral nectary, which, depending upon the species of hostplant, may be located on the leaves, buds, or flower parts. The caterpillars are solitary feeders, although more than one caterpillar (and various instars) may be found on the same plant. Depending on the site, the caterpillars are typically tended by *Ectatomma ruidum* and *E. tuberculatum* (Ponerinae), occasionally by *Camponotus sericeiventris,* sp. (Formicinae) and *Wasmannia* sp. (Myrmicinae), but rarely by ants in the Dolichoderinae. *Pupa*—dirty brown to brownish green and similar in shape to that of *Thisbe irenea,* but with head roundly bifid, flattened ventrally, first two abdominal segments wide and flattened dorsally, and a short, stout dorsolateral knob on abdominal segments. The pupae are tended by ants for a few days after pupation. *Note:* Specimens I reared on *Gustavia superba* flowers produced larger caterpillars, pupae, and adults than those reared on any other plants.

• **Adult:** Sexes dimorphic. *Male*—upperside entirely brown except for a few white areas at the FW apex and HW costa; underside dirty gray with a few black spots along HW margins and FW apex; distal margins dirty brown, and a scattering of dirty brown spots on postbasal areas of both wings. *Female*—upperside reddish brown with a wide white medial band, a few white spots usually present in the FW apex, and HW with a black margin bordered in white; underside pattern similar to upperside but overshot with white and bearing many irregular black and white rimmed spots at the wing margins and bases. Compare with *S. palaeste*, *Juditha molpe*, *J. dorilis*, *Pixus corculum*, *Thisbe irenea*.

Habits: In our area, this butterfly occurs commonly but not abundantly from sea level to 1450 m on both slopes, in association with almost any type of forested area. Encountered as solitary individuals generally throughout the year. During sunny days the males are encountered from 09:00 to 11:30 hrs in light gaps within the forest or at the canopy level along forest edges. Females oviposit from 11:00 to 13:30 hrs on plants that have vigorously growing shoots or flower buds. Plants that are acceptable to ovipositing females may grow in habitats ranging from open second growth to shady forest understory, and may or may not have ants on them. Both sexes visit flowers of *Croton*, *Lantana*, *Cordia*, *Serjania*, *Stachytarpheta*, *Asclepias*, *Psychotria*, and a variety of herbaceous Asteraceae.

Localities: [A]: Carrillos de Poas (March), San Antonio de Belen (June), Guacima (September), Guayabo (September). [C]: Tres Rios. [SJ]: Patarra (April, October), El Rodeo (July), Santana (June, July), Escazu (July–September), La Montura. [H]: La Selva (July, August), Chilamate (June, July), Santa Clara (September). [P]: Isla del Caño (March), Quepos (July), San Rosa de Puriscal, Palmar Norte (June), Puntarenas (June), Carrara (October), Esparta, Llorona, San Vito. [L]: Siquirres (March, April), Guapiles (January, April), Rio Victoria (September), Limon, Tortuguerro. [G]: Cañas (February), Cerro Ceibo de Guanacaste (September), Santa Rosa (June, November), and many other localities in our area.

Synargis ochra sicyon
(Godman and Salvin, 1878)
FW length: 18–19.5 mm   **Plate 18**
Range: Guatemala to Colombia, Peru. **Subspecies:** Guatemala to Panama
Hostplant: Unknown
Early stages: Unknown
• **Adult:** Sexes slightly dimorphic. *Male*—upperside pale yellow with the costa, apex, and wing margins bordered broadly with dark brown and inset with a thin yellow submarginal line; HW anal margin slightly produced; underside

pattern similar to the upperside, but with a submarginal row of oblong spots on the HW. *Female*—similar to the male color pattern, but with round FW apex and HW anal margins. Compare with *Juditha dorilis*, *Setabis cleomedes*, *Nymphidium haematostictum*.

Habits: In Costa Rica this butterfly is recorded between 600 to 1200 m elevation, from Atlantic slope forest in the Valley de Reventazon and the Carrillo Belt. In Panama, G. Small noted that the males perch around 15:00 hrs. In Costa Rica and Panama I found both sexes visiting flowers of *Croton* spp. (Euphorbiaceae) between 11:00 and 13:00 hrs. Judging from locality data, this butterfly appears to be very seasonal, with most specimens being captured during the commencement of the rains. Uncommon in Costa Rican collections.

Localities: [C]: Turrialba (May), Moravia de Chirripo (May). [H]: Chilamate (May). [L]: Bribri (August).

Synargis velabrum
(Godman and Salvin, 1878)
FW length: 19.5–22.5 mm   **Plate 21**
Range: Nicaragua to Colombia
Hostplant: Unknown
Early stages: Unknown
• **Adult:** Sexes similar. Distinguished by the brown upperside with a white medial band traversing both wings, and the prominent orange patch on the subapex of the FW. In both appearance and in behavior, this butterfly bears an uncanny resemblance to a small *Adelpha* (Nymphalidae).

Habits: In our area this butterfly is known from 700 to 1000 m on the Atlantic slope in association with the montane and flood plain forests of the Carrillo Belt. Typically found as solitary individuals or small groups at small, very local sites that are used traditionally by these butterflies from year to year. The males perch from 13:00 to 14:00 hrs high in the canopy on top of leaves growing at the tips of those branches overhanging rivers and ravines. The male-male chases are fast, frenetic, and their long, sweeping flights may take an interacting pair high into the air above the canopy in a manner reminiscent of some Hesperiidae. Uncommon in Costa Rican collections.

Localities: [A]: Cariblanco (June, August, October). [SJ]: La Montura (April). [H]: Chilamate (July), Tirimbina (March).

Synargis palaeste salvator
(Stichel, 1911)
FW length: 25–30 mm   **Plate 19**

Range: Costa Rica to Colombia. **Subspecies:** Costa Rica and Panama
Hostplant: Unknown, although L. E. Gilbert collected several prepupae at the nest entrance of a *Camponotus sericeiventris* ants in a *Lacmellea* (Euphorbiaceae) tree at Sirena.
Early stages: (Fig. 52c): *Mature caterpillar*—greasy gray with black bands across dorsum, and head with conspicuous, stout, forward-projecting head horns. At Sirena, I once found two caterpillars aggressively tended by *Camponotus sericeiventris* on a large branch fall that had an ant colony of the same species in it. *Pupa*—dull, dirty gray with an overall appearance similar to that of a very large *Synargis mycone*.
• **Adult:** Sexes dimorphic. *Male*—upperside dull black with a very broad gray-blue band on the distal half of the HW that is dissected by black radial veins; underside pale dirty brown with an indistinct, darker brown medial line on both wings. *Female*—upperside brown with a broad white or yellowish medial band across both wings, and a conspicuous red-brown submarginal band on the HW. The females are variable and much larger than the males. *Note:* In virtually all literature, the male has been placed in the genus *Pandemos*, and the female has been referred to as *Nymphidium grandis* and *Pseudopeplia grandis*. Compare with *Synargis nymphidioides*, *S. mycone*, *S. phylleus*.
Habits: This butterfly has been recorded in our area from several disparate rain forest habitats on both slopes that range from sea level to 1400 m. Such locality data suggest that the butterflies are local but may occur in more areas than are known at present. The males are encountered from 11:00 to 13:30 hrs as solitary individuals perching from 1 to 10 m above the ground along forest edges, rivers, and light gaps. The females have a slow, almost lazy flight that strongly resembles butterflies in the genera *Itaballia* and *Leptophobia* (Pieridae). On several occasions I observed females searching for oviposition sites between 11:00 to 12:30 hrs within recent tree falls and along forest edges, and once at the forest canopy level. On two occasions I noted that the female butterflies seem particularly attracted to nest entrances and aggregations of *Camponotus sericeiventris* ants. In Costa Rican collections the males are uncommon, and the females are rare.
Localities: [C]: Rio Catarata (October). [P]: Rincon de Osa (February, August), Llorona (March, April), Sirena (March, April, July, August, November), Palmar Norte (July), Monte Verde. [L]: Estrella (April).

Synargis nymphidioides
(Butler, 1872)
FW length: 26–30 mm   **Plate 19**
Range: Mexico to Panama
Hostplant: Unknown
Early stages: Unknown
• **Adult:** Sexes dimorphic. *Male*—upperside of FW dirty brown with two or three prominent yellow-white spots located posterior to the cell, HW discal area cream-yellow and brown at the base; underside dirty pale yellow with a row of two to three dark marginal spots at HW apex. *Female*—upperside dull white with dirty gray-brown at FW base, costa, apex and margin (except for costal area just distal to cell), and three dark spots at HW apical margin; underside patterns are washed out except for the spots at HW apex and tornus. *Note:* in some literature this species has been placed in the genus *Pandemos*, and it has also been considered a subspecies of *ethelinda*. Compare with *S. phylleus*, *S. palaeste*, *Hermathena candida*.
Habits: In our area this butterfly has been recorded from sea level to 1000 m on the Pacific slope in habitats ranging from second-growth forest to primary rain forest. Information from collections suggests that the adults are present throughout the year at most habitats, including the deciduous Guanacaste forest. Encountered as uncommon solitary individuals flying along forest edges, rivers, or even along fence rows in open areas. The females are active at midday and investigate vigorously growing shoot tips of seedlings, saplings, and shoots originating from cut stumps. I have a very distinct memory of the first time I encountered this butterfly. The individual female was flying around an *Acacia cornigera* plant investigating the shoot tips, alighting periodically, and then circling around again. My memory of this event is vivid for two reasons. First, I was surprised that a butterfly would be landing on a plant covered with aggressively stinging *Pseudomyrmex* ants. Second, when I collected the butterfly my net smashed into the tree, and I was stung several times on the face by the *Polybia* wasps that were nesting in the tree. Given its distinctively Pacific distribution and the gift of hindsight, I cannot help but wonder if this butterfly uses ant acacias as hostplants. While on the wing, the females may be mistaken for members of the common genera *Leptophobia* or *Itaballia* (Pieridae). For some reason, the females are more common in collections than the males.
Localities: [A]: Atenas (May, December), San Antonio de Belen (February, March, August), San Mateo. [SJ]: Santana (February, April,

September), El Rodeo (July). [P]: Sirena (March), Rio Lagarto (April), Puriscal. [G]: Santa Rosa (November), Cañas (March, May, October), Barranca (July).

Synargis nycteus
(Godman and Salvin, 1886)
FW length: 25–26.5 mm   **Plate 19**
Range: Costa Rica and Panama
Hostplant: Unknown
Early stages: Unknown
• **Adult:** Sexes dimorphic. *Male*—FW upperside red-brown with a few short, black medial bars in the cell, and a snowy white HW that has brown on the base and apical margin. *Female*— FW upperside snowy white with a red-brown band running from FW base to margin near tornus, dirty brown on FW apex and distal margin, and the HW entirely snowy white except for dirty gray spots at apical margin. Compare with *Synargis nymphidioides, S. palaeste, Calociasma lilina.*
Habits: In Costa Rica this butterfly is known from a single specimen (in the USNM) that originated from the Pacific slope in the Valle General. In Panama, however, G. Small took this species on both slopes. This suggests that the range of this butterfly in our area may eventually prove to be greater than is presently known. From its appearance, it is quite likely that during flight this butterfly could easily be confused with a species of Pieridae. Very rare throughout its range.
Localities: [P]: Terraba.

Synargis gela
(Hewitson, 1853)
FW length: 16–19.5 mm   **Plate 21**
Range: Costa Rica(?), Ecuador to Brazil
Hostplant: *Stigmaphyllon* spp (Malpighiaceae), *Acalypha* sp. (Euphorbiaceae)
Early stages: *Mature caterpillar*—in Ecuador I reared several individuals of this species and found them similar to *S. mycone*, but with a prominent reddish brown dorsal band that extends from behind the head to the anal shield. In Ecuador they were associated with *Ectatomma tuberculatum* and *Wasmannia* sp. ants (DeVries et al. 1994).
• **Adult:** Sexes similar. Distinguished by the prominent cream medial band running across both wings bordered broadly in a dark brown that covers the bases of both wings. Compare with *Synargis mycone, Juditha dorilis.*
Habits: There is a single specimen of this butterfly in the British Museum labeled "Costa Rica." As this species is quite common and widespread throughout the Amazon Basin of

South America, it may be that the putative Costa Rican specimen of this species is labeled erroneously. I include it here as a possibility in need of confirmation. In Ecuador the habits of this butterfly are similar to those described for *S. mycone.*

Genus **AUDRE** Hemming, 1934

To the casual entomologist these butterflies resemble members of the nymphalid subfamily Melitaeinae, particularly the genera *Thessalia, Chlosyne, Phyciodes,* and North American *Euphydryas.* Among butterflies in general, and riodinids in particular, *Audre* and its close relatives (*Ematurgina, Aricoris,* and *Eiseleia*) are unusual by having an apparently unique sexual dimorphism—the proboscis of the male is extraordinarily swollen, which in some species does not allow the insect to hold it tightly coiled. The exceptional development of the proboscis has been suggested to function as an evaporative cooling mechanism (Harvey 1987a). However, in light of the fact that most Lepidoptera cool by resting in the shade, it is not clear why *Audre* has evolved such a peculiar, sex-limited mechanism to do the same thing. As currently understood, the genus contains over twenty species, most of them occurring only in dry areas of montane Argentina and Chile. In Central America there are three species, only one of which has been recorded in Costa Rica. In much of the older literature these butterflies have been referred to under *Hamaeris,* a distantly related group that is confined to Europe.

The hostplants reported for *Audre* include members of the Asclepidaceae, Apocynaceae, Clusiaceae, and Fabaceae (in Argentina), and Central American oviposition records are on Turneraceae and Clusiaceae (Robbins and Aiello 1982). The caterpillars bear three complete sets of ant-organs, and unlike the caterpillars of *Synargis* and *Thisbe,* the first thoracic segment does not extend very far over the head. *Audre eupulus* (Cramer) was the first myrmecophilous riodinid species to have its caterpillars described in detail (Bruch 1926), and subsequent life history descriptions have been published for other species (Borquin 1953; Haywood 1973; Schremmer 1978). All of these accounts indicate that the caterpillars are typically found inside the nests of *Camponotus* or *Solenopsis* ants. My own observations on two Argentinean species showed that the caterpillars live inside the brood chambers of *Camponotus distinguendus* ants. In these species I could not induce the caterpillars to eat plant material, but there was no evidence that they were carnivorous on ant larvae or that they were fed regurgitations by adult ants (DeVries et al. 1994). Regardless, many specimens in collections are prone to become greasy (including Central American *domina* and *albina*), not unlike the carnivorous lycaenid genera *Liphyra*, *Euliphyra*, and *Feniseca* and the riodinid genus *Setabis*. Given their habit of living inside ant nests, perhaps some species of *Audre* will be found to have carnivorous caterpillars.

One anecdote on diapause of *Audre* caterpillars is worth relating. In Argentina I found a fifth instar *Audre* nr *aurinia* caterpillar in an ant nest and maintained it in a small container for nine months until it pupated. During that time the caterpillar did not eat but molted three times, each time getting slightly smaller. In other words, the caterpillar molted to fifth instar at least four times. This observation strongly suggests that in some habitats these butterflies may diapause in ant nests for considerable periods of time and further hints at the possibility that they may require a year or more to complete their life cycles.

Although at least one species (*domina*) can be locally abundant in Panama, these butterflies are inexplicably rare in Costa Rica. In the forests surrounding the Canal area in Panama, I encountered these butterflies along forest edges perching on low vegetation and found them not to be particularly fast or agile fliers. In a dry, montane desert of Jujuy Province, Argentina, however, I found that the species in that region were extremely fast and agile fliers, that individuals typically rested on the bare pebbled soil so common in that habitat, and their marbled underside rendered them nearly invisible.

Audre domina

(Bates, 1865)
FW length: 20–23 mm   **Plate 20**
Range: Costa Rica and Panama
Hostplant: Oviposition records on *Turnera ulmifolia* (Turneraceae), *Vismia baccifera* (Clusiaceae)

Early stages: *Egg*—blue, laid singly on stems of the hostplants (Robbins and Aiello 1982)
• **Adult:** Sexes similar. Upperside dull orange with indistinct black spots along the wing margin, submargin, base, and discal area, and the HW distal margin has a series of oblong orange spots with black pupils. Compare with *A. albina*.
Habits: In Costa Rica this species is recorded from a few specimens taken on the Pacific slope in the lowland drainage of the Valle General. At the beginning and end of the dry season in Panama, the butterflies may be locally common, and they are found typically as small colonies of ten to fifteen individuals. The males perch on top of low-growing vegetation from midmorning until early afternoon, always in direct sunshine. The butterflies are quite tame when perched, and easily approached. Close inspection of a perched male will reveal that the proboscis droops in a loose coil from between the palpi and lends the butterflies an almost comical appearance—as if the proboscis was borrowed from a larger species and then installed incorrectly. Robbins and Aiello (1982) found females ovipositing near colonies of *Ectatomma* ants, and observed that while laying eggs, the ants attacked the female! Very rare in Costa Rican collections.
Localities: [P]: Golfito (September), Terraba

Audre albina

(Felder and Felder, 1861)
FW length: 19–22.5 mm   **Plate 20**
Range: Costa Rica(?), Panama to Venezuela
Hostplant: Unknown
Early stages: Unknown
• **Adult:** Sexes similar. Upperside yellow-orange with broadly white discal areas on both wings, and black FW apex and margin. Underside pale orange with extensive white spots and bands on both wings. Compare with *A. domina*.
Habits: Unrecorded from Costa Rica as of this writing. However, its not uncommon presence in Panama suggests that it may eventually be found when our fauna is better known. I include it here as a possibility.
Localities: Not yet recorded for our area.

Tribe **NYMPHIDIINI** Bates, 1859

The butterflies embraced by this tribe are characterized by having the abdominal spiracle on segment 3 closer to the sternite than the tergite, a condition of the spiracles that is mirrored in the early stages. The butterflies here represent a diverse assemblage of nearly two hundred myrmecophilous species placed in some sixteen genera: *Parnes*, *Periplacis*, *Menander*, *Pandemos*, *Rodinia*, *Calociasma*, *Calospila*, *Adelotypa*, *Setabis*, *Pseudonymphidia*, *Theope*, and *Nymphidium*, which are found in our area, plus *Zelotaea*, *Dysmathia*, *Calliona*, and *Echenais*, which are entirely South American. Although little information is available, the butterflies here appear to use a range of hosts, including being carnivorous on scale insects; they may show obligate associations with particular ant taxa, and their caterpillars may be extraordinarily picturesque (e.g., *Menander, Setabis, Theope*).

Genus **PARNES** Westwood, 1851

These tiny butterflies—perhaps the smallest of all riodinids—are readily recognized by their striated undersides and the black eyespot in the apex of each wing. The genus ranges from Costa Rica southward throughout the Amazon Basin and contains only two species, one which occurs in our area. Although these butterflies can be locally common in South America, nothing is known about their hostplants or natural history.

Parnes nycteis
Westwood, 1851
FW length: 8–9 mm   **Plate 11**
Range: Costa Rica to the Amazon Basin and Guyana
Hostplant: Unknown
Early stages: Unknown
• **Adult:** Sexes similar. Distinguished by its tiny size, dark brown upperside, and the underside brown with many fine, wavy, yellowish lines, and two black spots bearing reflective blue pupils at FW and HW apex. Compare with *Adelotypa eudocia.*
Habits: This butterfly is reported in our area from three lowland rain forest localities—two on the Atlantic, the other on the Pacific slope. G. Austin informs me that in Costa Rica he found the butterflies flying very low to the ground in the deep shade of the forest interior. This has been my experience in Ecuador, where I found this butterfly to be active during the early afternoon in well-shaded primary forest on the periphery of large treefalls. These butterflies bear a resemblance to the common skipper *Ludens ludens* (Hesperiidae), although this skipper generally occurs only in sunny open areas. This butterfly is rare in Costa Rican collections, undoubtedly because it is easily overlooked.
Localities: [H]: Chilamate (May). [P]: Ruta 2, 9.2 km SE Chacarita (September). [L]: Hacienda Tapezco (March).

Genus **PERIPLACIS** Geyer, 1837

These butterflies strongly resemble members of the closely related genus *Menander*. However, *Periplacis* may be recognized by having a slightly produced terminal hook on the FW apex. The genus ranges from Costa Rica throughout the Amazon Basin and contains two, and perhaps three, species, one that occurs in our area. Nothing is known about the hostplants or early stages of *Periplacis*, but its close relationship to *Menander* suggests that the caterpillars probably feed on plants in the Marcgraviaceae.

Periplacis glaucoma splendida
(Butler, 1867)
FW length: 17.5–20.5 mm   **Plate 20**
Range: Costa Rica to Colombia, Brazil
Hostplant: Unknown
Early stages: Unknown
• **Adult:** Sexes dimorphic. *Male*—upperside a fine iridescent blue-green with black distal margins; HW with an extended anal lobe that bears a sparse covering of long androconial setae. *Female*—upperside reddish brown with a sprinkling of iridescent blue on the FW, an iridescent blue band in and around the HW cell, and an almost squarely cut posterior HW margin. Compare with *Menander menander* and *pretus.*
Habits: This butterfly is recorded in our area from sea level to about 400 m on both slopes in association with wet and rain forest habitats. The only experience I have had with this species was when I once observed a small flycatcher (Tyranidae) fly out from the outer edge of the forest canopy and catch an individual female of this butterfly. When the butterfly escaped, it fell straight downward from a considerable height, began flying a few meters from the ground, and then perched under a leaf only a few centimeters above the ground. Rare in Central American collections.
Localities: [H]: La Selva (April). [P]: Rio Catarata (September). [G]: El Libano.

Genus **MENANDER** Hemming, 1939

These butterflies have a short, robust body and thorax, a broad head with erect palpi, brilliant iridescent coloration on the upperside (only in males of some species), and a pale underside ground color checkered with dark spots in a manner that recalls the genus *Calospila*. Members of the genus are distributed from Mexico though Central and South America, and as currently understood *Menander* contains approximately ten species, three that occur in our area. In older literature these butterflies were known under the name *Tharops.*

Host records from Mexico, Costa Rica, Panama, Ecuador, and Brazil suggest that *Menander* caterpillars feed only on plants in the Marcgraviaceae, especially the genera *Marcgravia*, *Sourubea*, and *Norantea* (Callaghan 1977; DeVries et al. 1994). The caterpillars are covered with a prominent carapace that flares outward to the substrate and covers the body and legs like the shell of a turtle or an armadillo (Figs. 4a,b, 53). Of interest is that the spiracles are found underneath the carapace, thus indicating that the air trapped between the body and the carapace is used during respiration. Such morphology seems to suggest that the caterpillars are heavily armored, but against what is unclear. My observations on these caterpillars from Costa Rica, Panama, and Ecuador provide no suggestion that ants behave aggressively toward them. The caterpillars bear a complete set of ant organs and have been reported to be tended by a variety of ant genera. In my experience, the caterpillars are seldom attended enthusiastically by ants. The pupae are bluntly cylindrical, resemble a broken twig, and pupation may take place on or off the hostplant. Callaghan (1977) provides a life history description of Brazilian *M. felsina.*

These butterflies are fast, erratic fliers that produce an audible whirring sound while in flight. In South America they can, at times, be locally abundant. For example, Callaghan (1978) found *Menander felsina* abundant in a small, isolated patch of forest in Brazil. In Madre de Dios, Peru, I counted over thirty individual males of a species near *hebrus* (Cramer) in a single morning; they were perching along 100 m of a trail through lowland rain forest. It was amusing to observe that by slowly walking down the trail I could create an increasing wave of activity ahead of me; one individual would become disturbed and take wing, which caused another individual to chase it, which disturbed another, and so forth. While walking in the midst of this swirling cloud of butterflies, I recall quite clearly being able to hear them whizzing past my head. In Costa Rica and Panama, however, these butterflies are seldom, if ever, abundant.

The study of *M. felsina* by Callaghan (1978) provided important insights into the biology of these butterflies. The results of his mark-and-release study during the course of four years indicated that individuals may live up to four weeks, and that individual males tend to use the same perching areas for considerable periods of their lifetime. He also found that local populations tend to be composed predominantly of males that evidently confine themselves to patches of the hostplant, whereas the females appear to be more vagrant. Callaghan's study further suggests that local populations may become extinct due to inclement weather or parasitism, and are subsequently reestablished by females wandering in from other localities.

Menander menander purpurata
(Godman and Salvin, 1878)
FW length: 18–19 mm **Plate 20**
Range: Costa Rica to Brazil, Bolivia. **Subspecies:** Costa Rica to Colombia
Hostplant: *Sourubea* sp. (Marcgraviaceae)
Early stages: *Egg*—(Figs. 3c, 4a,b, 53)—pale green, deposited on stems or vigorously growing shoots. *Mature caterpillar*—pale, smooth green that perfectly matches the leaf color, and a black head that is recessed into the first thoracic segment. Early instars are flattened with a "carapace" that flares out over the substrate (like smooth trilobites), whereas the mature caterpillar is more cylindrical. The caterpillars may be tended by *Camponotus* and *Crematogaster* ants. *Pupa*—cylindrical and resembling a dead piece of wood.
• **Adult:** Sexes similar. Upperside dark iridescent blue with broad black FW apex and distal margin. The blue is very fine (almost mirrorlike) on the HW of the male, whereas it is broken by black bands in the female. Underside off-white with a scattering of short brown lines, and the HW apex and tornus bears two dark spots. Compare with *M. pretus* and *Periplacis splendida.*
Habits: This butterfly occurs from sea level to 900 m on both slopes in association with wet and rain forest habitats. Encountered as solitary individuals along forest edges and in light gaps. In Central America the males typically perch from 09:00 to 11:00 hrs either low to the ground or high in the subcanopy, and aggressively chase other insects that fly past. In Panama I found that individual males may repeatedly use the same perch over the course of several days, and that months later the same spot may be a traditional perching spot for other individual males. Females are most frequently encountered during midday, when they fly about in dense tangles of vegetation searching along forest edges or in light gaps for oviposition sites. The eggs may be laid on plants growing low to the ground or high in the subcanopy of the forest, in either direct

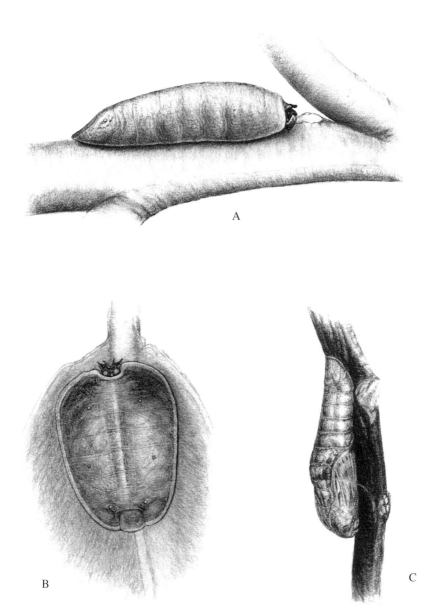

FIGURE 53. (A) Mature *Menander menander* caterpillar. (B) An early fourth instar *Menander menander* caterpillar. (C) *Menander menander* pupa. (Drawings by J. Clark)

sunshine or in shade. Infrequent in Costa Rican collections.
Localities: [C]: Juan Viñas (November), Turrialba (July). [H]: Magsaysay (December). [P]: Palmar Norte (August), Sirena (March), Llorona April). [L]: Guapiles (January).

Menander pretus picta
(Godman and Salvin, 1886)
FW length: 18–20 mm   **Plate 20**
Range: Guatemala to Colombia, Brazil. **Subspecies:** Guatemala to Panama
Hostplant: *Marcgravia nepenthoides, Sourubea* sp. (Marcgraviaceae)
Early stages: *Mature caterpillar*—dark green, with a dark brown head, two white spots on the thorax and two on the last abdominal segment; in overall shape, reminiscent of a smooth and flattened trilobite, and almost invisible while on the hostplant. All instars graze the epidermis of leaves. Tended by *Crematogaster* and *Camponotus* ants, albeit not very enthusiastically. *Pupa*—narrowly cylindrical in shape with the abdomen narrower than the thorax, and a broad, flattened cremaster.
• **Adult:** Sexes similar. Upperside iridescent green set with small, square black spots; underside washed in a pale reddish brown with the apex of both wings distinctly dark. The male has the HW distal margin drawn into a short lobe, whereas the distal margin of the female is rounded. Compare with *Periplacis superba* and *M. menander*.
Habits: This butterfly has been recorded in our area from sea level to 900 m on both slopes in association with wet and rain forest habitats. Encountered as solitary individuals flying along forest edges or in large light gaps. The males perch high in the subcanopy during midmorning or early afternoon and vigorously chase other insects that fly past. Females oviposit during midday on plants growing in the canopy, along forest edges, or in the understory in lightgaps. Both sexes visit flowers of *Miconia*, *Citrus*, *Lantana*, and *Cordia*.
Localities: [A]: San Mateo. [H]: La Selva (November), Plastico (July, August, October), Chilamate (March), Magsaysay (February). [P]: Palmar Norte (February). [L]: Sixaola (March).

Menander laobotas
(Hewitson, 1875)
FW length: 19.5–20 mm   **Plate 20**
Range: Nicaragua to Ecuador
Hostplant: *Marcgravia nepenthoides* (Marcgraviaceae)
Early stages: *Egg*—greenish white, globular; entire surface wrinkled and covered in a net of raised pentagons; micropyle consists of a circle of punctures. The egg is deposited singly on leaves, stems, and shoots.
• **Adult:** Sexes dimorphic. *Male*—upperside reminiscent of *Thisbe irenea*, but with two white spots near the end of the FW cell and broadly reflective blue on the upperside at the FW tornus and HW margins; the blue on the HW contains a wide, white medial band; underside washed chalky white with dark at the margins. *Female*—upperside gray-brown with two to three white costal spots near the end of the FW cell, and two brown, distinctly broken medial lines that run from the FW costa almost to the HW inner margin; underside as in the male. Compare with *M. menander*, *Thisbe irenea*, *Cremna umbra*.
Habits: This butterfly has been reported from sea level to 300 m on both slopes in association with wet and rain forest habitats. Encountered as rare, solitary individuals flying along shaded forest edges or in large shady light gaps. Once I watched a female oviposit single eggs near emerging shoots of a well-shaded plant that was growing in a tangled mass of vegetation in the forest between 10:00 and 10:15 hrs. For some unknown reason, more females (albeit few) of this species are represented in Central American collections than males, almost certainly reflecting a peculiarity in the perching sites of the males. *Note:* For some reason that is unclear to me, various authors have considered this species to be a member of the genus *Calospila*, something that it is decidedly not. Rare in Central American collections.
Localities: [C]: Turrialba (May). [H]: La Selva (May). [P]: Sirena (July), Rincon.

Genus PANDEMOS Hübner, 1819

Four species have been placed in this genus, all which are very large for riodinids, and all which are apparently quite rare. The group of species placed in *Pandemos* apparently do not share any singular characteristic that holds them together, and it may be that our single species is erroneously placed here (Harvey, pers. comm.). In fact, judging from its appearance, the palpi, and the sexual dimorphism, our species might be more correctly placed in the genus *Synargis*. Nothing is known about the hostplants or early stages of any species.

Pandemos godmanii
Dewitz, 1877
FW length: 32–33 mm **Plate 20**
Range: Mexico to Costa Rica
Hostplant: Unknown
Early stages: Unknown
• **Adult:** Sexes dimorphic. The large size and conspicuously produced FW apex make this species impossible to confuse with any other riodinid. *Male*—FW upperside warm reddish brown with a thin white transverse band running from costa almost to tornus; the area basal to white band dusted in blue-violet, and HW entirely a lustrous blue; underside dull brown with the FW area basal to white band almost black. *Female*—upperside entirely brown except for a white band that runs from FW costa across cell end almost to the tornus, and FW base almost black.
Habits: This spectacular butterfly is recorded in our area from a single collection taken in the Pacific lowland deciduous forest. In Belize I had the opportunity to briefly observe an individual female that was flying along a shady forest trail through deciduous forest. As it darted through the fairly dense woody vegetation, it flew in a fast zigzag pattern. When she landed, she did so on the underside of a branch about 4 m above the ground inside a tangle of branches. While at rest, the forewings were folded down into the hindwings in a manner that recalled the nymphalid genera *Libytheana* or *Catargynnis*, rendering the butterfly almost invisible. When I disturbed her by moving the branch slightly, she immediately flew upward above the canopy of the forest, and was lost from sight.
Localities: [G]: Parque Santa Rosa (December).

Genus CALOSPILA Geyer, 1832

These small-bodied butterflies are brightly colored on the upperside, have a monochrome underside that is set with many dots and streaks, and the sexes are typically strongly dimorphic. In *Calospila* the tendency is for the males to be distinctly patterned, whereas the females of many species all converge on a similar, drab color pattern. Museums often contain quite a few specimens where the sexes are not paired with certainty. Field workers could contribute toward a needed taxonomic revision by collecting pairs in copula, and by rearing series of specimens. Many of the species now placed in *Calospila* have been referred to under *Poly-*stictus and *Lemonias* in older literature. As currently understood, *Calospila*, which appears to be something of a catch-all genus, embraces about forty species, most of which are entirely South American, and it most likely contains undescribed species. In fact, there is little doubt that *Calospila* is in need of thorough revision. About a dozen species of *Calospila* have been reported from Central America, nine which occur in our area, and many of which are uncommon to rare.

Surprisingly little is known about the natural history of these butterflies. The only hostplant records to date are from the Malpighiaceae, yet these records are confined to a few species in a small section of *Calospila* (DeVries et al. 1994), and other sections may utilize other plant families. As far as is known, the caterpillars possess all three sets of ant-organs, they are very cryptic while on the hostplant, and they are reported to be attended by ants in the genera *Crematogaster*, *Pheidole*, *Solenopsis*, *Wasmannia*, and *Ectatomma*. The pupae are slender, roundly cylindrical, and do not bear any prominent projections. The little information available suggests that the early stages resemble those of *Adelotypa*.

In our area these butterflies are known to occur from sea level to approximately 1400 m in habitat types ranging from open second growth to primary forest. Some of the common species (*cilissa, lucianus*) are found in close association with their hostplants. However, most of the species are rare to uncommon, and little is known about them. In my experience these butterflies are occasionally found visiting plants that bear a profusion of small, white flowers (e.g., various Euphorbiaceae, Sapindaceae, Flacourtiaceae, Lauraceae).

Calospila lucianus lucianus
(Fabricius, 1793)
FW length: 12–13 mm **Plate 21**
Range: Costa Rica to Brazil, Trinidad. **Subspecies:** Costa Rica to Venezuela
Hostplant: *Stigmaphyllon* sp. (Malpighiaceae)
Early stages: Mature caterpillar—in overall appearance and behavior similar to that of *cilissa*, but darker green (record from Ecuador).
• **Adult:** Sexes dimorphic. *Male*—upperside dull orange-brown with a scattering of black comma marks on both wings; underside white with a scattering of black comma marks, and FW distal margin darker than ground color. *Female*—upperside similar to male except FW with entire discal area yellow-orange and HW brown-orange; underside more washed out than in the male. Compare with *C. cilissa, asteria*.

Habits: This butterfly has been reported in our area from sea level to about 600 m on the Pacific slope. In Panama and Ecuador I found this species common in open second growth adjacent to forest edges. This butterfly flies low to the ground and has similar habits and habitat preferences to *C. cilissa*.

Localities: [P]: Brujo de Buenos Aires (September), Palmar Norte (July), Rio Catarata (September), Golfito (June), Rincon de Osa (March), Villa Neily (July), Pozo Azul.

Calospila cilissa
(Hewitson, 1863)
FW length: 12–13 mm   Plate 21
Range: Honduras to Colombia
Hostplant: *Stigmaphyllon* spp (Malpighiaceae)
Early stages (Fig. 54b): *Egg*—tiny, greenish white, most frequently laid singly on developing shoot tips or leaves. *Mature caterpillar*—dull, pale green with a moderately well-developed prothoracic shield and a dark brown head. The body somewhat flattened, being widest at the thorax, tapering to the posterior, and terminating in a rounded lobe at the last abdominal segment. While on the plant, the caterpillars are incredibly cryptic, but they can generally be found at the extrafloral nectaries of young leaves tended by a clot of ants. Often each young leaf will have several caterpillars huddled around each extrafloral nectary. The caterpillars feed on young leaves, and in the last instars they rest in semirolled leaves. For their diminutive size the caterpillars produce a surprisingly robust call. *Pupa*—brown, elongate, somewhat cylindrical without projections or patterns. Pupation usually takes place inside a semirolled leaf away from the host. Occasionally the pupae may be found on the hostplant, but these are typically parasitized by tachinid flies.
• **Adult:** Sexes dimorphic. *Male*—upperside dark brown with orange discal areas on both wings; underside whitish with white ocelli set in indistinct dark margins. *Female*—upperside pale yellow with brown margins; underside as in male, only with ground color pale yellow. Compare with *C. lucianus, asteria.*
Habits: The most common and widespread *Calospila* species in our area. This butterfly occurs from sea level to 1200 m on both slopes, typically in association with open second growth in wet and rain forest habitats. The males perch under the leaves of low tangles of vegetation that is characteristic of open second growth between 10:00 and 11:30 hrs. The females oviposit on vigorously growing shoots of their hostplants during midday. Oviposition may take place on plants with or without the presence of ants. Both sexes visit flowers of various weedy Asteraceae, *Lantana,* and *Croton,* and while visiting flowers the butterflies pulse their wings open and shut.

Localities: [C]: Turrialba (June, July), Juan Viñas (May), Peralta, Pejivalle. [SJ]: Carrillo (May, October). [H]: La Selva (March, April, June, August), Chilamate (March, May–August), Santa Clara (April, September). [P]: Sirena (March, April, September), Rio Catarata (September), Las Cruces. [L]: Banana River (June, July), Limon (March), Guapiles (January, March, June, September), Siquirres (January), Rio Victoria (September, October), Germania (March, April), Puerto Viejo (March).

Calospila asteria
(Stichel, 1911)
FW length: 14.5–15 mm   Plate 21
Range: Costa Rica(?), Panama to Colombia
Hostplant: Unknown
Early stages: Unknown
• **Adult:** Sexes dimorphic. *Male*—upperside of both wings orange, bordered heavily in black, with a few white spots on the FW apex; underside of FW with pale yellow in discal area; HW discal area white with many black specks, and the distal margins faintly black. *Female*—upperside yellow with broad black margins, and a submarginal row of small white dots, and the HW discal area overshot with a dusting of black scales. Compare with *C. cilissa, Setabis cleomedes, Cariomothis poeciloptera.*
Habits: This butterfly has not yet been recorded in Costa Rica. However, its occurrence at a variety of Panamanian localities suggests that it will be found in our area when the fauna is better known. The montane areas in Parque Braulio Carrillo or in the Valle de Reventazon seem likely localities. In Panama, I found small populations of males perching high in the forest canopy from 10:00 to 13:00 hrs in montane wet forest at 800 m elevation.
Localities: Not yet recorded for our area.

Calospila martia
(Godman, 1903)
FW length: 20.5–22.5 mm   Plate 21
Range: Costa Rica to Colombia
Hostplant: Unknown
Early stages: Unknown
• **Adult:** Sexes dimorphic. *Male*—FW upperside purple with red-brown at the base; HW upperside red-brown with an orange crescent along the distal margin that runs from below the apex to the inner margin. *Female*—upperside gray-brown with a yellow FW band that runs

from costa, across the cell, and terminates at the margin just anterior to the tornus. Compare with *C. sudias, zeurippa, argenissa.*
Habits: In our area this butterfly has been recorded from a single Atlantic lowland rain forest site. In Panama, however, it also occurs in the Pacific lowlands during the dry season, suggesting that it may eventually be found in other areas of Costa Rica as well.
Localities: [H]: Magsaysay (August).

Calospila sudias
(Hewitson, 1858)
FW length: 19.5–20.5 mm   Plate 21
Range: Mexico to Panama
Hostplant: Unknown
Early stages: Unknown
• **Adult:** Sexes dimorphic. *Male*—FW upperside purple with a thin red-brown submarginal line; HW brown with the distal margin (excluding the apex) with a broad orange band that cuts almost straight from inner margin to subapex. *Female*—upperside gray-brown with a broad white FW band that runs from costa across the cell, then curves into the tornus without touching the distal margin. Compare with *C. martia, zeurippa, argenissa.*
Habits: This butterfly is recorded for our area on the strength of a single specimen in the USNM that bears no exact locality data. In Panama, G. Small took this species in wet forest habitats at about 700 m elevation on both slopes during the months of April and May, and in Guatemala J. Hall and K. Willmott took this species in the lowlands.
Localities: "Costa Rica."

Calospila argenissa
(Stoll, 1790)
FW length: 20.5–21.5 mm   Plate 21
Range: Costa Rica to Colombia
Hostplant: Unknown
Early stages: Unknown
• **Adult:** Sexes dimorphic. *Male*—upperside purple with a black submarginal line and several black, broken medial lines on the FW; HW purple with several short black bands along the costa. *Female*—upperside dirty brown with a broad yellow FW band that runs from the costa, across the cell, and ends squarely before it enters the tornus, or shows a distinct constriction as it enters the tornus. Compare with *C. martia, zeurippa, sudias.*
Habits: This butterfly has been recorded in our area from rain forest habitats on both slopes from sea level to about 1000 m. Encountered as rare, solitary individuals along forest edges,

light gaps, and streams. Both sexes visit plants with small white flowers.
Localities: [A]: Chachagua de San Carlos (September). [C]: Turrialba (July), Cachi (August). [H]: La Selva (October), Chilamate (September). [P]: Manuel Antonio (September). [L]: Estrella (April).

Calospila zeurippa lasthenes
(Hewitson, 1870)
FW length: 17–18.5 mm   Plate 21
Range: Mexico to Panama. **Subspecies:** Nicaragua to Panama
Hostplant: Unknown
Early stages: Unknown
• **Adult:** Sexes dimorphic. *Male*—FW upperside reddish brown with purple inside and around the cell and a red-brown submarginal band that is bordered distally by purple; HW upperside reddish brown with the posterior and part of the inner margin yellow-orange. *Female*—upperside pale brown with a yellow band on FW that begins at costa, runs across cell, and generally terminates just before tornus, except for a small intrusion that touches the inner margin. Compare with *C. sudias, argenissa, martia.*
Habits: This butterfly has been recorded in our area from both slopes in association with sea level mangrove habitats. Encountered as fast-flying, rare, solitary individuals along forest edges and rivers flying from 2 to 5 m above the ground. Both sexes visit flowers of herbaceous and woody plants that are typically associated with coastal mangrove habitats.
Localities: [P]: Quepos (August, September), Sirena (July). [L]: Limon (May, June).

Calospila parthaon pelarge
(Godman and Salvin, 1878)
FW length: 15–16.5 mm   Plate 21
Range: Mexico to Colombia, Ecuador, Trinidad.
Subspecies: Mexico to Panama
Hostplant: Unknown
Early stages: Unknown
• **Adult:** Sexes dimorphic. *Male*—FW upperside dark brown with blue spots at apex and margin and an orange spot near tornus; HW upperside bright orange with black margins; underside ground color blue-gray with indistinct black FW apex, margins, and speckles on discal area of both wings. *Female*—FW upperside brown with two fused white spots at end of cell and a distinct orange triangular shape in tornus; HW upperside almost entirely orange except for brown base and costal margin. Compare with *Cariomothis poeciloptera, Setabis cleomedes.*

Habits: This unusual butterfly has been recorded in our area from a single collection taken on the Pacific slope at 200 m. This locality was at one time covered in rain forest, but now is effectively devoid of natural vegetation.
Localities: [P]: Palmar Norte (June).

Calospila trotschi
(Godman and Salvin, 1901)
FW length: 15–16.5 mm   **Plate 11**
Range: Costa Rica to western Ecuador
Hostplant: Unknown
Early stages: Unknown
• **Adult:** Sexes dimorphic. *Male*—FW upperside dark red-brown with pale blue spots at subapex and along submargin; several medial white spots run from costa to distal end of cell; HW upperside red-brown from base to just beyond the end of cell, and the distal one-third of wing white; some blue medial spots at end of cell. The undersides of both wings are extensively white with several broken brown medial lines. *Female*—FW upperside brown with two or three white spots at distal end of cell near costa; HW upperside brown with distal margin broadly white and bearing a few brown spots; underside of both wings with extensive white, several broken brown medial lines, and broad, indistinct brown margins. *Note:* In older literature this taxon has been associated with the genus *Menander*. However, further study is needed to ascertain whether it is placed correctly here, or should be in the genus *Adelotypa*. Compare with *Lemonias agave, Roeberella lencates*.
Habits: This curious butterfly has been recorded in our area only from a single site on the Atlantic slope in association with rain forest. The solitary female that I collected was flying at the interface of primary forest and old second growth vegetation during midday. Very rare in Central American collections.
Localities: [H]: La Selva (April).

Genus RODINIA Westwood 1851

The butterflies in this genus are reminiscent of a robust *Rhetus*, but they may be recognized by their broad HW tails and very long palpi. Of the two species in *Rodinia*, one occurs in Central America. Nothing is known about the hostplants, early stages, or natural history of any species, and they are apparently rare throughout their range.

Rodinia calpharnia barbouri
(Bates, 1935)
FW length: 26–29 mm   **Plate 20**
Range: Costa Rica(?), Panama to Brazil. **Subspecies:** Costa Rica(?), Panama, Colombia
Hostplant: Unknown
Early stages: Unknown
• **Adult:** Sexes similar. Immediately distinguished by the long tail on the HW which has a broad blue distal margin, and a conspicuous red band that starts at the base of the HW and extends through the tornus and terminates at about the middle of the tail. *Note:* The first Central American specimen of this butterfly was described as *barbouri* Bates, 1935, from Barro Colorado, Panama (type in the Museum of Comparative Zoology, Harvard University), and considered a full species, although Bates suggested it was very similar to *delphinia* (Staudinger, 1887). However, it is now considered a subspecies of *calpharnia*. Compare with the females of *Rhetus arcius, jurgensenii, dysonii, periander*.
Habits: This butterfly has not been recorded from our area. However, in Panama it occurs very locally from the Darien almost to Bocas del Toro in a variety of rain forest habitats. I am therefore including it here as a possibility to be looked for, especially from habitats in the Atlantic lowlands near the Panamanian border. Along the canal area of Panama I found this butterfly during the dry season when the males were active, like clockwork, hill-topping from 12:00 to 13:30 hrs perching on the upper or underside of leaves along well-lighted forest edges. While flying, the butterflies made rapid, long sweeping flights across open light gaps, giving the impression of a small swallowtail in the genus *Eurytides* (Papilionidae) or a female of *Rhetus*.
Localities: Not yet recorded for our area.

Genus ADELOTYPA Warren ,1895

The butterflies currently placed in this genus (many of which were referred to under the name *Echenais*) have long formed a heterogeneous group that in some cases may be confused with members of *Charis, Lemonias*, or *Calospila*. Members of *Adelotypa* are found from Mexico through Central and South America, and the genus embraces over thirty species, three of which occur in our area. The Central American species may usually be recognized by their elongate forewing and a ground color set

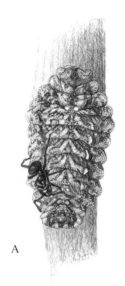
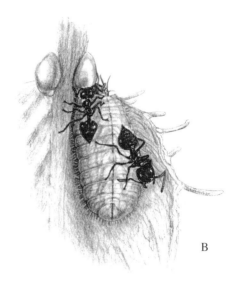

A

B

FIGURE 54. *Setabis lagus* caterpillar being tended by an *Azteca* sp. ant. (B) *Calospila cilissa* caterpillar being tended by *Crematogaster* sp. ants. Note that the caterpillar's head is over an extrafloral nectary. (Drawings by J. Clark)

with fine lines and spots as in *Chalodeta* or *Argyrogrammana*. However, unlike those genera, members of *Adelotypa* have slender, erect palpi, and the spiracle on abdominal segment 3 is shifted ventrally toward the sternite.

For a group of considerable size such as *Adelotypa*, there is surprisingly little information available on its hostplants or early stages. The only observations available (DeVries et al. 1994) indicate that *A. senta* in Ecuador feeds on *Bauhinia* (Fabaceae). The myrmecophilous caterpillars are tended by *Pheidole* ants and bear a strong similarity to *Calospila*: the body is covered with tiny granulations, bears a few long setae on the distal margin of the first thoracic segment, and other setae along the perimeter of the venter, the head is unadorned with the balloon setae or horns seen in *Nymphidium*, *Theope*, or *Synargis*, and the overall color ranges from yellow-brown to pale green. The caterpillars feed on leaf tissue between the main veins and rest with their head over extrafloral nectaries. The pupa is brown, with a slight dorsal keel that has its anterior end distinctly squared.

In Costa Rica, members of *Adelotypa* are found generally in lowland habitats and tend to be uncommon to rare. This is in contrast to South America, where some species may be abundant. An interesting observation on *A.*

senta is provided by D. Murray, who noted that males of *A. senta* feed on the extrafloral nectaries of their hostplant for extended periods of time (up to 24 hours), and that during this time, the ants frequently antennate the forelegs of the adult butterfly. These observations suggest a very close association between the butterfly population and its hostplant and may indicate ant-mediated oviposition in the females.

Adelotypa densemaculata
(Hewitson, 1870)
FW length: 12–14 mm   **Plate 11**
Range: Nicaragua to Colombia, Peru
Hostplant: Unknown
Early stages: Unknown
• **Adult:** Sexes slightly dimorphic. *Male*—upperside brown, set with a series of fine interwoven lines, and the distal margins of wings with a chainlike row of spots. *Female*—ground color a gray-brown that makes the series of lines more distinct. Compare with *A. glauca*, *eudocia*, *Chalodeta lypera*, and *C. candiope*.
Habits: In our area this butterfly has been recorded only from lowland areas on the Pacific slope between sea level and 500 m. I once observed this species during late afternoon in lowland rain forest, where several individual males were perching on vegetation about 2 m

above ground in a large light gap. The late G. Small found this species perching on tree trunks between 16:00 and 16:30 hrs. Rare in Costa Rican collections.
Localities: [A]: San Mateo. [P]: Villa Neily (June, October).

Adelotypa glauca
(Godman and Salvin, 1886)
FW length: 12.5–14.5 mm   Plate 11
Range: Costa Rica to Venezuela
Hostplant: Unknown
Early stages: Unknown
• **Adult:** Sexes slightly dimorphic. *Male*—upperside pale, shiny blue with small black rectangles in medial areas of both wings, and the FW apex and distal margins indistinctly black. Underside ground color a washed-out bluish white set with chainlike rows of spots across the discal areas and at the margins. *Female*—the blue on the upperside is paler and without a sheen. Compare with *Adelotypa densemaculata*.
Habits: In our area this butterfly has been recorded from 600 to 1600 m on both slopes in association with wet and cloud forest habitats. Encountered locally as solitary individuals flying along sunny forest edges and in large light gaps. The males perch between 08:00 to 09:30 hrs on the underside of leaves from 3 to 5 m above ground with their wings open, and make circular sorties from the perch, returning to the same leaf or one nearby. I found that individual perches are not used consistently through time, but a particular portion of a forest edge may generally be used as a perching arena. The behavior of the males recalls the slow, fluttery flight of *Nymphidium* or members of the lycaenid subfamily Polyommatinae that are common in open areas (e.g., *Hemiargus, Leptotes*). On sunny days the females are generally observed between 09:00 and 10:30 hrs flying almost at the subcanopy level. To my eye, the females have a slightly more rapid, circling flight than the males. I found both sexes visiting flowers of *Dendropanax* sp. (Araliaceae). Uncommon.
Localities: [A]: Cariblanco. [C]: Cachi, Juan Viñas. [P]: Las Alturas (March–August, December).

Adelotypa eudocia
(Godman and Salvin, 1897)
FW length: 9–10 mm   Plate 11
Range: Western Mexico to Costa Rica
Hostplant: Unknown
Early stages: Unknown
• **Adult:** Sexes similar. Upperside dull brown with darker brown spots that form broken me-

dial lines; distal margins of both wings have alternating brown and white fringe. Underside a light brown that causes the dark spots and lines to become more distinct. *Note*: This butterfly has in some collections been referred to as *tinea* (Bates 1868), a similar species that is not uncommon in Brazil, whereas in Costa Rica the habitat where it has been reported from contains species that are typical of Mexican faunas. Compare with *A. densemaculata, Charis hermodora, C. gynaea.*
Habits: This butterfly is known from our area on the strength of a single collection by W. Schaus from the Pacific slope at about 500 m elevation. To my knowledge this butterfly has not been collected since that time—over eighty years ago. However, its diminutive size strongly suggests that it could easily be overlooked.
Localities: [A]: San Mateo (October).

Genus CALOCIASMA Stichel, 1910

The butterflies in this genus have relatively narrow forewings and resemble members of the genus *Catocyclotis* and, like that genus, bear a slight resemblance to *Calospila*. The genus ranges from Mexico through Central and South America and contains four species, two of which occur in our area. In older literature these butterflies were referred to under the generic name *Echenais*. Nothing is reported on the early stages of any species.

Calociasma icterica
(Godman and Salvin, 1878)
FW length: 18.5–19.5 mm   Plate 21
Range: Costa Rica and Panama
Hostplant: Unknown
Early stages: Unknown
• **Adult:** Sexes similar. Upperside of FW brown with an irregular, broken yellow band running from the costa across the distal end of the cell, breaking into round spots at subapex and tornal margin; inner margin with irregular yellow band. The HW is yellow with a little brown at the base, two brown spots in the apex, and a thin, even brown distal margin. The underside is pale yellow with indistinct brown markings, and two brown spots at HW apex. The female is very pale yellow, almost white on the FW, and has the brown markings on the FW less sharply defined. Compare with *Catocyclotis aemulius, Synargis phylleus.*
Habits: This butterfly has been recorded in our

area from three lowland localities: one on the Atlantic slope, the other two on the Pacific. On the Osa Peninsula I once collected a female during midmorning that was flying around in a large, fresh treefall. Any information concerning the biology or abundance of this rare and unusual species would be worth publishing.
Localities: [A]: San Mateo (July). [P]: Sirena (August, October). [L]: Sixaola (March).

Calociasma lilina
(Butler, 1870)
FW length: 20–22 mm   **Plate 21**
Range: Mexico to Panama, Trinidad
Hostplant: Unknown
Early stages: Unknown
• **Adult:** Sexes similar. FW upperside pale blue with reddish brown spots; a conspicuous medial white triangular spot at costa; tornus and inner margin white; HW upperside white with small area of brown at base. Compare with *Synargis nycteus.*
Habits: This butterfly has been recorded in our area from 100 to about 1200 m on the Pacific slope in association with deciduous forest habitats. In Panama, G. Small found that the males perch at about 14:00 hrs on tree trunks. I have never seen it alive. Rare in Costa Rican collections.
Localities: [A]: San Mateo (October). [P]: Puriscal Mts. [G]: Cañas (June).

Genus SETABIS Doubleday, 1847

The butterflies in this genus are quite varied in appearance, and typically the sexes are strongly dimorphic. An interesting sexual dimorphism is shown by their antennae—the terminal segments in the males are noticeably thickened, whereas in the females they are only slightly thicker than the shaft. Many members of *Setabis* may be recognized by their bright blue, yellow, or orange coloration set in a black ground color. The genus apparently embraces upwards of thirty species, most which occur entirely in South America. Three species occur in Central America, all of which are treated here. In most literature, these butterflies have been referred to under the names *Orimba* or *Aricoris.*
Mimicry is important in this group. The females of *Setabis* can be brightly colored and involved in mimicry complexes with unpalatable

nymphalid butterflies (e.g., *Callicore*) and day-flying moths in the families Arctiidae, Notodontidae, and Geometridae (Figs. 19–21). Although the males typically have a more subdued coloration, they too may mimic certain arctiid moths. Moreover, the typically aposematic coloration and conspicuous flight behavior of some species suggest that a few of the butterflies in *Setabis* may be unpalatable to predators, and thus are Müllerian mimics.
Within the family Lycaenidae the caterpillars of some groups (e.g., Polyommatinae, Liphyrinae) are well known to be carnivorous on insects in the order Homoptera, or on the larvae of ants (Cottrell 1984). From cacao research done in Trinidad, Urich (in Kaye 1921) originally suggested that the caterpillars of *Setabis lagus* were carnivorous on scale insects. Recently, I. A. Chacon confirmed these observations by finding *Setabis lagus* caterpillars within the nest carton of ants feeding on nymphs of Membracidae and Jassidae (DeVries et al. 1994). Of special additional interest is that the abdomens of *Setabis* museum specimens are noticeably greasy—a trait found in some lycaenid butterflies that have carnivorous caterpillars (e.g., *Liphyra, Euliphyra*). These observations suggest that the carnivorous habit may be typical among members of *Setabis.*
In Costa Rica, members of *Setabis* are usually found only in lowland rain forest areas, except for *S. lagus*, which ranges into mid-elevation cloud forest habitats. The species in our area appear to be very local, never abundant, and two of the three species are quite rare.

Setabis lagus jansoni
(Butler, 1870)
FW length: 19.5–22.5 mm   **Plate 22**
Range: Honduras to Brazil. **Subspecies:** Honduras to Panama
Hostplant: Carnivorous on Membracidae and Jassidae (Homoptera) that have been found on *Annona* sp. (Annonaceae), *Doliocarpus* sp. (Dilleniaceae), *Conostegia xalapensis* (Melastomataceae), and *Vismia* sp. (Clusiaceae)
Early stages (Fig. 54a): *Egg*—blue with a highly sculptured chorion, laid on the carton that is produced by ants to cover their food resources. *Caterpillar*—overall coloration dull brown and similar to the color and texture of the nest carton that some ants build over the top of secretion-producing Homoptera and plant extrafloral nectaries (e.g., *Pheidole, Solenopsis, Wasmannia, Azteca*). Early instars are found inside the carton runs along stems and leaves, and the mature instars are found inside

the carton close to the main ant nest. All instars are carnivores on the nymphs of membracids or jassids. *Pupa*—overall beige, elongate in shape, with the abdomen and thorax forming the junction of two distinct curves; cremaster very flat and broad. Pupation takes place semigregariously within the carton near the main ant nest.
• **Adult:** Sexes dimorphic. *Male*—upperside deep blue with black margins, and a large white spot posterior to the end of the cell. The size of this white spot varies from specimen to specimen. The underside is brown, with the areas between the veins broadly white, and an obvious white spot near the FW cell. *Female*—FW upperside black with a broad, variable, transverse yellow band running from costa almost to the tornus. The HW upperside is deep blue in discal area with broad black margins. Underside dark brown with a conspicuous yellow band on FW; radial veins on HW gray, and distal margin of HW with white triangles between the veins. While in flight, the female resembles members of the nymphalid genus *Callicore*. Compare with *S. alcmaeon*.
Habits: This widespread butterfly is found in our area from sea level to 1500 m on both slopes in association with wet and rain forest habitats. Encountered as solitary individuals along trails, forest edges, streams, and in light gaps. Males perch from 1 to 8 m above the ground on the underside of leaves and make fast, circular sorties around the perching area between 12:30 and 14:00 hrs. In Panama, G. Small found populations that perched at about 15:00 hrs. The females are most frequently found in shady understory from midday until early afternoon. While flying, the females may be confused with the common nymphalid *Callicore lycas*. Between 11:00 and 12:00 hrs females oviposit on the main nest carton of arboreal ant colonies. Both sexes visit flowers of *Croton* (Euphorbiaceae), *Cordia* (Boraginaceae), *Tetrathylacium* (Flacourtiaceae), and *Serjania* (Sapindaceae).
Localities: [A]: Cariblanco (August), Reserva San Ramon (June), Atenas (April, August), 4.9 km S of Turucares (September), La Tigra de San Carlos (February, March). [C]: Turrialba (April, June–September), Juan Viñas (September), Moravia de Chirripo (April, June, July). [SJ]: Carrillo (March, April), El Rodeo (May, July–September), Rio Chirripo Pacifico, 5 km N of Rivas (September). [H]: Tirimbina (March), La Selva (April–June, August), Plastico (August, September). [P]: San Vito (April, August, September), Las Alturas (March, December). [L]: La Florida (March–October), Guapiles (May, July).

Setabis cleomedes
(Hewitson, 1870)
FW length: 17–19 mm   **Plate 22**
Range: Nicaragua to Panama
Hostplant: Unknown
Early stages: Unknown
• **Adult:** Sexes dimorphic. *Male*—upperside orange with broad, black wing margins and a few small white spots in FW apex. The orange on the FW is neatly outlined by the black costa and wing margins. *Female*—upperside yellow with a broad black area on the FW costa, apex, and both wing margins; two or three white dots set in the black FW apex that are most conspicuous on the underside. *Note:* based on the antennae and palpi, Seitz (1920) suggested that this species does not belong in the genus *Setabis*. Compare with *Calospila argenissa*, *Pachythone gigas*, *Monethe rudolphus*.
Habits: This butterfly is recorded in our area from sea level to 600 m on both slopes in association with rain forest habitats. Encountered as rare, solitary individuals along forest edges and rivers between 08:00 and 09:00 hrs. Both sexes perch under leaves with the wings open. In Costa Rica this species resembles moths in the families Arctiidae and Geometridae.
Localities: [C]: Turrialba (May, August). [P]: Rincon de Osa (April), Sirena (March), La Vacita (March).

Setabis alcmaeon alcmaeon
(Hewitson, 1876)
FW length: 20–23 mm   **Plate 22**
Range: Costa Rica to Colombia and Ecuador
Hostplant: Unknown
Early stages: Unknown
• **Adult:** Sexes dimorphic. *Male*—upperside black with blue on the FW base and inner margin, and then forming blue bands on the HW that run from base to distal margins; underside dark brown with indistinct white ray patterns between the veins. *Female*—FW with a broad white band with black veins, base of FW blue, and the areas between the HW veins dusted with blue and white; underside black with areas between the veins conspicuously white. Compare with *S. lagus*, *Brachyglenis esthema*, *Uraneis ucubis*.
Habits: This butterfly has been reported from our area from a single collection at 800 m on the Atlantic slope in association with rain forest. It is apparently a mimic of unpalatable, day-flying moths in the genus *Hypocritta* (Arctiidae). Judging from the series of specimens taken by G. Small in Panama, this species can be locally common.
Localities: [A]: Peñas Blancas (April).

Genus PSEUDONYMPHIDIA Callaghan, 1985

Beginning with its original description (Butler 1871), the placement of this butterfly has long been a taxonomic conundrum. Due to its superficial similarity to *Nymphidium*, the butterfly was historically placed in that genus even though it was recognized as being unrelated at the time of Butler's original description. The problem was partially solved when Callaghan (1982b) erected the monobasic *Pseudonympha* to contain it. However, the name *Pseudonympha* was preoccupied (and therefore invalid), and later the replacement name *Pseudonymphidia* was provided.

The monobasic genus *Pseudonymphidia* is separated from *Nymphidium* and relatives by its much-reduced last abdominal segment, and from other riodinid genera on the basis of its unusually stout thorax and abdomen, a characteristic of limited taxonomic use. The butterfly has been sporadically found from Mexico to Panama and is very rare throughout its range. Nothing is known of the early stages, but its systematic placement indicates that the caterpillars should form associations with ants.

Pseudonymphidia clearista
(Butler, 1871)
FW length: Male 21–22 mm   **Plate 22**
Range: Mexico to Panama
Hostplant: Unknown
Early stages: Unknown
• **Adult:** Sexes similar. Upperside snowy white with FW costa, apex, and distal margin broadly rich, warm brown; HW apex warm brown, and abdomen brown with white on the first few segments. Compare with *N. onaeum* and *Synargis nycteus*.
Habits: This utterly distinctive butterfly is unrecorded from Costa Rica. However, its geographical range and the types of habitats where it is found elsewhere in Central America make it virtually certain that this butterfly will be found in our area. According to the notes of G. Small (in Callaghan 1982b), in Panama the males are found in lowland forests, and may be encountered consistently at a particular spot perching high from 15:30 to 16:00 hrs. It has been recorded from March through June in a variety of habitats and localities in Mexico (de la Maza and de la Maza 1980). Considering the butterfly's rarity and the mysteries surrounding it, any observations on its early stages or biology would be worth publishing.
Localities: Not yet recorded for our area.

Genus THEOPE Doubleday, 1847

The butterflies in this genus are frequently mistaken by the casual entomologist for members of the Lycaenidae. On the whole, the majority of the *Theope* species are blue on the upperside, as in many lycaenids, but may be quickly recognized by the general tendency toward a dull monochrome underside. However, some species are yellow on the upperside (*eudocia*) or have prominent marks below (*cratylus, matuta*). Many of the species show pronounced sexual dimorphism.

Due to their great outward similarity, there has always been difficulty in assessing just how many species *Theope* contains, a problem that is very much in evidence today. For example, Seitz (1917) felt that most of the taxa were mainly forms or subspecies, and in some cases this has proved to be true. However, it is evident from the early stages and genitalia that there is a considerable number of undescribed species in the Central American fauna, some of which are currently placed under the same taxon that is thought to be widespread. In a more general context, we need only consider that more than half of all named species are thought to occur only in the Amazon Basin (many of which are extremely similar) and two things become evident: the number of species in this genus is probably seriously underestimated, and this group desperately needs a taxonomic revision. As currently understood, there are nearly fifty species of *Theope*, at least seventeen of which occur in our area, most of them rare.

The hostplant families for *Theope* include Sterculiaceae, Fabaceae, Bombacaceae, Cecropiaceae, Lecythidaceae, Euphorbiaceae, Convolvulaceae, and Cochlospermaceae (DeVries et al. 1994; Harvey 1987a). Available evidence suggests that particular species of *Theope* may utilize several families of plants, but as a group, the caterpillars are generally associated only with *Azteca* ants. The caterpillars have a prominent corona of balloon-setae circumscribing the head, and these inflated setae appear to provide some chemical stimuli to ants. For example, the *Azteca* ants that so belligerently tend the caterpillars may be observed to momentarily seize one of the balloons with their mandibles, release it, and then run about in an even more excited state than is normal for these ants. Such behavior on the part of the ants is similar to their response to their own alarm pheromones (see pp. 28–29). The caterpillars have well-developed vibratory papillae, produce strong calls, and one species (*matuta*) has two pairs of triple vibratory papillae—six in all (De-

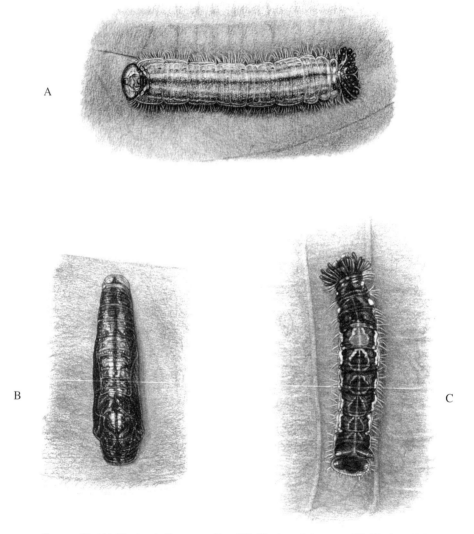

FIGURE 55. (A) *Theope virgilius* caterpillar. (B) *Theope matuta* pupa. (C) *Theope matuta* caterpillar. (Drawings by J. Clark)

Vries 1991c). The pupae are cylindrical, unadorned with any particularly obvious processes or colors, are often found in rolled edges of leaves, and superficially resemble those of *Nymphidium*.

In Central America, some of these butterflies generally perch on top of leaves in bright sunshine, their perching behavior strongly recalls members of the Lycaenidae, and the butterflies are seldom, if ever, abundant. Depending on the species these butterflies may fly low to the ground, or more frequently high in the forest canopy. As far as I am aware, all of the butterflies in *Theope* are fast, erratic fliers.

Theope virgilius
(Fabricius, 1793)
FW length: 17.5–19 mm   **Plate 23**

Range: Uncertain, but probably Mexico to Panama, Colombia
Hostplant: *Omphalea diandra* (Euphorbiaceae), *Inga* sp. (Fabaceae)
Early stages (Figs. 3e, 55a): *Egg*—white, rounded, flat lozenge shape that gives the impression of an overinflated inner tube contained in a coarse net that has been cut off around the slightly bulging dorsum, leaving a ropelike edge; the micropylar vents appear to be located under the ropy edge; lateral surface smooth, but the bulging dorsal surface is covered in a slightly raised pattern of polygons. The egg is laid singly on vigorously growing shoots and leaves, always in the presence of *Azteca* ants. *Caterpillars*—all instars have a pale green body; they fold leaf edges and rest inside the folds. *Mature caterpillar*—pale green with a scattering of small, indistinct white spots over dorsum; conspicuous anal plate with a horny texture, trimmed in black (including the tentacle nectary organ orifices); area between tentacle nectary organs dark brown; major area on dorsal part of anal plate whitish; body trimmed at lateral edges along vent with a skirt of white setae; head capsule shiny black with an inverted, white V-shape along the frontoclypeal sutures; a dense corona of prominent dark purple and black balloon setae that does not entirely obscure the head when viewed from above. When not feeding the later instar, caterpillars rest in leaves that may be some distance from the shoots. *Pupa*—uniformly brown, roundly cylindrical, and in overall form like that of *Nymphidium*. Pupation typically takes place inside the edge of a leaf that has been curled over and fixed with silk.
• **Adult:** Sexes dimorphic. *Male*—upperside blue with broadly black FW costa, apex, and distal margin such that the interface of the blue and black creates a straight edge cutting from the cell to the tornus; HW blue except for the distinctly black costal margin. Underside entirely creamy brown with a few, indistinct blue dots in the HW tornus. *Female*—upperside similar to male except the blue is paler, the blue and black interface on the FW is not as sharply defined, and one or two blue spots are set in the black FW subapex. The female also has more-rounded wings. *Note:* Several species may currently be placed under this name; in the absence of early stages, they can be separated only by details of the genitalia (D. Harvey, pers. comm.). Compare with *T. eupolis, publius, cratylus, speciosa.*
Habits: Specimens that appear to be of this species have been recorded from sea level to 800

m on both slopes. During March 1979, I found this butterfly to be especially abundant on Isla del Caño off the coast of the Osa Peninsula. Both sexes visit flowers of *Casearia, Terminalia, Psychotria, Cordia, Pentaclethra, Inga,* and herbaceous Asteraceae.
Localities: [H]: Chilamate (July). [P]: Cauhita (December), Palmar Norte (September), Isla del Caño (March), Sirena (February). [G]: La Cruz (November).

Theope eupolis
Schaus, 1890
FW length: 15–19 mm   Plate 23
Range: Uncertain, but probably Mexico to Costa Rica and Panama
Hostplant: Unknown
Early stages: Unknown
• **Adult:** Sexes dimorphic. *Male*—FW upperside black with pale blue confined to a small area from base to halfway across the inner margin; HW upperside pale blue with black on the costa, apex, and very broadly black at the distal margin such that the black bows into the blue toward the end of cell. *Female*—FW upperside black with pale blue extending from base, into and slightly beyond cell, then posterior toward the inner margin; HW upperside pale blue with indistinct gray-blue margin. Underside of both sexes similar to *virgilius.* Compare with *T. virgilius, publius, cratylus, speciosa.*
Habits: This butterfly has been recorded in our area from a single collection from an Atlantic lowland rain forest habitat. According to Seitz (1917) this species is apparently common in Mexico.
Localities: [H]: Magsaysay (September).

Theope speciosa
Godman and Salvin, 1897
FW length: 13–16.5 mm   Plate 24
Range: Costa Rica to Colombia
Hostplant: Unknown
Early stages: Unknown
• **Adult:** Sexes dimorphic. *Male*—upperside of FW black overshot with two shades of blue: deep royal blue in the subapex and at the base, and a pale, pearly blue along inner margin; except for the extreme margins, the HW upperside entirely pearly blue. *Female*—FW upperside pale blue with black margins and apex, with an almost circular black area in the tornus; HW upperside pale blue with a narrow black apex and distal margin. The underside of both sexes is similar to *virgilius. Note:* The female was described as *phineus* by Schaus (1913) from Costa Rica.

Habits: This butterfly has been recorded in our area from a single collection—the holotype of *phineus* housed in the U.S. National Museum. However, it will probably be found more extensively along the Atlantic lowlands as our fauna becomes better known.
Localities: Limon [TL of *phineus*].

Theope cratylus
Godman and Salvin, 1886
FW length: 19–21.5 mm   **Plate 23**
Range: Costa Rica and Panama
Hostplant: Unknown
Early stages: Unknown
• **Adult:** Sexes dimorphic. *Male*—FW upperside shining purple-blue with the broad black apex and margins defining an almost square area of blue; the distinctive FW apex sharply elongate; underside creamy tan colored with a few tiny black dots in the HW tornus. *Female*—upperside paler blue and the square area on FW less confined than the male, and the radial veins highlighted in black. Compare with *virgilius*, *eupolis*, *speciosa*.
Habits: This butterfly has been recorded in our area from sea level to 500 m on both slopes in association with rain forest habitats. In Panama, G. Small found it during the dry season and early rainy season in several localities in the canal area.
Localities: [A]: Rio Virilla de Guacima (September). [H]: Chilamate (March). [L]: Guapiles (March), Germania (September).

Theope eleutho
Godman and Salvin, 1897
FW length: 20–23 mm   **Plate 23**
Range: Mexico to Panama
Hostplant: *Inga* sp. (Fabaceae)
Early stages: *Mature caterpillar* (Figs. 7a,e,f, 56b)—head reddish brown with a white inverted V-shape along the frontoclypeal sutures, the center of which is darker; an extremely exaggerated corona of dark brown and black balloon setae surrounds the head; dorsal area of body brownish green with a broad, dark brown band at the interface of the dorsolateral areas; lateral areas pale green; the conspicuous anal plate is wider than the body and black in color, with marbled white on either side of a broad black midline; tentacle nectary organs conspicuously pink when everted. The caterpillars are tended tenaciously by *Azteca* ants. *Pupa*—uniformly brown, elongate, tapering from head to last abdominal segment, much like that of *Nymphidium*. Pupation takes place inside a leaf that is curled by the caterpillar prior to pupation.

• **Adult:** Sexes dimorphic. *Male*—FW upperside a shining blue with a broad black FW apex that cuts the blue in an oblique line from inside cell almost to tornus; the tip of FW apex bears a slight notch; HW upperside shining blue with a black costa that proceeds in a straight line from anterior edge of cell to the distal margin. The distinctive underside is a rich marbled brown with a grayish area on FW near end of cell, a dark wavy medial line that runs from the FW apex across the medial area of both wings, and curves basally to terminate at HW inner margin; five conspicuous white medial spots (two in the FW cell, and three in the HW discal area). The HW tornus produced into a short, curved tail. *Female*—upperside similar to male except paler blue, a blue subapical bar in the FW, and a HW tornus that is acuminate but not produced into a tail. Compare with *basilea*, *publius*.
Habits: This distinctive butterfly has been recorded in our area from sea level to 600 m elevation on both slopes in association with rain forest habitats. In Panama, G. Small found this butterfly in a variety of lowland forest sites, and in Mexico it has been found in premontane wet forest (de la Maza and White 1990). Uncommon.
Localities: [C]: Turrialba (July). [P]: Sirena (April), Palmar Sur (July).

Theope basilea
Bates, 1866
FW length: 20–21 mm   **Plate 23**
Range: Nicaragua to Colombia
Hostplant: Unknown
Early stages: Unknown
• **Adult:** Sexes dimorphic. *Male*—FW upperside dark blue and sharply confined by a broad black apex that bears an ill-defined brownish patch at end of cell; HW dark blue with the costal margin broadly and sharply defined black, and the distal margin narrowly black; underside reddish brown with a distinct medial line running from FW apex to HW inner margin, three white spots (two in the FW cell, one at the distal end of the HW cell), and the HW tornus acuminate. *Female*—upperside paler blue than in male, a blue rectangle in FW apex, the black borders confining the blue less sharply, and HW tornus rounded; underside with medial line as in male. Compare with *eleutho*, *publius*.
Habits: In our area this butterfly has been recorded from sea level to about 400 m on both slopes in habitats ranging from rain forest to deciduous forest. In Panama, I found both sexes visiting *Croton* flowers between 10:00 and

A

B

FIGURE 56. (A) *Theope* nr *publius* caterpillar being tended by *Azteca* sp. ants. At close quarters I observed the female oviposit the egg but was unable to capture her. The caterpillar died during pupation. (B) *Theope eleutho* caterpillar being tended by an *Azteca* sp. ant. Note the extremely prominent balloon setae around the head. (Drawings by J. Clark)

10:30 hrs. Uncommon in Costa Rican collections.
Localities: [P]: Carrara (October), Rio Catarata (September). [L]: 5.8 km S of Rio Blanco (September). [G]: Cañas (January).

Theope publius
Felder and Felder, 1861
FW length: 16.5–18 mm   **Plate 23**
Range: Costa Rica to Colombia, Venezuela
Hostplant: *Cassia* sp. (Fabaceae)
Early stages: Unknown, but see Figure 56a.
• **Adult:** Sexes dimorphic. *Male*—dark blue on the FW upperside roundly confined by a broad black apex that bears a distinct brown patch at end of cell; HW upperside almost entirely blue except for a thin black costa; underside with a wide, smeary medial line, no white spots in the cell areas, and a slightly produced HW tornus. *Female*—upperside pale blue, FW apex broadly black typically (but not always) with a white and blue rectangular subapical bar, and a rounded HW tornus; underside with medial line as in male. Compare with *basilea, eleutho.*
Habits: In our area this butterfly has been recorded from sea level to 700 m on both slopes in association with wet and rain forest habitats.

I found males during midday as rare, solitary individuals along well-shaded forest streams and rivers perching about 4 m above the ground. In Panama, G. Small found males perching between 14:00 and 15:00 hrs. On the Osa Peninsula, L. E. Gilbert collected a female that was ovipositing near an *Azteca* nest.
Localities: [A]: Florencia de San Carlos (August). [SJ]: Santa Rosa de Puriscal (May). [P]: Rincon de Osa (July), Manuel Antonio (September), Sirena (July), Rincon (July). [L]: Limon. [G]: Rio Piedras de Cañas (September, December).

Theope thebais
Hewitson, 1870
FW length: 17.5–20.5 mm   **Plate 24**
Range: Costa Rica to eastern Ecuador, Brazil, and Guianas
Hostplant: Unknown
Early stages: Unknown
• **Adult:** Sexes dimorphic. *Male*—upperside an intense, uniform deep blue that is sharply confined by broad black costa, apex, and margin on both wings; underside violet-brown with indistinct medial and postmedial bands that appear as a ray pattern where the brown crosses at each vein, and the base of each wing (espe-

cially the FW) with dull red; FW apex and HW tornus acuminate. *Female*—upperside a paler blue than the male; underside ray pattern indistinct and almost dirty looking, and the FW apex and HW tornus rounded. Compare with *matuta*.
Habits: In our area this butterfly has been recorded from both slopes in association with lowland rain forest habitats from sea level to about 300 m elevation. I have observed males perching high in the forest canopy in light gaps and along edges. The females fly along forest edges, in light gaps at ground level, and at the canopy level during midday. Both sexes visit flowers of *Tetrathylacium* and large *Serjania* vines in the canopy.
Localities: [H]: Chilamate (July), La Selva (December). [P]: Sirena (June).

Theope matuta
Godman and Salvin, 1897
FW length: 17.5–20.5 mm   **Plate 24**
Range: Costa Rica to Colombia, Venezuela
Hostplant: *Pseudobombax septenatum* (Bombacaceae)
Early stages (Figs. 3f, 8f, 55b,c): *Egg*—white with a flat micropylar area, heavily sculptured along the sides, and laid in small clusters. *Mature caterpillar*—head capsule shiny black with a conspicuous corona of dark purple balloon setae, and the unusual trait of bearing three pairs of vibratory papillae; body velvety black covered with inverted V-shapes on dorsum of each segment that are outlined in white; reddish brown lines at posterior edge of segments T2–3, A2–3; an irregular white band running along lateral edge of segments A2 and A3, interrupted at A4, and then present again along segments A5 and A6; venter a purplish pink that is conspicuous the full length of the body on lateral areas above the legs; black anal plate well developed with distal margins trimmed with purplish pink. *Pupa*—roundly cylindrical as in other congeners and uniformly brown in color. Pupation takes place inside the partially rolled edge of a leaf.
• **Adult:** Sexes dimorphic. *Male*—upperside an intense deep blue that is sharply confined by broad black costa, apex, and margin on both wings; HW with pale blue at base near costa that extends to distal end of cell; underside violet-brown with indistinct medial and postmedial bands that appear as a ray pattern where the brown crosses at each vein, and the base of each wing (especially the FW) with dull orange. The FW apex and HW tornus are acuminate. *Female*—upperside a paler blue than the male without being sharply confined

by black on the FW, underside ray pattern almost dirty looking, but with the radial veins distinct, and the FW apex and HW tornus rounded. *Note*: It is probable that this species is the one recently described by D'Abrera (1994) as *zyzyxoxyx*. Compare with *thebais*.
Habits: In our area this distinctive butterfly is recorded from a single Pacific lowland rain forest locality. In Panama I observed males perching high in the forest canopy in light gaps and along edges. The females fly along forest edges, in light gaps at ground level, and at the canopy level during midday. Both sexes visit flowers of *Tetrathylacium* and large *Serjania* vines at the canopy level.
Localities: [P]: Sirena.

Theope acosma
Stichel, 1910
FW length: 12.5–13.5 mm   **Plate 24**
Range: Costa Rica to Colombia
Hostplant: Unknown
Early stages: Unknown
• **Adult:** Sexes similar. Upperside orange-yellow with black on FW that begins at costa near base, extends broadly across apex (without entering the cell), then narrows along distal margin to stop at tornus. Underside entirely orange-yellow except for a few dark scales on the HW fringe. *Note*: This species has been considered a form of *eudocia*, and its status can perhaps be resolved by a comparative study of the genitalia or of the early stages when they are known. Compare with *eudocia*.
Habits: This butterfly has been recorded in our area from a single Atlantic lowland rain forest locality. In Panama, G. Small found this butterfly during the dry season at several sites ranging from sea level to about 600 m.
Localities: [H]: La Virgen de Sarapiqui (March).

Theope eudocia pulchralis
Stichel, 1910
FW length: 14–14.5 mm   **Plate 24**
Range: Nicaragua to Peru. **Subspecies:** Nicaragua to Panama
Hostplant: *Theobroma cacao* (Sterculiaceae)
Early stages: Kirkpatrick (1953) reported that the caterpillars in Trinidad feed on new leaves. *Mature caterpillar*—body apple green with a darker dorsal stripe, and covered with minute, pale setae (a few are black) and a lateral fringe of longer pale setae. Prothorax with nearly one hundred balloon setae projecting forward over the head; some of the setae are black, others brown, of varying sizes, with some long pale setae among them. Meso-

thorax with purplish subdorsal stripes, small purple subdorsal spots at the posterior margin of the metathorax and first seven abdominal segments, and a purple dorsal stripe on segments 7–9 that expands laterally on segment 8 to form a cross. The dorsum of segment 9 is enlarged into a flat saddle that covers segment 10. Invariably tended by ants.

• **Adult:** Sexes dimorphic. *Male*—FW upperside orange-yellow with black along costa starting from the base, extending broadly across one half of wing and entering the cell, and then terminating broadly along distal margin at tornus; the black FW apex set with a distinctive blue patch; HW upperside entirely yellow-orange. *Female*—upperside yellow-orange with no blue in FW apex, and black on FW that begins at the base and broadly covers apex and distal margin. Both sexes have dark fringe on HW distal margin. Compare with *acosma*.

Habits: In our area this butterfly has been recorded from sea level to about 1000 m on both slopes. Judging from locality records, it appears to fly during dry periods. Although I have never seen it alive, one could imagine that the casual entomologist might mistake this butterfly for a species of *Eurema* (Pieridae).

Localities: [L]: Limon (February), Banana River (March). [G]: Rincon de la Vieja (September), Miravalles.

Theope thestias decorata
Godman and Salvin, 1878
FW length: 11.5–12 mm   **Plate 24**
Range: Nicaragua to Bolivia. **Subspecies:** Costa Rica and Panama
Hostplant: Unknown
Early stages: Unknown
• **Adult:** Sexes dimorphic. *Male*—upperside black with a deep lustrous blue area confined to an irregular bar along the anal margin; HW upperside deep lustrous blue with indistinct black margins; underside yellow-gray with cream yellow at the base of both wings (especially the FW) and a reflective blue semicircle (best seen in oblique light) extending from the FW costa and curving below apex almost to distal margin. *Female*—paler blue on the upperside, and without the blue semicircle on the FW underside. Compare with *guillaumei*.

Habits: This butterfly has been recorded in Costa Rica on both slopes from two disparate rain forest localities, one in the Reventazon Valley, and the other from the Osa Peninsula. As has been pointed out to me by J. Hall, almost all specimens of this butterfly are females. Rare in Central American collections.

Localities: [C]: Turrialba. [P]: Llorona (January), Sirena (March, June).

Theope guillaumei cecropia
DeVries and Hall, 1996
FW length: 11.5–12 mm   **Plate 25**
Range: Costa Rica and French Guiana. **Subspecies:** Costa Rica
Hostplant: *Cecropia peltata* (Cecropiaceae)
Early stages: *Mature caterpillar* (Fig. 57b)—body gray with a rich maroon broad dorsal midline that has the distal edges somewhat jagged and bordered by white; a conspicuous black dot on the posterior margin of all abdominal segments; anal plate with a distinct central black triangle with the apex directed toward posterior; areas distal to this triangle pale pink; the areas surrounding the tentacle nectary organs rich maroon; head brown, surrounded by a sparse corona of short brown balloon setae; the anterior edge of the first thoracic segment, the interface of all abdominal segments, and the venter with fairly long white setae. The caterpillars are semigregarious and skeletonize the underside of the leaf near the radiating central veins. Interestingly, these caterpillars are not tended by the *Azteca* ants that inhabit the *Cecropia* tree, but rather by *Solenopsis* (the *Diplorhoptrum* group) ants that form small colonies in the radiating leaf veins at the base of the petiole. The caterpillars are loosely gregarious. Pupation takes place in a curled edge of the hostplant leaf.

• **Adult:** Sexes dimorphic. *Male*—perhaps simlar to female, but the unique male is badly crumpled, and imperfectly known (see DeVries and Hall 1996). *Female*—upperside pale blue with broad black on FW costa, apex, and distal margins; veins on HW with conspicuous black elongate triangles where they meet the distal margin; underside semishiny, light brown, with an indistinct yellowish cast along distal margins of both wings; FW costa golden yellow from base almost to end of cell. The species may be distinguished by not having the reflective blue on the underside of the FW, and the yellow not extending to base of both wings. Compare with *decorata*.

Habits: This diminutive butterfly is known in our area only from a single Atlantic lowland rain forest locality. The species originally came to light during the course of J. Longino's study on *Cecropia* and *Azteca* ant interactions (see Longino 1991). In 1989 at La Selva he pointed out a group of riodinid caterpillars to me on an individual *Cecropia* tree and suggested that it might be something of interest. It clearly was. Intermittently over the subsequent two

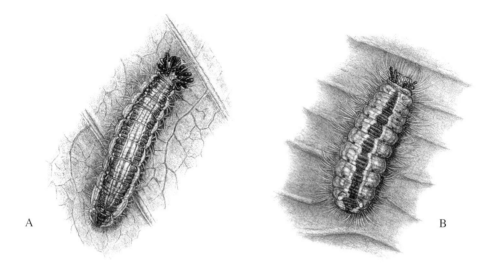

A

B

FIGURE 57. (A) *Theope lycaenina* caterpillar. (B) *Theope guillaumei cecropia* caterpillar. (Drawings by J. Clark)

years I examined this individual tree and many others in the area without finding more caterpillars. I have never seen this butterfly in any Central American collection or in nature as an adult. Obviously quite rare.
Localities: [H]: La Selva (February, March).

Theope barea
Godman and Salvin, 1878
FW length: 12.5–14 mm   Plate 24
Range: Costa Rica to Colombia
Hostplant: Unknown
Early stages: Unknown
• **Adult:** Sexes dimorphic. *Male*—FW upperside black with dark blue along the inner margin running from base to tornus, and filling most of the cell; HW upperside blue; underside entirely pale yellow. *Female*—FW upperside dusty black with a large pale blue triangular area that runs from base, along inner margin, and then to end of cell; HW upperside pale blue with broad dusty black costa and apex. *Note*: This taxon has been referred to under the synonym *caenina* Godman and Salvin, 1878 (G. Lamas, pers. comm.). Compare with *herta*, *pedias*.
Habits: This butterfly has been recorded in our area from three distinct habitats: Atlantic lowland rain forest, mid-elevation wet habitat, and

Pacific lowland deciduous forest. Uncommon in Costa Rican collections.
Localities: [A]: Alajuela (March). [C]: Tuis (March). [G]: Bagaces.

Theope herta
Godman and Salvin, 1886
FW length: 13–14 mm   Plate 24
Range: Costa Rica(?) and Panama
Hostplant: Unknown
Early stages: Unknown
• **Adult:** Sexes dimorphic. *Male*—FW upperside dull black with blue along the inner margin; HW upperside dirty gray-black with a dusting of blue scales from base into the cell; underside silver-gray with tiny black spots between veins on HW distal margin, and a blush of yellow on FW costa. *Female*—FW upperside similar to male except paler blue; HW upperside blue-gray on distal three-quarters, much like lycaenids in the subfamily Polyommatinae; underside as in male. Compare with *lycaenina* and *barea*.
Habits: As far as I am aware, this butterfly has not been formally recorded in our area. However, as it was originally described from Bugaba in Panama, it is likely to be found in areas near the Osa Peninsula. In the original description (Godman and Salvin 1886) and

the subsequent treatment by Seitz (1917), this butterfly has been considered rare. In Panama, G. Small found this butterfly on both slopes in several lowland rain forest localities. **Localities:** Not yet unrecorded for our area.

Theope pedias isia
Godman and Salvin, 1878
FW length: 13–14 mm   **Plate 24**
Range: Mexico to Brazil. **Subspecies:** Mexico to Panama
Hostplant: Unknown
Early stages: Unknown
• **Adult:** Sexes dimorphic. *Male*—FW upperside deep blue circumscribed by a broad black margin, costa, and tornus in such a manner that the blue is confined from base, along half of the inner margin, and through discal area beyond cell. Underside entirely dull violet. *Female*—upperside deep blue with broad black FW costa and margin, and a thin black HW margin; underside as in male. Compare with *phaeo* and *barea*.
Habits: This butterfly has been recorded in our area from sea level to 1500 m on both slopes in association with forest types ranging from lowland rain forest to semideciduous forest. Encountered as solitary individuals from 12:30 to 15:00 hrs along forest edges, gaps, or in open pastures visiting plants with small white flowers.
Localities: [A]: San Mateo (December). [C]: Juan Viñas (June). [H]: La Selva (May, December), Chilamate (December). [P]: Rincon (February), Las Alturas (March).

Theope phaeo folia
Godman and Salvin, 1886
FW length: 14.5–16 mm   **Plate 24**
Range: Nicaragua to the Amazon Basin. **Subspecies:** Nicaragua to Colombia
Hostplant: Unknown
Early stages: Unknown
• **Adult:** Sexes dimorphic. *Male*—FW upperside deep blue with broad black margin, especially at the produced apex; HW deep blue with black at the apex; tornus acuminate and accented by a small scallop in the anal margin; underside dirty gray overshot with a violet-pink that is best seen when viewed obliquely. *Female*—FW upperside deep blue with a deep intrusion of black at distal margin that runs just posterior to cell; HW deep blue with white along anal margin; underside similar to male but overshot with more pink. Compare with *pedias*.
Habits: I am aware of only one collection of this butterfly from our area taken by O. Pagels on

the Atlantic slope in premontane forest. In eastern Panama, G. Small found this butterfly at several premontane forest localities. Rare in Central American collections.
Localities: [H]: Bajo Rodriguez.

Theope lycaenina
Bates, 1868
FW length: 13–14.5 mm   **Plate 25**
Range: Costa Rica, Panama to eastern Brazil
Hostplant: *Maripa panamensis* (Convolvulaceae)
Early stages: *Mature instar* (Fig. 57a)—head capsule shiny black with inverted white V-shape along suture lines of frons and clypeus; a dense corona of dark purple to black balloons, with a few white balloons at posterior edge The body with wide pale green dorsal band bordered on either side by a mottled band of purplish, reddish, and white dots; each of these lateral bands has seven to eight white dots at the posterior margins of the abdominal segments; the band is bordered ventrally by a pale green band that has a white longitudinal stripe running its entire length; anal plate transparent on posterior and lateral edges except for a black band that starts at the area between the tentacle nectary organs and then runs to posterior edge as a medial band; body trimmed at lateral edges at ventrum with a skirt of white setae. The caterpillars are tended tenaciously by *Azteca* ants. *Pupa*—pale green, often folded inside a leaf of the hostplant, but it may even be covered with a thin layer of carton built by the *Azteca* workers.
• **Adult:** Sexes dimorphic. *Male*—FW upperside blue confined by broad black costa, apex, and margins with radial veins highlighted in black; HW sparsely blue with indistinct black margins; underside entirely a dull industrial gray, with cream-yellow on FW costa near base, and a few tiny black dots on HW margin near tornus; legs cream-yellow. *Female*—similar to male except paler blue on upperside, and the cream-yellow FW costa on underside less distinct. Compare with *herta*.
Habits: This butterfly has been recorded in our area from a single lowland Pacific locality. In Panama this butterfly is not uncommon in areas surrounding the canal, including the more urban parts of Panama City. Both sexes are active from midmorning until early afternoon. The females are frequently observed fluttering above the new shoots of the hostplant which are growing near large colonies of *Azteca* ants. During oviposition the ants will occasionally disturb the butterfly, although I have never seen them attack her aggressively.
Localities: [P]: Sirena (March).

Genus NYMPHIDIUM
Fabricius, 1807

The butterflies in this genus typically have a conspicuous white or yellow medial band across both wings, long antennae, a tendency for the FW to be slightly elongate, and the sexes similar. The elongate antennae of *Nymphidium* generally separates them from similar species of *Synargis*, *Juditha*, *Pixus*, and *Pseudonymphidia*. Members of *Nymphidium* are found from Mexico throughout Central and South America, and by far the greatest number of species occur in the Amazon Basin. As currently understood, over thirty species are embraced by *Nymphidium*. Of the six or seven species that occur in our area, about half are rather rare. Pertinent literature on the genus includes Callaghan (1985, 1986c, 1988, 1989).

The host plants of *Nymphidium* are predominantly Fabaceae, especially the genus *Inga*, with some records from the Convolvulaceae, Malpighiaceae, Sapindaceae, Passifloraceae, Lecythidaceae (DeVries et al. 1994), and Loranthaceae (DeVries, unpublished). The caterpillars are naked, have a full compliment of ant organs, no prominent head horns, and typically bear only a few balloon setae on the first thoracic segment. However, at least one species (*mantus*) has a well-developed corona of balloon setae much like those found in *Theope* (Figs. 58c, 59a). All the caterpillars have vibratory papillae, but some species are unable to produce a call due to a peculiar arrangement of mushroomlike setae on the epicranium that apparently do not allow the vibratory papillae to contact the head (DeVries 1991c). *Nymphidium* is the only genus known where the presence of vibratory papillae does not always correlate with the ability to produce calls. The caterpillars are most frequently encountered drinking extrafloral nectar at the prominent nectaries on the new shoots of *Inga*. Available evidence indicates that the caterpillars generally associate with a wide diversity of ants. The pupae are cylindrical, unadorned with any particularly obvious processes or colors, are often found in rolled edges of leaves, and resemble those of *Theope*.

In Costa Rica these butterflies are typical denizens of most types of forest habitats below 1500 m. As a rule, all of the species have a weak and fluttery flight. Although the butterflies can be common, especially during their periodical population explosions at local sites, I have seldom noticed marked perching times for most of our species.

Nymphidium mantus
(Cramer, 1775)
FW length: 14–14.5 mm   **Plate 22**
Range: Costa Rica to Venezuela and Brazil
Hostplant: *Maripa panamensis* (Convolvulaceae), *Inga ruiziana* (Fabaceae), the flowers of *Gustavia superba* (Lecythidaceae) and *Serjania mexicana* (Sapindaceae)
Early stages (Figs. 58c, 59a,b): *Egg*—tiny, white, laid singly (although repeatedly) on leaves and stems, always in the presence of *Azteca* ants. *Mature caterpillar*—body dull green with a tinge of purple, and a thin white line that runs along the entire interface of the venter and lateral segments; anal plate pale green; head capsule dark brown with either a prominent white spot in the center of the face (most common), or occasionally with a white ring on the face (the white circle being mostly filled in). Depending on the individual, the balloon setae may be of two color forms. Typically the area behind the head has conspicuous balloon setae, with the lateral ones white and the dorsal ones deep purple. However, some caterpillars may have all of the balloon setae redbrown. The middle of the first thoracic segment is not covered with balloon setae. *Note*: The well-developed balloon setae are reminiscent of those found typically on *Theope*, perhaps suggesting that this butterfly may be better placed in another genus. The caterpillars feed only on soft young leaves, and when not feeding they roll the edge of a leaf into a semitube and hide inside. They are always tenaciously tended by *Azteca* sp. ants. *Pupa*—pale green without any noticeable adornments. Pupation generally takes place inside a semirolled leaf edge where the caterpillar has previously fed.
• **Adult:** Sexes similar. Distinguished by the beautiful reflective blue on the upperside of both wings, and the wide white band running from FW subapex to HW inner margin, including across the first few segments of the abdomen. Compare with *olinda*.
Habits: This butterfly has been recorded in our area from a single specimen in the C. Lankester collection housed in the British Natural History Museum, and judging from the associated material, it is likely that the specimen originated from the Atlantic lowlands. In the canal area of Panama, this butterfly is present throughout the year, and I typically encountered it as solitary individuals flying from 3 to 4 m above the ground along forest edges, roadcuts, and streams, and occasionally inside the forest. The females were frequently ob-

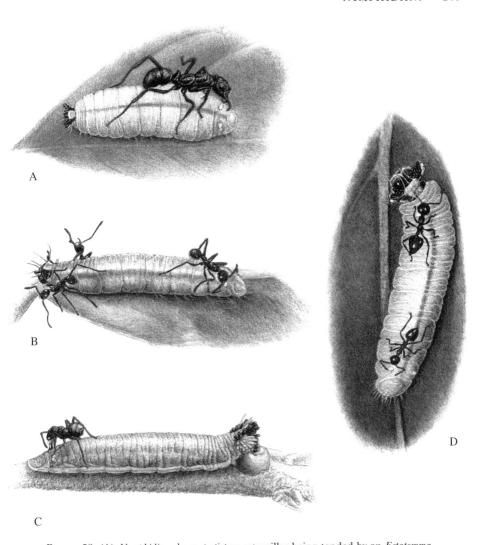

FIGURE 58. (A) *Nymphidium haematostictum* caterpillar being tended by an *Ectatomma ruidum* ant. (B) *Nymphidium onaeum* caterpillar being tended by *Pheidole* sp. ants. (C) *Nymphidium mantus* caterpillar tended by an *Azteca* sp. ant. Note that the corona of balloon setae strongly recall those of the genus *Theope*. (D) *Nymphidium ascolia* caterpillar being tended by *Crematogaster* sp. ants. (Drawings by J. Clark)

served to oviposit between 11:30 and 14:00 hrs, always in the presence of *Azteca* ants. I never observed the ants attack the butterfly even when she landed in the midst of them. A female typically lays a single egg on a plant, flies a short distance away to a sun fleck (often alighting under a leaf), rests for a few minutes, then returns to the same place to lay more single eggs.

Localities: "Costa Rica."

Nymphidium olinda
Bates, 1865
FW length: 16–16.5 mm   **Plate 22**

Range: Costa Rica(?), Panama to Venezuela, Brazil
Hostplant: Unknown
Early stages: Unknown
• **Adult:** Sexes similar. Similar to *mantus*, but without the reflective component in the blue on the upperside, and the distal margin of HW narrowly white. Compare with *mantus* and *lenocinium*.
Habits: This species has not been recorded from our area, but a record from the old locality "Bugaba" and its occurrence elsewhere in Panama suggest that it should be in areas near the Osa Peninsula. Judging from what I have observed in Ecuador, the behavior of the adult is similar to those described for *mantus*. In Panama near the canal area, it has been recorded for most months of the year.
Localities: Not yet recorded for our area.

Nymphidium lenocinium
Schaus, 1913
FW length: 13–13.5 mm   **Plate 22**
Range: Costa Rica to Colombia
Hostplant: Unknown
Early stages: Unknown
• **Adult:** Sexes similar. Upperside white with the dark wing margins inset with black scalloping along the distal margins; underside white with grayish blue FW costa and distal margin, and HW margins with dark lunules between veins at the distal margin. Compare with *olinda*.
Habits: In Costa Rica this butterfly has been recorded from sea level to 600 m on both slopes in association with rain forest habitats. Once at 13:20 hrs I collected a male that came to rest on the underside of a sunlit leaf about 3 m above the ground along a secondary forest edge. Prior to alighting it flew fairly fast for a member of *Nymphidium*, but it showed the characteristic zigzag flight typical of the genus. During flight the butterfly ranged from 1 to about 4 m above the ground, always flying in direct sunshine. Rare in Central American collections.
Localities: [C]: Turrialba (April), La Florida [TL]. [P]: Pirris (March).

Nymphidium azanoides occidentalis
Callaghan, 1986
FW length: 21–22 mm   **Plate 22**
Range: Costa Rica to Panama, Ecuador, Brazil.
Subspecies: Costa Rica to Ecuador
Hostplant: *Inga* spp. (Fabaceae)
Early stages: *Egg*—white, deposited singly in small clusters of five to six on new shoots, stems, or buds of sapling plants. *Mature caterpillar*—body pale green with a white dorsal mid-line; head shiny brown with a sparse corona of brown balloon, and a few long white setae that project over the head. The caterpillars are tended by *Pheidole biconstricta* and *Pheidole* sp. ants.
• **Adult:** Sexes similar. Upperside white with both wing margins and FW costa mottled black; HW with a conspicuous reddish orange submarginal band set into the mottled black border that varies in length from specimen to specimen. Underside overshot with a dull cast, and FW cell with three to four elongate black triangles thinly bordered with white. Compare with *onaeum, ascolia, Pixus corculum*.
Habits: This butterfly is found in our area from sea level to 400 m on the Atlantic slope in association with primary and secondary forest habitats. Both males and females are active from 11:00 to 14:00 hrs in shaded understory along trails, rivers, and streams. Their slow, fluttery flight makes them quite obvious to the casual observer. At times these butterflies may be encountered as small, localized colonies around saplings or sucker sprouts of the hostplants. The females oviposit single eggs, then fly away to rest for a few moments to sit in the sun, and then return to ovipositing. An individual female may lay up to ten eggs on a single shoot during the course of an hour. In Panama, G. Small found males perching between 14:00 and 15:00 hrs. Both sexes visit flowers of *Lantana, Psychotria, Cordia, Croton,* and other small white flowers. Common.
Localities: [C]: Turrialba (August). [H]: Magsaysay (August, November), Tirimbina (February), La Selva (February–April, September), Chilamate (May–July). [L]: Siquirres (January, March, September), Guapiles (April), La Florida (March–June, October), Bannanito Sur (September).

Nymphidium haematostictum
Godman and Salvin, 1878
FW length: 19–20 mm   **Plate 22**
Range: Costa Rica and Panama
Hostplant: *Inga* spp. (Fabaceae)
Early stages (Fig. 58a): *Egg*—white, deposited singly in clusters of three to four on new shoots, stems, or buds of sapling plants. *Mature caterpillar*—body pale, translucent green; dorsum of first thoracic segment green with white along anterior edge, and flanked on either side with a few dark balloon setae; head shiny black. The caterpillars do not produce a call, even though they possess vibratory papillae. Associated with *Crematogaster* sp. (Myrmicinae) ants.
• **Adult:** Sexes similar. Upperside pale yellow

with FW costa, apex, and distal margin broadly brown; subapex with a small yellow spot set in the brown; HW distal margin with conspicuous red-orange submarginal band at the tornus (the width of the band is variable, and typically wider south of Costa Rica). *Note*: It may be that this taxon is a synonym of the South American species *chimborazium* Bates, 1868, which occurs in Colombia and Ecuador. Compare with *onaeum*, *ascolia*, *Pixus corculum*. **Habits:** In Costa Rica this butterfly is known only from the Atlantic slope in association with lowland rain forest. In our area this butterfly is curiously rare. In Panama, however, I made numerous observations on this butterfly where both males and females were encountered as solitary individuals from 11:00 to 14:00 hrs in shaded understory along trails, rivers, and streams. The females were commonly found fluttering around the vigorously growing shoots of *Inga* saplings. Both sexes visit flowers of *Croton, Cordia, Alibertia*, various Asteraceae, and other low-growing plants with white flowers. Although rare in Costa Rican collections, I suspect that it may be found to be locally abundant in the areas around Bribri, and in the Valle de Estrella. **Localities:** [L]: Sixaola.

Nymphidium ascolia ascolia
Hewitson, 1853
FW length: 19–20 mm Plate 22
Range: Guatemala to Brazil, Bolivia. **Subspecies:** Guatemala to Brazil
Hostplant: *Inga* spp. (Fabaceae)
Early stages (Figs. 3d, 58d): *Egg*—white, globular with a distinctly flattened dorsum; heavily sculptured with wavy, inset rows of ellipses; the flattened dorsum has a smeary raised area that is reminiscent of cake frosting, and the central micropyle consists of a single, deeply recessed pore. The egg is typically deposited in small clusters of eight to fifteen against a prominent vein or on newly emerging leaves and stems, although a female may deposit smaller clusters. *Mature caterpillar*—body overall a pale yellow-green with broad white bands on either side of the dorsal midline; head capsule shiny black with a white inverted V on the face; first thoracic segment white on dorsum, flanked on either side by a few dark balloon setae. The caterpillars roll the dorsal edges of leaves and hide inside when not feeding, and are frequently found drinking at extrafloral nectaries. The caterpillars do not produce a call, even though they have vibratory papillae. Associated with *Paratrechina* sp. (Formicinae), *Crematogaster* sp., *Pheidole* sp., *Solenopsis* sp., and

Megalomyrmex foreli (Myrmicinae) ants. *Pupa*—pale green, cylindrical with widest portion at the head, and a dark spot over the eyes. Pupation typically takes places inside a semirolled leaf and occurs either on or off the hostplant. • **Adult:** Sexes similar. Upperside pale yellow with broad, dirty-brown margins on both wings, and a short red-orange submarginal band confined to the HW tornus. However, this submarginal band is variable and may be absent on some specimens. *Note*: In much literature this taxon has been referred to as *cachrus ascolides*, a combination of a different species (*cachrus*) and a synonym (*ascolides*). Compare with *onaeum* and *haematostictum*. **Habits:** In our area this butterfly occurs commonly from sea level to 1400 m on both slopes in virtually all moist or wet forest habitats. I have found it especially common in areas around the Osa Peninsula. Curiously, Godman and Salvin (1886) had abundant material from Nicaragua and Panama, but none from Costa Rica. This suggests either that collectors simply did not bother with it, or that there has been as increase in abundance (reflected as a range extension) since that time, perhaps due to extensive deforestation in recent years. Encountered as solitary individuals along forest edges, light gaps, roadcuts and streams from 09:30 to 14:00 hrs. The females generally oviposit between 11:00 and 12:30 hrs, and may do so on plants with and without the presence of ants. In Panama, G. Small found males perching between 14:00 and 15:00 hrs. Both sexes visit flowers of *Lantana camara, Cordia, Psychotria, Croton*, and various herbaceous Asteraceae.
Localities: [A]: San Mateo (October), Atenas (February–April, August, September). [SJ]: El Rodeo (July, August), Desamparados (September), Desamparaditos (September). [H]: Chilamate (September), La Selva (April). [P]: Carrara (May), Piedras Blancas (June), Sirena (February, April, July), Quepos (January, February, July), Monte Verde (September), San Vito (April–June, September–November), Las Alturas (September, December), Parrita (December), Rincon de Osa (February), Rio Catarata (September), Rio Cacao (September), Chacarita (September), Avangarez. [L]: Bananito (April, September), Tortuguerro (July), Limon.

Nymphidium onaeum
Hewitson, 1869
FW length: 15–20.5 mm Plate 22
Range: Honduras to Panama

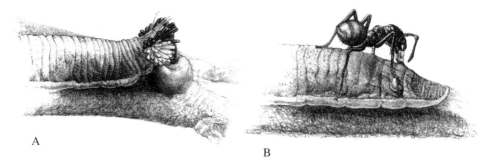

A

B

FIGURE 59. (A) Detail of *Nymphidium mantus* caterpillar drinking extrafloral nectar from its *Inga* sp. hostplant. (B) Detail of an *Azteca* sp. ant drinking from an everted tentacle nectary organ of a *Nymphidium mantus* caterpillar. (Drawings by J. Clark)

Hostplant: *Inga* spp. (Fabaceae), *Cassia fruticosa* (Fabaceae), *Heteropteris* sp. (Malpighiaceae) **Early stages** (Fig. 58b): *Egg*—white, lozenge shaped, laid in small clusters of five to ten on new shoots and stems. *Mature caterpillar*—very similar to that of *ascolia* except often with a brownish green cast to body and indistinct bands on either side of dorsal midline. The caterpillars do not produce a call, even though they have vibratory papillae. Associated with *Pheidole* and *Solenopsis* ants.
• **Adult:** Sexes similar. Upperside white area on the FW distinctly triangular, and broadly bordered with dark brown along costa and distal margin; FW often with two short red bands in cell, and a short, red submarginal band in FW tornus (red may be absent in specimens to the south); HW broadly white with dark brown distal margins; HW always with short, red submarginal band in tornus. *Note:* This taxon has been referred to in older literature as a subspecies of *chione* Bates, 1867. Compare with *azanoides, ascolia, Juditha molpe, Pixus corculum.*
Habits: In our area this butterfly has been recorded from sea level to 1000 m mainly on the Atlantic slope in association with rain and wet

forests. However, I collected an ovipositing female from the mountain pass between Volcan Miravalles and Volcan Santa Maria, suggesting that the butterfly crosses to the Pacific slope in appropriately moist habitats. Encountered as solitary individuals from 10:00 to 13:00 hrs along forest edges, gaps, or deep in the forest. In Panama, G. Small found males perching between 15:30 and 17:00 hrs. Typically the butterflies fly less than 3 m above the ground, but they may occasionally ascend into the subcanopy along forest edges. An individual female may oviposit many eggs on the same new shoot after resting between oviposition bouts. Both sexes visit flowers of *Psychotria, Croton,* and herbaceous Asteraceae.
Localities: [A]: San Gabriel Dos Rios (May), Grecia (December), Cariblanco (March–July, September, October). [C]: Tapanti (November), Juan Viñas (January); Cachi (February, March), Moravia de Chirripo (February, April), Turrialba (March, May, June), Rio Chitaria (March). [SJ]: Carrillo (February, May, September). [H]: La Selva (February, March), Tirimbina (September). [L]: Guapiles (March, May, September).

SOME MAJOR COLLECTING LOCALITIES IN COSTA RICA

The following localities are listed by province and represent some of the best known sites in Costa Rica with respect to the Riodinidae. However, this list is far from comprehensive and differs slightly from that found in DeVries (1987). The elevation for montane areas and the latitude-longitude bearings are approximated. For example, in Parque Corcovado, the single coordinate point will locate the general area, but it is not meant to impose exact boundaries. Other useful references for Costa Rican geography and locality descriptions may be found in Noriega (1923), Selander and Vaurie (1962), Holdridge (1967), and Blutstein et al. (1970).

Some of the localities listed here include more than one life zone. Those instances separated by a hyphen represent a series of life zones, whereas those separated with a comma indicate separate life zones. The life zones are taken from the Holdridge Life Zone system map printed by the Tropical Science Center, San José, Costa Rica. Each number refers to a distinct life zone, as follows: 1, tropical dry forest; 2, tropical dry forest, moist province transition; 3, tropical moist forest; 4, tropical moist forest, prehumid province transition; 5, tropical moist forest, premontane belt transition; 6, tropical wet forest; 7, tropical wet forest, premontane belt transition; 8, premontane moist forest; 9, premontane wet forest, basal belt transition; 10, premontane wet forest; 11, premontane wet forest, basal belt transition; 12, premontane wet forest, rain forest transition; 13, premontane rain forest; 14, lower montane moist forest; 15, lower montane wet forest; 16, lower montane rain forest; 17, montane wet forest; 18, montane rain forest; 19, subalpine rain paramo.

An asterisk (*) indicates a locality worked extensively by William Schaus, a dagger (†) indicates a locality worked extensively by I. A. Chacon, and a black dot (•) indicates a locality worked extensively by P. J. DeVries.

ALAJUELA PROVINCE

Locality	Elevation (meters)	Latitude/Longitude	Life Zone
Abangares	100	10°15n–85°00w	2
Atenas	500	09°58n–84°23w	8
Cariblanco•	850	10°16n–84°10w	7
Colonia Blanca	500	10°50n–85°10w	6
Virgen del Socorro†	700	10°14n–84°12w	7
La Cinchona	1300	10°13n–84°09w	13
La Libertad	600	10°50n–85°05w	7
Parque Volcán Poas	2000–2700	10°12n–84°15w	16,17
San Mateo*	500	09°56n–84°31w	5
San Ramon	700	10°05n–84°39w	3

CARTAGO PROVINCE

Curridibat	1400	09°55n–84°02w	8
Cachi*	1100	09°50n–83°48w	10
Estrella	1600	09°48n–83°57w	15
Juan Viñas*	1300	09°54n–83°45w	15
La Carpintera	1850	09°53n–83°58w	15
La Suiza	800	09°51n–83°37w	10
Moravia de Chirripo†	1000	09°52n–83°25w	10
Orosi	1300	09°48n–83°51w	13
Redondo	1300	09°59n–83°58w	12

CARTAGO PROVINCE (*cont.*)

Locality	Elevation (meters)	Latitude/Longitude	Life Zone
Tapanti	1400	09°46n–83°48w	13
Tres Rios*	1400	09°54n–83°41w	12
Tuis*	1200	09°51n–83°35w	13
Turrialba•	600	09°54n–83°41w	11
Parque Volcán Irazu	2800–3400	09°58n–83°53w	17,18
Volcán Turrialba	2800–3400	09°02n–83°46w	17,18

SAN JOSÉ PROVINCE

Bajo La Hondura	1600	10°04n–84°00w	13
Copey	2000–2600	09°39n–83°54w	15
Desamparados	1000	09°54n–84°04w	8
Hacienda El Rodeo	600	09°55n–84°16w	8
El Empalme	1800	09°44n–83°52w	15
Escazu	1000	09°51n–84°10w	8
Guatuso†	1300	10°42n–84°50w	8
Madre Selva	2700	09°40n–83°50w	17
Parque Braulio Carrillo•†	300–2700	10°05n–83°58w	6,7,13,17
Parque Chirripo	2800–3850	09°29n–83°30w	17–19
San José	1200	09°52n–84°07w	8
Villa Mills	2800–3000	09°33n–83°42w	18

HEREDIA PROVINCE

Barba	1200	10°04n–84°07w	10
Finca la Selva•	50–100	10°26n–83°59w	11
Chilamate	100	10°26n–84°02w	6
Plastico†	500–850	10°20n–84°00w	13
Magsaysay	200	10°25n–84°03w	6
Volcán Barba	2500–3000	10°08n–84°06w	16,17

PUNTARENAS PROVINCE

Barranca	100	09°59n–84°43w	3
Parque Carrara	0–350	09°47n–84°40w	5
Esparta	100	09°59n–84°40w	3
Las Alturas•	1400–1700	08°56n–82°51w	12
Las Mellizas	1500	08°52n–82°45w	10
Monte Verde	1300–1600	10°06n–83°26w	13–16
Parque Corcovado•†	0–600	08°32n–83°35w	7,13,16
Paso Real	700	08°59n–83°15w	3
Punta Quepos	0–50	09°27n–84°09w	12
Rincon de Osa	0–100	09°55n–84°13w	6
San Vito•	1000–1300	08°47n–83°00w	13
Villa Neily	550	08°37n–82°57w	6

LIMON PROVINCE

Bribri	100	09°38n–82°47w	11
Cairo*	100	10°07n–83°31w	11
Guapiles*	150–300	10°13n–83°46w	6
Florida*	200	10°05n–83°02w	6
Limon*	0–50	10°00n–83°02w	11

LIMON PROVINCE

Locality	Elevation (meters)	Latitude/Longitude	Life Zone
Siquirres	100	10°06n–83°30w	11
Sixaola*	100	10°06n–83°30w	11
Parque Tortuguerro	0–50	10°35n–83°47w	6
Zent District*	0–100	10°02n–83°16w	4

GUANACASTE PROVINCE

Arenal	700	10°29n–84°53w	10
Cañas	100	09°14n–83°25w	2
Parque Rincon de la Vieja†	700–1800	10°55n–85°22w	10–13
Parque Santa Rosa†•	0–100	10°57n–85°37w	2,3
Taboga	80	10°20n–85°13w	1

HOST RECORDS FOR GENERA OF RIODINIDAE IN COSTA RICA

Subfamily *Genus*	*Hostplant Family*
CORRACHIINAE	
Corrachia	?
EUSELASIINAE	
Methone	?
Hades	Simaroubaceae
Euselasia	Myrtaceae, Clusiaceae, Melastomataceae
RIODININAE	
Mesosemiini	
Peropthalma	Rubiaceae
Leucochimona	Rubiaceae
Mesosemia	Rubiaceae
Eurybiini	
Eurybia	Marantaceae, Zingiberaceae
Incertae sedis	
Hermathena	Bromeliaceae
Cremna	Orchidaceae
Napaea	Bromeliaceae
Voltinia	?
Riodinini	
(Ancyluris section)	
Lyropteryx	Vochysiacae
Necyria	Vochysiacae, Melastomataceae, Gesneriaceae
Cyrenia	?
Ancyluris	Melastomataceae, Euphorbiaceae
Chorinea	Hippocratiaceae, Flacourtiaceae, Celastraceae
Rhetus	Combretaceae,
Ithomeis	Olacaceae
Isapis	?
Brachyglenis	?
Monethe	?
Melanis	Fabaceae
(Riodina section)	
Notheme	?
Metacharis	Olacaceae, Flacourtiaceae, Loranthaceae
Cariomothis	Loranthaceae
Lepricornis	Malpighiaceae, Combretaceae
Syrmatia	Zingiberaceae
Chamaelimnas	?
Baeotis	?
Caria	Ulmaceae, Bromeliaceae
Chalodeta	Melastomataceae, Sterculiaceae, Asteraceae

Subfamily	Genus	Hostplant Family
	Parcella	?
	Charis	Dead leaves, Asteraceae
	Calephelis	Asteraceae
	Lasaia	Fabaceae
	Exoplisia	Bombacaceae
Symmachiini		
	Mesene	Sapindaceae, Fabaceae, Violaceae
	Mesenopsis	Melastomataceae
	Xenandra	?
	Esthemopsis	?
	Chimastrum	?
	Symmachia	Ulmaceae, Melastomataceae
	Phaenochitonia	?
	Pterographium	Melastomataceae
	Stichelia	Melastomataceae(?)
Charitini		
	Sarota	Lejuniaceae
	Anteros	Melastomataceae, Vochysiaceae
Emesini		
	Argyrogrammana	Clusiaceae
	Calydna	?
	Emesis	Sterculiaceae, Nyctaginaceae, Euphorbiaceae, Flacourtiaceae, Ranunculaceae, Olacaceae, Fabaceae, Myrtaceae
	Pachythone	?
	Pixus	?
	Apodemia	Rosaceae, Polygonaceae, Krameriaceae, Fabaceae
Lemoniini		
(Lemonias section)		
	Lemonias	Euphorbiaceae
	Thisbe	Euphorbiaceae, Fabaceae
	Uraneis	Loranthaceae
(Synargis section)		
	Catocyclotis	?
	Juditha	Fabaceae, Passifloraceae, Dilleniaceae, Malpighiaceae, Sapindaceae, Simaroubaceae, Membracidae(?)
	Synargis	Fabaceae, Lecythidaceae, Sapindaceae, Polygalaceae, Bignoniaceae, Dilleniaceae, Euphorbiaceae, Sterculiaceae, Loranthaceae, Membracidae(?)
	Audre	Fabaceae, Asclepidaceae, Rosaceae, Turneraceae, regurgitations of ants(?)
Nymphidiini		
	Parnes	?
	Periplacis	?
	Menander	Marcgraviaceae
	Pandemos	?
	Calospila	Malpighiaceae
	Rodinia	?
	Adelotypa	Fabaceae
	Calociasma	?

Setabis	Membracidae, Jassidae
Pseudonymphidia	?
Theope	Euphorbiaceae, Bombacaceae, Cecropiaceae, Convolvulaceae, Lecythidaceae, Fabaceae, Sterculiaceae
Nymphidium	Fabaceae, Convolvulaceae, Sapindaceae, Lecythidaceae, Malpighiaceae, Passifloraceae,
Stalachtini	
Stalachtis	Simaroubaceae, Fabaceae, Sapotaceae

NOTE: Some records are from outside Central America. Sources include records summarized in K. Brown (1993), DeVries et al. (1994), Harvey (1987a), and DeVries (unpublished observations).

TRIBAL AND SUBFAMILY CHARACTER DIAGNOSES OF RIODINIDAE

(CONDENSED FROM HARVEY 1987a)

SUBFAMILIES

Styginae Ehrlich, 1958: fustrum egg; recurrent veins in cell of forewing; extra vein inking Sc + R1 to Rs on hindwing (variable).

Euselasiinae Kirby, 1871: m1–m2 join M2 smoothly, without any angle; sexual dimorphism in number of radial veins in FW; presences of scales on lateral surface of valvae of males; lateral projections on the tegumen of male genitalia.

Corrachiinae Stichel, 1928: fustrum-shaped egg; fusion of Sc and R1 to edge of forewing.

Riodininae Grote, 1895: antero-ventral placement of first abdominal spiracle on caterpillar; contact of pupal segments M2 and A1; a pedicel connecting the aedeagus to the base of the valve; presence of a costal vein on HW basal margin.

TRIBES OF RIODININAE

Mesosemiini Bates, 1859: silk girdle on pupa crosses A2; male genitalia with split base of pedicel; consistently hairy eyes; absence of tibial spurs.

Eurybiini Reuter, 1897: bristlelike scales on medial surface of palpi; extraordinarily long proboscis (*Eurybia*).

Incertae sedis (of Harvey 1987a): all have five radial veins in FW, but are not included in the Mesosemiini or Eurybiini. *Not considered monophyletic.*

Riodinini Grote, 1895: posterior margin of male tegumen with a deep invagination that is visible in dorsal view; FW R2 originates beyond cell and arises from a common stalk with R3 and R4 (Ancyluris section); ostium bursa of female is placed asymmetrically on right side of abdomen.

Symmachiini Bates, 1859: male with androconial scales on tergites 4 through 7; erectile androconial scales on HW.

Charitiini Stichel, 1911: female with spatulate scales surrounding the ovipositor lobes.

Emesini Stichel, 1911: all riodinids with four radial veins, but not with any apomorphies for other tribes. *Not considered monophyletic.* Also note that the name is a homonym of the widespread tribe of the Reduviidae (Heteroptera)—Emesini Amyot and Serville, 1843.

Lemoniini Kirby, 1871: males with bifurcate rami that underlie valvae of genitalia.

Nymphidiini Bates, 1859: abdominal spiracle on segment 3 closer to sternite than tergite (correlated with spiracle position in caterpillars).

Stalachtini Bates, 1861: both sexes with long tufts of scales on abdominal segment 8 (see Fig. 20).

CHECKLIST OF COSTA RICAN RIODINIDAE

SUBFAMILY CORRACHIINAE

Corrachia
leucoplaga Schaus, 1913

EUSELASIINAE

Hades
noctula Westwood, 1851

Methone
cecilia chrysomela (Butler, 1872)

Euselasia
bettina (Hewitson, 1869)
aurantia (Butler and Druce, 1872)
leucophryna (Schaus, 1913)
chrysippe (Bates, 1866)
matuta (Schaus, 1913)
regipennis regipennis (Butler and Druce, 1872)
euoras (Hewitson, 1855)
corduena anadema Stichel, 1927
gyda gydina Stichel, 1919
procula (Godman and Salvin, 1885)
sergia sergia (Godman and Salvin, 1885)
mystica (Schaus, 1913)
hieronymi (Salvin and Godman, 1868)
inconspicua (Godman and Salvin, 1878)
leucon (Schaus, 1913)
labdacus reducta Lathy, 1926
argentea argentea (Hewitson, 1871)
eucrates leucorrhoa (Godman and Salvin, 1878)
portentosa Stichel, 1927
amphidecta (Godman and Salvin, 1878)
hypophaea (Godman and Salvin, 1878)
onorata (Hewitson, 1869)
midas crotopiades Stichel, 1919
rhodogyne patella Stichel, 1927
aurantiaca (Salvin and Godman, 1868)
angulata Bates, 1868
subargentea Lathy, 1904

RIODININAE

MESOSEMIINI

Perophthalma
tullius (Fabricius, 1787)
lasus (Westwood, 1851)

Leucochimona
lepida (Godman and Salvin, 1885)
lagora (Herrich-Schaeffer, 1853)
vestalis leucogaea (Godman and Salvin, 1885)

Mesosemia
hesperina hesperina Butler, 1874
esperanza Schaus, 1913
coelestis Godman and Salvin, 1885
albipuncta Schaus, 1913
zonalis (Godman and Salvin, 1885)
carissima Bates, 1866
grandis Druce, 1874
gaudiolum Bates, 1865(??)
ceropia Druce, 1874
hypermegala Stichel, 1909
lamachus Hewitson, 1857
telegone telegone (Boisduval, 1836)
asa asa Hewitson, 1869
harveyi DeVries and Hall, 1996

INCERTAE SEDIS

Napaea
eucharila (Bates, 1867)
theages theages (Godman and Salvin, 1886)
umbra (Boisduval, 1870)

Voltinia
theata Stichel, 1910
radiata (Godman and Salvin, 1886)

Cremna
thasus subrutila Stichel, 1910

Hermathena
oweni Schaus, 1913
candidata (Hewitson, 1874)

EURYBIINI

Eurybia
caerulescens fulgens Stichel, 1910
cyclopia Stichel, 1910
unxia Godman and Salvin, 1885
patrona persona Staudinger, 1876
elvina elvina Stichel, 1910
lycisca Westwood, 1851

RIODININI (ANCYLURIS SECTION)

Lyropteryx
lyra cleadas Druce, 1875

Necyria
beltiana Hewitson, 1870
ingaretha (Hewitson, 1872)

Cyrenia
martia pyrippe Godman and Salvin, 1878

Ancyluris
inca inca (Saunders, 1850)
jurgensenii jurgensenii (Saunders, 1850)
cacica cacica (Felder and Felder, 1865) (??)

Rhetus
arcius castigatus Stichel, 1909
dysonii caligosus Stichel, 1929
periander naevianus Stichel, 1910

Chorinea
octauius bogota (Saunders, 1859)

Ithomeis
eulema imatatrix Godman and Salvin, 1878

Brachyglenis
esthema Felder and Felder, 1862
dinora (Bates, 1866)
dodone (Godman and Salvin, 1886)
nr *dodone*

Monethe
rudolphus rudolphus Godman & Salvin, 1885

Melanis
pixie sanguinea (Stichel, 1910)
cephise (Menetries, 1855)
electron melantho (Menetries, 1855)

Isapis
agyrtus hera Godman and Salvin, 1886

RIODININI (RIODINA SECTION)

Notheme
erota diadema Stichel, 1910

Metacharis
victrix Hewitson, 1870
umbrata Stichel, 1929

Lepricornis
strigosa strigosa (Staudinger, 1876)
bicolor Godman and Salvin, 1886 (??)

Cariomothis
poeciloptera poeciloptera (Godman and Salvin, 1878)

Syrmatia
nyx (Hübner, 1817)
aethiops Staudinger, 1888

Chamaelimnas
villagomes xanthotaenia Stichel, 1910(??)

Baeotis
nesaea Godman and Salvin, 1889
zonata zonata Felder, 1869
sulphurea macularia (Boisduval, 1870)

Caria
rhacotis (Godman and Salvin, 1878)
domitianus domitianus (Fabricius, 1793)
lampeto Godman and Salvin, 1886

Chalodeta
chaonitis (Hewitson, 1866)
lypera (Bates 1868)
candiope (Druce, 1904)

Parcella
amarynthina (Felder and Felder, 1865) (??)

Charis
auius (Cramer, 1776)
iris (Staudinger, 1875)
velutina (Godman and Salvin, 1878)
hermodora Felder and Felder, 1861
gynaea (Godart, 1824)

Calephelis
sixaola McAlpine, 1971
fulmen (Stichel, 1910)
schausi McAlpine, 1971
browni McAlpine, 1971
sodalis Austin, 1993
costaricicola Strand, 1916
exiguus Austin, 1993
argyrodines (Bates, 1866)
inca McAlpine, 1971
laverna parva Austin, 1993

Lasaia
agesilas (Latreille, 1809)
sessilis Schaus, 1890
sula sula Staudinger, 1888
oileus Godman, 1903
pseudomeris Clench, 1972

Exoplisia
cadmeis (Hewitson, 1866)
hypochalbe (Felder and Felder, 1861) (??)

SYMMACHIINI

Mesene
phareus rubella Bates, 1865
mygdon Schaus, 1913
croceella Bates, 1865
silaris Godman and Salvin, 1878
margaretta semiradiata Felder and Felder, 1865

Mesenopsis
melanochlora Godman and Salvin, 1878
bryaxis (Hewitson, 1870)

Xenandra
caeruleata (Godman and Salvin, 1878)
helius (Cramer, 1779)
desora Schaus, 1928

Esthemopsis
clonia Felder and Felder, 1865
colaxes Hewitson, 1870

Chimastrum
argenteum argenteum (Bates, 1866)

Symmachia
rubina rubina Bates, 1866
threissa Hewitson, 1870 (??)
accusatrix Westwood, 1851
leena leena Hewitson, 1870
probetor belti Godman and Salvin, 1886
tricolor hedemanni (Felder, 1869)
xypete (Hewitson, 1870)

Pterographium
elegans Schaus, 1913

Stichelia
sagaris tyriotes (Godman and Salvin, 1878)
phoenicura (Godman and Salvin, 1886) (??)

Phaenochitonia
ignicauda (Godman and Salvin, 1878)
ignipicta Schaus, 1913

CHARITINI

Anteros
allectus Westwood, 1851
cumulatus Stichel, 1909
chrysoprastus roratus Godman and Salvin, 1886
formosus micon Druce, 1875
kupris kupris Hewitson, 1875

carausius carausius Westwood, 1851
renaldus indigator Stichel, 1911

Sarota
gyas (Cramer, 1775)
myrtea Godman and Salvin, 1886
gamelia Godman and Salvin, 1886
estrada Schaus, 1928
spicata (Staudinger, 1888)
psaros psaros (Godman and Salvin, 1886)
chrysus (Stoll, 1781)
subtessellata (Schaus, 1913)
dematria (Westwood, 1851)
turrialbensis (Schaus, 1913)

EMESINI

Argyrogrammana
holosticta (Godman and Salvin, 1878)
venilia crocea (Godman and Salvin, 1878)
leptographia (Stichel, 1911)
barine (Staudinger, 1887)

Calydna
venusta Godman and Salvin, 1886
sturnula hegias Felder, 1869

Emesis
tenedia tenedia Felder and Felder, 1861
lacrines Hewitson, 1870
cypria paphia Felder, 1869
ocypore aethalia Bates, 1868
lupina Godman and Salvin, 1886
tegula Godman and Salvin, 1886
mandana mandana (Cramer, 1780)
fatimella nobilata Stichel, 1910
lucinda aurimna (Boisduval 1870)

Pachythone
gigas (Godman and Salvin, 1878)
nigriciliata Schaus, 1913

Pixus
corculum (Stichel, 1929)

Roberella
lencates (Hewitson, 1875)

Apodemia
multiplaga Schaus, 1902
walkeri Godman and Salvin, 1886

LEMONIINI (LEMONIAS SECTION)

Thisbe
irenea (Stoll, 1780)
lycorias lycorias (Hewitson 1853)

Lemonias
agave Godman and Salvin, 1886(??)

Uraneis
ucubis Hewitson, 1870

Lemoniini (Synargis section)

Juditha
molpe molpe (Hübner, 1808)
dorilis dorilis (Bates, 1866)

Catocyclotis
aemulius adelina (Butler, 1872)

Synargis
phylleus praeclara (Bates, 1866)
mycone (Hewitson, 1865)
ochra sicyon (Godman and Salvin, 1878)
velabrum (Godman and Salvin, 1878)
palaeste salvator (Stichel, 1911) comb. nov.
nymphidioides (Butler, 1872)
nycteus (Godman and Salvin, 1886)
gela (Hewitson, 1853) (??)

Audre
domina (Bates, 1865)
albina (Felder and Felder, 1861) (??)

NYMPHIDIINI

Pames
nycteis Westwood, 1851

Periplacis
glaucoma splendida (Butler, 1867)

Menander
menander purpurata (Godman and Salvin, 1878)
pretus picta (Godman and Salvin, 1886)
laobotas (Hewitson, 1875)

Pandemos
godmanii Dewitz, 1877

Calospila
lucianus lucianus (Fabricius, 1793)
cilissa (Hewitson, 1863)
asteria (Stichel, 1911) (??)
martia (Godman, 1903)
sudias (Hewitson, 1858)
argenissa (Stoll, 1790)
zeurippa lasthenes (Hewitson, 1870)

parthaon pelarge (Godman & Salvin, 1878)
trotschi (Godman & Salvin, 1901)

Rodinia
calpharnia barbouri (Bates, 1935) (??)

Adelotypa
densemaculata (Hewitson, 1870)
glauca (Godman and Salvin, 1886)
eudocia (Godman and Salvin, 1897)

Calociasma
icterica (Godman and Salvin, 1878)
lilina (Butler, 1870)

Setabis
lagus jansoni (Butler, 1870)
cleomedes (Hewitson, 1870)
alcmaeon alcmaeon (Hewitson, 1876)

Pseudonymphidia
clearista (Butler, 1871) (??)

Theope
virgilius (Fabricius, 1793)
eupolis Schaus, 1890
speciosa Godman and Salvin, 1897
cratylus Godman and Salvin, 1886
eleutho Godman and Salvin, 1897
basilea Bates, 1866
publius Felder and Felder, 1861
thebais Hewitson, 1870
matuta Godman and Salvin, 1897
acosma Stichel, 1910
eudocia pulchralis Stichel, 1910
thestias decorata Godman and Salvin, 1878
guillaumei cecropia DeVries and Hall, 1996
barea Godman and Salvin, 1878
herta Godman and Salvin, 1886
pedias isia Godman and Salvin, 1878
phaeo folia Godman and Salvin, 1886
lycaenina Bates, 1868

Nymphidium
mantus (Cramer, 1775)
olinda Bates, 1865(??)
lenocinium Schaus, 1913
azanoides occidentalis Callaghan, 1986
haematostictum Godman and Salvin, 1878
ascolia ascolia Hewitson, 1853
onaeum Hewitson, 1869

NOTE: (??) = needs to be confirmed for Costa Rica.

BIBLIOGRAPHY

Ackery, P. R. 1984. Systematic and faunistic studies on butterflies. *Symp. R. Ent. Soc. Lond.* 11: 9–21.

Ackery, P. R. 1988. Hostplants and classification: A review of nymphalid butterflies. *Biol. J. Linn. Soc.* 33: 95–203.

Ackery, P. R. 1990. Biocontrol potential of African lycaenid butterflies entomophagous on Homoptera. *J. African Zool.* 104: 581–591.

Ackery, P. R. 1991. Hostplant utilization by African and Australian butterflies. *Biol. J. Linn. Soc.* 44: 335–351.

Ackery, P. R., and R. I. Vane-Wright. 1984. *Milkweed Butterflies: Their Cladistics and Biology.* British Museum (Nat. Hist.), London.

Alcock, J. 1988. The mating systems of three territorial butterflies in Costa Rica. *J. Res. Lep.* 26: 89–97.

Alonso-Mejia, A., and M. Marquez. 1994. Dragonfly predation on butterflies in a tropical dry forest. *Biotropica* 26: 341–344.

Auclair, J. L. 1963. Aphid feeding and nutrition. *Ann. Rev. Ent.* 8: 439–490.

Austin, G. T. 1993. Three new taxa of *Calephelis* from Costa Rica (Lycaenidae: Riodininae). *J. Res. Lep.* 30: 237–244.

Baker, H. K., and I. Baker. 1975. Studies of nectar constitution and plant-pollinator coevolution. In L. E. Gilbert and P. H. Raven, eds., *Coevolution of Animals and Plants*, pp. 100–140. University of Texas Press, Austin.

Baker, H. K., and I. Baker. 1976. Analysis of amino acids in nectar. *Phytochem. Bull.* 9: 4–7.

Baker, H. G., P. A. Opler, and I. Baker. 1978. A comparison of the amino acid compliments of floral and extrafloral nectars. *Botanical Gazette* 139: 322–332.

Barcant, M. 1970. *The Butterflies of Trinidad and Tobago.* Collins Press, London.

Baroni-Urbani, C., M. V. Buser, and E. Schilliger. 1988. Substrate vibration during recruitment in ant social organization. *Insectes Sociaux* 35: 241–250.

Bates, H. W. 1859. Notes on South American butterflies. *Trans. Ent. Lond.* 5: 1–11.

Bates, H. W. 1862. Contributions to an insect fauna of the Amazon Valley, Lepidoptera: Heliconidae. *Trans. Ent. Lond.* 5: 218–245.

Bates, H. W. 1868. A catalogue of the Erycinidae, a family of diurnal Lepidoptera. *J. Linn. Soc. Lond.* 9: 367–459.

Baylis, M., and N. E. Pierce. 1991. The effects of host-plant quality on the survival of larvae and oviposition by adults of an ant-tended butterfly, *Jalmenus evagoras*. *Ecol. Ent.* 16: 1–9.

Beizanko, C. M., O.H.H. Mielke, and A. Wedderhoff. 1978. Contribution to the faunistic study of the Riodinidae of Rio Grande do Sul, Brazil (Lepidoptera). *Acta. Biol. Par., Curitiba* 7: 7–22.

Benson, W. W. 1971. Evidence for unpalatability through kin selection in the Heliconiinae (Lepidoptera). *Am. Nat.* 105: 213–226.

Benson, W. W. 1972. Natural selection for Müllerian mimicry in *Heliconius erato* in Costa Rica. *Science* 176: 936–939.

Bernard, G. D. 1979. Red-absorbing visual pigments of butterflies. *Science* 203: 1125–1127.

Beutelspacher, C. R. 1972. Some observations on the Lepidoptera of bromeliads. *J. Lep. Soc.* 26: 133–137.

Blutstein, H. I., L. C. Anderson, E. C. Betters, J. C. Dombrowski and C. Townsend. 1970. *Area Handbook for Costa Rica.* Government Printing Office, Washington D.C.

Bolton, B. 1994. *Identification Guide to the Ant Genera of the World.* Harvard University Press, Cambridge, Mass.

Boppré, M. 1984. Chemically mediated interactions between butterflies. *Symp. Roy. Ent. Soc. Lond.* 11: 64–77.

Borquin, F. 1953. Notas sobre la metamorfosis de *Hamearis susanae* Orfila, 1953 con orgua mirmecofila (Lep.: Riodin.). *Rev. Soc. Ent. Argentina* 16: 83–87.

Borror, D. J., C. A. Tripplehorn, and N. F. Johnson. 1989. *Introduction to the Study of Insects.* Harcourt-Brace-Jovanovich College Publishers, Orlando, Florida.

Boyden, T. C. 1976. Butterfly palatability and mimicry: experiments with *Ameiva* lizards. *Evolution* 30: 73–81.

Brevignon, C. 1992. Elevage de deux Riodininae guyanais *Napaea beltiana* Bates et *Cremna thasus* Stoll. *Alexanor* 17: 403–4134.

Bridges, C. A. 1988. *Catalog of Lycaenidae and Riodinidae (Lepidoptera: Rhopalocera).* Printed by the author.

Brower, A.V.Z. 1994a. Phylogeny of *Heliconius* butterflies inferred from mitochondrial DNA sequences (Lepidoptera: Nymphalidae). *Molec. Phylog. Evol.* 3: 159–174.

Brower, A.V.Z. 1994b. Rapid morphological radiation and convergences among races of the butterfly *Heliconius erato* inferred from patterns of mitochondrial DNA evolution. *Proc. Nat. Acad. Sci.* 91: 6491–6495.

Brower, A.V.Z. 1995. Locomotor mimicry in butterflies? A critical review of the evidence. *Phil. Trans. Roy. Soc. Lond.* B 347: 413–425.

Brower, J.V.Z. 1958a. Experimental studies of mimicry in North American butterflies, part 1, The monarch, *Danaus plexippus,* and the viceroy, *Limenitis archippus archippus. Evolution* 12: 32–47.

Brower, J.V.Z. 1958b. Experimental studies of mimicry in North American butterflies, part 3, *Danaus berenice* and *Limenitis archippus floridensis. Evolution* 12: 273–285.

Brower, L. P. 1984. Chemical defenses in butterflies. *Symp. Roy. Ent. Soc. Lond.* 11: 110–134.

Brower, L. P., ed. 1988. *Mimicry and the Evolutionary Process.* University of Chicago Press, Chicago.

Brower, L. P., and J.V.Z. Brower. 1964. Birds, butterflies, and plant poisons: A study in ecological chemistry. *Zoologica* (N.Y.): 137–159.

Brower, L. P., J.V.Z. Brower, and J. M. Corvino. 1967. Plant poisons in a terrestrial food chain. *Proc. Nat. Acad. Sci.* 57: 893–898.

Brown, K. S., Jr., 1981. The biology of *Heliconius* and related genera. *Ann. Rev. Entom.* 26: 421–456.

Brown, K. S., Jr., 1984. Adult-obtained pyrrolizidine alkaloids defend ithomiine butterflies against a spider predator. *Nature* 309: 707–709.

Brown, K. S., Jr., 1992. Borboletas da Serra do Japi: Diversidade, habitats, recursos ailmentares e variacao temporal. In *Historia natural da Serra Japi: Ecologia e preservacao de um area florestal no sudeste do Brasil*, pp. 142–186. FAPESP, Campinas.

Brown, K. S., Jr., 1993. Neotropical Lycaenidae: An overview. In T. R. New, ed., *Conservation Biology of Lycaenidae (Butterflies)*, pp. 45–61. ICUN, Gland, Switzerland.

Brown, W. L. 1973. A comparison of the Hylean and Congo-West African rain forest ant faunas. In B. J. Meggers, E. S. Ayensu, and W. D. Duckworth, eds., *Tropical Ecosystems in Africa and South America: A Comparative Review*, pp. 161–185. Smithsonian Institution Press, Washington, D.C.

Bruch, C. 1926. Orugas mirmecofilas de *Hameris epulus* signatus Stichel. *Rev. Soc. Ent. Argentina* 1: 2–9.

Brues, C. T. 1924. The specificity of food-plants in the evolution of phytophagous insects. *Am. Nat.* 58: 127–144.

Callaghan, C. J. 1977. Studies on Restinga butterflies, I. Life cycle and immature biology of *Menander felsina* (Riodinidae), a myrmecophilous metalmark. *J. Lep. Soc.* 20: 36–42.

Callaghan, C. J. 1978. Studies on Restinga butterflies, II. Notes on the population structure of *Menander felsina* (Riodinidae). *J. Lep. Soc.* 32: 37–48.

Callaghan, C. J. 1982a. A study of isolating mechanisms among neotropical butterflies of the subfamily Riodininae. *J. Res. Lep.* 21: 159–176.

Callaghan, C. J. 1982b. Three new genera of riodinids from Mexico and Central America. *Rev. Soc. Mex. Lep.* 7: 55–63.

Callaghan, C. J. 1982c. Notes on immature biology of two myrmecophilous Lycaenidae: *Juditha molpe* (Riodininae) and *Panthiades bitias* (Lycaeninae). *J. Res. Lep.* 20: 36–46.

Callaghan, C. J. 1985. A preliminary revision of the genus *Nymphidium* (Rhopalocera, Riodinidae). Part I, Introduction: Mantus-Baoetia complex. *Bull. Allyn Mus.* 98: 1–21.

Callaghan, C. J. 1986a. Notes of the biology of *Stalachtis susanna* (Lycaenidae: Riodininae) with a discussion of riodinine larval strategies. *J. Res. Lep.* 24: 258–263.

Callaghan, C. J. 1986b. Studies on Restinga butterflies: The biology of *Synargis brennus* (Stichel) (Riodinidae). *J. Lep. Soc.* 40: 93–96.

Callaghan, C. J. 1986c. A preliminary revision of the genus *Nymphidium* (Riodinidae). Part II, The azanoides complex. *Bull. Allyn Mus.* 100: 1–7.

Callaghan, C. J. 1988. A preliminary revision of the genus *Nymphidium* (Riodinidae). Part III, The omois group. *Bull. Allyn Mus.* 119: 1–6.

Callaghan, C. J. 1989. Notes on the biology of three riodinine species: *Nymphidium lisimon attenuatum, Phaenochitonia sagaris satinus*, and *Metacharis ptolomaeus* (Lycaenidae: Riodininae). *J. Res. Lep.* 27: 109–114.

Callaghan, C. J. 1991. Notes on the immature biology of two riodinine butterflies: *Metacharis ptolomaeus* and *Napaea nepos orpheus* (Lycaenidae). *J. Res. Lep.* 30: 221–224.

Callahan, P. S., and J. B. Chapin. 1960. Morphology of the reproductive systems and mating in two representative members of the family Noctuidae, *Pseudaletia unipuncta* and *Peridroma margaritosa*, with comparison to *Heliothis zea*. *Ann. Ent. Soc. Am.* 53: 763–782.

Calvert, W. H., L. E. Hendrick, and L. P. Brower. 1979. Mortality of the monarch butterfly (*Danaus plexippus* L.) due to avian predation at five overwintering sites in Mexico. *Science* 204: 847–851.

Carpenter, G.D.H. 1942. Observations and experiments by the late C.M.F. Swynnerton on wild birds eating butterflies and the preferences shown. *Proc. Linn. Soc. Lond.* 154: 10–46.

Carroll, S. B., J. Gates, D. N. Keys, S. W. Paddock, G. Panganiban, J. Selegue, and J. Williams. 1994. Pattern formation and eyespot determination in butterfly wings. *Science* 265: 109–114.

Chai, P. 1986. Field observations and feeding experiments on the response of rufous-tailed jacamars (*Galbula ruficauda*) to free-flying butterflies in a tropical rainforest. *Biol. J. Linn. Soc.* 29: 166–189.

Chai, P. 1990. Relationships between visual characteristics of rainforest butterflies and the response of rufous-tailed jacamars (*Galbula ruficauda*) to free-flying butterflies in a tropical rainforest. In M. Wickstein, ed., *Adaptive Coloration in Invertebrates*, pp. 31–60. Texas A & M University, College Station.

Chai, P. 1996. Butterfly visual characteristics and ontogeny of responses to butterflies by a specialized tropical bird. *Biol. J. Linn. Soc.* (in press).

Chew, F. S., and R. K. Robbins. 1984. Egg laying in butterflies. *Symp. Roy. Ent. Soc.* 11: 65–79.

Claassens, A.J.M., and C.G.C. Dickson. 1977. A study of the myrmecophilous behaviour of the immature stages of *Aloeides thyra* (L.) (Lep.: Lycaenidae) with special reference to the function of the retractile tubercles and with additional notes on the general biology of the species. *Ent. Record and J. Variation* 19: 195–215.

Clark, G. C. and C.G.C. Dickson. 1956. Proposed classification of South African Lycaenidae from early stages. *J. Ent. Soc. S. Africa* 19: 195–215.

Clark, G. C., and C.G.C. Dickson. 1971. *Life Histories of Southern African Lycaenid Butterflies*. Purnell, Cape Town, South Africa.

Clench, H. H. 1972. A review of the genus *Lasaia* (Riodinidae). *J. Res. Lep.* 10: 149–180.

Clench, H. K., and L. D. Miller. 1976. How to prepare slides of sclerotized parts of the Lepidoptera. (A widely circulated article published in-house by Section of Insects, Carnegie Museum of Natural History, Pittsburgh.)

Coen, E. 1983. Climate. In D. H. Janzen, ed., *Costa Rican Natural History*, pp. 35–46. University of Chicago Press, Chicago.

Common, I.F.B., and D. F. Waterhouse. 1972. *Butterflies of Australia*. Angus and Robertson, Brisbane, Australia.

Comstock, J. A. 1928. Studies in Pacific Coast Lepidoptera (cont.). *Bull. S. Calif. Acad. Sci.* 27: 80–82.

Comstock, J. A., and C. H. Dammers. 1932. Early stages of *Melitaea wrightii* Edw. and *Calephelis nemesis* Edw. (Lepidoptera). *Bull. S. Calif. Acad. Sci.* 31: 9–15.

Costa, J. T., and N. E. Pierce. 1996. Social evolution in the Lepidoptera: Ecological context and communication in larval societies. In J. C. Choe and B. J. Crespi, eds., *Social Competition and Cooperation in Insects and Arachnids*, vol. 2, *Evolution of Sociality*. Princeton University Press, Princeton, N.J.

Cottrell, C. B. 1984. Aphytophagy in butterflies: Its relationship to myrmecophily. *Zool. J. Lond. Soc.* 80: 1–57.

Cripps, C., and T.H.E. Jackson. 1940. The life history of *Lachnocnema bibulus* (Fab.) in Kenya (Lep. : Lycaenidae) (with a note on the larval gland by Dr. H. Eltringham F.R.E.S.). *Trans. Roy. Ent. Soc. Lond.* 90: 449–453.

Curry, K., L. McDowell, W. Judd, and W. Stern. 1991. Osmophores, floral features and systematics of *Stanhopea* (Orchidaceae). *Am. J. Botany* 78: 610–623.

Cushman, J. H., V. K. Rashbrook, and A. J. Beattie. 1994. Assessing benefits to both participants in a lycaenid-ant association. *Ecology* 75: 1031–1041.

D'Abrera, B. 1994. *Butterflies of the Neotropical Region*, vol. 4, Riodinidae. Hill House, Victoria, Australia.

de la Maza, R. G., and R. H. de la Maza. 1976. Ciclo de vida de *Calephelis perditalis* Barnes and Macdng. (Riodinidae). *Rev. Soc. Mex. Lep.* 2: 91–96.

de la Maza, R. G., and R. H. de la Maza. 1980. Notas y descripciones sobre la familia Riodinidae en Mexico. *Rev. Soc. Mex. Lep.* 6: 7–19.

de la Maza, R. G., R. de la Maza, and D. Turrent. 1977. Un nuevo *Calephelis* de la Cuenca Superior del Rio Balsas, Mexico (Riodinidae). *Rev. Soc. Mex. Lep.* 3: 85–90.

de la Maza, R. G., and A. White. 1990. Rhopalocera de la Huasteca Potosina, su distribucion, composicion, origen y evolucion. *Rev. Soc. Mex. Lep.* 13: 29–88.

Dempster, J. 1984. The natural enemies of butterflies. *Symp. Roy. Ent. Soc. Lond.* 11: 97–104.

DeSalle, R., J. Gatesy, W. Wheeler, and D. Grimaldi. 1992. DNA sequences from a fossil termite in Oligo-Miocene amber and their phylogenetic implications. *Science* 257: 1933–1936.

Dethier, V. G. 1963. *The Physiology of Insect Sense.* Methuen, New York.

DeVries, P. J. 1977. *Eumaeus minyas*: An aposematic lycaenid butterfly. *Brenesia* 12: 269–270.

DeVries, P. J. 1984a. Of crazy ants and the Curetinae: Are *Curetis* butterflies tended by ants? *Zool. J. Linn. Soc.* 80: 59–66.

DeVries, P. J. 1984b. Butterflies and Tachinidae: Does the parasite always kill its host? *J. Nat. Hist.* 18: 323–326.

DeVries, P. J. 1987. *The Butterflies of Costa Rica and Their Natural History.* Princeton University Press, Princeton, N.J.

DeVries, P. J. 1988a. The use of epiphylls as larval hostplants by the neotropical riodinid butterfly *Sarota gyas. J. Nat. Hist.* 22: 1447–1450.

DeVries, P. J. 1988b. The larval organs of *Thisbe irenea* (Riodinidae) and their effects upon attending ants. *Zool. J. Linn. Soc.* 94: 379–393.

DeVries, P. J. 1988c. Stratification of fruit-feeding nymphalid butterflies in a Costa Rican rainforest. *J. Res. Lep.* 26: 98–108.

DeVries, P. J. 1990. Enhancement of symbioses between butterfly caterpillars and ants by vibrational communication. *Science* 248: 1104–1106.

DeVries, P. J. 1991a. Ecological and evolutionary patterns in riodinid butterflies. In C. Huxley and D. F. Cutler, eds., *Ant-Plant Interactions*, pp. 143–156. Oxford University Press, Oxford.

DeVries, P. J. 1991b. The mutualism between *Thisbe irenea* and ants, and the role of ant ecology in the evolution of larval-ant associations. *Biol. J. Linn. Soc.* 43: 179–195.

DeVries, P. J. 1991c. Call production by myrmecophilous riodinid and lycaenid butterfly caterpillars (Lepidoptera): Morphological, acoustical, functional, and evolutionary patterns. *Am. Mus. Novitates* 3025: 1–23.

DeVries, P. J. 1991d. Detecting and recording the calls produced by butterfly caterpillars and ants. *J. Res. Lep.* 28: 258–262.

DeVries, P. J. 1992. Singing caterpillars, ants and symbioses. *Scientific American* 267: 76–82.

DeVries, P. J. 1994. Patterns of butterfly diversity and promising topics in natural history and ecology. In L. McDade, K. S. Bawa, H. Hespenheide, and G. Hartshorn, eds., *Ecology and Natural History of a Neotropical Rainforest*, pp. 187–194. University of Chicago Press, Chicago.

DeVries, P. J., and I. Baker. 1989. Butterfly exploitation of a plant-ant mutualism: Adding insult to herbivory. *J. N.Y. Ent. Soc.* 97: 332–340.

DeVries, P. J., and G. E. Martinez. 1993. The morphology, natural history, and behavior of the early stages of *Morpho cypris* (Nymphalidae: Morphinae) — 140 years after formal recognition of the butterfly. *J. N.Y. Ent. Soc.* 101: 515–530.

DeVries, P. J., J. Schul, and N. Greig. 1987. Synchronous nocturnal activity and gregarious roosting in the neotropical skipper butterfly *Caelenorrhinus fritzgaertneri* (Lep.: Hesperiidae). *Zool. J. Linn. Soc.* 89: 89–103.

DeVries, P. J., R. B. Cocroft, and J. A. Thomas. 1993. Comparison of acoustical signals in *Maculinea* butterfly caterpillars and their obligate host *Myrmica* ants. *Biol. J. Linn. Soc.* 49: 229–238.

DeVries, P. J., I. A. Chacon, and D. Murray. 1994. Toward a better understanding of host use and biodiversity in riodinid butterflies (Lepidoptera). *J. Res. Lep.* 31: 103–126.

DeVries, P. J., and J. Hall. 1996. Two new butterflies from Costa Rica (Riodinidae). *Trop. Lep.* 7: 87–90.

dos Passos, C. F. 1936. The life history of *Calephelis borealis* (Lepidoptera). *Can. Ent.* 68: 167–170.

Downey, J. C. 1961. Myrmecophily in the Lycaenidae (Lepidoptera). *Proc. N. Central Branches, Entom Soc. Amer.* 16: 14–15.

Downey, J. C. 1966. Sound production in pupae of Lycaenidae *J. Lep. Soc.* 20: 129–155.

Downey, J. C., and A. C. Allyn. 1973. Butterfly ultrastructure, 1. Sound production and associated abdominal structures in pupae of Lycaenidae and Riodinidae. *Bull. Allyn Mus.* 14: 1–48.

Downey, J. C., and A. C. Allyn. 1975. Wingscale morphology and nomenclature. *Bull. Allyn Mus.* 31: 1–32.

Downey, J. C., and A. C. Allyn. 1978. Sounds produced in pupae of Lycaenidae. *Bull. Allyn Mus.* 48: 1–14.

Downey, J. C., and A. C. Allyn. 1980. Eggs of Riodinidae. *J. Lep. Soc.* 34: 133–145.

Downey, J. C., and A. C. Allyn. 1981. Chorionic sculpturing in eggs of Lycaenidae, part I. *Bull. Allyn Mus.* 61: 1–29.

Downey, J. C., and A. C. Allyn. 1982. Chorionic sculpturing in eggs of Lycaenidae, part 2. *Bull. Allyn Mus.* 84: 1–44.

Durden, C. J., and H. Rose. 1978. Butterflies from the middle Eocene: The earliest occurrence of fossil Papilionoidea (Lepidoptera). *Pearce-Sellard Series* (Texas Memorial Musuem, Austin) 29: 1–25.

Edwards, W. H. 1878. Notes on *Lycaena pseudargiolus* and its larval history. *Can. Ent.* 10: 1–14.

Ehrlich, P. R. 1958a. The comparative morphology, phylogeny, and higher classification of the butterflies (Lepidoptera: Papilionoidea). *Univ. Kansas Sci. Bull.* 39: 305–370.

Ehrlich, P. R. 1958b. The integumental anatomy of the monarch butterfly *Danaus plexippus* L. (Lepidoptera: Papilionoidea). *Univ. Kansas Sci. Bull.* 39: 305–370.

Ehrlich, P. R., and A. H. Ehrlich. 1982. Lizard predation on tropical butterflies. *J. Lep. Soc.* 36.

Ehrlich, P. R., and P. Raven. 1965. Butterflies and plants: a study in coevolution. *Evol.* 18: 596–604.

Eisner, T. 1970. Chemical defense against predation in arthropods. In E. Sondheimer and J. B. Simeone, eds., *Chemical Ecology*, pp. 157–217. Academic Press, New York.

Eisner, T., and J. C. Meinwald. 1965. Defensive secretion of a caterpillar (*Papilio*). *Science* 150: 1733–1735.

Elfferich, N. W. 1988a. Zuchterfahrungen mit *Maculinea alcon* (Denis and Schiffermüller, 1775) (Lep.: Lycaenidae). *Mitt. Ent. Gesellschaft Basel* 38: 134–150.

Elfferich, N. W. 1988b. Gerauschproduktion bei Lycaeniden-Puppen (Lepidoptera). *Mitt. Ent. Gesellschaft Basel* 38: 156–168.

Eliot, J. N. 1973. The higher classification of the Lycaenidae (Lepidoptera): A tentative arrangement. *Bull. Brit. Mus.* (Nat. Hist.) 28: 371–505.

Elmes, G. W., J. C. Wardlaw, and J. A. Thomas. 1991a. Larvae of *Maculinea rebeli*, a large-blue butterfly, and their Myrmica host ants—wild adoption, and behaviour in ants' nests. *J. Zoology* 223: 447–460.

Elmes, G. W., J. C. Wardlaw, and J. A. Thomas. 1991b. Larvae of *Maculinea rebeli*, a large-blue butterfly, and their Myrmica host ants—patterns of caterpillar growth and survival. *J. Zoology* 224: 79–92.

Eltringham, H. 1910. *African Mimetic Butterflies*. Clarendon Press, Oxford.

Emmel, T. C., and G. T. Austin. 1990. The tropical rainforest butterfly fauna of Rondonia, Brazil: Species diversity and conservation. *Trop. Lep.* 1: 1–12.

Emmel, T. C., L. D. Miller, and H. K. Clench. 1975. The neotropical metalmark *Hermathena oweni* (Riodinidae): New records and major range extension of the known range from Costa Rica to El Salvador and Mexico. *J. Lep. Soc.* 29: 108–111.

Emmel, T. C., M. C. Minno, and B. A. Drummond. 1992. *Florissant Butterfles.* Stanford University Press, Stanford, Calif.

Endler, J. A. 1993. The color of light in forests and its implications. *Ecol. Mon.* 63: 1–27.

Erwin, T. L. 1982. Tropical forests: Their richness in Coleoptera and other arthropod species. *Coleopterist's Bull.* 36: 74–75.

Evans, H. C. 1982. Entomophagous fungi in tropical forest ecosystems: An appraisal. *Ecol. Ent.* 7: 47–60.

Fahn, A. 1988. Secretory tissues in vascular plants. *New Phytologist* 108: 229–257.

Farquharson, C. O. 1921. Five years' observations (1914–1918) on the bionomics of Southern Nigerian insects, chiefly directed to the investigation of lycaenid life-histories and the relation of Lycaenidae, Diptera, and other insects to ants. *Trans. Ent. Soc. Lond.* 1921: 319–448.

Farrell, B. D., and T. L. Erwin. 1988. Leaf-beetle community structure in an Amazonian rainforest canopy. In P. Joliviet, E. Pettpierre, and T. H. Hsiao, eds., *Biology of Chrysomelidae*, pp. 73–90. Kluewer Academic Publishers, Amsterdam.

Fiedler, K. 1991. Systematic, evolutionary, and ecological implications of myrmecophily within the Lycaenidae (Insecta: Lepidoptera: Papilionoidea). *Bonner Zool. Mon.* 31: 1–210.

Fiedler, K., and C. Saam. 1995. A "microbial" cost of butterfly-ant mutualisms. *J. Lep. Soc.* 49: 80–84.

Fisher, R. A. 1930. *The Genetical Theory of Natural Selection*. Clarendon Press, Oxford.

Fitzgerald, T. D. 1993. Sociality in caterpillars. In N. E. Stamp and T. E. Casey, eds., *Caterpillars*, pp. 372–403. Chapman Hall, New York.

Forey, P. L., C. J. Humphries, I. J. Kitching, R. W. Scotland, D. J. Siebert, and D. M. Williams. 1992. *Cladistics: A Practical Course in Systematics*. Clarendon Press, Oxford.

Futuyma, D. J., and M. Slatkin, eds. 1983. *Coevolution*. Sinauer Associates, Sunderland, Mass.

Gilbert, L. E. 1976. Post mating odor in *Heliconius* butterflies: A male contributed antiaphrodisiac. *Science.* 193: 419–420.

Gilbert, L. E. 1983. Coevolution and mimicry. In D. Futuyma and M. Slatkin, eds., *Coevolution*, pp. 263–281. Sinauer Associates, Sunderland, Mass.

Godfray, H.C.J. 1994. Pacasitoids: Behavioral and Evolutionary Ecology. Princeton University Press, Princeton, N.J.

Godman, F. D., and O. Salvin. 1879–1901. *Insecta, Lepidoptera, Rhopalocera (Biologia Centrali Americana)*, vols. 1–3. London.

Gomez, L. D., and J. M. Savage. 1983. Searchers on that rich coast: Costa Rican field biology, 1400–1980. In D. H. Janzen, ed., *Costa Rican Natural History*, pp. 1–11. University of Chicago Press, Chicago.

Grimaldi, D. 1993. The care and study of fossiliferous amber. *Curator* 36: 31–49.

Grimaldi, D. 1995. On the age of Dominican amber. In K. B. Anderson and J. C. Crelling, eds., *Amber and Resenites*, pp. 1–11. American Chemical Society Symposium, Washington, D.C.

Grimaldi, D. 1996. *Amber: Window to the Past*. Harry N. Abrams, New York.

Guilford, T. 1986. How do "warning colours" work?—Conspicuousness may reduce recognition errors in experienced predators. *Animal Behav.* 34: 286–288.

Guppy, J. 1904. Notes on the habits and early stages of Trinidad butterflies. *Trans. Ent. Soc. Lond.* 1904: 225–228.

Harvey, D. J. 1987a. The higher classification of the Riodinidae (Lepidoptera). Ph.D. diss., University of Texas, Austin.

Harvey, D. J. 1987b. Riodinidae. In F. Stehr, ed., *Immature Insects*, vol. 1. Kendall/Hunt, Dubuque, Iowa.

Harvey, P. H., and M. D. Pagel. 1991. *The Comparative Method in Evolutionary Biology*. Oxford University Press, Oxford.

Hawkins, B. A., and W. Sheehan, eds. 1994. *Parasitoid Community Ecology*. Oxford University Press, Oxford.

Hayward, K. J. 1973. Catologos de ropaloceros Argentinos. *Opera Lilloana* 23: 7–191.

Hemming, F. 1967. The generic names of the butterflies and their type species (Lepidoptera: Rhopalocera) *Bull. Brit. Mus.* (Nat. Hist.), *Ent. Suppl.* 9: 1–509.

Hennig, W. 1966. *Phylogenetic Systematics*. University of Illinois Press, Champagne-Urbana.

Henning, S. F. 1983. Chemical communication between lycaenid larvae (Lep.: Lycaenidae) and ants (Hymen.: Formicidae). *J. Ent. Soc. S. Africa* 46: 341–366.

Hinton, H. E. 1946. A new classification of insect pupae. *Proc. Zool. Lond.* 116: 282–382.

Hinton, H. E. 1951. Myrmecophilous Lycaenidae and other Lepidoptera—a summary. *Proc. Trans. S. Lond. Entom. and Nat. Hist. Soc.* 1949-1950: 111–175.

Hinton, H. E. 1981. Biology of Insect Eggs. Pergamon Press Ltd., Oxford.

Holdridge, L. R. 1967. *Life Zone Ecology*. Tropical Science Center, San Jose, Costa Rica.

Hölldobler, B., and E. O. Wilson. 1990. *The Ants*. Harvard University Press, Cambridge, Mass.

Honda, K. 1983. Defensive potential of the components of the larval osmeterial secretion of papilionid butterflies against ants. *Physiol. Ent.* 8: 173–179.

Horvitz, C. C., and D. W. Schemske. 1984. Effects of ant-mutualists and an ant sequestering herbivore on seed production of a tropical herb, *Calathea ovandensis* (Marantaceae). *Ecology* 65: 1369–1378.

Horvitz, C. C., C. Turnbull, and D. Harvey. 1987. Biology of immature *Eurybia elvina* (Lepidoptera: Riodinidae), a myrmecophilous metalmark butterfly. *Ann. Ent. Soc. Am.* 80: 513–519.

Huston, M. 1979. A general hypothesis of species diversity. *Am. Nat.* 113: 81–101.

Huxley, J. S. 1940. *The New Systematics*. Clarendon Press, Oxford.

Jackson, T.H.E. 1937. The early stages of some African Lycaenidae (Lepidoptera), with an account of the larval habits. *Trans. Roy. Ent. Soc.* 86: 201–238.

Janzen, D. H. 1967. Why mountain passes are higher in the tropics. *Am. Nat.* 101: 233–249.

Janzen, D. H. 1973a. Comments on host-specificity of tropical herbivores and its relevance to species-richness. In V. H. Heywood, ed., *Taxonomy and Ecology*, pp. 201–211. Academic Press, New York.

Janzen, D. H. 1973b. Sweep samples of tropical foliage insects: Effects of seasons, vegetation types, elevation, time of day, insularity. *Ecology* 54: 687–708.

Janzen, D. H., ed. 1983. *Costa Rican Natural History*. University of Chicago Press, Chicago.

Johnson, G., and B. Johnson. 1980. *This Is Hong Kong: Butterflies.* Hong Kong Government Printer, Hong Kong.

Jorgensen, P. 1932. Lepidopterolisches aus Südamerika. *Dt. Ent. Z. Iris, Dresden* 46: 37–66.

Kaye, W. J. 1921. *A Catalogue of the Trinidad Lepidoptera Rhopalocera (Butterflies).* Government Printing Office, Trinidad, B.W.I.

Kendall, R. O. 1959. More larval foodplants from Texas. *J. Lep. Soc.* 13: 221–228.

Kendall, R. O. 1976. Larval foodplants and life history notes for some metalmarks (Lepidoptera: Riodinidae) from Mexico and Texas. *Bull. Allyn Mus.* 32: 1–12.

Kirkpatrick, T. W. 1953. *Notes on Minor Pests of Cacao in Trinidad.* Ann. Report on Cacao Research, 1953, pp. 67–72. ICTA, Trinidad.

Kitching, I. J. 1984. The use of larval chaetotaxy in butterfly systematics, with special reference to the Danaini (Lepidoptera: Nymphalidae). *Syst. Ent.* 9: 49–91.

Kitching, I. J. 1985. Early stages and the classification of milkweed butterflies (Lipidoptera: Danainae). *Zool. J. Linn. Soc.* 85: 1–97.

Klots, A. B. 1931. A generic revision of the Pieridae (Lepidoptera) together with a study of the male genitalia. *Ent. Am.* 12: 139–242.

Klots, A. B. 1956. *Lepidoptera.* In Tuxen, ed., *Taxonomist's Glossary of Genitalia in Insects,* pp. 97–110. Munksgaard, Copenhagen.

Kristensen, N. P. 1976. Remarks on the family-level phylogeny of butterflies. *Z. Zool. Syst. Evolforsch.* 14: 25–33.

Lamas, G. 1981. La fauna de mariposas de la Reserva de Tambopata, Madre de Dios, Peru (Lepidoptera, Papilionoidea y Hesperoidea). *Rev. Soc. Mex. Lepid.* 6: 23–40.

Lamas, G. 1985. Los Papilionoidea (Lepidoptera) de la Zona Reservada de Tambopata, Madre de Dios, Peru. I: Papilionidae, Pieridae y Nymphalidae (en parte). *Rev. per. Ent.* 27: 59–73.

Lamas, G., R. G. Robbins, and W. D. Field. 1995. *Bibliography of Butterflies.* Scientific Publishers, Gainesville, Florida.

Lamborn, W. A. 1915. On the relationship between certain West African insects, especially ants, Lycaenidae and Homoptera. *Trans. Ent. Soc. Lond.* 1913: 436–498.

Lande, R., S. Engen, and B. Saether. 1994. Optimal harvesting, economic discounting and extinction risk in fluctuating populations. *Nature* 372: 88–90.

Lande, R. 1996. Statistics and partitioning of species diversity, and similarity among multiple communities. *Oikos* 75 (in press).

Lane, R. 1984. Host specificity of ectoparasitic midges on butterflies. *Symp. Roy. Ent. Soc. Lond.* 11: 105–108.

Lanza, J. 1988. Ant preferences for *Passiflora* nectar mimics that contain amino acids. *Biotropica* 20: 341–344.

Lawton, J. H., and R. M. May. 1995, eds. *Extinction Rates.* Oxford University Press, Oxford.

Leong, K.L.H., H. K. Kaya, M. A. Yoshimura, and D. F. Frey. 1992 The occurrence and effect of a protozoan parasite, *Ophryocystis elektroscirrha* (Neogregarinida: Ophryocystidae), on overwintering monarch butterflies,

Danaus plexippus (Lepidoptera: Danaidae) from two California winter sites. *Ecol. Ent.* 17: 338–342.

Liebherr, J. K., ed. 1988. *Zoogeography of Caribbean Insects.* Cornell University Press, Ithaca, N.Y.

Longino, J. T. 1991. *Azteca* ants in *Cecropia* trees: Taxonomy, colony structure and behavior. In C. Huxley and D. Cutler, eds., *Ant-plant Interactions*, pp. 271–288. Oxford University Press, Oxford.

Longino, J. T., and N. Nadkarni. 1990. A comparison of ground and canopy leaf litter ants (Hymenoptera: Formicidae) in a tropical montane forest. *Psyche* 97: 81–94.

Longstaff, G. B. 1912. *Butterfly Hunting in Many Lands.* Longmans, Green and Co., London.

Lorkovic, Z. 1990. The butterfly chromosomes and their application in systematics and phylogeny. In O. Kudrna, ed., *Butterflies of Europe*, pp. 332–396. AULA Verlag, Wiesbaden.

Malicky, H. 1969. Versuch einer Analyse der okologischen Beziehungen zwischen Lycaeniden (Lepidoptera) und Formiciden (Hymenoptera). *Tijdschrift voor Entomologie* 112: 213–298.

Malicky, H. 1970. New aspects of the association between lycaenid larvae (Lycaenidae) and ants (Formicidae, Hymenoptera). *J. Lep. Soc.* 24: 190–202.

Mallet, J. B., and L. E. Gilbert. 1995. Why are there so many mimicry rings? Correlations between habitat, behavior and mimicry in *Heliconius* butterflies. *Biol. J. Linn. Soc.* 55: 159–180.

Mallet, J. B., and M. C. Singer. 1987. Individual selection, kin selection, and the shifting balance in the evolution of warning colours: Evidence from butterflies. *Biol. J. Linn. Soc.* 32: 337–350.

Malo, F. 1961. Phoresy in *Xenufens* (Hymenoptera: Trichogrammatidae) a parasite of *Caligo eurilochus* (Lepidoptera: Nymphalidae). *J. Econ. Entom.* 54: 465–466.

Martin, J. A., and D. P. Pashley. 1992. Molecular systematic analysis of butterfly family and some subfamily relationships (Lepidoptera: Papilionoidea). *Ann. Ent. Soc. Am.* 85: 127–139.

Maschwitz, U., M. Wüst, and K. Schurian. 1975. Blaulingraupen als Zuckerlieferanten für Ameisen. *Oecologia* 18: 17–21.

Mayr, E., and P. D. Ashlock. 1991. *Principles of Systematic Zoology.* McGraw-Hill, New York.

McAlpine, W. S. 1938. Life history of *Calephelis muticum* (McAlpine): Lepidoptera. *Bull. Brooklyn Ent. Soc.* 33: 111–121.

McAlpine, W. S. 1971. A revision of the butterfly genus *Calephelis* (Riodinidae). *J. Res. Lep.* 10: 1–125.

McDade, L. A., K. S. Bawa, H. Hespenheide, and G. Hartshorn, eds. 1994. *La Selva: Ecology and Natural History of a Neotropical Rainforest.* University of Chicago Press, Chicago.

McLaughlin, R. E., and J. Myers. 1970. *Ophryocystis elektroscirrha* sp. n., a neogregarine pathogen of the monarch butterfly *Danaus plexippus* (L.) and the Florida queen butterfly *Danaus gilippus berenice* Cramer. *J. Protozool.* 17: 300–305.

Miller, J. S. 1987. Phylogenetic studies on the Papilioninae (Lepidoptera: Papilionidae). *Bull. Am. Mus.* 186: 365–512.

Miller, J. S. 1991. Cladistics and classification of the Notodontidae (Lepidoptera: Noctuoidea) based on larval and adult morphology. *Bull. Am. Mus.* 204: 1–230.

Miller, J. S. 1996. Phylogeny of the neotropical moth tribe Josiini (Notodontidae: Dioptinae): A hidden case of Müllerian mimicry. *Zool. J. Linn. Soc.* 177 (in press).

Miller, J. S., and L. D. Otero. 1994. Immature stages of Venezuelan Diptinae (Notodontidae) in *Josia* and *Thirmida*. *J. Lep. Soc.* 48: 338–372.

Miller, L. D. 1970. Nomenclature of wing veins and cells. *J. Lep. Soc.* 8: 37–48.

Mitter, C. 1988. Taxonomic potential of some internal reproductive structures in Catocala (Lepidoptera: Noctuidae) and related genera. *Ann. Ent. Soc. Am.* 81: 10–18.

Moschler, E. 1916. A classification of the Lepidoptera based on characters of the pupa. *Bull. Illinois State Lab. Nat. Hist.* 12: 15–159.

Müller, F. 1879. *Ituna* and *Thyridia*: A remarkable case of mimicry in butterflies in Brazil (trans. R. Mendola). *Proc. Ent. Soc. Lond.* 1879: 20–29.

Munroe, E. 1953. The phylogeny of the Papilionidae. *Proc. 7th Pacific Sci. Congr. Auckland* (1949) 4: 83–87.

Munster-Swendsen, M. 1991. The effect of sublethal neogregarine infections in the spruce needleminer, *Epinotia tedella* (Lepidoptera: Tortricidae). *Ecol. Ent.* 16: 211–219.

Myers, N. 1986. Tropical deforestation and a Mega-extinction spasm. In M. E. Soule, ed., *Conservation Biology*, pp. 394–409. Sinauer Associates, Sunderland, Mass.

Narstedt, A., and R. H. Davis. 1981. The occurrence of cyanoglucocides linamarin and lotustralin in *Acraea* and *Heliconius* butterflies. *Comp. Biochem. Physiol.* 68B: 575–577.

Narstedt, A., and R. H. Davis. 1983. Occurrence, variation and biosynthesis of the glucocides linamarin and lotustralin in species of the Heliconiini. *Comp. Biochem. Physiol.* 75B: 65–73.

Nijhout, H. F. 1991. *The Development and Evolution of Butterfly Wing Patterns.* Smithsonian Institution Press, Washington, D.C.

Noriega, F. F. 1923. *Diccionerio Geografico de Costa Rica.* Imprenta Nacional, San Jose, Costa Rica.

Norris, M. J. 1936. The feeding habits of the adult Lepidoptera: Heteroneura. *Trans. Roy. Ent. Soc. Lond.* 85: 61–90.

Odendaal, F. 1990. The dry season influences parameters in female butterflies. *Biotropica* 22: 100–102.

O'Hara, J. E. 1995. Henry Walter Bates—his life and contributions to biology. *Arch. Nat. Hist.* 22: 195–219.

Oldroyd, H. 1958. *Collecting, Preserving and Studying Insects.* Macmillan, New York.

Olson, D. 1994. The distribution of leaf-litter invertebrates along a neotropical altitudinal gradient. *J. Trop. Ecol.* 19: 129–150.

Opler, P. A., G. W. Frankie, and H. K. Baker. 1976. Rainfall as a factor in the release, timing, and synchronization of anthesis by tropical trees and shrubs. *J. Biogeography* 3: 231–236.

Owen, D. F. 1980. *Camouflage and Mimicry.* University of Chicago Press, Chicago.

Pasteur, G. 1982. A classificatory review of mimicry systems. *Ann. Rev. Ecol. and Syst.* 13: 169–199.

Peterson, A. 1962. *Larvae of Insects, and Introduction to Neararctic Species,* part I, *Lepidoptera and Plant-infesting Hymenoptera.* Edwards Brothers, Ann Arbor, Michigan.

Peterson, M. A. 1995. Unpredictability in the facultative association between larvae of *Euphilotes enoptes* (Lep.: Lycaenidae) and ants. *Biol. J. Linn. Soc.* 55: 209–223.

Pierce, N. E. 1983. The ecology and evolution of symbioses between lycaenid butterflies and ants. Ph.D. diss. Harvard University, Cambridge, Mass.

Pierce, N. E. 1984. Amplified species diversity: A case study of an Australian lycaenid butterfly and its attendant ants. *Symp. Roy. Ent. Soc. Lond.* 11: 196–200.

Pierce, N. E. 1985. Lycaenid butterflies and ants: Selection for nitrogen-fixing and other protein rich food plants. *Am. Nat.* 125: 888–895.

Pierce, N. E. 1987. The evolution and biogeography of associations between lycaenid butterflies and ants. *Oxford Surveys Evol. Biol.* 4: 89–116.

Pierce, N. E., and M. A. Elgar. 1985. The influence of ants on host selection by *Jalmenus evagoras,* a myrmecophilous lycaenid butterfly. *Behav. Ecol. Sociobiol.* 16: 209–222.

Pierce, N. E., R. L. Kitching, R. C. Buckley, M.F.J. Taylor, and K. F. Benbow. 1987. The costs and benefits of cooperation between the Australian lycaenid butterfly, *Jalmenus evagoras,* and its attendant ants. *Behav. Ecol. and Sociobiol.* 21: 237–248.

Platt, A. P., S. J. Harrison, and T. F. Williams. 1984. Absence of differential mate selection in the North American tiger swallowtail, *Papilio glaucus. Symp. Roy. Ent. Soc. Lond.* 11: 245–250.

Poulton, E. B. 1908. *Essays on Evolution.* Clarendon Press, Oxford.

Poulton, E. B. 1924. Mimicry in butterflies of Fiji considered in relation to the Euploeine and Danaine invasions of Polynesia and the female forms of *Hypolimnas bolina* L. in the Pacific. *Trans. Ent. Soc.* 1924: 564–691.

Price, P. W., T. M. Lewinsohn, G. W. Fernandez, and W. W. Benson, eds. 1991. *Plant-Animal Interactions: Evolutionary Ecology in Tropical and Temperate Regions.* Wiley and Sons, New York.

Punnett, R. C. 1915. *Mimicry in Butterflies.* Cambridge University Press, Cambridge, U.K.

Raguso, R. A., and J. Llorente-Bousquetes. 1991. The butterflies (Lepidoptera) of the Tuxlas Mountains, Vera Cruz, Mexico revisited: Species-richness and habitat disturbance. *J. Res. Lep.* 29: 105–133.

Reavey, D. 1993. Why body size matters to caterpillars. In N. E. Stamp and T. M. Casey, eds., *Caterpillars,* pp. 248–279. Chapman and Hall, New York.

Reuter, E. 1896. Über die Palpen der Rhopaloceran. *Acta Soc. Scientiarum Fennicae* 22: 1–577.

Rhode, K. 1992. Latitudinal gradients in species diversity: The search for the primary cause. *Oikos* 65: 514–527.

Ricklefs, R. E., and D. Schluter, eds. 1993. *Species Diversity in Ecological Communities.* University of Chicago Press, Chicago.

Ritland, D. B., and L. P. Brower. 1991. The viceroy butterfly is not a Batesian mimic. *Nature* 350: 497–498.

Robbins, R. K. 1981. The false head hypothesis: Predation and wing pattern variation of lycaenid butterflies. *Am. Nat.* 118: 770–775.

Robbins, R. K. 1982. How many butterfly species? *News of the Lep. Soc.* 1982: 40–41.

Robbins, R. K. 1985. Independent evolution of "false head" behavior in Riodinidae. *J. Lep. Soc.* 39: 224–225.

Robbins, R. K. 1988. Comparative morphology of the butterfly foreleg coxa and trochanter (Lepidoptera) and its systematic implications. *Proc. Ent. Soc. Wash.* 90: 133–154.

Robbins, R. K., and A. Aiello. 1982. Foodplant and oviposition records for Panamanian Lycaenidae and Riodinidae. *J. Lep. Soc.* 36: 65–75.

Ross, G. N. 1964. Life history on Mexican butterflies, III. The early stages of *Anatole rossi*, a new myrmecophilous metalmark. *J. Res. Lep.* 3: 81–94.

Ross, G. N. 1966. Life history studies of a Mexican butterfly, IV. The ecology and ethology of *Anatole rossi*, a myrmecophilous metalmark. *Ann. Ent. Soc. Amer.* 59: 985–1004.

Salt, G. 1937. Experimental studies in insect parasitism, V. The sense used by *Trichogramma* to distinguish between parasitized and unparasitized hosts. *Proc. Roy. Ent. Soc. B* 122: 57–75.

Saunders, W. W. 1859. On the genus *Erycina*, Linn., with descriptions of some new species. *Trans. Ent. Soc. Lond.* (II) 5: 94–110.

Schaus, W. 1913. New species of Rhopalocera from Costa Rica. *Proc. Zool. Soc. Lond.* 24: 339–374.

Schremmer, F. 1978. On the bionomy and morphology of the myrmecophilous larva and pupa of the neotropical butterfly species *Hamaeris erostratus* (Lep.: Riodinidae). *Entomologica Generalis* 4: 113–121.

Scoble, M. J. 1992. *The Lepidoptera.* Oxford University Press, Oxford.

Scott, J. A. 1986. *The Butterflies of North America: A Natural History Field Guide.* Stanford University Press, Stanford, Calif.

Scudder, S. H. 1887. Note on the group Eumaeidi. In F. D. Godman and O. Salvin, *Biologia Centrali Americana. Insecta, Lepidoptera, Rhopalocera.* Vol. II, pp. 110–112. London.

Scudder, S. H. 1889. *Butterflies of the Eastern United States and Canada with special reference to New England.* 3 vols. Cambridge, Mass.

Seitz, A. E. 1916–20. Erycinidae. In *Macrolepidoptera of the World*, vol. 5, pp. 617–738. Alfred Kernan, Stuttgart.

Selander, R. B., and P. Vaurie. 1962. A gazetteer to accompany the "Insecta" volumes of the "Biologia Centrali Americana." *Am. Mus. Nat. Hist. Novitates* 2099: 1–70.

Sepp, J. 1828–48. *Surinaamsche Vlinders.* J. C. Sepp en Zoon.

Shapiro, A. M. 1976. Beau geste? *Am. Nat.* 110: 900–902.

Sherry, T. W. 1983. Galbula ruficauda. In D. H. Janzen, ed., *Costa Rican Natural History*, pp. 579–581. University of Chicago Press, Chicago.

Shields, O. 1976. Fossil butterflies and the evolution of Lepidoptera. *J. Res. Lep.* 25: 132–143.

Simpson, G. G. 1945. The principles of classification, and a classification of mammals. *Bull. Am. Mus. Nat. Hist.* 85: 1–350.

Simpson, G. G. 1961. *Principles of Animal Taxonomy.* Columbia University Press, New York.

Singer, M. C. 1983. Multiple host use by a phytophagous insect population. *Evolution* 37: 389–403.

Singer, M. C. 1984. Butterfly host-plant relationships: Host quality, adult choice and larval success. *Symp. Roy. Ent. Soc. Lond.* 11: 81–88.

Singer, M. C., and C. Parmesan. 1993. Sources of variation in patterns of plant-insect associations. *Nature* 361: 251–253.

Singer, M. C., C. D. Thomas, H. L. Billington, and C. Parmesan. 1994. Correlates of speed of evolution of host preferences in a set of twelve populations of the butterfly *Euphydryas editha. Ecoscience* 1: 107–114.

Smith, K. M. 1967. *Insect Virology.* Academic Press, New York and London.

Smith-Trail, D. R. 1980. Behavioral interactions between parasites and hosts: Host suicide and the evolution of complex life cycles. *Am. Nat.* 116: 77–91.

Sokal, R. R., and P.H.A. Sneath. 1963. *The Principles of Numerical Taxonomy.* W. H. Freeman, San Francisco.

Stamp, N. E. 1981. Behavior of parasitized aposematic caterpillars: Advantageous to the parasitoid or the host? *Am. Nat.* 118: 715–725.

Stamp, N. E., and T. M. Casey, eds. 1993. *Caterpillars: Ecological and Evolutionary Constraints on Foraging.* Chapman and Hall, New York.

Stehr, F. W. 1987. *The Immature Insects.* Kendall/Hunt, Dubuque, Iowa.

Stern, W., K. Curry, and A. Pridgeon. 1987. Osmophores of Stanhopea (Orchidaceae). *Am. J. Bot.* 74: 1323–1331.

Stichel, H. 1910–11. *Riodinidae. Genera Insectorum.* P. Wytsman.

Stichel, H. 1928. Nemobiinae. *Das Tierreich* 51: 1–330.

Stichel, H. 1930–31. *Lepidopterorum Catalogus.* Pars. 40, 41, 44. W. Junk, Berlin.

Swofford, D. L. 1993. *PAUP: Phylogenetic Analysis Using Parsimony,* version 3.1.1. Illinois Natural History Survey, Champaign-Urbana.

Swynnerton, C.M.F. 1915. A brief preliminary statement of a few results of five years' special testing on the theories of mimicry. *Proc. Ent. Soc. Lond.* 1915: 21–33.

Thomas, J. A., G. W. Elmes, J. C. Wardlaw, and M. Woyciechowski. 1989. Host specificity among *Maculinea* butterflies in *Myrmica* ant nests. *Oecologia* 79: 452–457.

Turner, A. H. 1924. On the numerical aspect of reciprical mimicry (diaposematic resemblance). *Trans. Ent. Soc. Lond.* 1924: 667–675.

Turner, J.R.G. 1984. Mimicry: The palatability spectrum and its consequences. *Symp. Roy. Ent. Soc. Lond.* 11: 141–161.

Tuxen, S. L., ed. 1970. *Taxonomist's Glossary of Genitalia of Insects.* Munksgaard, Copenhagen.

Tyler, H., K. S. Brown, and K. Wilson. 1994. *Swallowtail Butterflies of the Americas.* Scientific Publishers, Gainesville, Florida.

Vane-Wright, R. I. 1972. Precourtship activity and a new scent organ in butterflies. *Nature* 239: 338–340.

Vane-Wright, R. I. 1976. A unified classification of mimetic resemblances. *Biol. J. Linn. Soc.* 8: 25–56.

Vane-Wright, R. I. 1978. Ecological and behavioural origins of diversity in butterflies. *Symp. Roy. Ent. Soc. Lond.* 9: 56–70.

Vane-Wright, R. I. 1980. On the definition of mimicry. *Biol. J. Linn. Soc.* 13: 1–6.

Vane-Wright, R. I., and P. R. Ackery, eds. 1984. The Biology of Butterflies. *Symp. Roy. Ent. Soc.* 11: 1–429.

Vane-Wright, R. I., and M. Boppré. 1993. Visual and chemical signalling in butterflies: Functional and phylogenetic perspectives. In R. K. Butlin, T. Guilford, and J. R. Krebs, eds., The Evolution and Design of Animal Signalling Systems. *Phil. Trans. Royal Soc.* B 340: 197–205.

Velez, J., and J. Salazar. 1991. *Mariposas de Colombia.* Villegas Editores, Bogota, Colombia.

Wagner, D. 1993. Species-specific effects of tending ants on the development of lycaenid butterfly larvae. *Oecologia* 96: 276–281.

Walbauer, G. P., and J. G. Sternberg. 1975. Saturniid moths as mimics: An alternative explanation of attempts to demonstrate mimetic advantage in nature. *Evolution* 29: 650–658.

Wickler, W. 1968. *Mimicry in Plants and Animals.* World University Library, London.

Wiley, E. O. 1981. *The Theory and Practice of Phylogenetic Systematics.* John Wiley and Sons, New York.

Woodhall, S. 1992. *A Practical Guide to Butterflies and Moths of Southern Africa.* Lepidopterists' Society of Africa, Florida Hills, Transvaal, South Africa.

Woods, C. A., ed. 1989. *Biogeography of the West Indies: Past, Present and Future.* Sandhill Crane Press, Gainesville, Florida.

World Wildlife Conservation Monitoring Center. 1992. *Global Biodiversity, Status of the Earth's Living Resources.* Chapman and Hall, London.

Zikán, J. F. 1949. Observacoes sobre os componentes dos generos *Phaenochitonia* Stichel e *Pterographium* Stichel, com descicao de uma nova especie e criando um novo genero (Riodinidae—Lepidoptera). *Rev. de Entomologia* 20: 535–539.

Zikán, J. F. 1953. Beitrage zur Biologie von 19 Riodiniden-Arten (Riodinidae—Lepidoptera). *Dusenia* 4: 403–413.

INDEX